C000069471

# REMINISCENCES AND REMEMBRANCES

*Reflections After Age 80*

"Proof of the Pudding"
(from the Edge of Bankruptcy to one of the
Finest Small Universities in the Country)

## E. BRUCE HEILMAN

AuthorHouse™
1663 Liberty Drive
Bloomington, IN 47403
www.authorhouse.com
Phone: 1 (800) 839-8640

Because of the dynamic nature of the Internet, any web addresses or links contained in this book may have changed
since publication and may no longer be valid. The views expressed in this work are solely those of the author and do not
necessarily reflect the views of the publisher, and the publisher hereby disclaims any responsibility for them.

This book is printed on acid-free paper.

ISBN: 978-1-5462-5274-0 (sc)
ISBN: 978-1-5462-5275-7 (e)

Library of Congress Control Number: 2019904103

Print information available on the last page.

Published by AuthorHouse  12/18/2019

authorHOUSE®

# A NOTE TO READERS

This publication is a culmination of two years of work writing, rewriting, editing, and most importantly, remembering and reminiscing the life of Dr. E. Bruce Heilman. It is memories of the important parts of his life including his successes, his family, his life as a veteran Marine and his travels. His continued involvement in life continued long past the age when most would assume they have been as productive as they can be and take the rest of their life sitting down. Dr. Heilman never retired from either work or life.

It is with a heavy heart and a joyful soul that this book has been published. On October 19, 2019, Dr. E. Bruce Heilman passed away. My heart is heavy in that he will not see the completion of his book. He had made some final revisions of this book prior to his passing and together we were in the process of finalizing it for printing when he passed.

However, my heart is joyful in that ten days before he passed, I promised him that I would make sure this book, his Remembrances and Reminiscences, would be completed in the manner in which he had envisioned. It was his way of reliving some of the highlights of his career, his life, and his family as well as passing on to others his knowledge and experiences.

Working with him for these past few years, I was able to get to know him well and he exuded positivity, kindness, and knowledge. He always had a kind word for all who met him and a smile that would light up a room. He worked hard to the very end, never stopping even for illness. His work on behalf of education, the military, veterans and WWII veterans in particular, was never ending. Days before he passed, he addressed a group of students in Washington, D.C. The energy he put into his relationships and work was constant until the day he passed.

Dr. Heilman, I will miss you dearly, but your legacy, words and knowledge will continue in the pages of this book for others to learn from your example.

Joy Caporale

# A VERY SPECIAL DAD

I was lucky enough later in my career to become the Director of Development at my mother and father's alma mater Campbellsville University. In the final year of dad's life the The National WWII Museum in New Orleans asked my father to be their guest on their "Victory in the Pacific" Tour. He was able to invite someone to accompany him and he chose me. We were able to share so many great memories together on Iwo Jima as we walked up Mount Suribachi. We met Keiko, a survivor of the atomic bomb in Hiroshima. Keiko was about ten years old when dad was about eighteen years old and on occupation duty in Hiroshima during WWII. On the final night of our tour we had the opportunity to sit around the dinner table and listen to the both of them talk to each other about their shared experiences. She lamented about how she still to this day regretted stepping over the dead bodies and dad spoke about the friendships he made with the Japanese families there. They both cried together and it was a very moving experience for everyone around the table. I was blessed to have a father like the one I had . He taught me many great lessons and my only regret is that I could never be a Marine like him.

A loveable batch of Great Grand Children

I dedicate these memoirs to my late wife, Betty, my children, my grandchildren and my great grandchildren, all of whom have been so meaningful to me throughout their lifetimes and mine.

My daughters Terry and Sandy at the height of innocence.

Eight of my great grandchildren

Betty & Bruce Heilman

Dr. E. Bruce Heilman, one of this country's greatest generation, willingly expected to die in the invasion of Japan when the A-bomb ended the war. However, the former high school dropout and son of a Kentucky sharecropper set out on an education career he never dreamed of: becoming a visionary president of a college and university raising hundreds of millions of dollars for programs, buildings and faculty and transforming the lives of thousands of students.

Even in "retirement" he has served as chancellor of the University of Richmond for three decades, serves on numerous boards and at 93 still takes trips on his black Harley-Davidson, Electra special edition motorcycle with the Marine Corps logo on the Aztec. His optimism, philosophy of life, and faith continue to serve him well, some 75 years after the war. One would be hard pressed to find a more enlightening, entertaining and inspirational autobiography.

—*Dr. Randy Fitzgerald, University professor and writer*

I have always heard that when one needs help, one seeks the advice of a specialist. If ever there was a specialist in higher education, it's Dr. E. Bruce Heilman. His book attests to that fact.

—*Art Powers, publisher, Johnson City Press*

As the university's first chief executive officer, Dr. Heilman was willing to risk and make the risk work. He worked seven days a week, twenty-four hours a day. While the task was awesome to the staff, Heilman led with nothing but a positive, can-do attitude. It has been said that leadership is more than process, it is inspiration and charisma. Dr. Heilman had both in abundance. That spirit is evidenced throughout his memoirs.

—*H. Gerald "Jerry" Quigg, vice president for development and university relations, University of Richmond, 1969–1997*

Dr. Heilman is the epitome of a trustee … I consider him a friend and recognize him as one of the top professionals I have ever known. His memoirs reflect this characteristic in his many years as a leader in higher education.

—*Major General Harold G. Glasgow, USMC (Ret.), former president, Marine Military Academy*

Bruce Heilman … is an outstanding and defective educator, fund-raiser, and counselor with a broad base of support and one who has the respect of all constituents not only within his own institution but throughout the larger community and across the nation. This is reinforced throughout the pages of his autobiography.

—W. Christian Sizemore, University of Richmond alumnus and former president of William Jewell College

Former rectors and other administrators continue to speak of his vitality and indomitable spirit. The consummate professional in every sense, he has continued to work tirelessly in the promotion of the university. Bruce Heilman is our best ambassador, tirelessly winning important new friends for the university, and we are grateful for his continued services.

—*Dr. William E. Cooper, former president of the University of Richmond*

Overall comments from the editor:

"This is more than a memoir. It's a continuation of a long life lived, a life that experienced war, love, family, higher education, leadership, and much more. This book continues a previously published book about the author's life adventures, taking readers into the details of his role as president of the University of Richmond, his childhood memories, his travels, and his youthful mind even in his 90s. The following quote from p. 570 captures the theme of the book: "The greatest risk of all is to die bored or to fail to live life to its fullest."

The writing is professional and straightforward as the author shares compelling glimpses into his life."w

Dr. E. Bruce Heilman preparing to leave one of his cross country rides highlighting the Gold Star Families.

# TABLE OF CONTENTS

## THE UNIVERSITY OF RICHMOND
## BUILDING A UNIVERSITY ANEW
## ON A SOLID FOUNDATION
## A MIRACLE

# MEREDITH COLLEGE—ANOTHER MIRACLE

# MARINE MOTORCYCLE MAN AND MISSION

# FAMILY

# LEADERSHIP

# TRAVEL

# THE MILITARY

# AGING

# MEASURING SUCCESS BY THE ACKNOWLEDGEMENTS OF OTHERS

# FOREWORD

### By Dr. Jerry Davis,

### President of The College of the Ozarks

Almost 50 years ago I became acquainted with Dr. E. Bruce Heilman. He was well known and highly respected for his leadership in higher education. With his success at Meredith College and the University of Richmond came national prestige, which continues to the present. At 93 years of age, he's inspiring to be around because he never really retired. He simply changed titles (from President to Chancellor) and never slowed down, a veritable "Miracle Man" of leadership.

Many have wondered how Dr. Heilman became so successful. His rise from Kentucky farm boy to a leader of national prominence is truly an example of the "American Dream." His life reflects how adversity led to hard work, strong character, and hope for a meaningful future.

Like so many of the "Greatest Generation," Heilman wanted to serve his country. In joining the U.S. Marine Corps, he risked everything. Once I asked him if, while sitting in a ship offshore near Japan, he was really prepared to die for his country. "Yes," was his quick answer, adding, "and many of my friends did." I've never doubted that he meant what he said.

To say that Dr. Heilman came out of the Marine Corps as a different man is an understatement. Self-confident and forward looking, he entered Campbellsville University and met his wife Betty along the way. He wasted no time in climbing the ladder of success—first serving as head of the Tennessee Higher Education Commission, followed by successful presidencies at Meredith College (North Carolina) and the University of Richmond (Virginia). His leadership in the management of a diverse organization was matched by his communication skills.

He's the kind of person who can make you feel special. When E. Bruce visits, he says such nice, complimentary things. Although I know them to be overstated, I feel good anyway! No wonder he was so successful in raising tens of millions of dollars.

Most college or university presidents fade away after retirement. I don't know many former executives who continue making meaningful contributions past the age of 80, let alone 90! As well as being Chancellor and goodwill ambassador for the University of Richmond, Dr. Heilman travels all over the country (and the world). Always looking for a new adventure, he even rides his Harley motorcycle across the United States on behalf of worthy organizations such as the Gold Star Families and the Greatest Generation Foundation—a contemporary "Paul Revere." Wherever he goes, he spreads a message that needs to be heard.

Throughout his lifetime of service, Heilman has been a family man, who gives and has drawn support from his children and grandchildren. They, like many others, seek his advice and respect his wisdom. His mentorship has been invaluable and his counsel held in high esteem.

As a builder, manager, leader, and communicator, E. Bruce Heilman is one of a kind. You will enjoy knowing more about his life and accomplishments. In him you will see a reflection of the core values of the "Greatest Generation."

The remarkable person of E. Bruce Heilman will no doubt be remembered by buildings in three states that bear his (and wife Betty's) name. Of greater significance will be the impact on the lives of those who have known him. We see in him a shining example of a life that has experienced and reflected honor, courage, commitment, faith, and hard work.

America is better off because of leaders like Dr. E. Bruce Heilman. He truly reflects the motto of the United States Marine Corps.

*Semper fidelis.*

Jerry C. Davis, President
College of the Ozarks

# PREFACE

## THE UNFOLDING OF A MIRACLE

More than fifty years ago, a miracle began to unfold. It saved the University of Richmond and made all things seem possible for those who became a part of the university in the years that followed. Unfortunately, the story of this miracle has faded with time, but it remains fresh in the memory of those who were involved, and it should never be forgotten.

At a trustee meeting in 1967, E. Claiborne Robins ('31) listened intently as president George Modlin outlined the University of Richmond's precarious position. Tuition and fees were no longer enough to pay the bills. The facilities on campus were grossly inadequate, and the institution was facing increased competition from state-supported colleges. In short, it would take a miracle to save the university.

The question, of course, was how much this miracle was going to cost. Modlin, a professor of economics, walked to the blackboard and wrote $25,000,000–$50,000,000.

The situation continued to deteriorate in the months that followed, but Claiborne started thinking about making a large gift to the university. He had built the A. H. Robins Corporation into a highly profitable entity and major manufacturer of pharmaceuticals, and he dreamed of seeing his alma mater transformed into one of the nation's finest institutions of higher learning. He discussed this dream with his wife, Lora, and their first inclination was to donate $25 million. After more discussion, they decided to make it $50 million. At the conclusion of commencement ceremonies in May 1969, president Modlin announced the miraculous gift. The people in the crowd gasped, and then they jumped to their feet, clapping and shouting.

When I was elected president of the university in 1971, I found—to my amazement—that the Robins family was to be as important in participation as in philanthropy. Claiborne, Lora, and their children were my strongest advocates, supporters, and mentors. Whenever I needed a friend, they were there. Whenever the university needed money, they were there, often agreeing to match major gifts to close deals.

The entire family set a new standard for transformative philanthropy. Only $10 million of the $50 million gift was a challenge grant, but alumni and other supporters matched the entire $50 million by 1980. This was an incredibly ambitious undertaking, and some of my supporters advised against it—including some of the university's trustees. They were afraid the effort would come up embarrassingly short. Some would ask, "Why does the university need more money when the Robins family just gave $50 million?" Claiborne did not see it that way—and neither did the alumni. The Robins gift inspired greater generosity among all interested in the university, and their generosity further inspired Claiborne and the family.

Over the years, the Robins family donated more than $200 million (in today's dollars, more than three-quarters of a billion dollars) to the university. Typically, the family responded to critical needs with few strings—or no strings—attached, but their contributions have been far more than monetary. They have been intimately involved in every aspect of Richmond's development. They built dormitories, the Robins Center, and a major expansion of the business school. They endowed scholarships and filled leadership positions. E. Claiborne Robins Jr. ('68 and recipient of an honorary degree) chaired a $60 million-campaign from 1982–1987, the largest fundraising effort to that point.

E. Claiborne Robins Sr. died in 1995, but he said not long before that he lived long enough to see his dream come true. I am glad he felt that way, but I personally believe the miracle that began with the Robins gift is still unfolding on the campus today. Tens of thousands of alumni and friends have answered Claiborne's call to support education and build towers of strength on historically solid foundations from the past. All gifts, large and small, continue to ensure Claiborne and his family's vision.

In no small measure, private philanthropy has created the institution known today as one of the finest small universities in the country, and it happened because Claiborne Robins and his family believed strongly enough in the possibility to make it happen.

*"One of the joys of giving is to be able to see the results of your giving"*

E. CLAIBORNE ROBINS

1910-1995

DISTINGUISHED TRUSTEE AND ALUMNUS

OF THE UNIVERSITY OF RICHMOND

# INTRODUCTION

*It is not the years in your life but the life in your years that counts.*
*—Abraham Lincoln*

Ninety-Three Years of Grand Adventures

The unfolding of a miracle presented in the preface of this book sets the stage for my ninety-three years of fulfilling adventures. The miracles as described became major events in my life and stand at the top of a number of extraordinary opportunities that have transpired over my sixty-six years of leadership in higher education and have been a central focal point in my life.

Claiborne Robins inspired the University of Richmond's miracle, and his words gave clarity and confirmation to the level of our success. In a letter dated October 18, 1978, seven years into my presidency, he wrote, "More has taken place in the past seven years than all the previous one hundred and forty years combined." At the end of my presidency of sixteen years, he was quoted in *Richmond Magazine* as declaring, "More has happened than I ever dreamed possible." Thus, with such positive affirmations of the results by the one who inspired it all, I acknowledge my leadership role as the defining example of the best of my professional success.

My life story, *An Interruption That Lasted a Lifetime: My First Eighty Years*, was published in 2008. It is no longer my life story; it is only the first eighty years of that story. The title of this extended portion of *My Life Beyond Eighty* should attract the interest of those who believe that life at such an age could be only about infirmities of one kind or another—or transition into a retirement home with paid-up services as age and health issues require.

Writing "the rest of my story" as an extension of my 626-page book containing the part of my life I considered worthy of sharing and completed thirteen years before is a challenge. However, as I enter my my 93rd year, I realize I miscalculated on how much more life would have to offer after eighty—and how much I would be engaged in its living.

My five wonderful children.

My children all grown up.

Grandchildren on the Kentucky Farm.

Grandsons Chris and Matt.

Chinese Alumnus John Wu and Chief and Mrs. Dillard.

Daughter Terry.

Riding on my Kentucky Farm.

More family photos.

A host of grandchildren.

First Lady, Betty Heilman.

From my higher age level, I can see more clearly that which engaged my energies in the past, and I can reflect upon a life that has, in many ways, been an exception to the rule. With an average life span of seventy-eight years, relatively few people live to be ninety-three. Most do not have the opportunity to reflect from such a mature perspective. These pages contain recollections from my entire life as well as activities that have given meaning to the eleven years—from eighty to ninety-three—unhampered by the limitations often brought about by age.

For those reading this updated part of my life without the benefit of the content of the original publication, I share three letters conveying reactions common to hundreds of readers of the original. Perhaps reading these will inspire the acquiring of a copy of *An Interruption that Lasted a Lifetime: My First Eighty Years,* from the internet, the University of Richmond, or elsewhere.

Earl Hamner, a writer and producer of the television program "The Waltons," is an alumnus of the University of Richmond. In my role as president of his alma mater, I became acquainted with him and his outstanding accomplishments. Recently, and after knowing Earl for many years, I received the following letter, which I hope will serve as an introduction to *An Interruption that Lasted a Lifetime: My First Eighty Years.*

This letter and the one to follow were unsolicited, but they came from very astute individuals who know me and my background. They read the book with serious interest in its content and volunteered their reactions to its message.

Dear Dr. Heilman.

What a pleasant surprise it was to receive your book *An Interruption That Lasted a Lifetime.* I cannot imagine how I missed it earlier, but I was not aware of it. Had I been, I certainly would have bought and read it immediately. I thank you sincerely for the gift as well as the read.

As you point out the parallels in our lives are extraordinary. Not only did we have the same first name, but also for a while, each of us was dubbed "June" in your case, "Junnie" in mine. And the time and circumstances in which we grew up, the family unity, the Baptist religion. One exception. We didn't have a rain barrel. As I read, I was constantly reminded of the long-term effect of the Depression. To quote a good writer, "It was the reality that colored all of life and changed forever the outlook of two generations."

For all the similarities the circumstances of our military service are, to my discredit, quite different. You admirably volunteered into a dangerous branch of the service. Cowardly old Earl waited to be conscripted and ended up overseeing the dispersal of food and clothing to other servicemen in the Paris area.

I admire so many things in the book. For a resident of the academic world, you sure are an adventuresome party, always in the thick of things, taking chances, observing with fascinating detail other societies and cultures, and writing about them in a most engaging and vivid style. Incidentally, another parallel—the letters sent home. My mother kept each one. And, a sidelight, I recently received a note from a lady in an assisted living home in Detroit, Michigan, who asked if I would like her to return all the love letters I had sent her during the war. At eighty-eight, she remembered—and so did I!

I have to tell you one parallel in our lives that might surprise you. I have read that you are a motorcycle enthusiast. Well, when Jane and I first moved into our present home here on our California hillside, several fathers and sons had bikes. I invested in a rather tame little dirt bike but which I enjoyed immensely. There is a photo of me taken just as I come over a berm at extreme speed, and the expression on my face would be right at home as an illustration in *Dante's Inferno*. I remember once it stalled on Mullholland Drive, and I couldn't get it started. Suddenly an immense group of Hells Angels zoomed by, saw that I was in trouble, then zoomed back and asked if I needed help. I was a little nervous because the guys had a bad reputation. However, a couple of them got to work on the bike, had it fixed within seconds, then roared on and off to what I imagined was all sorts of wonderful mischief.

I am running on, but I cannot close without confirming what you know—that had it not been for the scholarship at the University of Richmond, I might have ended up an embittered clerk at a county grocery store, frustrated and still dreaming of becoming a writer. And of course my gratitude for the extraordinary work you did in bringing the university up to its present distinguished place in the universities of our country.

I still have a few chapters to go, but I allow myself a few pages at a time. Much of it reads like a novel. If you have any such inclination, you should give that a try in your spare time!

Sincerely,

Earl

Robert S. Jepson, a distinguished graduate and major donor to his alma mater, the University of Richmond, funded the Jepson School of Leadership Studies among other facilities and programs, wrote the following letter.

Dear Bruce:

What a wonderful surprise the mail has brought to our office today!  I have just opened "An Interruption that Lasted a Lifetime – My First Eighty Years" and must admit to being in awe of your undertaking and your achievement. What a spectacular book that so artfully tells of the life of one of my favorite people!

Dear friend, I thank you for the gift and for your thoughtful inscription. Without you, our Leadership School would never have come to life and, as a consequence, you and I would have missed the joy of seeing so many young lives changed in such a meaningful way.

I intend to take your book to Gregorie neck Plantation and enjoy its every page through the Thanksgiving holidays. Should you feel an additional presence with you at Thanksgiving, it will be my thoughts and grins as I discover your glorious life through your written word.

Congratulations on this monumental task and all the best wishes to you and your family for a joyous Thanksgiving holiday.

Warm regards,

Bob

General Hal Glasgow, a two-star Marine Corps general, was a longtime president of the Marine Military Academy.

Dear Bruce:

I wanted to let you know I have just finished reading *An Interruption That Lasted a Lifetime* for the second time. I enjoyed it the first time through some three years ago; however, at the time, I was traveling around from Illinois back through the Southeast involved in family research and reading the book in spurts, losing my place, getting colleges mixed up, etc. The second reading was word by word and page by page and a priceless experience.

You were born in 1926, while I arrived in February 1929, and your description of life in La Grange and Oldham County, Kentucky, at the time was almost the same as mine in Heflin and Cleburne County, Alabama. I still have in my possession the steelyards used to weigh cotton, beef, and pork; my grandfather's shoe last, which made the shoes for a family of ten; and Mother's butter mold, which she filled from the churn, and I delivered to neighbors who returned a nickel (most of the time, five pennies) to my mother for her efforts.

I was impressed by your openness in describing the events of your life. Our entry in the Marine Corps was different, but it appears to have played a significant part in both of our lives.

You volunteered, while I was drafted. For some reason, I thought you had gone through boot camp at Parris Island—I was not aware you were a "Hollywood marine." Your description of the drill instructor and the purpose of boot camp is superb.

The boot camp at Parris Island where I began my Marine Corps career is identical to the training you went through in San Diego. You departed San Diego in May 1945 aboard the USS *Laurens* on your way to World War II, while I followed over six years later in the nineteenth draft out of the same port in December 1951 aboard the USS *Wiegle* with 3,700 marines headed for Korea. We sailed into Osaka, Japan, dumped our sea bags into a storage area (which I never saw again), reloaded two days later, and sailed to Inchon, Korea. Your description of marines traveling at sea and advancing to combat areas is exemplary.

You have received so many well-earned plaudits for all of your accomplishments throughout your lifetime, I feel like a tadpole in a frog pond expressing my comments and gratitude for all you have done for me and my family. There is nothing that could have been more beneficial to my entire family than their association with your family on the many trips we were able to be a part. I will always be grateful and, by the way, I was not aware the trips began while you were at Meredith College. Further, I wish this book had been written before I went to the Marine Military Academy— I would have carried it with me like the Guidebook for Marines we carried in boot camp.

You may recall early in my time at MMA you spoke to the board for three hours in Houston, setting forth the need for a plan for the academy and a plan for raising the funds necessary to make the plan happen—basically as you have stated in your book. At any rate, your comments were taped, and I returned to the academy and drafted a five-year plan to improve the financial status of the academy, improve the academic area, build an auditorium, and commence the removal of the old Harlingen Air Force buildings.

I presented it to the board at the next meeting and added the need for a fund-raising campaign to raise not less than ten million dollars. You would have thought the building was going to explode. Two-thirds of the board were opposed and wanted to know where this idea came from. If I had been able to have had your book, I could have saved the day and not waited until you became chairman of the board.

Back to the book, I was deeply impressed by your letters to your mother and the continuous credit you gave to Betty as an equal part of your team. I was already aware of this fact, but maybe others who read the book will understand a man is not likely to be successful without a dedicated wife. I also found the many pictures included very interesting. In fact, I noticed several mutual friends.

I hope this wordy letter has not taken too much of your time. I merely wanted to let you know how much I enjoyed the content of your book and how much richer my life is having been in your association. I was also impressed by your rifle score of 323. I thought my 321 wasn't all that bad. I also believed your three doves with a single shot was lucky, but I now know you were using Kentucky windage. Carol joins me in sending our best with the hopes the Heilman family has a Merry Christmas and a continuously productive New Year.


Semper Fi,
Hal


And yet another commentary on my memoirs was written by General Al Gray, a former commandant of the Marine Corps in respect to the passing of my wife, Betty. Such a distinguished individual as General Gray having read my memoirs twice speaks to its relevance, its historic worth, and its points of personal identity with a broad range of readers.


After hearing about your heartbreaking loss, I went back and read your book again—you and Betty had a wonderful life together, and she was the perfect person for you and all that you believe in.

Please stay in touch; let me know if there is anything we can do.

Love and Semper Fidelis,
Al and Jan


If the reading of these letters sparks a fire of interest, you may want to enjoy the story of the Great Depression through World War II followed by all the adventures made possible by the G.I. Bill and all the opportunities given to those of us who fought for freedom and received the rewards of our service and benefits of a free society.

Growing up on a farm during the Great Depression with little or no interest or capability in education and nothing to suggest that my circumstances might change did not bode well for any prospect for leadership in my future. So, having begun the extension of my life after eighty with references to highlights of ultimate successes, I reflect back to my earlier life and the bleak prospects for any level of success beyond farm labor or a day job in a factory due to the circumstances of the times.

Born in 1926, I spent my early years growing up in Oldham County, Kentucky. We were not in the hustle and bustle of the county seat of La Grange but some distance away in the very unsophisticated community of Ballardsville. We didn't even enjoy the luxury of electricity in our house not to mention the appliances and other benefits that would later come with it. This was my world during the Depression years, and because only a few of us now survive to tell our story, the history of that period has survived. Unfortunately, our story will, to a large extent, be buried with us.

Being born and growing up during the Great Depression was either an obstacle to be overcome or a circumstance to be conquered. Fortunately, much literature conveys the unique circumstances growing out of the times referred to as the Great Depression. *The Grapes of Wrath* by John Steinbeck, for example, captures the essence of its unyielding impact where the Okies and others were so desperate that "death was a friend and sleep was death's partner." Life expectancy in the United States was fifty-four years as compared to seventy-seven today. Only 6 percent of youngsters graduated from high school. I didn't make the cut and fell into the 94 percent not completing the requirements. Today, 83 percent graduate from high school and 27 percent from college.

At the height of the Depression in 1932, when I was six years old, 273,000 families were evicted from their homes. William Manchester in *The Glory and the Dream*, wrote, "Poverty was considered shameful. One could never be sure about the smartly dressed young lawyer who left home every morning. He may have been off to sell cheap neckties, or magazines, or vacuum cleaners, or other door-to-door pandering in a remote neighborhood."

Nearly 28 percent of the population during those Depression years was without any income at all, not including the eleven million farm families who, like mine, were suffering in their own way. Few could afford a $450 new Chevrolet or could borrow enough to build a $3,000 house. Ten thousand banks closed, 175,000 school systems failed to open, and millions more closed their doors in 1933.

Today tenant farmers and sharecroppers are often thought of as second-rate farmhands who settle for a demeaning role short of success or accomplishments. But in those lean years, those who could support their families were highly regarded for what then was called keeping the family out of the poorhouse. I honed my capacity for hard work, my determination to see through to the finish, and never despair during those Depression years. So, with the goodwill of others playing their part, I accomplished what my talents and ambition made possible by way of my own efforts.

The thirteen years since my eightieth birthday have afforded interesting opportunities that have allowed me to do what few others could or would do at my age. Continuing to serve as chancellor of the University of Richmond results from a judgment I made at the time I accepted the presidency forty-nine years ago. I declared that I would stay just ten years because I realized that there was so much to be done—and the demands were so great in leading the university to become one of the finest in the nation—that it would substantially exhaust my energy. By the end of ten years, I would either be worn out, or because I would have to push everyone so hard that I would make not only friends but enemies, and thus my effectiveness would be impaired.

The harsh reality was that I did of necessity drive people forcefully to do what was essential to success in fulfilling the vision of Claiborne Robins. So, rather than moving on to other opportunities, forty-nine years afterward, I continue to occupy the physical space I had moved into as president forty-nine years earlier. At the end of ten years, true to my commitment, I did resign by letter to the board of trustees. Immediately, the chairman called a luncheon meeting at the president's home, including prominent trustees like Claiborne Robins, Lewis Booker, Carlyle Tiller, and others, to proclaim to me that they would not accept my resignation. I would allay their concerns, they said, if I would agree to stay a minimum of another five years. If so, they would affirm that I could spend the rest of my life in some capacity at the university where I could be meaningfully engaged.

The chairman of the board, at a called meeting of the board and the faculty, announced the board's request that I stay on, resulting in the unanimous support of the faculty. So, I accepted their challenge along with its conditions that I might serve in some capacity acceptable to the board and to me.

Although invited to consider other presidencies periodically, I was always persuaded to stay on. Many years after I became chancellor, I talked to Claiborne Robins about a presidency that held a special interest. He responded without hesitation, "If you should take another presidency, you would do a disservice to yourself and to the University of Richmond." I didn't persist. Hopefully, my staying has proved valuable in many ways as it continues today.

In these thirteen years since my first eighty, a lot of people may wonder what I have been doing. Many know what has been publicly declared in many newspapers throughout the country:

that I ride my Harley from coast to coast serving the university and a host of nonprofit and veterans' organizations. What I do educationally speaking for the university is not unusual; therefore, it doesn't get highlighted as much as my motorcycle riding. Rather than being recognized as an educator, I am often just the "Motorcycle Man," which highlights the university with lots of publicity as a result of my title as chancellor.

I see and serve a lot of alumni, friends, donors, and fellow educators even while in leathers, and I serve a noble purpose interacting with veterans, politicians, business leaders, civic clubs, and educators across the country and the world, always identifying myself as the chancellor of the University of Richmond. To my knowledge, without any credit or discredit, I am the only president in the history of the university who has served in the military. So, while every president during wartime has contributed some valuable service that benefitted the nation, none have been active militarily. Those who know me and my successes as expressed by the current reputation of the University of Richmond will judge me by what I have done to elevate the character and visibility of an already credible university where I have served for forty-nine years.

When I began my journey to being ninety-three years old, I had already completed eighty years of living from birth to a level or maturity physically, intellectually, socially, and spiritually. I had passed through the various stages of education and experience in preparation for my years of productive leadership and service. This period of activity is fully recorded in my previously published memoirs.

Having extended my life another thirteen years, it seemed logical to update my autobiography, to highlight who I am, what I have done, and the attributes that made possible my accomplishments during these past ninety-three years. I am reflecting upon the past as well as showing the nature of activities defined by an age when many have retired from personal engagement due to age limitations—actual or perceived.

In writing *My First Eighty Years,* I gave no thought to an extension in case life carried forward in such an active and engaging manner. Much like those who built their houses to serve their needs for their lifetimes but later find reason to adapt and adjust their facilities to their changing lifestyles, so it is with adjustments in lifestyle upon discovery of new interests and capabilities in later years.

I won't claim that this period has represented a new beginning, but it has altered my perception of what to expect in regard to my overall physical and even mental capabilities based upon historic perceptions of age. Unanticipated new, interesting, and even exciting adventures have presented themselves. Age limitations have been found to be few. I have continued to participate in a broad range of activities during this period almost without restriction. Rather than yielding to presumptions of limitations due to age, I have continued at age ninety-three most everything I've done at seventy or eighty.

My current age finds me in good health in spite of some hazards along the way. Having been cured of cancer of the esophagus over a three-year period and having experienced radical surgery for prostate cancer twenty years ago, I declare good fortune health wise. My continuing association as chancellor of the University of Richmond, my membership on a variety of boards, my extensive speaking as a goodwill ambassador, and my functioning throughout the country and the world as national spokesperson for the Greatest Generations Foundation and the Spirit of '45 tend to identify me as the face of the university where that sector of society is concerned.

Natural happenings have impacted the whole family during this thirteen year period. The most distressing has been, by far, the loss of the mother of my children, the grandmother of my grandchildren, the great-grandmother of my great-grandchildren, and for me, my wife, Betty. After sixty-five years of marriage, nothing could leave a larger space in my heart or empty space in my life during the years since she passed away. Though she has been gone for five years, it seems she has both been gone forever, and at the same time, in my thoughts, she remains just out for the day and will be back soon. Her impact in my life and as First Lady of the University of Richmond and Meredith College is later highlighted in these pages.

In the meantime, my five wonderful children, my eleven loveable grandchildren, and now my nine great-grandchildren starting another life cycle bring joy and help offset the loss of the one missed by us all. Life has taken on new dimensions as grandchildren have matured and assumed leadership roles in their professional arenas. Also, their marriages have fostered my nine great-grandchildren. Every advance familywise makes clear the legacy of the wife, mother, grandmother, and great-grandmother, bringing to fruition the greatest fulfilling adventure of my life—my marriage and family. The fact that twenty-three members of my family are graduates of the University of Richmond impacts us all in a powerful way.

It may be that I am beyond most maladies of age and hazards of health having had cancer twice, having survived an airplane crash, having lived through three automobile wrecks, with two deaths, having survived World War II combat unscathed, and living through more than 100,000 motorcycle miles while traveling through all fifty states, and visiting 145 countries along with many cities of the world. I have lived through and beyond risks not common to most. I have overcome these sufficiently to continue to live my life with only minor restrictions in my activities or disruption to my lifestyle.

While I present first and highlight strongly my University of Richmond experience, this great adventure is only one of the facets of my life about which I share in the cover of the book divided by sections to include Meredith College, my military engagements, my family, motorcycling, aging, traveling, and a miscellaneous section. Each holds interest to some, and some hold interest to all.

I began writing some of these words while sitting on the porch of a Cracker Barrel restaurant in one of their comfortable rocking chairs. A passing lady asked, "Are you getting your sermon ready for tomorrow?" It was Saturday afternoon, so what could have been more logical? Who I am and what I represent in the minds of strangers passing results from the fact that I usually wear a coat and tie.

On that day, I was also wearing a bright red cap that highlighted "United Sates Marines." As a result, the waitress, at my leaving, announced, "Some folks have already paid for your lunch." Because a lady leaving earlier thanked me for my service, perhaps she was the one who paid, but another also thanked me. I did not know who to thank. But as a veteran, I am proud to be acknowledged for my service because that represents much of who I am.

Because many have enjoyed my use of verses and quotations within the pages of my earlier book, I continue to embody appropriate ones in this extension. Further, I draw from my earlier memoirs thoughts, illustrations, pictures, and even paragraphs and stories that clarify, amplify, or illustrate and confirm that which is further highlighted in this extension of my life expressed as life's opportunities beyond age eighty or ninety-one years of fulfilling adventures, including two miracles.

In my earlier memoirs, I sought to present a balance to my life, trying not to highlight the highs or lows, the good or the bad, or play down or fail to highlight what others did in making possible my successes. However, ten years later, at age ninety-one, with expanded wisdom fostered by age, I have little inclination for recalling negatives. Instead, I choose to reflect on the most positive aspects of my life that are most representative of these thirteen years of maturity when most of my critics are deceased and most of my remaining friends, and even members of my family, more mature, are inclined to be positive.

Readers of these pages and *An Interruption That Lasted a Lifetime* will, I hope, reflect on Longfellow's words: "We judge ourselves by what we feel capable of doing while others judge us by what we have already done." It is my hope that, after forty-six years of association with the University of Richmond and my sixty-seven years in higher education, the following reflections will call to mind a successful journey of great progress in building new towers on sound foundations.

By way of my inaugural address, restated in these pages, I shared what I intended to do.

In the interim, I did that which I embodied in the address, and I am, in the chapters of this book, directing readers' attention to the results, which are self-evident of what I and others have done to bring to fruition Mr. Robins's dream.

Highlighted are the successes I have enjoyed, the remembrances of the good things in life, the results of which I am most proud, the cards, letters, comments, and conversations that most positively elevate my ego, even if fostered by my own hard work and reinforced by my wife and family. I have lived my life to my own satisfaction by doing my best with a positive attitude and a confident spirit.

In these forty-nine years of my association with the University of Richmond, I have played a variety of parts with many different actors making a great difference in the outcome of the production. Together we have led a transition almost unparalleled in history. We planned the play based upon certain prescribed factors and we have completed the different stage settings to the satisfaction of the audience over time.

The achievements of so many performers need no great elaboration by me as the coordinator of actions over some of those years. Without the cast in its full contingent, my efforts would have been for naught. But, as the director drawing upon the superior talents of the cast available to me, we have had great success.

I've written this book by putting in a positive framework the outcomes that are credible, hoping that I have been fair and honest casting of everything in proper perspective. My enjoyment of life, the goodwill of others, the blessing of having a good family, good friends, and excellent professionals who made me look good, and the blessings and rewards of succeeding in worthwhile things that have made life fulfilling. I give credit to everyone from the Supreme Being to the most invisible individual on the universe who may have contributed to the positive outcomes of my life.

# A UNIVERSITY

THERE ARE FEW EARTHLY THINGS MORE BEAUTIFUL THAN
A UNIVERSITY.
IT IS A PLACE WHERE THOSE WHO HATE IGNORANCE MAY STRIVE TO
KNOW, WHERE THOSE WHO PERCEIVE TRUTH MAY STRIVE
TO MAKE OTHERS SEE; WHERE SEEKERS AND LEARNERS ALIKE, BANDED
TOGETHER IN SEARCH FOR KNOWLEDGE, WILL HONOR
THOUGHT IN ALL ITS FINER WAYS, WILL WELCOME THINKERS
IN DISTRESS OR IN EXILE, WILL UPHOLD EVER THE
DIGNITY OF THOUGHT AND LEARNING AND WILL EXACT
STANDARDS IN THESE THINGS.
THEY GIVE TO THE YOUNG IN THEIR IMPRESSIONABLE YEARS,
THE BOND OF A LOFTY PURPOSE SHARED, OF A GREAT CORPORATE
LIFE WHOSE LINKS WILL NOT BE LOOSED UNTIL THEY DIE.
THEY GIVE YOUNG PEOPLE THAT CLOSE COMPANIONSHIP FOR
WHICH YOUTH LONGS, AND THAT CHANCE OF THE ENDLESS
DISCUSSION OF THE THEMES WHICH ARE ENDLESS,
WITHOUT WHICH YOUTH WOULD SEEM A WASTE OF TIME.
THERE ARE FEW EARTHLY THINGS MORE SPLENDID THAN A
UNIVERSITY.
IN THESE DAYS OF BROKEN FRONTIERS AND COLLAPSING VALUES, WHEN
THE DAMS ARE DOWN AND THE FLOODS ARE MAKING MISERY, WHEN
EVERY FUTURE LOOKS SOMEWHAT GRIM AND EVERY ANCIENT
FOOTHOLD HAS BECOME SOMETHING OF A QUAGMIRE,
WHEREVER A UNIVERSITY STANDS, IT STANDS AND SHINES; WHEREVER IT
EXISTS, THE FREE MINDS OF MEN, URGED ON TO FULL AND
FAIR INQUIRY, MAY STILL BRING WISDOM INTO HUMAN AFFAIRS.

JOHN MASEFIELD

Poem entitled A University by John Masefield

# CHAPTER ONE

## THE UNIVERSITY OF RICHMOND
## BUILDING A UNIVERSITY ANEW
## ON A SOLID FOUNDATION
## A MIRACLE

This section includes the details of my election as president, my inaugural address, looking back from today after years of success, a definition of the presidency, notable contributions of my successors, and the role and fulfillment of that role by Betty as the First Lady.

It has been said many times, in many ways, that "the quickest way to change an institution is to change its leadership." It may not satisfy every need, but it is the single most effective measure of all the rest that can be undertaken.

\*\*\*

# I

# BEING ELECTED PRESIDENT OF THE UNIVERSITY OF RICHMOND

*Never despair, but if you do, work on in despair, looking always*
*upon the bright side and you will find your way.*
*—Edwin Burke*

While this book is not intended to be a history of the University of Richmond becoming one of the finest small universities in the country, it is intended to embody the defining adventure of my lifetime in higher education. Thus, the miracle highlighted in the preface of this book and further expanded in my introduction serves as a beacon toward other activities engaged at the university during my forty-nine years as president and chancellor. Thus, with an ambitious challenge to provide the leadership for making the university one of the finest anywhere, I've waited all these years to declare this adventure an unqualified success.

After being elected president, I presented the case and articulated the challenge based upon the expectation fostered by the Robins' gift of $50 million. The school's future success depended on nurturing confidence that the ambitious outcome desired could be realized. How I did that required selecting leaders capable of facilitating the miracle by raising money and enlisting and managing the staff to make it happen.

# The New President

With a surprise spring snowstorm sweeping across the state, the University's Board of Trustees met March 26, in the Fine Arts Center and elected a young, enthusiastic college administrator the fifth president of the University of Richmond.

Dr. E. Bruce Heilman, President of Meredith College in Raleigh, N. C., since 1966, will take office as the University's chief administrator on Sept. 1. President George M. Modlin will retire June 30 and become Chancellor.

Meredith College has an enrollment of approximately 1,200 women, and is affiliated with the Baptist Church.

Battling the snow all the way from Raleigh, Dr. and Mrs. Heilman reached the campus in time for a news conference and a short get-acquainted session with faculty, administrators and student leaders.

(Continued)

It is not reported in the minutes of the board of trustees that when offered the presidency, I declined. Two weeks later, the board pursued the prospect of my revisiting the university to discuss the offer further. I declined that invitation as well, even though every committee with which I had met gave me their full support.

However, upon reflection and with the encouragement of representatives of the board, I made a judgement that proved to be a wise one. I would come back to Richmond to discuss the presidency further—but only with the one who was to contribute the large gift. I had not yet met Mr. Robins since he was not engaged in discussions with the prospective new president and was not on the committee. This, to me, was a mistake on the part of the university because Mr. Robins's pledge to give $50 million to his alma mater was certainly the most powerful influence on anyone considering the position.

Thus, it was arranged that I would meet with Mr. Robins privately to discern whether he could impress upon me what the university committees had not, up to that time, been successful in doing. I knew that making Richmond one of the finest small universities in the country was a big order, and I would need to press everybody hard to bring that to fruition. I knew I needed someone of influence on my side.

After two hours of private conversation with Claiborne Robins, he said, "If you will accept the presidency of my alma mater, I will personally guarantee you that you will never regret it." With that guarantee, I revisited the campus and accepted the offer. That was forty-nine years ago, and with Claiborne being true to his word, I never regretted my decision. In a real sense, it was he who employed me as president after I declined the invitation of those with legal authority.

The following excerpts are from a section of board minutes entitled "Presidential Election of March 26, 1971." The following are quotes from the board's minutes:

Ninety-five individuals had been suggested to the selection committee.

After careful consideration, the committee placed thirteen in group A. Exploratory letters were written to those individuals asking if they would be interested in learning about the University of Richmond and considering the position as president. Eight of the thirteen individuals indicated that they might be interested, and they were visited by representatives of the committee.

The committee came to the conclusion that Dr. E. Bruce Heilman was the best qualified. However, he first stated that he was not interested in leaving Meredith College where he was president. Members of the selection committee visited him in Raleigh on two occasions, and he had been to Richmond three times. The selection committee and the faculty advisory committee were unanimous that Dr. Heilman be elected as president. The deans, president, and treasurer had met Dr. Heilman, and they were all favorably impressed by him. The student government presidents had also met with Dr. Heilman, and they unanimously endorsed him.

Dr. Theodore F. Adams spoke enthusiastically concerning Dr. Heilman and moved that the board receive the report of the selection committee and the recommendations that Dr. E. Bruce Heilman be elected president of the University of Richmond effective September 1, 1971.

Mr. E. C. Robbins stated that Dr. Heilman appealed to the faculty, students, and trustees and that the university would be indeed fortunate to secure Dr. Heilman as president and seconded the motion.

Judge J. W. Dillion stated that he had met Dr. Heilman and was very impressed with him and commended him to the board and also seconded the motion.

The following comments were made in the discussion of the motion:

Justice Harold F. Sneed stated that he had the privilege of meeting Dr. Heilman and felt that he possessed all of the qualities needed for a president of the University of Richmond.

Dr. L. D. George, as a member of the selective committee, endorsed all the comments that had been made by the individuals and felt that Dr. Heilman was a keen intellect.

Dr. E. L. Hans asked what Dr. Heilman's church relationship was, as nothing was stated concerning this in the biographical sketch distributed to the board. He also stated that the press release dated March 19 concerning Dr. Heilman disturbed many members of the board because they were unaware of the committee's decision. Mr. Marsh stated that Dr. Heilman was a Baptist and had been deacon in four Baptist churches and the press release was unauthorized, and it was very unfortunate that the newspaper printed it.

Dr. E. H. Prudent stated that he was college pastor at Meredith and that the university would be very fortunate if they could secure Dr. Heilman as president. He stated that Dr. Heilman is a very aggressive person and gets things done. Dr. R. C. Pitts asked, "What was the feeling of the Baptist leadership in North Carolina concerning Dr. Heilman and his relationship with the Baptist Convention?" Dr. Prudence stated that Dr. Heilman had the very best relationship with the state convention, that he had kept in very close contact with the leaders of the convention. Dr. Adams stated that the North Carolina Baptist Convention was generous with all the Baptist colleges and schools in the state and that Dr. Heilman had obtained the respect of the entire business community of Raleigh.

The board unanimously elected Dr. E. Bruce Heilman as president effective September 1, 1971.

Following the board action taken by the University of Richmond, there was much displeasure at Meredith expressed in various ways with Dr. Heilman having served only five years.

Irrespective of that unhappiness on the part of the board of Meredith, in gratitude for what had been accomplished, the accompanying resolution was presented to me, a building was named for me, and I was named a founder of the college.

Having been elected already as a college president, I found myself in line for consideration for the presidency of the University of Richmond with some ninety-five others. Why were ninety-five people willing to be considered for such a job and why would one who had already enjoyed the privileges, honors, prestige, and pains of the presidency be willing to go through the risk of selection, the trauma of change, and the pressure of beginning again? I doubt if anyone really knows. I don't but unusual opportunities and challenges cause strange reactions.

The Inaugural
Address

The
Inaugural
Address

University of Richmond

# CAPITALIZING ON CONFIDENCE
# FOR OUR TIME IN HISTORY

E. Bruce Heilman
Saturday, October 30
1971

*** 

All the great things are simple . . .
Freedom, justice,
Honor, mercy,
Duty, hope.

—*Winston Churchill*

# II

# MY INAUGURAL ADDRESS

Saturday, October 30, 1971

Upon having been selected to lead the charge toward the challenge presented by Claiborne Robins and the board of trustees, I accepted my role of creating and sustaining the momentum essential to making the University of Richmond "one of the finest small universities in the country." Convinced it was the right choice to give up a successful presidency at Meredith, where the board would have done anything that Richmond offered, I was in the driver's seat with my new constituents awaiting my first move.

While in transition between institutions, I put my anticipated actions into words in order to adequately motivate positive support as I assumed office. I began this by way of my acceptance comments.

Next came the important process of articulating all that was about to happen. No longer was I confirming what might happen, but what was already in the process of happening.

I presented my inaugural address as a future already underway in spirit and anticipated action. How would we know how to get there unless we knew where we were going? That's what my address was all about.

## CAPITALIZING ON CONFIDENCE FOR OUR TIME IN HISTORY

My much beloved predecessor, Dr. Modlin, and Mrs. Modlin, both of whom are my most ardent supporters, Rector Marsh, honored platform guests, members of my family, former colleagues from Meredith College, representatives of colleges, universities, and learned societies, trustees, fellow administrators, colleagues of the faculty, staff, students, alumni, alumnae, neighbors in the community, friends of the university, ladies, and gentlemen.

Dr. and Mrs. Modlin in Cannon Memorial Chapel

Dr. E. Bruce Heilman with Visitor During First Day
as President of UR.

Making Music with
Chaplain David Burhans.

Leland Melvin, R'86
Rhodes Scholar nominee
All-American Candidate.

As is: Trustee George Wellde, B'74;
trustee Paul Queally, R'86; Tim Leahy, BR '98;
and Ryan FitzSions, BR'01 in New York City

An inauguration is many things to many people. To the one being inaugurated, it's an occasion unlike any other and represents the formal initiation of his administration. To the inaugural committee, it's a demanding responsibility and a challenging opportunity to turn the spotlight on the university. Certainly, the entourage gathered here speaks well for the efforts of this group.

To trustees, the inauguration signifies a transfer of leadership and the beginning of a new era. To faculty, students, graduates, the denomination, the community, and all other members of the university family, this is a time to be proud of the past, an opportunity to take note of the present, and an occasion for reaffirming dedication, loyalty, and support.

To those who have been invited to take part in this celebration, it is as many things as the number of individuals involved. But to each and every one, we at the University of Richmond extend our warmest welcome and express our deepest appreciation for your presence and participation. We are proud to reflect with you on an illustrious past, to indulge with you in the exciting present, and to anticipate in your company a future that promises to be among the finest years in the life of the university.

We are privileged to have the governor of our state represented and the mayor of our city present with us, along with many other political, civic, social, and church leaders, and delegates from many colleges, universities, and learned societies. We respond with gratitude to the expressions of good will tendered by representatives of the principal communities of the University of Richmond.

In my second month of office and on my sixtieth day, I can't speak as if I've been around forever or even for a long time. Nonetheless, I shall endeavor to express something of the atmosphere and of the character of the university, as well as the spirit and posture of the administration assuming office. I shall also remember that an inauguration is not for the president and the cultivation of his already healthy ego, but to give exposure to the university and possibly to make some contribution to higher education generally.

Since my first contact with the presidential selection committee, I've heard over and over again from many sources that this institution aspires to be a great university. These expressions have caused me to reflect on the several colleges and universities that I've served and to remember that, without exception, they aspired to greatness. Certainly they did, and why not?

For without such aspirations, no institution is worth the salt of its existence.

Most recently, in preparation for this address, I remembered the history of higher education, and I recalled that much mention is made of *the* great universities. I also observed that very little is said of the conditions that made them great or the criteria for greatness. There seems to be, however, a particular thread that runs true throughout all of history in identifying college and university greatness. That thread embroiders on the institution a clear evidence of selfconfidence and uncompromising self-expectation to the point of clearly saying to all, "*We are* a distinctive institution."

The fact of such confidence is not surface or peripheral but dips into the trunk and roots of the institution and exudes from every aspect of its being. Some may read it as arrogance, but anything bordering on conceit does not compliment a truly great university. The kind of confidence that is observable in the institutions I have in mind grows out of the generally recognized assumption that there's a relationship between what others expect of them and what they expect of themselves. Both self-respect and expectation on the part of others result from continuing performance at a level beyond the ordinary.

A few colleges and universities have been great even in poverty, but not many. Many have been great because they had great resource, but not all. Most have been great because they believed in themselves in such a way that their confidence in self spread to others, making greater and greater achievement possible. Strength built on strength, and the university moving of its own volition found direction under able leaders who were attracted by the special excitement created under such conditions.

Has this university called Richmond *been* a great university? In a measure, I think we would all say it has been. Great things have been accomplished throughout its history. But it's obvious that this university has the possibility of building higher towers on these strong foundations because those who are the university conceive of a measure of greatness not yet attained. We who are now responsible must improve upon the excellent record of the past and make it outstanding if we are to do justice to the new opportunities resulting from the generosity of the Robins family and others who have been generous to the university over the years. We cannot do less than run the risk of building strength far above a level ever dreamed of prior to the recent magnificent contributions from the Robins family, including endowments and facilities, which with the matching portions will total more than seventy million dollars, making this an unprecedented act in the history of this university or any other.

But aspirations are only emotions put into words unless we discover the ingredients necessary to success in bringing about the greatness of which we speak. Certainly it won't be money alone, although that provides a measure of possibility not before attained. It won't be human resources alone because people can create or perpetuate weakness as well as strength. It won't be more students because size doesn't make greatness. It won't even result from a winning football or basketball team. A university's greatness depends neither upon presence nor upon the absence of any particular thing at any particular time. Rather, it depends upon an attitude, a spirit, and a posture of a kind embodied in confidence.

I believe confidence to be the only certain ingredient that will bring us toward, and carry us into, a new level of greatness. We must have a new confidence, a clear confidence, and a confidence far beyond that achieved prior to this time. I believe so strongly that "capitalization on confidence" is our best approach to success in the months and years ahead that I've made the title of this address "Capitalizing on Confidence for Our Time in History." If a lack of confidence can cause crises, as John Gardiner has so clearly observed, then the presence of confidence should keep us free from the pangs of crisis and catapult us toward our goal. This confidence should say to us, "If you are going to be something, be something special." But to do so, we must translate our confidence into specifics. So, let me share with you what I believe about confidence specifically.

*I believe we who are responsible for the university must have confidence in ourselves.* I would be the wrong person for the presidency of the University of Richmond if I had any doubt as to the possibility of greater progress and more outstanding achievements in the months and years ahead. The faculty, staff, trustees, students, alumni, community, denomination, and administration would be poor risks in doing their jobs for the university if they expected anything less. Confidence must be our state of mind, our spirit, and our attitude. It must make us face up to our responsibilities, and it must make worthwhile our efforts to achieve our ambitions.

Yes, I believe all of us who are the university must have confidence in ourselves if we are to live up to the level of expectation obvious at this point in time. We must envision the rewards and satisfactions of our efforts if we are to deal with the challenge and opportunities, and we must believe fully in our ability to fulfill the demands, whatever they may be. The most obvious evidence of institutional confidence is self-confidence on the part of its leadership.

*I believe we must have confidence in our purposes and objectives.* Thornton Wilder said, "Our young people are being prepared for a world in which every good and excellent thing stands moment by moment on the razor's edge of danger and must be fought for. There is not an hour in the education of our young people that is not trembling with destinies. We are the leaders in preparing for these destinies. We must define our purpose clearly, and it should not be faulty compromise with expediency."

Thomas Braden said, "Only when men and institutions do not know what they want or have forgotten what their purpose was, do pressures become dangerous … for pressures of whatever sincerity and from whatever source can be dealt with—can be resisted or welcomed— as long as an institution and the men who make it up know what they want and have a purpose and a goal … When there is no purpose, pressure takes its place. And institutions which ought to help define the ends and aims of life are themselves defined by pressure."

We at the University of Richmond must put ourselves to the stern test of gauging results in terms of human behavior, dignity, and freedom. Our priorities must be appraised against their contributions to this overriding purpose. This university has a background that gives it special reason to be sensitive to such considerations, and we must have confidence that these commitments justify our best efforts.

*I believe we must maintain mutual confidence between the university and the general public.* Arnold Toynbee has said, "The world's greatest need … is mutual confidence … confidence may be risky, but it is nothing like so risky as mistrust." Plato said, "We can forgive a child who is afraid of the dark; the real tragedy of life is when men are afraid of the light." But many will continue to be afraid of the light unless we in the forefront of education can win their confidence anew. To do this, we must talk to them in terms they can understand, give more emphasis to our positive achievements, and disclaim responsibility for what we have not brought about or what we should not be expected to control.

But confidence, like prestige, sought directly is almost never gained. It must come as a by-product of that which is sought and achieved for its own sake and recognized as valid and valuable by others. We cannot maintain confidence simply by verbal expressions of objectivity. Our credibility must come through in practice. Objectivity is not in disregarding or flouting the views of others even those off campus. We can't become great by putting down those who would not agree with us. A university must be open-minded, and that image should exist neither to deceive nor to placate others, but simply to express an honest intent to broaden our own narrow views.

While outside forces should not tell us what we may teach, how we must teach it, or what kind of speakers we may have on campus, we *must* have the willingness to make a part of our posture a stance of listening, learning, and inviting suggestions. We have the ability and the responsibility to convince our constituents that we deserve both support and respect. We do not condescend to others in so doing, but rather we extend our image of integrity beyond ourselves.

In order to have others listen to us, we must first win their confidence. It is only as we pay attention to others that we get them to pay attention to us.

John Stuart Mill said, "Every conceivable shade of opinion should be tolerated in a university." In a social or political sense, this means that the university as an institution is neutral. In a good university, however, even neutrality is dynamic, and if it is, there are some who will need to be assured of the legitimacy of that posture. That will take continuing effort because the confidence that is built by many acts is often lost by one.

*I believe we must maintain confidence in leadership and in constituted authority necessary to effecting that leadership.* No great movement has reached its peak without a leader having the authority necessary to fulfill the expectations of the movement. Confidence in leadership is critically important to success in any university. This includes confidence in the president, but it extends throughout the institution. Unless there is confidence in leadership, there is excessive over-the-shoulder looking, which hinders the necessary risk-taking that is essential if an institution is to build and grow in strength and service. If every critic is free to check every move of those selected for leadership, then the leader will seek only to please, not to lead. Such a practice is analogous to regularly pulling up flowers to see how the roots are growing. They may continue to live as plants, but they will do very little blooming.

Every institution with aggressive ambitions must create and honor some reasonable structure of authority. If it ceases to do so, then it moves toward no authority or ultimately it reverts to total authority, neither of which is desirable. Educational institutions are particularly vulnerable in their authority structure because they must allow a wide latitude for dissent.

Governance is a great concern of the present and of the future in the life of the university. Trustees, administrators, students, professors, staff, alumni, and the public all have an interest. It's easy to underestimate or exaggerate the influence of any one of these. It's impossible that all should decide everything or be consulted on each issue. But there must be a sharing of information and responsibility and a readiness to subject all authority to the requirements of a well-defined system of accountability.

John Stuart Mill said, "Men often submit willingly, even cheerfully, to authority when they believe it to be exercised well and responsibly in the pursuit of ends of which they approve and whose benefit they would justly share." Total consensus is not a viable alternative on the campus today. We must maintain a healthy confidence in each other, and we must have guidelines that treat rights and responsibilities simultaneously under leaders whose constituted authority is clear and present.

*I believe we must continually seek and endeavor to maintain the confidence of our supporting church.* The Christian community must believe in institutions that aspire to uphold Christian principles and traditions. The University of Richmond was born of dedicated churchmen. Its history of some 140 years has been blessed with this relationship. They who have blessed the university must not be disregarded.

Perhaps a university and its church relationship is analogous to a parent and a child. The child is conceived and nurtured by the parent. As the child matures, he grows more and more independent. Nonetheless, he never disowns his parent, and if he seeks to do so, his action reflects upon himself. The wise parent seeks not to dominate his maturing child but endeavors to find those attributes that are complementary, recognizing that perfection is a goal not a reality. In turn, the child sows hospitality and appreciation toward the parent by fostering a meaningful relationship that enriches the lives of both.

Frederick deBolman of the Esso Foundation, said, "The university is a protective shield beneath which all points of view can be expressed and cherished. Unlike the church, its mission is not to propagandize or to preach some particular gospel. Its mission is rather to tolerate."

The University of Richmond, although a church-related institution, has been privileged to function in an unusually free atmosphere. As testimony to the liberality of this university, I quote from a speech made by Dr. Modlin some years ago: "Faculty and students have never been restricted here in their search of truth. Everyone has been free to follow the inquiries of his mind and the dictates of his conscience without fear or interference or recrimination. On this campus, there have been breadth of opinion and freedom of expression to a degree that is rare at a churchrelated institution."

Dr. Frederick W. Boatwright, speaking in defense of the university and its teaching practices in 1930, said, "We must encourage our teachers and students to think, and we should not be surprised when they do not think alike. The inquiring mind will question established customs in every field of human action … a college is more concerned with teaching students how to think than with telling them what to think."

As far back as 1890, Dr. Robert Ryland, the first president of the University of Richmond, returning from retirement to deliver an alumni address, pointed out that the college is a "Baptist college in no narrow, bigoted sense. Pupils of every creed and no creed have been and will be received on the same terms and treated with equal justice and consideration." Baptists in Virginia have, over the years, held high expectations for their university as they have been both tolerant of its actions and proud of its results.

After 140 years of contribution to the university, the Baptist denomination deserves to know that the relationships growing out of the roots of its existence are not taken lightly. At the same time, the university cannot be run by the church, and as a result, the church cannot assume responsibility for what the university does. Together, I believe the Baptists of Virginia and the University of Richmond have much to give to each other in the years ahead. We must have their confidence, and in turn, I hope we give them no doubt as to ours.

*I believe we must have confidence in our faculty and its ability to continually change the university constructively.* A university campus is many things—a physical place, a shifting scene of people, a set of functions, a series of traditions, a body of rules, and much else. But it is also a spirit. This spirit has been in the past, and needs to be in the future, a healthy tolerance, respect for the contrary views of others, and goodwill toward each other as individuals. It also must embody the supremacy of persuasion, concern for hard facts and careful analysis, devotion to the well-being of mankind around the world, and a means of thought directed toward the end of wisdom. This spirit and the preservation of freedom that it implies is particularly in the care of the faculties of a university. As they nurture it and guard it well, it endures; if they do not, it decays. From its place within the hearts and minds of the faculty, it emerges just at the right time to cast itself upon young minds, creating a positive confidence in self and one's place in society.

A very heavy responsibility thus falls upon faculty members, for they are at the heart of all academic endeavors. The quality of campus life depends upon their performance. They need to be alert to grievances, ready to accept constructive change, willing to cope with the problems of detecting dissent and preventing disruption, and devoted to the preservation of independent scholarship and teaching.

Education is a stimulating occupation. Confidence in its nature in a university setting is essential if the faculty is to meet the enormous challenge. None of us who have faculty responsibility can look forward to rest, for as we seek and find we open new doors of inquiry.

What we find today will be taken for granted or rejected tomorrow, and the search will begin anew. We must have confidence in that search and instill confidence on the part of those who make it possible.

*I believe we must have confidence in our youth.* "We live," as Dickens said, "in the best and the worst of times" and in the greatest paradox ever. Never before have we had such strength of good, yet so little knowledge of how to use it. The power of religion, once dominant in people's lives has declined to a point of nominal significance to many. Family stability continues its decline. We are in an age of uncertain moral values. The one clear line between violence, lawlessness, and destruction and the world of builders, cooperators, and constructive forces has become blurred. We are reaping the harvest of failure to challenge youth with ideals, values, and standards of conduct. Why shouldn't they fail to measure up to some of our expectations?

Most of the world's great issues are yet to be resolved, and our young people know it. They have become aware of the fact that these problems cannot all be resolved by research. Somewhere in their background, they acquired the idea that life is more than objectivity, that human concern plays a part. With such a spirit stimulating our young people, we should be encouraged to mobilize our intellectual and spiritual talents to overcome some of the problems of the past and present. As we do this, we give hope to our young people as we both educate them to a mission and leave a foundation on which they can build their lives.

The older generation owes the younger generation what all older generations have owed younger generations— love, some protection, and respect when they deserve it. We also owe them an education based upon our experiences but not saturated with our prejudices. But above all else and in spite of every reason we may have to do otherwise, we owe them our confidence, and having given that confidence, our help in building a better world.

*I believe we must have confidence in the old adages regarding response to challenge.* Professor Arnold Toynbee said that civilizations rise to greatness only when faced with some desperate challenge. Where there is challenge, there is action, and action is a great building for confidence.

Man is a complicated animal. He simplifies only under pressure. Put him under pressure in almost any situation, and he will scream in anguish—then he will come up with a plan that, to his own private amazement, not only solves his past problem but also creates a new and better way of dealing with his own original objective.

The greatest source of satisfaction is the act of creation, whether it be a work of art, a garden, social reform, or business or professional achievement. Throughout it all, a love of excellence lifts one's sights and makes even the smallest task a source of satisfaction. Such is the need in attitude of those who would make this university greater.

All through history, the proper challenge has caused men and women to strive impatiently and restlessly for results that appear worthwhile to them. In the process, they have achieved great religious insights, created works of art, uncovered secrets of the university, and established standards of conduct. "Our chief want in life," said Emerson, "is someone who will make us do all that we can, whether we like it or not." People who fail to do all they can have clearly not seen the alternatives. I believe that our cause is vital enough to point up these alternatives and draw out the best in those who must support it. It is my feeling that men and women of today are just as capable of devotion, courage, and response to challenge as has ever been true in the past.

In conclusion, let me say that the task of presiding over a private institution of higher learning in the sentries will be arduous, awesome, and exciting.

Arduous because the maintenance of a truly independent college or university of high quality grows more difficult with each passing year. In the face of stiff competition from taxsupported institutions, many private universities and colleges are becoming mediocre or secondrate.

The task is awesome because the prospect of America slumbering placidly while its private colleges and universities suffer from malnutrition is preposterous but a real threat. The University of Richmond and other private, independent institutions must be made even stronger, for they are the fountainheads of freedom and free enterprise in this country. If we allow these institutions to grow weak, we will have contributed, I am convinced, to the weakness of the country at large.

The task is exciting because all of us joining in this common cause can give the University of Richmond the forward thrust she must have. Despite difficulties that confront us, the vistas of opportunity are real and vast. Our opportunities are limited only by our vision of what can be and by our ability to share this vision with others.

As I respond to the challenge before me, I do so without modesty, but with much humility. I accept the full weight of responsibility, knowing that as president I represent the University of Richmond. I realize further that the demanding charge carries with it commensurate honor and satisfaction.

Here I expect to find maximum fulfillment. I do not anticipate that we will perform miracles or create a paradise. But we will do our best. Step by step, throughout the history of this institution, those who have gone before us have made possible all that this new administration will build upon. Our heritage is a rich one indeed. Our past is behind us. That which is ahead is a responsibility for each of us. God grant us the wisdom to fulfill our aspirations.

I believe our trustees are at a high level of readiness; our administrators have the knowhow and commitment to do the job; our faculty and staff are anxiously contributing their best effort; the alumni and alumnae have shown what they can and will do; the church is giving strong support, and the community, students, parents, and all the rest appear willing to promote an ambitious undertaking and invest in something that will continue as a worthwhile and successful enterprise.

In Revelation 3:8, we read, "Behold I have set before thee an open door, and no man can shut it." I believe that we who hold the future of this university in our hands must believe that destiny has for us an open door that no man can shut. How far we advance through that door is up to us. The advance will require painstaking preparation: helping each other to grow; high aim; long days; and sleepless nights. According to J.C. Holland,

Heaven is not reached by a single bound, But we built the ladder by which we rise
From the lowly earth to the vaulted skies, And we mount to its summit round by round.


Life for this university must be lived in the spirit of reaching for the summit. Otherwise, our accomplishments will not be worthy of the investment of human effort that such confidence as that expressed here today can muster. Many hold keys that open the doors to the future of this university to make our time in history—the time when we set out to mount to the summit of the destiny of this university.

\*\*\*

I cannot review these words of forty-nine years ago without being amazed at how clearly they represent the challenges as they were seen by me then. Certainly times have changed, and the words as interpreted then do not mean exactly the same thing in the context of today. For example, the value of the dollar has been reduced by about four or five times so that the $50 million-dollar Robins gift would be about $300 million today.

Our relationship to the church is different, and our overall financial strength can hardly be compared. How the university is perceived, the breadth of recognition, its enrollment diversity, its selective status, and much else are different. Yet, it all was a part of the ambition perceived when my address was given. We have indeed capitalized upon our confidence of that time, and we have reaped the ambitions that were ours then.

Fifteen years after this address, Mr. Robins observed, "More has happened than I ever thought possible." What would he say today? But with these words in my inaugural address, the foundation was laid for all that has happened to bring us to where we are today.

\*\*\*

# III

# HOW I SAW IT THEN FROM THE PERSPECTIVE OF TODAY

It's been forty-nine years since I became president of the University of Richmond, so I have to stretch my memory in order to garner the details from my ninety-three-year-old mind. In the meantime, I have spent half of my life as president and chancellor of this university.

I arrived here long before current students and many faculty members were born, and much that was a challenge to me as president had been rectified before they became associated with the university.

Forty-nine years ago, when I was offered the presidency of the university, I declined the offer. How brash. Why would I have refused an opportunity to be president of such a prestigious institution as seen through the eyes of those living today? The answer to that is that I was not seeing through eyes of today but through the eyes of a seasoned educational administrator already having served in senior positions in colleges and universities in four states, including a statewide system of higher education and in every senior position definable in higher education.

When offered the presidency of the University of Richmond, I was already a college president. In five years, my colleagues and I had transformed Meredith College from a negative trajectory to a robust and positive position of breaking trends and setting records of dynamic growth, strengthening financial health, and enthusiastic anticipation for the future. So, I had no reason to accept the presidency of a university with questionable conditions similar to those I had already helped remedy at Meredith.

So, what specifically caused me to say no to the opportunity of serving as president of a university that today has 11,000 applicants anxious to fill 750 spaces and that clearly is recognized as among the finest in the country and the world?

I had come to Richmond at the invitation of the chairman of the board and the chairman of the faculty to discuss whether I would be interested in considering the presidency of the university. I thought of my visit as a means of helping the board and the faculty to better determine who they might discover qualified to fill the position as president. I was happy where I was and generally not interested in the University of Richmond—although an alumnus of UR had generously tendered a $50 million gift that offered some incentive.

Of the ninety-seven candidates already vetted, none were finally presented for election to the position. When the board decided to open the search again, and I was the first to be contacted. I wasn't even on the list of the first group.

After two days of interacting with committees of students, faculty, alumni, trustees, and others, each declaring unanimously that I was their choice to be president, I responded that I would reflect a few days and respond.

I returned to North Carolina and Meredith College and met with my board, anticipating a strong negative reaction to my even thinking about leaving. The response was, "You don't need to go to Richmond—whatever they will do for you, we will do for you here." I responded to the University of Richmond, indicating that I had decided to continue as president of Meredith.

Two weeks later, an emissary from the University of Richmond was dispatched to persuade me to come back and talk further. My response was that I had talked to everybody and had turned down a unanimous offer, so what could come of my talking with them again? The representative said, "I want you to sleep on this thought: The University of Richmond is going to become one of the finest universities in the country in ten to fifteen years, and you may look north thinking, I could have been president of that university. I will call you in the morning to see whether you will come back and talk some more."

I didn't sleep very well because I thought his advice made sense. The next morning, he called, and I said, "I don't need to come back to the university. I am, however, willing to talk with the man who has committed to giving $50 million and who has about $600 million more at his command. I believe he will make a greater impact upon my becoming president there than anybody on campus."

So, a meeting was arranged for just the two of us to talk privately at the Commonwealth Club in Richmond. After two hours of discussions, the man whose statue is on campus, Mr. E. Claiborne Robins, said, "If you will accept the presidency of my alma mater, I will personally guarantee you that you will never regret it." Hearing that, after learning of his vision and commitment, caused me to go immediately to the campus and accept the invitation to become president. Thus, in a real sense, Claiborne Robins employed me as president of the University of Richmond.

So, why had I originally rejected the offer?

As a seasoned college and university administrator—and especially with my experience as the chief business officer of three colleges—I observed what might have been harbingers of other less than positive conditions as follows:

- The main boiler in the heating plant was in need of replacement, a major cost factor.
- Faculty and staff salaries were very low, and there were no funds yet available to make a serious difference.
- Two dorms were under condemnation and required to be made safe before opening in the fall.
- The Health Department mandated immediate correction of unacceptable conditions in Food Services.
- The library did not meet accreditation standards.
- There was no student center as such.
- The science facilities were less adequate than local high schools.
- There were not enough applicants to fill dorms, although charges were only $2,000 a year for room, board, and tuition.
- There was a hole in the screen door in the administration building that no one seemed to notice but me. I had already declined one presidency upon seeing a hole in the screen door of the president's home.
- There were no phones in the wooden classroom buildings and only one in a threestory building.
- Nothing was air-conditioned.
- Athletic facilities were inadequate.

And on I could go on seeing such as the above everywhere I turned.

Being aware of all this—but with the blessing of Mr. Robins—I set out to face the challenge that was simply "to make the university one of the finest of its kind in the nation." While that sounded like a reasonable charge, especially with $50 million, I knew better. I realized the size of the hole we would have to climb out of before building the towers of strength that would define the university as one of the finest.

Having committed to lead the university in climbing to the heights of quality as it exists today, I was to arrive on campus in March 1971 to have lunch with the board and be formally elected president. The board was on time and in session, anticipating my arrival. Following lunch, I was to speak to the board, the media—TV, radio, and newspaper—and the faculty and staff. My arranged flight from Raleigh was canceled after it started snowing, and heavy coverage was predicted.

So, with no other choice, Betty and I headed north by automobile. By the time we arrived in Richmond at three o'clock, the snow was thirteen inches deep—and the Virginia Highway Patrol was looking for us. The luncheon had been completed, I had been elected in absentia, the press had gone home, and the faculty, staff, and everybody else had disbanded. I was about the loneliest new president ever, and all the glitter was vanquished.

At the launching of "Our Time" campaign:
Robert T. Marsh Jr., President Heilman,
E. Claiborne Robins (from left).

**Vanderbilt Game Tailgate**
Will Campbell, R'90, Dortch Oldham, R'41;
Sara Hardison Reisner, W'91 and University
Chancellor E. Bruce Heilman, H'86, enjoyed
a tailgate party before the Richmond vs.
Vanderbilt football game in September.
The Nashville Alumni Chapter sponsored the
event, which organizers termed "a tremendous
success."

In the new Robins Center with
the First Lady front and Center.

"To make the
University
of Richmond
one of the best small
private universities
in the nation."

It would be a long summer before I assumed the office early in September when the academic year was about to open. The circumstance I had anticipated was abysmal since the essential financial resources had not yet begun to flow in order to immediately take corrective action. The situation was a dilemma. But, as is almost always a fact, we do what we have to do. I worked with my colleagues day and night to do what had to be done.

My uniqueness as president was that in the history of the university, I—with the aid of colleagues and board members—raised more money than all other presidents put together since the university's beginning. But because presidential history had not contained the practice of fund-raising, it was not the most endearing action for the president from the perspective of many—if not most—faculty. Raising money was not what past presidents had done, which was why the university was in such a financial dilemma. But old impressions die hard, and what was new for the president did not conform to the dignified presence on campus where past presidents were always accessible.

On October 19, 1971, just a month after taking office, I spoke to an alumni group to let them know I needed lots of money to fulfill what was required to begin our journey of success. I noted that much has been done at the university over the years but much more was required in the future. A new athletic center was already under construction, and a new dorm was being planned for the women's college. These would begin to satisfy some of our ambitions.

In the years immediately ahead, we needed a new science center, greatly expanded library facilities, a new administration building, air-conditioning campus wide, improved streets, walks, parking areas, and utilities such as campus lighting. We needed to replace all temporary structures on campus and make like new those grand old structures that had over many years been worn down from use and exposure.

The plan anticipated everything we could muster to create what the university ought to be. It embodied a vast program of renovation and updating. Not so much because the university was not able to function but because its future would require being far sighted. Academic programs, student services, and physical facilities all would be expected to represent the best— and not just meet minimum requirements.

To make this possible, we needed multiplied millions of dollars more than anyone had ever dreamed of before. Part of our challenge was to overcome the image that we were newly rich, which was not the case. The Robins family didn't give $50 million to make life easy for everyone else. They gave it to challenge everyone else to do their part in transforming the whole university.

We moved forward with a major capital campaign, increased student financial aid, and continued to upgrade the overall quality and capacity of the campus and every aspect of its operations. All this meant new resources. Thus, we expanded our estate planning and deferred giving program, increased our charges, and found ways to encourage every constituent to do more in support of those efforts.

And so, with the guideline for my leading the board, the faculty, the alumni, and everybody else to make this one of the finest small universities in the country, we were off and running. I announced we would have a $50 million campaign to match the Robins family's $50 million. That was a real challenge to the board because the university had never had a campaign over $3 million, and that was a failure.

When I presented the proposal, one of our wealthiest trustees rose and said, "That's the craziest thing I ever heard. My alma mater, the University of Pennsylvania, is seeking $30 million and failing at that."

I retorted, "If that's the way others of the board feel, then I may have come to the wrong place. It will take multiplied many times more than another $50 million to make this university what together we have aspired for it to become." I sat down, and Mr. Robins rose and moved that we go forward with the $50 million proposed. The support was unanimous except for the one member who later gave $50,000. Others later admitted that they too wondered whether I was crazy.

Having submerged myself in my role and to provide some objectivity of how my leadership appeared to others, I interject a statement published by the public relations officer of the university, Randy Walker, as he observed my activities in the early stages and share his impressions and opinions. He begins with my addressing the board of trustees and senior officers.

His first address to the trustees was inspiring and exciting, as he himself described the meeting: "a significant rallying point for the trustees and administration as we join with faculty, students, alumni, church, community, and all of our other constituents and publics to bring into focus all the forces necessary to fulfill the purposes and to bring to fruition the highest expectation of those who are the university."

There followed in quick succession, addresses to faculty, the students, the opening convocation of school, and later audiences at Homecoming, Parents' Day, and other functions.

The inaugural on October 31 was a significant occasion, attracting more than two thousand to the Greek Theater where Rector Marsh placed the new university chain of office on Dr. Heilman's shoulders. The crowd braved a misty, damp morning to hear Dr. Heilman discuss a new era of the University of Richmond. See the special insert for the full text of the inaugural address.

To list all the organizations he has addressed would take more space than is available. But among those groups are the Junior Chamber of Commerce, the Rotary Club, the Baptist General Association of Virginia, alumni and alumnae chapters scattered across the East Coast, and many others.

Sandwiched between speaking engagements has been visits to the city manager and mayor of Richmond as well as other local government officials. He dined in Washington with Senator

William Spong, Senator Harry F. Byrd Jr., and others on a national level. He makes regular visits with dozens of other persons interested in aiding the University of Richmond in accomplishing his mission.

Mealtimes are pleasant occasions for Dr. Heilman to do business. He breakfasts regularly with civic and business leaders, lunches at the university or elsewhere with others including alumni and other special guests. Home football games gave him the opportunity to have guests for a luncheon or dinner prior to the game where he could discuss the university with board members, faculty members, or others.

Calm and unruffled, always with a smile, he is a man in motion. He stops (he's never too busy to chat with the students on the campus) only occasionally. But it's never to catch his breath. It's only to line up the next task.

# THE PRESIDENT: DR. E. BRUCE HEILMAN

In recent years, few independent colleges in the country have made the strides the University of Richmond has made in terms of physical improvements, faculty, academic programs, athletics and endowment.

The man behind this success is Dr. E. Bruce Heilman, who became the president of the University in 1971. During Dr. Heilman's tenure, the reputation of the University of Richmond has grown nationally year by year. The national respect which the University has gained under Dr. Heilman's leadership was exemplified when U.S. News & World Report in its November 28, 1983 issue listed UR as one of the best universities in the nation for undergraduate study. The ranking was based on a survey of college presidents.

Dr. Heilman is the first to acknowledge that the catalyst in the University's magnificent rise has been a $50 million gift in 1969 from the E. Claiborne Robins family. At that time, the gift was the largest benefaction from one family to an institution of higher education.

Through all of the changes, however, the University's campus has retained a tranquil beauty which is unmatched elsewhere. Today, more than 46 major buildings surround the central University Lake. New buildings constructed during the Heilman regime include the Robins Center, the President's home, residence halls for men and women, the Gottwald Science Center, University Townhouses, the University Dining Hall and the Tyler Haynes Commons, an architectural conversation, combining the Gothic tradition and modern functionalism. Major renovations over the last 13 years have included the transformation of the old Science Quadrangle into an up-to-date academic/administrative complex.

As the University has grown, it has maintained its central commitment to the liberal arts and sciences—an educational commitment judged particularly appropriate to a small, traditional university with a heritage of Christian values.

Instrumental in this commitment to academic excellence is the largest faculty in the school's history. Including the business and law schools, the University now has the full-time equivalent of over 240 faculty members. It is a faculty far better paid than ever before, and one which is able to claim a new diversity in age, background and academic interests.

Perhaps nowhere has success been more obvious at the University of Richmond in the last 13 years than in the area of endowment. In his first year at Richmond, Dr. Heilman launched a $50 million fundraising campaign, "Our Time in History," to strengthen the academic program and to enlarge and improve the physical facilities of the University. The campaign was successfully completed two and a half years ahead of schedule with a total of $54 million.

In 1982, the University launched the "Cornerstones for the Future" campaign for $55 million to increase the endowment and to achieve the goal of making the University of Richmond one of the strongest small private universities in the nation.

Under the direction of Dr. E. Bruce Heilman, this goal has clearly become a reality.

To Papa, a man of great honor.

# IV

## DR. MARY LYNCH JOHNSON

He's fond of quoting Edgar Guest's poem "It Couldn't Be Done," and the university community has learned from this enthusiastic man that, by golly, it can be done.

In his announcement to alumni of the selection of Dr. Heilman as our new president, Rector Robert T. Marsh, Jr., made the statement: "We need a man who can lead the University of Richmond in taking advantage of the opportunity for excellence made possible by the financial beneficence of the E. Claiborne Robins family. In Dr. Heilman, we have that man. Indeed, we are fortunate to obtain the services of this highly qualified leader and administrator."

And now we know he is right.

A university news release ten years after I was elected president clarifies the level of support and goodwill in response to a letter of resignation I submitted to the board.

FOR IMMEDIATE RELEASE

Dr. E. Bruce Heilman, who has just completed a ten-year term as president of the University of Richmond, has agreed to serve at least another five years at the unanimous request of the board of trustees.

When he was appointed president in 1971, Dr. Heilman announced his intention of staying ten years, which he said at the time he believed was the term during which he could be "most productive" in office.

At the end-of-the-year faculty meeting Monday morning (May 11), the outgoing rector, F. Carlyle Tiller, announced that the trustees had rejected Dr. Heilman's offer to resign at the end of this academic year and had persuaded him that his leadership as chief executive officer was essential for the continuing progress of the university in the near future. Tiller added that the board was also looking into the possibility of dividing up the present duties of the presidency so that Dr. Heilman would remain as chief executive officer, but that some aspects of the presidency would be taken over by another officer.

A significant consideration for the immediate future, Tiller told the assembled faculty, is the governance study now underway. This study is being carried out by a committee consisting of trustees, faculty members, and administrators and is expected to be completed by the spring of 1982. It could have far-reaching effects on how the university is governed, Tiller said.

Another major undertaking that the trustees felt needed Heilman's leadership is a new fund-raising campaign to begin this fall.

The Director of Public Relations

Dear Mr. President: I commend to your attentional Jack Wilberger's article in the current issue of the *Collegian*. It is an interview he conducted with the presidents of student governments of Richmond College, Westhampton College, and the business school. I was impressed with the enthusiasm of the three presidents and particularly with their cordial attitude toward the present administration. I have not known so much harmony on this campus in the past ten years.

Surely any such interview conducted at any time in the past ten years would have been devoted to a great extent to griping and, as we marines sometimes say, "bitching."

The students feel that this administration is interested in their problems. They are beginning to see the great future that extends beyond our present horizons.

Sincerely,

Joseph E. Nettles

One of a number of complimentary notes

The incoming rector, attorney Lewis T. Booker, who served a fouryear term in this office before Tiller took over as rector in 1977, told the faculty that fund-raising was of necessity going to have to be a high priority for the university over the next four years, and that "every institution of higher education in the country, public and private," was in the same position because of the state of the economy.

In an address to the faculty following the announcement of the action of the board, Heilman said, "I consider the major accomplishment of my presidency to be holding the trajectory high, aiming the barrel of our efforts far afield rather than turning it down and fighting skirmishes immediately before our eyes ... Because we have been working on so many big issues, the immediate issue of the moment might appear to have been overlooked. But I believe we have accomplished the greater goals, and now we can deal with the so-called lesser issues without contradicting that which is our ultimate goal."

Fast-forwarding to fifteen years later, after I had led the university toward being one of the finest, a resolution was drawn up by the Richmond College Alumni Association, the University Law School Alumni Association, the Westhampton Alumni Association, and the E. Claiborne Robins School of Business alumni as follows:

Resolutions of Appreciation
Honoring
E. Bruce Heilman

WHEREAS E. Bruce Heilman for fifteen years has served the University of Richmond as its fifth president; and

WHEREAS the University during that time has attained national prominence, as evidenced by two rankings in *U.S. News & World Report* as "one of the best colleges in America; and

WHEREAS the number of faculty members holding terminal degrees as risen to 90 percent; and

WHEREAS the yearly output of scholarly books, articles and papers published by the faculty has more than doubled; and

WHEREAS eight endowed distinguished faculty professorships have been created; and

WHEREAS the average SAT scores by entering UR freshmen have risen to some 235 points above the national average; and

WHEREAS merit-based scholarships have increased with such programs as the Oldham Scholars, the University Scholars, the CIGNA scholars and the Virginia Baptist scholars; and

WHEREAS. Bruce Heilman has managed the magnificent $50 million Robins family gift and has led campaigns that have brought in an additional $200 million in gifts and pledges; and

WHERAS UR's endowment is nearly $200 million and ranks in the top two percent of all American universities; and

WHEREAS some $65 million has been spent on new buildings and renovations that fit into a consistent Collegiate Gothic Architecture and the campus's traditional natural beauty; and

WHERAS a unique $1.5 million Chair of the Chaplaincy has been created under the leadership of E. Bruce Heilman, helping to preserve UR's spiritual heritage; and

WHEREAS the athletic programs have achieved national success as exemplified in the football team's recent number one ranking, the basketball team's two visits to the NCAA playoffs, the golf team's conference title, the baseball team's conference title and participation in the NCAA tournament; and

WHEREAS that success was achieved while nearly 100 percent of scholarship athletes have graduated or are on schedule to graduate; and

WHEREAS all of those accomplishments are a source of great pride for the alumni/ae of the University; and

WHEREAS those accomplishments make even more valuable an already valuable degree;


Therefore


BE IT RESOLVED that the alumni/ae associations of the University of Richmond hereby pass this resolution in grateful appreciation of E. Bruce Heilman for his leadership during 15 of the most exciting years in the University's proud 156-year history;

BE IT FURTHER RESOLVED that the alumni associations of the University of Richmond thank E. Bruce Heilman for agreeing to continue to work for the University in the role of Chancellor and wish him continued success in that new role, passed on this 31st day of May, 1986

Richmond College Alumni Association

University of Richmond Law School Association

Westhampton College Alumnae Association

E. Claiborne Robins School of Business Alumni Association

At this juncture, I resigned as president and was elected chancellor by the board of trustees. I took six months' leave, and at the end of the six months, our chairman came to me and informed me that my successor had resigned—and the board, having considered all other options, judged that the best one was for me to assume the office of interim president while they began another search for my successor. I served in the capacity of chief executive for another year, a total of sixteen years. I was then succeeded in the presidency at age sixty, by Dr. Richard Morrill, after I had served twenty-one years as president, including my five at Meredith College.

My sixteen years as president of the University of Richmond were composed of moving mountains, which had been the case at Meredith as well. In both institutions, my successor would have to make fertile the soil where mountains had stood. While it was my role to build confidence, enthusiasm, and excitement, it was now time for another to do constructive analysis and wholesome critique essential to consolidation of forces necessary for the next major advance.

# Center Opens Before 10,000 Fans

**ROBINS WATCH SPIDERS**

*—Staff Photo by Butterfield*

E. Claiborne Robins Jr. (Front Left) And Sr. (Middle) Watch Spiders In Action. Accompanying The Robins Are Alumni Secretary John Clayton (Front Right) And Dr. And Mrs. Heilman.

Alumnus Referr John Moreau signals for a foul; Center Opens Before 10,000 Fans

In my presidency, we marketed the essential elements of expecting and attempted great things, and the results spoke for themselves. We agreed to look beyond our horizons without forgetting the strengths of the past upon which the university was built. We decided to add strength on strength rather than size to mediocrity.

A university's past importance is in the fact that it is a stage, a platform and even a launching pad for its future. Its future is in its new leader, its board, its faculty, its administration, its alumni, and certainly the students for which it exists plus the financial requirements essential to leveraging the momentum of progress.

In a real sense, we had been able to jump high buildings in a single bound, walk on water even when being pulled down, and keep our heads while some about us were losing theirs. An article by Virginia LeSueur Carter, entitled "Spectacular Accomplishments, Heightened Expectations," covers the period quite clearly.

> Journalists covering education would call the University of Richmond during the Heilman era a "counter-trend" story:
>
> Applications for admission at most colleges and universities have been declining; those at Richmond College have increased by 35 percent since 1970, and Westhampton College applications have tripled.
>
> While College Board scores for entering freshmen across the nation have shown a steady decline in recent years, UR scores have been increasing.
>
> Faculty salaries nationally have not kept up with inflation; UR has moved its salaries from the 40th to the 70th percentile on the American Association of University Professors' scale.
>
> Many small universities routinely lose their best administrators to business or larger universities; UR has attracted and kept a first-rate staff.
>
> Hundreds of universities have trimmed back their academic offerings; UR has been enriching its curriculum, and the percentage of its faculty holding PhDs has gone up from 57 to 85 percent.
>
> Campus buildings at scores of private institutions show the peeling paint of reduced maintenance; UR has remodeled, refurbished, and airconditioned virtually every older building on campus.
>
> In a decade when new college construction has slowed dramatically, UR has completed an $8 million science center, a $10 million sports complex, a $4 million student center, a $4 million library addition, and new dormitories for nine hundred students.
>
> Fund campaigns even at some prestigious institutions have failed or been stretched over longer-than-planned periods; UR is closing in on its $50 million goal two years ahead of schedule.
>
> Community agencies as well as colleges around the country report fewer volunteer workers; UR has strengthened its board of trustees and recruited a virtual army of volunteer fund-raisers, donors, and alumni leaders.

What has made it possible for UR to swim against the tide? How, in this time of cutbacks, has the university been able to move steadily toward its goal of becoming one of the nation's best small private universities?

The most visible factors have been the generosity of the E. Claiborne Robins family, the leadership of E. Bruce Heilman, and the good counsel of Rector Lewis T. Booker and F. Carlyle Tiller. Equally responsible have been the thousands of people who have responded to this leadership and worked for a stronger, better university.

I am proud to have been president and chancellor and have watched this university go from a low ebb basically to a high level of superb quality and to proudly proclaim with the support of the alumni and the students, and all whose day to day efforts made it what it has become: one of the finest small universities in the country. Still with a trajectory of becoming greater and, as the world moves forward, so must the university keep moving as well or lose what we have gained.

A great measure of our success is that an endowment of a little over $8 million when Mr. Robins made his gift has increased to $3.5 billion today. Thus, we are financially a different university, allowing many students to attend irrespective of their ability to pay. Another measure of our success is that, during my time as president, thirteen of the administrators who were employed to help us during those sixteen years became presidents of other colleges and universities. I am proud of my judgment in bringing to U of R such superb administrators that other institutions sought them out to help do for other colleges and universities some of what they did as leaders at U of R.

As I look back over the sixty-six years of my total administrative experience in four states, I don't need to defend myself against arrogance when I say that I have been successful. In every aspect of my life, I appropriately and correctly acknowledge that I did not independently climb to the heights. I was lifted, and in some cases pushed and shoved, by good people.

Another ingredient of our success has been our mission and our clear purpose— reinforced with passion and made secure by a heavy layer of performance. That was my guideline. I had been given the mission, and it became my purpose. I was passionate to the extent that even though every night I was up late, I couldn't wait to get up early the next morning. My motivation, excitement, and enthusiasm along with lots of others was the foundation that made the university succeed in becoming what it is today.

I am, I realize at age ninety-three, ancient history to today's students, and I have been a participant in aspects of history that affected its forebears from the Great Depression to the greatest of all military conflicts where many students left the university to fight for their country and military training took place on our campus. After the war, many returned under the G.I. Bill to prepare for the rest of their lives.

I have a paper, stating for certain eyes only, that outlines the anticipated invasion of Japan citing all the hazards and risks that were known to all, which ultimately led to the use of the atom bomb. In the plan, it was announced that the battle would engage the entire Marine Corps. I was one of those marines on the front line, ready to move in and most likely to die with hundreds of thousands predicted of the millions of Americans and Japanese.

But our lives were saved while others suffered by the use of the atom bomb. So, rather than landing with guns blazing, we entered Japan to disarm the military and many of us walked in the ashes of Hiroshima and Nagasaki.

During the final battle of Okinawa, I was in combat at eighteen years of age, was disarming Japanese at nineteen, and was a sergeant at twenty. I have spent sixty-seven years as an educator because my country for which I fought made acquiring an education possible for me. All in all, my forty-nine years as president and chancellor at the University of Richmond has been another grand adventure.

\*\*\*

# Can a school dropout be a college president? Ask Dr. Heilman

## DIVERSIONS

### By Steve Clark

This Christmas is turning out to be one of the merriest ever for Dr. E. Bruce Heilman, the University of Richmond's president since 1971.

First and foremost, Dr. Heilman and his wife have their five children and seven grandchildren home for the holidays. This gathering of the family truly is joyful because the Heilmans' children are widely scattered. One daughter lives in West Germany. Another daughter lives in San Francisco.

Then there was UR's basketball victory Saturday night over the University of Virginia in the championship game of the Times-Dispatch Invitational Tournament. It was the first time the Spiders have won the 10-year-old tournament and the first time UR has beaten U.Va. in basketball since 1968.

"Some of our alumni are calling it our biggest win ever," Dr. Heilman said. "I'm not sure about that. But beating The University is mighty big."

### 'Those planes could land anywhere'

We scarcely had started our conversation yesterday morning in his office when Dr. Heilman had to leave the room to take a message. He soon returned wearing a big smile.

"We just got word we're getting a $150,000 gift we've been working on for some time," he said.

To the president of a private university where raising money is crucial, this news had "Merry Christmas" written all over it.

There's still another reason that Dr. Heilman is in an upbeat mood this Christmas season. One night last week, he watched a television show that brought back a flood of memories. The Public Broadcasting System show, "The Plane That Changed the World," was a tribute to the Douglas DC-3 airplane, which is celebrating its 50th birthday.

Like many men who served in World War II, Dr. Heilman has a special affection for the DC-3, which, as a military plane, was the C-47 to the Army and the R-4D to the Navy and Marine Corps.

Dr. Heilman

"Those planes could land anywhere. And often did," Dr. Heilman said. "I have vivid memories of landing in one in a cow pasture in Japan. I remember another landing in zero visibility when we hit the runway before we saw it."

Dr. Heilman's memories of the DC-3 go back to the days when he was a young non-commissioned officer in the U.S. Marine Corps. They're good memories because it was a time when he learned that life has numerous open doors, even for a country boy from Kentucky who had dropped out of high school.

Earl Heilman, as he was known in those days, enlisted in the Marines in the spring of 1944, before he graduated from high school in Ballardsville, Ky., a small town near Louisville. He likes to say he dropped out of high school before he flunked out.

"The farthest thing from my mind in those days was going to college," he said. "So I joined the Marines and went to boot camp in San Diego. Except for a couple of trips across the state line into Indiana, it was the first time I'd ever been out of Kentucky."

After boot camp, he trained to be a tail gunner, and in the spring of 1945, he found himself on a troop ship headed for the South Pacific and the invasion of Okinawa. His outfit got there after the main assault, so he was involved in the mopping-up exercises.

When the war with Japan ended, Dr. Heilman remained in the Pacific about six months to help in the transition from war to peace. He was stationed at a naval base at Yokosuka, Japan, where he fell in love with the DC-3.

"I was a radio operator on an old beat-up R-4D after the war, and we flew it all over the area on a variety of assignments," he recalled.

### Plenty of memories

He still has black-and-white photographs of the plane and colorful memories.

He remembers the time he was a passenger on an Army C-47 that crashed on takeoff on a flight from Iwo Jima back to Japan. He still has the letter he sent his mother to describe that experience. In it, he wrote:

"Next morning we had a ride on an Army transport to Japan, so we all piled on, and the plane was really filled up with passengers. We started out, and got off the ground a little when the tail dropped down and hit the deck because it was loaded too heavy in the rear. It bounced back up, and we went on up a little more when a pretty high crosswind came under our right wing and just flipped us over. . . . We hit on the left wing and bounced around for a while and scooted to a stop. Not a one was hurt, but it scared a couple of years out of us all."

One thing about that harrowing experience made a big impression on him.

"Most of the men on that plane were high-ranking officers, and I remember they were just as scared as I was," he said.

After getting out of the Marines, Dr. Heilman went home and enrolled at Campbellsville Junior College in Kentucky.

"It had 200 students, and in that little setting, I found out for the first time in my life that I could compete in academics," he said.

He went on to earn a Ph.D. and become a college president. He is convinced this never would have happened if it weren't for the Marine Corps. He tells people: "The greatest accomplishment in my life was being promoted to buck sergeant." He means it.

"Before I joined the Marines, I was a farm boy from Kentucky who was totally disinterested in education. The Marines opened my eyes and gave me a great perspective of the world. I became motivated. My message to young people is that average people can do great things if they're highly motivated."

**THE RICHMOND NEWS LEADER** / Tuesday, December 24, 1985

Grandaughter receives her degree at
Campbellsville University.

President Carter and Other
administrative leaders at
Campbellsville University,
one of my Alma Maters.

## ᴜᴿ *On Campus*

# Dr. Heilman's Decade: Ten Golden Years

### By Alison Griffin

Dr. E. Bruce Heilman became the fifth president of the University of Richmond on Oct. 31, 1981.

In the ten years since E. Bruce Heilman became the fifth president of the University of Richmond, changes have taken place at a faster rate than at any other period in the institution's 151-year history. In fact, few independent colleges in the country have made such outstanding strides in terms of physical improvements, faculty, academic programs and endowment.

Dr. Heilman himself would be the first to acknowledge that the chief catalyst in all of this has been the Robins family gift of $50 million in 1969 — at that time the largest benefaction from one family to an institution of higher education.

Ten years after his inauguration in October of 1971, Dr. Heilman can look back on what all would agree has been a "decade of progress:"

— A campus that retains the tranquil sylvan beauty that has left nostalgic memories with generations of students since 1914, yet has managed to accommodate over the past ten years the addition of handsome new facilities, along with major renovations of existing buildings — bricks-and-mortar benefits that have helped to enhance the life of the entire campus community from freshmen to support staff. The new buildings include the Robins Center, the President's Home, residence halls for men and women, the Gottwald Science Center, and the University Commons Building that has become an architectural conversation piece, with its graceful combination of the Gothic tradition and modern functionalism. Major renovations over the decade have included the transformation of the old Science Quadrangle into an up-to-date academic/administrative complex that retains the pleasant architectural symmetry of the old quad.

— A continuing central commitment to the liberal arts and sciences — an educational commitment judged peculiarly appropriate to a relatively small, traditional, independent university with a strong heritage of Christian values.

— An expanded faculty (now the full-time equivalent of 242, including the business and law schools); a faculty far better paid than ever before and able to claim a new diversity in age, background and academic interests.

— Improved and up-dated academic programs, including expanded opportunities for superior students — such as the program of interdisciplinary studies; independent studies and honors programs; undergraduate grants for individual research; Women's Studies and the Scholars' Program, aimed at recruiting academically superior freshmen with generous scholarships awarded entirely on merit, with the annual incoming group of about 15 Scholars acting as a kind of academic leavening agent for the entire student body.

— A stronger, more cohesive, more diverse Board of Trustees than ever before in the University's history — board described consistently by the president as "extraordinary of its kind," a board that works harder than ever before.

59

# V

# THE NATURE OF A UNIVERSITY PRESIDENT

I cannot give you the formula for success, but I can give you the
formula for failing—which is: try to please everybody.
—*Herbert B. Swope*

The kings, the queens, the lords, the earls
They gave their crowns, they gave their pearls
Until Philander had enough And hurried homeward with the stuff.
He ran the college, built the dam
He milked the cows, he smoked the hams He stoked the furnace, rang the bell
And spanked the naughty freshmen well.
—*Philander Smith*

Vartan Gregorian, former president of Brown University said, "The only things in life that are really important are your dignity and your integrity. Integrity is what you have left when everything else you've ever been taught has been forgotten." To be a successful university president, one must be trustworthy. I can't imagine a really great school that isn't known first of all for its standards, its values, and its integrity. "Honor and character is all I ask—and I ask God for no more," said William Blake.

The presidency of a college or university is a position that is not often anticipated or prepared for in a special manner compared to ambitions to be a doctor, a lawyer, an accountant, an airplane pilot, or a minister. The presidency is not a profession or job to be passed on to a member in a family as may be the case of an executive in a family corporate enterprise. The enthusiastic anticipation of "I am studying to be ___ and fill in the blank," holds little chance that the blank will be filled with the words "a university or college president."

And though my children and grandchildren have all grown up on campuses, are graduates of a university where their father and grandfather has been president, and are familiar with my profession as head of two institutions of higher education, I've never heard even one of them suggest an ambition of becoming a college or university president like their dad or their grandpa. Perhaps the long years of preparation and the intensity of the requirements are more than they are willing to commit to a lifetime filled with many less demanding yet rewarding opportunities.

Clearly, there is a certain mystique even with a lack of clarity in regard to what the presidency is all about. One adds a level of prestige to the usual requirement of a PhD. The position and its incumbent is notable and respected, and only a limited number of opportunities are available. Thus, such a position may be seen as an impossible dream.

Perhaps most who become presidents do so purely by accident, never having planned or anticipated the prospect over time. I could never have speculated that I might be a college or university president. I did not educate myself to that end, and my background of having failed high school would have suggested that I would be out of the mix of possibilities. So, how do I describe the nature of a college and university president or the presidency?

John Ruskin said, "Education is not just learning what you previously didn't know, but it is behaving in a way you didn't previously behave." I believe John Ruskin would have identified the presidency similarly in that behavior is greatly related to how one sees or even accomplishes the presidency.

Following is a statement entitled "The Last Word on the Presidency." It presents the points that finishes the statement and answers the question: What is a college or university president? This statement was published in September and October 1984 in the *Magazine of the Association of Governing Boards*.

Quigg, Vice President; Patterson, Assistant to the President;
Withers, Associate Vice President

"President Heilman welcomes Charles L. Brown, Chairman of the Board
of AT&T, as the keynote speaker for the fifth annual Winter Business Forum"

Presented by Dr. E. Bruce Heilman,
Chancellor of the University of Richmond

I had written it as a part of a speech, and it was so well received that it was published nationally. As I read it today, more than thirty years later, I wouldn't change a thing. It fits well my descriptive message on the nature of the presidency as follows:

## The Last Word

A college or university president is …

… a person of culture. It is appropriate that the person and the office be identified with the symphony, ballet, museums, opera, and other aspects of the "higher things in life."

… an intellectual, a person of letters who is knowledgeable and wise.

… a symbol of the college or university on or off campus. No matter what he or she says or does, it reflects upon the institution's image; the president and spouse are public property: they are always news, good or bad.

… a person of strong character expected to set moral and ethical standards on campus and in the community.

… an influential public figure often asked to serve on corporate boards, the chamber of commerce, and any number of other enterprises and activities.

… an entertainer who speaks about everything and to everybody on every occasion.

… an endlessly accessible individual. Presidents, in fact, do not want even to *appear* inaccessible.

… an admissions officer. There is no escape from being the court of last resort; the time never seems to come when it is not necessary to deal with special admissions.

… a defender and protector of what the institution represents— someone who must uphold the freedom and flexibility of the academy.

… a person who is youthfully vigorous without being immature. The chief executive must continue to learn from young people; be young in heart, mind, and spirit; and remain adaptable.

… a salesman and procurer. Obtaining resources is an art and a science; the president must be the catalyst and coordinator for cultivating major donors and instilling confidence in the institution.

… a public relations professional and press agent. Public relations cannot be avoided; to do the job well, the president must relate effectively to the public and the institution's administration. Inquiries must be always answered with good humor, judgement, dispatch, and diplomacy.

… a coach. He or she must be prepared to assume responsibility for all of the losses in college athletics and leave to the coaches credit for the wins.

     … a politician and lobbyist before the state legislature.

     … a prophet and seer. The world at large wants to know what is going to happen to the university or college and the president must be ready to conjecture.

     … a dreamer. Dreams—grown from one's convictions, ambitions, and aspirations—make the presidency exciting and give it life; they override the negative factors.

\*\*\*

The president and the presidency must be flexible enough to endure the dips and peaks of social and other changes that create adjustments in policy and practice within the broader guidelines and policies essential to the present purposes of the institution.

     To add balance, including some humor, I include another descriptive verse that comes from the publication "Going Around in Academic Circles" written by Richard Armour. (Today the "he" is as apt to be a "she.")

He has such perquisites as these An inside track to LLDs
A large and handsome rent-free house
A par- time maid to help his spouse
A special fund for entertaining
Fare paid first class whenever plane-ing Two secretaries well-equipped
Sharp-minded and sharp pencil-tipped.
And memberships in sundry clubs
With steam baths and relaxing rubs
Much else, in fact, too much to mention Besides a quiet substantial pension What does he do to earn all these?
He merely pacifies trustees
And students, faculty, and grads
Townspeople also moms and dads
And keeps his health and keeps his sanity
And isn't heard to use profanity
But living in a gold fishbowl
Next day, can be filet of sole
Unlike professors whom he hires He has no tenure, walks on wires And if he falls, he's out, he's gone, While some still sad and glad stay on.

University of Richmond Chancellor Bruce Heilman (left), who served in the Marine Corps during World War II, joked with C. Kenneth Wright as Wright's daughter, Nancy Wright, looked on after a ceremony at the Virginia War Memorial on Thursday.

With Claiborne Robins Jr.

# Casual Phone Call Turns Into $1 Million

RICHMOND (AP)—University of Richmond President E. Bruce Heilman was working busily in his office this week when his telephone rang.

A voice on the other end of the line asked whether Heilman could accept an anonymous gift for the university.

Sure, said Heilman.

Then he almost fell out of his chair.

The caller said he was giving $1 million to the university development program.

It was for real, all right. Heilman announced the gift to the faculty later in the day, but true to the wishes of the donor, nobody is making public his — or her — identity.

Richmond's new AD Chuck Boone (l),
President Dr. E. Bruce Heilman meet Press

Graduate and Major Donor, Marcus Weinstein

I initiate my commentary with these two descriptions because I believe, along with the humor in Armour's verse, it also is realistic. Along with my "Last Word" from the Association of Governing Boards article, the presidency is rather well defined. I have filled in the blank spots so that most anyone will identify what it really means to be the president of a college or a university, a position I experienced in two institutions for twenty-one years.

I also experienced senior administrative positions from my early days right out of college when I became an administrator. In the meantime, I have held every definable position in higher education in four states, including heading the statewide system of higher education in Tennessee. I am able to state with some clarity what it is all about even if my time as a president has been some years ago.

The responsibilities that are significant in the presidency are understanding the mission of the institution, believing in it intensely, and adopting it as the guideline. That includes establishing and maintaining the essential atmosphere, being the dreamer, fanning the flame of enthusiasm, settling the disputes, losing sleep over the real issues, trying to maintain rationality with the students, and sometimes the faculty, controlling the podium in the center of whatever is happening, seeking to maintain credible relationships with the board, convincing the surrounding community that campus activities are reasonable, living twenty-four hours a day in the midst of whatever is happening at the university and finally, and raising money twenty-four hours a day.

A newspaper citation from early in my presidency at the University of Richmond included the following commentary about my early actions:

At one of his first meetings with trustees, he outlined his views about university administration and about where UR was headed. He spoke frankly:

"Trustees of this university, if they ever have assumed such a role, must abandon the role of being the mere conservator of the financial resources of this institution and must adopt as a first and overriding responsibility the increase in very substantial amounts of these resources."

Heilman also spelled out his theory, supported by quotes from authorities in the field, on how trustees should and must relate to the university through the president. He made it clear that they were to set policy; he was to run the institution.

And, he warned, board members "must be prepared for longer working sessions … meaning a day or two rather than a couple of hours."

He is gregarious, persuasive, aggressive, and optimistic. ("There are always those who will see the problems; let us deal with the opportunities.")

Another headline: "A Tough Act to Follow" leads into the following story.

After fifteen years as president of the University of Richmond, E. Bruce Heilman stepped up on September 1 and officially took over as chancellor of the Virginia University. His tenure at the university is referred to as "The Heilman Years" and the growth that occurred during that time is unparalleled in the school's history.

Realistically Heilman will be a tough act to follow. Only the fifth president in the university's 155-year history, he has been largely responsible for an unprecedented growth of the university's national reputation, its academic program, its physical plant, and its endowment. Since his inauguration, the number of faculty members holding doctoral degrees has risen from 60 percent to 90 percent, faculty publications have more than doubled, and faculty salaries have risen dramatically. Eight distinguished faculty chairs have been created.

The average student's SAT scores has risen to some thirty-five points above the national average. There has been an increase in merit-based scholarships. During his tenure, approximately $65 million was spent on new buildings and renovation of existing buildings, and the university's endowment increased from $38 million to $162 million, placing UR in the top 2 percent of all universities in the country.

He is so well respected that the university's alumni publication, *The University of Richmond Magazine,* dedicated a special issue to him last spring: "The Heilman Years." In that publication, Tiller noted that Heilman's leadership ability stems first from confidence in himself derived from his great inner strengths and secondly from his confidence in his fellow man.

When I was elected president, the headline was "A college president with $50 million" by Randy Walker.

Chairman of the Board Robert T. Marsh Jr. of University of Richmond in announcing Heilman's appointment described him a wonderful organizer, builder, and forward planner. He is dynamic with a pleasing personality, added Marsh.

The University of Richmond is most fortunate to secure as president such an able, experienced college administrator, Dr. Bruce Heilman. He possesses all the qualities to lead the university during the important years ahead, said Dr. Modlin. During his five years at Meredith, Heilman saw enrollment increase by 40 percent to its present 1,200, he has credited to raising $4 million toward a $5 million fund-raising goal, Meredith College was cited in the Carnegie Mission on Higher Education as one of twelve institutions in the US that are not in financial trouble. The estimates were made from studies of forty-one institutions across the country. An editorial in the *Raleigh North Carolina News Observer* on January 12, 1971, praised Dr. Heilman's leadership in bringing Meredith to its present excellent fiscal shape. The editorial said Dr. Heilman and others at Meredith know how to distinguish brass from gold.

Heilman Brings New Optimism

When asked by the columnist in the university's student newspaper what are the major problems occurring in the University of Richmond, Heilman responds, "There really are none. The only problem we have are those we create for ourselves." The columnist said, "So, you have no idea how difficult it is to accept an individual with such optimism as Dr. Heilman. Richmond has been spared the situation of other universities that crumbled into disarray and could only be reconnected through some system of strict university governance." And the columnist quotes Heilman, "I have no illusions about keeping students in the background. I will not choose to keep their responsibility from them. We must think of students as part of a responsible community. Neither the students nor any other constituent should have the option in determining the nature of the university. They are the many voices that must be heard."

\*\*\*

**Vietnam Era Restlessness**

The mid-to-late sixties ushered in the height of unrest on college campuses nationwide. The Vietnam War very much affected the attitude and spirit of young people and bred a general distrust of all authority. Nearly every night, newscasts pictured students burning down buildings and staging sit-ins at colleges or universities across the country. The usually serene setting of Meredith was not exempt from a flurry of student demonstrations.

I remember well our brush with "Power to the People," when young women staged a sitin in the president's office. In early spring of 1969, I had issued some regulations regarding alcohol consumption on campus and also had admonished the students about undue "public displays of affection," which today, long after, is remembered as my PDA speech. I spoke with the authority of a president who was fully backed by the board of trustees, but my remarks whetted the appetite for resistance by some of the students.

During a convocation, a confrontational outburst erupted. Some students became emotional, angry, and even rude, and I found myself in the position of having to apply a strategy I have learned is essential to success. I managed to remain calm and stable, while continuing reasonable dialogue when I would have preferred to let off a little steam myself.

Protests and sit-ins in the president's office followed. These tactics attracted hordes of male students from other colleges and universities in the area. Encouraged by the young women who thought it was folly and who considered it a legitimate panty raid, some five thousand men from the University of North Carolina, North Carolina State, and Duke invaded Meredith's campus and ran on a rampage through dormitories, shrubbery, and anything else they found in the way. Faced with a decision of how most effectively to react, I took the course of least resistance, a tactic that paid off in spades. I sat in my office and let the demonstration run its course. I realized that our two or three campus security police officers would do nothing but incite the crowd even further; with no one to fight against, the youthful exuberance burned out of its own steam.

I believe that the ability to maintain self-control is one of the most essential of all traits for a leader. In this case, it took real emotional restraint to keep my indignation from inflaming an already volatile situation. After the convocation and the noisy reception to our strengthened alcohol policy, I received numerous letters from students who supported my position of leadership and respected my deliberately calm response. One group of students wrote:

> Dear Dr. Heilman:
> We as interested students would like to express our support of your thoughtful and sincere effort in bringing before the student body the recent actions of the board of trustees. We realize that the only response to this vote of confidence lies in our mature acceptance of the responsibilities it entails. We hope that the lack of judgment and self-control shown by some students on Wednesday is not indicative of the entire student body.

Another student wrote, just a few days after the meeting:

> I am very sorry that a bunch of immature hotheads have insulted the student body in their insults toward you.

And from a faculty member, I received this endorsement:

> You managed the situation at Chapel Wednesday, extremely well. Your presence of mind and calmness of manner are commendable, especially when you had every provocation to lose your temper.

Over the years, I have found that nothing can be gained by confrontation and angry outbursts— and that almost everything can be worked out through convincing dialogue.

**Changing Attitudes**

I managed to retain a congenial rapport with most of the student body, so much so that the 1970 yearbook, *Oak Leaves*, was dedicated to me by the senior class. Members of that class were the very ones who in earlier years had given me the most trouble. One letter I received in 1970 from a fellow educator helps explain the special pleasure I derived from being honored in the yearbook:

> Dear Bruce,
> I have just received a copy of the Meredith College Oak Leaves for 1970. It is very beautifully done annually, and there are a great many college presidents these days who are not getting student publications dedicated to them. Congratulations to you for this deserved honor!

Students are the core of a school who add to the pleasure of the presidency as they add vitality and a degree of unpredictability to an institution. Even during the sixties, when young people had a tendency to distrust authority, the students at Meredith—along with their families—were a constant source of support and stimulation.

I had been at Meredith a little less than one year when I received a letter from Professor Gates, bolstering my ego and affirming my rapport with the student body. She asked her history class to select two individuals, living between the time of the French Revolution and the present, who embodied the characteristics of a good leader. As a second part of the assignment, students were asked to name a living person who demonstrated their ideas of good leadership. When my name was selected by several of the students, Professor Gates wrote to me. "You will be pleased to know that you were mentioned a number of times in reply to this question." And pleased I was.

Although I could not make myself readily available for every individual who sought an appointment with me, I did continue my policy of scheduling private time with anyone who requested it—often over the breakfast table. I found breakfast meetings of this type to be extremely valuable in helping maintain a personal touch and communicate directly, especially with students and faculty. Most invitations for a six thirty or seven thirty breakfast were turned down unless there was a real desire for a meeting. So, if someone wanted to see me enough to rise and shine early in the morning, I knew I needed to make myself available. Over bacon and eggs, almost no problem seems unsolvable.

The nature of the presidency is expressed in many ways. Communications from all sectors of the constituents internally and externally give impressions of how the president and his or her role is perceived. From a collection of memos and letters received over time, some impressions can be formed concerning relationships between the president and colleagues.

One faces many forces of contradicting dispositions. One college president complained that during the course of the year, he had heard from half the country's wise men and all of its lunatics—and they refused to talk to anyone else. During my presidency, my secretary received a call from someone in New York who said he was in prison for extortion, claimed he knew Bruce Heilman, and asked that I return his call. He refused to talk to anyone else. Another asked for a Spider cap, and we sent him one!

From a professor who was also a marine:

> As this first academic year of our association draws to a close, I would like to express to you my feeling of satisfaction in the way the year has gone.
>
> You have more than lived up to our expectations, and you have certainly created an atmosphere of confidence for the future of the university. This confidence is especially felt by us in the Natural Sciences who had earlier been given little real hope of rapid improvement. Your work has begun a new existence in a new era in faculty-administrator relationships. You are to be applauded. Your sincerity and patience are appreciated.

> Dear Dr. Heilman, I don't ordinarily write fan letters but your comments in the *Times-Dispatch* were as a stream of clear cool water in a parched wasteland of current comments concerning higher education generally and the liberal arts in particular.
>
> I congratulate and applaud you for your lucid and cogently presented ideas. I believe that my sentiments are shared by many of our colleagues and the university community as we all strive together to achieve the goal of becoming one of the finest small universities in the nation.

Professors are often reluctant to pay compliments to the president due to the appearance of seeking favors. The following represents an acknowledged appreciation for the president's actions from a professor.

> I suppose it is in the nature of things that your office receives more criticism than it does praise. All the more reason then to pass along something positive when it crops up.
>
> A couple of weeks ago, I had occasion to go through some old files and found a copy of a list of department needs we had compiled at the administration's request about a year after the

Robins' gift was announced. To my great surprise, I discovered that something like 80 percent of the requests on that list have since that time albeit with all delivered speed been granted. That's not too bad a record.

I thank you for having been instrumental in its attainment. We are always more aware of our needs than our possessions, of our failures, more than our successes. So, sharing a reflection of how far we have come is probably useful in whatever deliberations any of us engage in about the future.

Please don't feel obligated to answer this letter, and I would prefer that it remain a private communication. Thanks again for your help.

He signed his first name. This wonderful person is now deceased, so I haven't given anything away. Out of four to six hundred professors, no one could know who this might have been. I've received many, but most are protective of their privacy.

From another of my outstanding senior administrators:

Dear Bruce, I've heard many speeches of yours, and each was better than the one before. Simply, your words about - - - were the best yet. I know they came from the heart. It was your "finest hour."

From an assistant:

It's an honor to work for you. Each day I don't feel like I come to work. I feel like I am doing what I enjoy. Not many people can say that they look forward to going to work, yet I believe in the theory that if you enjoy what you are doing, you don't work a day in your life. That's how I feel each morning as I enter the campus. Assisting you is my pleasure, and I look forward to working with you for many more years. You have become a part of the family, and I always look forward to seeing you when you come into the office.

From a staff member:

Since you are completing your first four-year term and beginning another one, we wanted to be the ones to say we are glad that you considered and accepted another term. Your support and disposition are at a tremendously high level and the university just wouldn't be the same without you.

From the Boy Scouts:

> Dr. Heilman, yesterday we received a lifetime treasure: your powerful and inspirational speech on behalf of the Boy Scouts. We will read and reread it with a great deal of joy and many happy memories. Thanks for the gift of your presence and your fantastic speech. You are wonderful."

From a colleague:

> You have been a friend, a mentor, and a supporter of me throughout these last fourteen years, many of which have been the best of my life, and you have been an inspiration to me about how to act as a representative of the university, about how to keep a positive attitude, and about how to reach for great accomplishments. Many people have done great things here at the University of Richmond, but the university is what it is today only because of you.

> Dear President Heilman,
> I have just read with great interest the *University of Richmond Magazine* on your retirement. What a wonderful leader you have been. I can't think of any other in any area in which you weren't the best leader ever. How will they ever find a leader to follow you?

And from a neighbor:

> If it hadn't been for you taking a chance on me, I wouldn't be who I am today. As hard as things were in the early years, it has produced some of the best memories of my life. Had it not been for folks like you, I wouldn't have been able to do that, and I thank you. You actually have served as more of an inspiration than you realize. During rough periods of my life, I've often thought of what you have accomplished in much harder conditions, and I soon stop my complaining and just do what is expected of me.

And I receive notes frequently when speaking to groups:

> Dr. Heilman, I cannot begin to tell you how much the members of the club enjoyed and appreciated your presentation. It was the topic of conversation all evening. Thank you for the gift of your time and sharing your more recent experiences.

> Dear Bruce: I wish to thank you personally for the Dunlora Society for your delightful and so moving talk yesterday. Your experiences are incomparable even by standards of our other presidents and presented by you with candor and with polish. The nostalgia element joined of course with that of each person in the room and it was sweet to enjoy your memories as they bound up with ours. This was one of our largest crowds, and we appreciated spending the time with you. We all came away a little more firmly loyal to the great university we serve.

> You are a remarkable person; driven to succeed and you have, in most every situation! I think your intelligence, your ability to adjust and your positive attitude are major traits that contributed to making a good life for you and your family.   Jerry

> An excerpt from a letter from a fellow educator who was a college and university administrator with whom I have had a long friendship "I have always admired tremendously your exceptional talent for seeing administration the way you do and for accomplishing the things you envision. More than that, though I have admired your style, the image part of all of that, that is you your personality, the way you say things, the energy that pours out of you like a never failing stream. You are one of these Bruce and I want you to know it.

John"

> From a graduate of Meredith College during my presidency who lives in Richmond most of my presidency at the University.

Dear Dr. Heilman, I finished your first 80 years on New Year's Day. I truly enjoyed every aspect of your adventure, parts made me laugh, and parts made my eyes fill with tears but most of all it made me very very proud of you your accomplishments both personal and professional.

Because I had the good fortune to be one of your Meredith angels and to live in Richmond, since 1969 I have witnessed the growth of Meredith and UofR. I know the before and after of both institutions and have always believed Meredith would not exist today if it were not for your vision and determination. Linda"

From Carlyle Tiller, Chairman of the University board while I was president, "You did your family and many friends around the world a big favor by putting your experiences and achievements in print for them to enjoy."

And from a hotel proprietor who purchased my book in Gallup, New Mexico, "I have been really enjoying your book and can't wait to finish it so I can start it over again."

From a letter from Dr. Sam Clagg, former president of Marshall University and a retired lieutenant in the Marines "I would stack your book up with any I have read. It is a delightful and full story of the first eighty years."

Speaking to High School Students.

High school students reaction to World War II Speech.

Speaks for itself

At the naming of a building at my Alma Mater, Campbellsville University.

At my alma mater, Campbellsville University

Calls for Cheer

This headline headed an editorial in the newspaper during the earlier days of my presidency:

> Good news has been in woefully short supply this spring but some came from out Westhampton Way yesterday and it is truly a joy for rejoicing. At the University of Richmond commencement, President E. Bruce Heilman announced that the privately supported university has completed its tenyear, $50 million development campaign two years ahead of time.
>
> That's a big paragraph, that's a big tribute to UR, its vitality and that of its supporters at a time of financial stress for colleges and schools in general. Some skeptics thought the goal helplessly ambitious but by refusing to keep their aspirations small, UR's officials and backers have secured commitments topping $54 million, which is being used to improve the physical plant and update the academic program.
>
> Dr. Heilman, who became president of the university just one year before the ten-year campaign was launched, F. Carlyle Tiller, president of Wheat Securities who headed the $30 million first phase of the drive and who is now UR rector, and Joseph Jennings of the board of the United Bank Shares who led the second phase are to be commended.
>
> And a very special mention of E. Claiborne Robins, chairman of the A.H. Robins Company whose family's unprecedented gift of $50 million provided the inspiration and challenge for others to match.

From a student graduating (after I had written him a letter):

> I hold you in highest esteem that I cannot put into words how sincerely I appreciate your praise. I feel very fortunate to have gotten to know you over the course of these few years, and I have every hope that my graduation will not mark the end of our relationship.

And finally, the proof of the pudding is in the tasting or in the presidency. It is the actions that speak louder than words. Some commentary from a student who followed me for a day tells its own story of the intensity of the activities included:

Our lasting impression of Dr. Heilman was that he totally lived his job. Whereas many people rise at five thirty, have breakfast, and go to work, the president wakes up at six thirty already at work. He typically has a breakfast meeting, manages to work a full day with lunch and dinner meetings interspersed, and usually turns in about midnight. He does not eat at home alone with his family very often—possibly once a week. Whenever he travels by car, he asks someone to accompany him, and will normally dictate letters or speeches into his portable tape recorder, or reflect on problems concerning the university.

Betty entertaining Mrs. Lynda Johnson Robb, the VCU First Lady and friend, Nan Vulgamore

His schedule is hectic. During the week, he met with the various university vice presidents, administrators, faculty, students, alumni/ae, trustees, lawyers, members of the board of associates, and community leaders. He had breakfast meetings with the athletic council in the refectory, the trustee selection committee at his home, and two lawyers, the vice president for student affairs, and the dean of administration in the president's dining room at Westhampton; lunches with A.H. Robins for a board meeting, with Westhampton college students, and with a representative from the College Entrance Examination Board.

During the day, he spoke with faculty, trustees, and alumni, met with a student representative to the athletic council in his office, and interviewed a job applicant for superintendent of buildings and grounds. Through all this, Dr. Heilman appeared to be in control of both his time and that of others—the consummate businessman operating in an academic climate.

So, after all is said and done as expressed in these pages—representing commentary from the press, notes from faculty, students and administrators and other sources—some sense of the nature of the position of president should be evident: "But more than realized by many, the president of this, the University of Richmond, operates in the corporate and academic spheres with equal aplomb."

The prior sentence I quote from a story by Peter McPherson in *Style* magazine of September 24, 1985 under the heading, "The Selling of a University." The story continues as follows to provide objective impressions of the presidency and the president:

The elegantly appointed president's dining room at the W. Tyler Haynes Commons building at the University of Richmond would not be out of place in any corporate suite in Richmond. And the president of the university himself would not be out of place. For one thing, E. Bruce Heilman has a lot in common with the leaders of the local business community. His undergraduate and graduate degrees in business administration from Vanderbilt University—prepared him to join their ranks. He is a southerner (though he comes from rural Kentucky) and a World War II veteran. He lives in a graciously furnished, palatial house on River Road with his wife, Betty.

Indeed, he is not out of place in Richmond's corporate community, moving skillfully and diplomatically among its members in his constant quest for funds for his university. A lot of persuading is done over breakfast in his dining room in the Commons building.

By any conventional measure, Heilman has been a successful university president. When he assumed the presidency of the University of Richmond fourteen years ago, the school's endowment was $48 million. Today, that figure stands at $150 million. During that time, ten new buildings, additions, and major renovations have been completed at the university's West End campus.

Heilman's phenomenal success is the result of a number of factors. According to Lewis T. Booker, a senior partner at the law firm of Hunton and Williams and a member of the University of Richmond's board of trustees, "Everybody recognizes that he's an outstanding leader and can articulate what the University of Richmond can do for the community." In 1983, for example, Wheat First Securities, United Virginia Bankshares, and CSX gave the university $250,000 each to endow business school professorships. Former Gov. John Dalton, who also serves on the University of Richmond's board of trustees, said, "He knows all the CEO-type people in Richmond," and has branched out into other parts of the country. Heilman talks matter-of-factly about chatting with J. Richard Munro, the chief executive officer of Time, Inc. "Not everyone with influence on our board has money," he says, "but everyone on our board has influence."

It would be easy to stereotype Heilman as a conservative corporatist, who is able to get his well-heeled friends and connections in the business community to give to the school. But Heilman cannot be that simply categorized. While he lives in a big house, he drives a small Japanese car. He is a thoughtful man who is candid enough to make himself seem totally sincere, yet not so candid as to be overly provocative. And Heilman has managed to remain accessible to faculty and students. According to Joseph F. Kent III, chairman of the department of mathematics and computer science and president of the university faculty counsel at UR, "I think he's respected, and he does a good job ... I think people are quite pleased with where we've come compared to where we were."

Like so many men of his generation, World War II changed Heilman's life. Until he crossed the river into Indiana on his way to California to join the marines, he had never left the Kentucky farm where he was raised. Seeing the world transformed him, he says, "but it has not been like the lightning on the road to Damascus. It has been a transformation that perhaps would hardly be noticed by people I've associated with over a period of years.

"We were a very localized group and therefore I [had] a very narrow point of view, socially, religiously, sociologically, educationally, and almost every other way—very parochial. Now if you wanted to use classifications like conservative or liberal ... I suppose in an educational setting I would tend toward, in the minds of faculty, being conservative. But compared to what I might have been when I left the farm and what I have moved from, while I might not be liberal ... I am very open. I am not an absolutist in any sense of the word. In fact, there are people I know well who think of themselves as being very liberal who are the most dogmatic people I know. Conservatism is supposed to be identified with dogmatism. It's not. The dogmatists are on both extremes."

He attributes his open-mindedness to sixty-six years in college and university life: "You cannot survive in the presidency by being a dogmatist … I think I've realized that I don't have all the answers even in those things that might have been dear to me at one point … Today I recognize that a lot of people accept what they think of as absolutes and everything isn't absolute."

Heilman previously served as president of Meredith College in Raleigh, North Carolina. He has been involved with both public and private universities. One gets the feeling from talking to Heilman that he prefers the private presidency, choosing to direct events rather than having them dictated. "I think the difference [is] that in a private school you can see the result of your actions much easier than you can at a public institution. I say that having been the coordinator of the state system of higher education in Tennessee. I have had the experience of deciding to take some action [and] I might have been retired before it came [about] because of the all the bureaus and political realities of life … Here at this institution or at a small college … as president if I take an action, I can actually see the results … We have an executive committee meeting today, and we'll take action on what we discuss today. We won't worry about whether the governor will approve them, or the legislature. If we approve them and we act on them and we assume that we have the support of the faculty and the students (and I don't mean by that that we have to ask the faculty and students—we like to have them involved), if we act on it today, then it will be implemented.

"I feel more like a leader than I would in the larger public sector … The private sector president has more of a personal investment in the result of his or her actions," he said. "The public president can frequently say to the faculty, 'Okay, I recommended to the legislature that you get a 12 percent increase in salary, but the legislature and governor wouldn't approve it. I'm the good guy, they're the bad people.' If I say to my faculty, 'You're going to get only a 2 percent pay raise,' I can't blame someone else. As a private sector president, I am on the line for having succeeded or failed."

Yet Heilman is completely self-effacing about the accomplishments that have occurred during his tenure as president. "Here I've gotten an awful lot of credit in fourteen years for a lot of success. We've had a lot, though clearly most of it can be identified with specific people."

The Richmond area has two large universities, and Heilman insists that it is possible to advance one without retarding the other. "We go to the corporate enterprises in Richmond but not with an approach that is negative toward our neighbor VCU. I never say, 'Don't support VCU' because I support it with my tax money, and so do you. That would be totally counterproductive.

We do acknowledge that VCU, Virginia Tech, and [the university of] Virginia get perhaps $50 million a year from the state, right up front. Therefore, if you're supporting these institutions in addition to that, fine. But remember, when you support us, that's our first dollar ... Don't overlook the fact that we're free enterprise like you in business and industry, and if you don't support us, we're out of business ... VCU and the University of Richmond are great complements [for] each other. We give a broad base of what's important to a city so we don't demean each other in the process."

VCU's president, Edmund F. Ackell, said of Heilman, "We're friends," and says that Heilman is "persuasive and persistent" to partially explain his success at fund-raising. But Ackell does acknowledge that the two institutions are competitors. "To a certain extent, it's true," Ackell said, "due to the nature that both institutions are in Richmond. The dollars are limited, and everybody's competing for a piece of the pie."

The Heilman message is almost invariably upbeat. His job is to sell, and a good salesman knows the message has to be positive. And once the sale is completed, there is plenty of good cheer for the customer. One does not hear Heilman making disparaging remarks about the university's various corporate benefactors or other wealthy givers, which include Phillip Morris and the Robins family. Heilman staunchly defends both the family and the besieged pharmaceutical company, saying that most people simply don't have all the facts regarding A.H. Robins's problems. He says, "I think that anybody that's really familiar with the situation—that the Robins have given $100 million to this university over a fifteen-to-twenty-year period— that everybody who's ever been here or who's here today is benefitting ... it's not just a question of the university taking the money, every student pays $1,000 to $2,000 less by virtue of that ... everybody who is here is taking from the Robins."

Joseph Kent says that Heilman meets regularly with groups of students at his home and is generally regarded as having decent relations with the students. "I can't think of anything more pleasant than interacting with the students," he says. "I don't mean that the students agree with me. They don't. But they give me the benefit of the doubt, like I try to give them the benefit of the doubt."

But there was a time when relations between Heilman and his students were less favorable. And may have been not so much a failure of Heilman's abilities as a sign of the times. "I did not enjoy," Heilman said, "the confrontational period of the Vietnam War. That was not pleasant, but it was not a matter of disagreement. Of course, as an old marine, we weren't for folks going to Canada to avoid the draft or anything like that. I thought they ought to fight for their country. But they faced a very different kind of war than I knew ... But when students were forcing their way in numbers, I had five thousand students on the campus of Meredith College from the University of North Carolina, North Carolina State, and Duke. They were rampaging through the dorms and shrubbery and destroying things, and there was no way of mediating, controlling, and discussing. They were just mean. Mad and mean … Students would not speak to me on campus, literally. It was an ugly attitude, kind of like a terrorist mentality. … In fact, if that had not corrected itself, I would not have stayed long in the presidency.

"By the time I arrived here [in 1971], things had settled down, but when I was interviewed here, I was interviewed by five student government presidents, and they were very sharp and condemning of the past administration … at that time, they still had long hair and they had the posture of confrontation," though the anti-war fervor was beginning to wear itself out by then, according to Heilman.

Bruce Heilman is not a scholar, by his own admission. He thinks that a scholar can be a university president but cannot be an active scholar while president. Heilman's business and administrative background, however, do not prevent him from having interesting opinions about education. "Education," Heilman said, "may well not be a platform or foundation for leadership in international understanding for which we give it credit. It may be a foundation for parochialism and propaganda and even for confrontation. The Russians go through a teaching and learning process and come out one way. Our people go through a teaching and learning process and come out another way. And in Saudi Arabia, they go through a teaching and learning process and come out another way, and yet we talk about education as something that does good for everybody. Well, we sit down together, and none of us can even communicate. We don't believe the same thing, we're not rational in the same way, so education is not as universal and international as we perceive it to be, except in the fact that teachers teach, and students learn. But the end results are very different."

Heilman's accomplishments at the University of Richmond have been considerable, and neither he nor the board have expressed any interest in terminating what appears to be an ideal relationship. As John Dalton said,

"We want him to continue to do what he's doing."

But Heilman did say this: "I came here at age forty-five. At fortyfive, a person still has a lot of vigor, vim, vitality, and excitement. The excitement never really goes away, contrary to what young people think. I feel just as excited today as I was when I was ten years old … about life and what happens. But the energy level is not the same, and I've got as much energy as anybody my age. Or the ability to look ahead twenty or thirty years is not the same. When I came here, I could look at this university, and I could see … so much that had to be done, that it would consume me, and I was willing to be consumed … At this point in history, I can't look forward with the same objective, open point of view. What do we do for the next twenty years? Well, at some point I'm not the one to deal with the next twenty years. Every institution periodically needs new high octane … An old president can fade away, but a university does not deserve to participate in the fading process. Rather it should be accelerated by new blood, new energy, and new aspirations under the leadership of someone not blinded by imagined limitations developed in the minds of those who have spent their vigor.

While most presidents render a notable and noble service in time over time, one may confuse the office and the man holding the appointment.

Many honors come to the one holding the office of president. Few, if any, would come to the one as John Q. Citizen unless he were a great scholar, soldier, or statesman in his own right. Once realized, the president can step down from the podium and again become himself with pride in past accomplishments.

\*\*\*

## SPEAKING OF PEOPLE
*October 21, 1982. The Courier-Journal, Louisville, Ky.*

# Kentuckian is pushing Virginia school ahead

**Joan Kay**

*Courier-Journal columnist*

Shortly after becoming president of the University of Richmond in 1971, Dr. E. Bruce Heilman, a Ballardsville, Ky., native, spearheaded an ambitious fund-raising campaign for the Virginia institution.

Several years earlier, the E. Claiborne Robins family of Richmond had given $50 million to the university in hopes it would be seed money to make the private institution one of the finest in the country.

Heilman says he "simply suggested that if one family could give $50 million, we ought to go to the whole world for another $50 million." Within eight years, by 1980, the university raised $54 million, two years ahead of schedule.

Heilman talked about the college on a visit to Louisville for an alumni gathering last weekend and the University of Richmond-University of Louisville football game.

E. Claiborne Robins, a UR alumnus, is chairman of the A. H. Robins

Co., a pharmaceutical firm in Richmond. In 1968, the family's gift of $50 million was the largest gift by any one family in the country to a university. Since then, the Robins family has added another $30 million.

With its current hefty endowment of $105 million, the university could aim to establish a reputation based on size of enrollment or to develop specialized schools. "We simply don't choose to," says Heilman. UR has stuck with its commitment to providing a quality liberal-arts education, with limited professional educational opportunities.

The University of Richmond actually is five colleges: Richmond College for men, about 1,300 students; Westhampton College for women, about 1,200; T. C. Williams School of Law, about 425; E. Claiborne Robins School of Business, roughly 600 graduate and undergraduate students, and University College, about 600. There are about 225 full-time faculty members for the whole university.

Enrollment is limited and virtually has stayed the same over the past 12 years. There were five applications last year for every slot. "We have really resisted growth," says Heilman.

The Robins family money went into the endowment fund to earn interest so faculty salaries could be

increased. The fund drive's money was earmarked to rehabilitate buildings and build new facilities.

After the fund drive was launched, the university began recruiting students from all over the country. Fourteen years ago 85 percent of UR's student body was from outside Virginia. Now 65 percent come from outside Virginia. "So we've become a national institution," attracting the same students who apply to Tulane, Vanderbilt and private schools in the East.

Three weeks ago a second fund drive was begun with a goal of $55 million in five years. At the kickoff, almost $21 million had been raised

from corporations in the Richmond area, selected alumni and trustees. This money will be used predominantly to strengthen academic programs, establish professorships and provide scholarships for top-notch students who can't afford tuition.

Heilman spends a lot of his time raising money. "When you ask for a $2 million gift, the president of the university must be the one (to ask). Actually, you get money from people who intend to give it" because of their commitment to serve society, "but they haven't decided where. So what presidents do — they hope they have something to market and that they market it well."

The Heilmans have five children, all graduates of UR, plus three sons-in-law who are alumni, "so we feel it's a great place to educate young people," says Mrs. Heilman, the former Betty June Dobbins of Louisville.

Heilman, 56, who is only the sixth president since UR's founding in 1830, is a dynamic, persuasive spokesman for his university, while retaining a down-home, informal manner. He grew up outside Ballardsville on a farm and recalls that "we came to Louisville once or twice a year to get shoes. Otherwise, we went to La Grange on Saturday."

He attended La Grange High

School, which preceded Oldham County High, and joined the Marine Corps in 1944. After completing duty, he went to Campbellsville College, then a junior college. He met his wife there, and they were married as students in 1948.

Heilman received a bachelor-of-science degree in business administration from George Peabody College for Teachers in Nashville in 1950 and a year later got a master's degree. After completing a Ph.D. in educational administration at Peabody in 1961, he came to Louisville to help establish the now-defunct Kentucky Southern College. For two years he was vice-president and dean, helping establish the curriculum.

Then he was administrative vice-president at Peabody and president of Meredith College in Raleigh, N.C., before going to the University of Richmond.

In the summers, the Heilmans spend time at their farm in Henry County, where Heilman's parents, Mr. and Mrs. Earl B. Heilman, live. And they take a break from campus life every summer with a trip abroad.

For 15 years now, Heilman has negotiated with travel agents for a tour to some part of the globe, and he and his wife act as guides to 15 to 30 university trustees, alumni or other friends.

Last year the group traveled by the Trans-Siberian railroad from Moscow to Irkutsk, Siberia. They went to China the year before, and Egypt is on the agenda next summer. "We've been to Africa, Eastern Europe, Scandinavia, the South Pacific," says Heilman. "We've not missed in 15 years so we've touched most of the world."

Staff Photo by Pam Spaulding

Dr. and Mrs. E. Bruce Heilman visit the Henry County farm of his parents every summer.

# VI

## THE PRESIDENT SELLING THE UNIVERSITY

The Selling of a University by Pete McPherson
*Style Magazine*

Don't confuse office and man.

The president of the University of Richmond operates in the corporate and academic spheres with equal aplomb. The elegantly appointed president's dining room at the W. Tyler Haynes Commons building at the University of Richmond would not be out of place in any corporate suite in Richmond. And the president of the university himself would not be out of place. For one thing, E. Bruce Heilman has a lot in common with the leaders of the local business community. His undergraduate and graduate degrees in business administration from Vanderbilt University prepared him to join their ranks. He is a southerner (though he comes from rural Kentucky) and a World War II veteran. He lives in a graciously furnished, palatial house on River Road with his wife Betty.

Indeed, he is not out of place in Richmond's corporate community, moving skillfully and diplomatically among its members in his constant quest for funds for his university. A lot of persuading is done over breakfast in his dining room in the Commons building.

But Heilman did say this: An old president can fade away but a university does not deserve to have a president fade away.

\*\*\*

*Before commencement on May 8 Nathan S. Gumenick, left, talked with J. Richard Munro, center, and Dr. Heilman. Gumenick was awarded an honorary Doctor of Commercial Science degree and Munro, the commencement speaker, received an honorary Doctor of Letters degree. During the ceremony at the Robins Center four additional honorary degrees were awarded and two Trustees' Distinguished Service Awards were presented.*

## Dr. and Mrs. E. Bruce Heilman

Dr. E. Bruce Heilman was elected the fifth president of the University of Richmond in March, 1971. His tenure has been marked by unprecedented growth in the University's national reputation, its academic programs, its physical plant, and its endowment. In his fifteen years of leadership, he has built a strong administration and faculty and enhanced dramatically the quality of the student body.

Bruce Heilman will be remembered by us, his fellow trustees, as an educational leader of bold vision, a tireless champion of private higher education, an imaginative administrator who challenged us and countless others to a new level of service to the University of Richmond.

He and Betty together have captured our hearts with their willingness to make their home our home. They have shared in our lives and caused us to rediscover the excitement of giving so that others might be served. They have helped us to dream as we sought to make the University an even finer place in which to live and learn.

On this seventh day of March, 1986, we offer our sincerest thanks to you, Bruce and Betty, for these years of accomplishment. As together we continue building on the strong foundation set during your presidency, we extend our best wishes for good health and happiness.

In the *Richmond News Leader* of Tuesday, July 17, 1979, eight years after I assumed the presidency of the University of Richmond, Allan McCreary, news leader education writer, published a rather elaborate story with the bold letters "Heilman Brought Golden Touch to University." This was a very detailed citation of perspectives, dispositions, interpretations, and happenings relative to what was then and had been occurring in respect to the transformation of the university. A great deal of space was given to impressions of faculty, staff, alumni, students, the community, and board members—both positive and negative.

None of this was unusual at a university that had been so ambitious as to seek transformation from an institution known relatively little beyond its immediate environment to one of the finest small universities in the country, literally to become known throughout the world. The story was so filled with reality and was so clearly presented in respect to what had been transpiring from 1971 until 1979 that it better described the situation than I, as president, could have done myself. I let the story speak for itself.

My inaugural address had outlined what was to be done and by now, much of that which had been outlined and defined had been initiated or completed. In fact, Mr. Robins had noted after seven years that more had happened in these few years at the university than all of its 140 prior years. While that may have been an ambitious exaggeration in time, it certainly highlighted the bold story heralding that "Heilman Brought Golden Touch to the University."

Certainly not all of the story left the impression that I was altogether a golden boy. In fact, it suggested a great deal more in some respects and less in others. But all in all, up to that period, it presented a transition unlike any other—or at least of only a few in such a dramatic trajectory that was continuing and would not slack even to this day, forty-nine years later.

The story states much of reality, including some disaffection on the part of some who might have done things differently out of their restlessness to take certain actions appealing especially to them. Cited are disappointments on the parts of some and excitement on the parts of others, all of which was a natural consequence of a president asserting actions unlike any other over the prior 140 years. Expectations had become so dramatically greater for the institution that there would be those who would praise the results, but others who would criticize happenings because of the change in style in comparison to past presidents.

To some, I seemed not to be as academically focused as my predecessors because I was moving the institution forward, requiring the garnering of resources unlike any other time in history. Therefore, by being so busy, I was unable to sit in my office, satisfying the personal interests that many had taken for granted with prior presidents whose lack of efforts in fundraising common in these years had left the university at risk financially. I had to move so rapidly that I did not communicate as warmly everything to everybody simply because of the lack of time.

From this story, I share enough to convey that it was the way things were and that the writer stated it substantially as I would have conveyed the reality of the time myself. I have tried to balance enough of its contents

UR Ranked Among America's Best Colleges

Dr. E. Bruce Heilman —photo by Wertheimer

For the Heilmans, part of Christmas at home means seeing the grandchildren. Dr. Heilman holds Hilary Sylvester while Mrs. Heilman holds Hilary's twin sister Natalie. Corey June Heilman is between them. In front of them, left to right, are Christopher Hudgins, Whitney Sylvester and Matthew Hudgins.

Dr. Heilman presents Helen Boehm with a certificate of honor for her gifts to the University

to provide a message of the time from an objective view point. Attached to the first page of the long article "Heilman Brought Golden Touch to University" was a photo with the caption: "UR president E. Bruce Heilman works like a piece of machinery."

One of Bruce Heilman's first cars was a 1946 Hudson, a well-worn taxi cab with 97,500 miles on the odometer. He paid four hundred dollars for it and later spent six hundred trying to get it in condition to provide dependable transportation but he couldn't get it right. He later sold it to a dealer for $400.

The Hudson was one of Heilman's few bad investments. He later bought a new Ford off the assembly line and paid for it by ferrying fellow US marines between North Carolina and Washington. In more recent times he learned that salvaging colleges and universities with other people's money is a safer gamble than salvaging ailing cars with his own money.

In 1966, he took over limping Meredith College in Raleigh, North Carolina, raised about $5 million in private gifts, and left the college on sound financial footing with double enrollment when he moved to Richmond in 1971.

The University of Richmond also needed an overhaul. A few years before, former President George M. Modlin had told the board of trustees that the university might face disaster in the 1970s. At U of R, dormitories, classrooms, office buildings, and science facilities needed major renovation or replacement. The library needed more space and money for new books and materials. Faculty salaries needed to be boosted.

The $7 million endowment fund was not producing enough income to keep the university solid without sizeable tuition increases. Dr. Modlin mentioned the possibility of merging with a public institution or closing the university. As an afterthought, he also mentioned the possibility of a major gift to the university one trustee recalls, but he was not optimistic about that.

Then, at the commencement exercise in 1969, Dr. Modlin announced that E. Claiborne Robins, an alumnus, met with the board of trustees and announced his gift of $50 million to give the university a new lease on life. Robins, chairman of the pharmaceutical manufacturing A. H. Robins Company, hoped his gift would stimulate other giving and enable the university to become one of the best small liberal arts institutions in the country.

The trustees began looking for somebody who could rebuild the campus and carry out a successful fund drive for more millions. Dr. Modlin announced his intention to retire in 1971, and Dr. Heilman was brought on the campus for an interview. The pinstripe-clad country boy with a hillbilly twang and a reputation for being able to sniff money across a crowded room or hundreds of miles away looked like a good prospect for the job. Dr. Heilman, part salesman, part evangelist, part faith healer, sized up Richmond and decided he could raise $50 million. The trustees hired him, paid him a beginning salary of $50–60,000 a year, gave him a car, built him a large house at 7000 River Road, and arranged a generous expense allowance. At that time, Dr. Heiman was believed to be the highest-paid college president in the state. His salary was only 10–20 percent lower than the salaries paid to presidents of Harvard and Stanford University, campus sources said. F. Carlyle Tiller, rector for the board of trustees, said, "Whatever he is paid is not enough. He works like a piece of machinery." When Dr. Heilman is on campus, he works hard, associates say. But he is off campus a lot to raise funds and to attend to other university business.

One faculty member stated, "He is unpopular with a vocal minority, but I've worked with him in several committees, and I am convinced that he has the best interest of the university at heart." Another professor, chairman of a department, said, "He doesn't know many faculty members who do not believe they need more money for department expenses."

"In the long run," said one professor, "I think the university's pretty well managed." It's impossible to do everything to everybody. Multiply some small requests by two hundred faculty members, and you can have $1 million or so."

# Heilman resigns presidency

By William B. Lindsay
Editor

University of Richmond President E. Bruce Heilman announced Friday that he will resign from office and assume the position of chancellor effective Sept. 1, 1986.

Heilman made his announcement to faculty, staff, administrators and student leaders at a special convocation, following the Board of Trustees semi-annual meeting.

Heilman, 59, said that although he is 10 years younger than his predecessor, George M. Modlin, when he retired from the presidency, he probably wouldn't lead the University in the future as vigorously, effectively or as positively as Modlin has for the last 15 years.

Explaining his request for the change in position, the President said that "the University deserves not just able, effective and mature leadership at this time, but youthful, forceful, dynamic and imaginative direction, which can best be provided by an objective and unaffected perspective."

"Old presidents should never be allowed to fade away," Heilman said. "They should either die, retire or take a position where they can continue to serve well in support of the policies of the Board and the leadership of a new president. The latter appeared for me the best choice."

He looks forward to supporting and reinforcing the new leadership and he hopes that the future will show even greater progress than seen to date, Heilman said.

"The next president can build new towers on the foundations laid."

Looking back at the perceptions of students and the dreams of the faculty when he assumed office in 1971, Heilman said that today's students perceive things differently and the dreams of the faculty of 15 years ago would seem shallow and short-sighted to the faculty of today.

When Heilman became president, less than 40 percent of the current faculty and less than 10 percent of the current administration and staff were at the University.

The fifth president in the University's 155-year history, Heilman's tenure has been marked by unprecedented growth in UR's national reputation, academic programs, physical plant and endowment.

The number of faculty members holding doctorates or terminal degrees has risen from 60 percent in 1971 to 90 percent today. Faculty publications and salary have more than doubled and faculty salaries have risen dramatically, according to F. Carlyle Tiller, Rector of the Board of Trustees.

The Heilman years have seen the average student SAT scores rise 235 points above the national average as well as the creation of eight distinguished faculty chairs and a substantial increase in merit-based scholarships, Tiller said.

In the last 15 years, approximately $65 million has been spent on new buildings and renovations around campus, Tiller said. Since Heilman's arrival, the University has gained: the $10 million Robins Center, the $8 million Gottwald Science Center, the $5 million Tyler Haynes Commons, the $5 million dining hall, Lora Robins Court, Gray Court, a new president's home and additions to and renovations of the Boatwright Library, the T.C. Williams School of Law, E. Claiborne Robins School of Business Administration and Sarah Brunet Memorial Hall.

The University's endowment has increased from $38 million in 1971 to $162 million today, placing UR in the top 2 percent of all universities in the country, Tiller said.

On Sept. 1, 1986, Heilman will become chancellor, replacing Modlin who will become chancellor emeritus. In the role of chancellor, Heilman will be involved in projects and activities "consistent with his special talents and within the needs of the University as judged by the Board, the president, and himself," according to Tiller.

Tiller said that Heilman will take a sabbatical leave next fall, after the new president takes office.

The Board of Trustees expects to be inundated with applications for Heilman's present job. "It will

Dr. Heilman announces change of position.    photo by Michele Marin

be one of the most sought after positions in higher education," Tiller said.

According to Tiller the search for a successor to Heilman, headed by Joseph A. Jennings, chairman of the executive committee of the Board, is already underway. The Trustees have set Dec. 31 as the application deadline, but Tiller added that worthy candidates will be considered beyond that point. A screening committee, to review applications and narrow the field, and a selection committee, to choose the next president, have been established by the Trustees.

Prior to coming to UR, Heilman was president of Meredith College in Raleigh, N.C., from 1966 to 1971. He has also been coordinator of higher education for the state of Tennessee.

"Heilman resigns presidency."

Few faculty remembered a library that was not fully accredited, and science facilities that were less adequate than the high schools in the area, and on and on I could go. Faculty members are not savvy to many things outside of their departments and fail to understand that the president has to do things that might not seem to others the proper action at a given time.

In the meantime, while some faculty may have thought their salaries should have increased even more rapidly, we were moving from the fortieth percentile to the seventieth percentile nationally and doing so rapidly. Further, with all the actions being taken, the enrollment as trending upward.

> Several faculty members credited Dr. Heilman with having done an outstanding job in raising funds and improving campus facilities. However, others have been concerned about his ability to function as an academic leader in some difficult years ahead. One department chairman "sees Dr. Heilman as very bright, clever, with a high degree of native intelligence. He is good at working with complex issues in the context of groups with their divergent interests."

So, having cited some perspective shared by a news reporter giving lots of opportunities for faculty members to express their views, a picture emerges of second-guessing, which, after forty-nine years, if one reads my inaugural address, was just that as there is almost nothing negative to be said for where we have come from where we started on the path to transformation as a university recognized as one of the best.

All has taken place within the context of a vision, a purpose, and with a passion as the board of trustees speaking through the president judged to do what was done at a given time, utilizing the resources available in the best way to bring us to where we are today. Even those who were critics in the past came to realize that the dispersal of our resources, the accumulation of our endowment, the programs we have fostered, the quality of the faculty have brought to the university, the student quality levels, and everything that we perceived should happen has happened.

A measure of the level of success during my presidency is the fact that from the senior administrators employed during my presidency, thirteen became presidents of other institutions.

McCreary's article noted, "It is the job of a faculty to advocate for better conditions and the job of the president to serve as a scapegoat and take the flak from anybody who is dissatisfied with the university." He suggested that the University of Richmond was controversial with the church, alumni, faculty, and others because everybody has a slice of it and everybody wants to have something to say about what happens. The president, the writer observes, has taken considerable more time to deal with faculty concerns. When he might otherwise have raised another $1 million in gifts in that time but thought it was worth more than the money to deal with the faculty.

The writer of a story entitled "Expertise" cited says,

> Whatever the merits of Dr. Heilman's financial management thus far, several faculty members and trustees believe his fund-raising expertise would be a critical factor in the future. Watch him at a cocktail party some time suggested a Richmond banker. If you are standing there with some loose change in your pocket, he will walk right by you and never blink. He knows exactly who to put the touch on.

During this period of time, there were also complaints from our Baptist constituency. That was not new, of course, for a church-related institution. After dealing with a major issue, a professor said, "We've come through this and are a better school because of the strength and integrity of the faculty." There was a remarkable outpouring of public support locally among friends of the school and concerned citizens. The professor was convinced of the president's commitment to the university and to academic freedom. "I think I came to know him in a way few faculty members have," he said.

> Few faculty members are aware of what the president and the board and senior administrators are doing and why they are doing it—no matter how much they may state the fact in publications or at faculty meetings. For example, when a campaign was launched for the University of Richmond after the Robins gift, for another $54 million, it was among the twenty most ambitious college university development campaign in the country being conducted at that time. The university could never have succeeded at that without subjecting itself to some of the criticisms cited. The president was totally submerged in getting the resources to do the many things the faculty wanted

done and were done as a result of the campaign taking place. The funds were, among other things, to correct the inadequacy of the library and the science facility, as well as housing for students to get rid of the old World War II barracks on campus, and to improve food service.

These things that didn't impress the faculty even though upgrading the library, science, and other facilities was essential to improving the academic program. That should have been something they applauded that might have highlighted the privilege of operating in the new environment.

Many stories were written during the period of dramatic change to fulfill our ambitions. From the beginning, if all could have looked ahead, we would have been praising each other all along because today we agree that a miracle that happened.

The administration and faculty members function in many ways like politicians. We were for or against based upon where we stood in self-interest. We did not seek to see the other's position as well as we should or we who have the legal responsibility do our best to live up to the adventures we create, the ambitions we perceive, and the challenges we are given. Faculty members have more flexibility in judging without the responsibility for the ultimate outcome.

# Banks resigns; Heilman back

Samuel A. Banks

**Mary M. Fehm**
*Editor*

Chancellor and former President E. Bruce Heilman will serve as interim chief executive officer of the University of Richmond until a new president can be found.

Heilman was president of the University from 1971 until Dec. 1, 1986, when he became chancellor. His appointment follows the early retirement of former President-elect Samuel A. Banks.

The executive committee of the board of trustees requested that Heilman be appointed on an interim basis while a search for

a new president is conducted, John Roush, assistant to the president, said.

With Heilman's leadership at this time of transition, the University is not likely to lose momentum, Joseph A. Jennings, rector of the University, said. Jennings also said that the University would move quickly but prudently to find a new president.

The search process will not begin until the board of trustees meets on Oct. 1 and 2.

Zeddie Bowen, vice president and provost, served as chief operating officer from Aug. 15 until Sept. 1, when Heilman assumed the position.

Banks' retirement came as a surprise to members of the University community. There were no preliminary warnings, Thomas Pollard, dean of admissions, said. "It was a shock in terms of notification."

Leonard S. Goldberg, vice president for student affairs, said he didn't find out about Banks' health problem until the third or fourth week of May. Banks told him that he had been travelling to the Hershey Medical Center in Pennsylvania and that he was having trouble with his

see BANKS page 8

also GREETINGS page 5

E. Bruce Heilman

# VII

# NOTABLE CONTRIBUTIONS OF MY SUCCESSORS

"Someone said "If we are going to kill giants, we must believe we are bigger than they are. If not, they will kill us."

1979: E. CLAIBORNE ROBINS WAS NAMED "THE GREATEST LIVING PATRON" OF THE UNIVERSITY OF RICHMOND AS THE SESQUICENTENNIAL CELEBRATION OPENED AT THE BEGINNING OF THE 1979-80 ACADEMIC YEAR, AND THE UNIVERSITY'S SCHOOL OF BUSINESS WAS NAMED THE E. CLAIBORNE ROBINS SCHOOL OF BUSINESS.

I could claim, and I believe be proved correct, that one of my attributes was in selecting good colleagues, and that was confirmed by the thirteen who later became presidents of other colleges. I selected them because I knew they had talent and would serve me and the institution I served well for a period of at least five years, giving their best. The individuals who were clearly in the top of their league in this regard were Jerry Quigg, Chris Withers, Lou Molchert, Charlie Glasick, Herb Peterson, Bill Leftwich, and others who made the difference. One who made a broad difference at the institution was in the chaplaincy headed by Dr. David Burhans. He positively affected the entire administrative team.

I alone defined the position and recruited the chaplain who served more than thirty years. Some of what we do as leaders is make judgments. A judgment might not always be supported by the faculty, staff, students, or the community. It may not be proved as the right action for years to come. One must have the long view in order to hold the position of president. Spirit is essential along with deep conviction in order to operate against opposition that can sometimes be strong. But, in the end, a leader is selected to lead and not to follow the opinion of the community.

After all these years of its operating as it was defined, I now conclude that my judgment in establishing the chaplaincy at the university was unique and helped create an environment that was conducive to the open spirit that exists at the university today.

I may be presumptuous in reserving a place in my book for "notable contributions of my successors." The university is what it is today not only because I laid the foundation following the Robins gift but because capable individuals who succeeded me each accepted and responded to Claiborne's challenge to make the University of Richmond one of the finest small universities in the country. Each built on the foundations laid during the sixteen years of my presidency and of each succeeding president.

I shall present a thumbnail sketch of the very obvious contributions of each of my successors to highlight the leadership results and impact upon what the university has become by virtue of their actions over the years since my days as president.

## Dr. Richard Morrill

Dr. Morrill picked up the reigns of leadership for the university with a background that few presidents can claim. He had already served as a senior administrator at several institutions. He was educated at first-rate colleges and universities—Brown University and Duke—and had interacted with educators as a leader among leaders wherever he served.

I had observed Dr. Morrill in professional relationships when he was president of Centre College in Kentucky. He had also served as president of Salem College in Winston-Salem, North Carolina. In social relationships, he functioned comfortably as was true in his leadership in professional and educational activities and in his articulation and publication of educational ideas.

On an occasion—I believe it was the annual meeting of the Southern Association of Colleges and Schools— we chatted long enough for me to broach the subject of my imminent retirement from the presidency of the University of Richmond. I suggested that he would be a good successor to me. So, when the committee was formulated at Richmond for selecting my successor, I suggested Dr. Morrill's name as an able prospect.

As the search proceeded, I was invited by the committee to comment further about him, after which he was contacted. He stated that his short tenure at Centre made it impossible to consider another presidency so soon. Therefore, the committee turned in another direction, and after considering many possibilities, they settled on the president of Dickenson College, Dr. Sam Banks, as president to succeed me.

As my retirement activities proceeded, I suggested that having already been selected to be chancellor of the university, I should have a six-month leave from the campus completely so that the incoming president would have no misapprehensions as to who was in the driver's seat as the senior leader of the university. I assured the board that I would be off the campus so that the new president and anyone else would not think of me as the chief executive after fifteen years.

At that time, there was a gift of a house given by Marcus Weinstein, several blocks from the campus. He indicated that it might be used for a home for the chancellor. I left the campus, moved into the chancellor's home, and went about my business independent of the university while the new president was being situated, oriented, and incorporated into the leadership role that was his.

Skipping the next months, I had a call from Lewis Booker, the chairman of the board. He would shortly arrive at the chancellor's home for a discussion. Upon his arrival, we initiated a private conference concerning action just taken by the board to accept the resignation of the president for health reasons and to cite the best option to temporarily fill the vacant position while seeking the next president. In the end, they decided I should serve in the interim. "We need you to come back into the presidency in an acting capacity for perhaps a year as we seek another successor as president."

I immediately responded in that I was functioning as chancellor at the discretion of the board. Thus, if it was their desire, I would immediately assume the interim role of chief executive. Since I had already relocated to the chancellor's home, I would stay there and entertain from the president's home since that seemed appropriate.

I was welcomed back by my colleagues, vice presidents, and others with a generous spirit while the board looked for my successor. Dr. Richard Morrill's name came up again before the committee, and I suggested that

Dr. Morrill might feel that he had been at Centre College long enough to consider another presidency. He was contacted by the committee, and he indicated that he would consider that possibility. He ultimately was selected and elected to succeed me as the new president of the University of Richmond.

Rich Morrill brought a constructive period of leadership, filling in the many gaps that he could see needed to be filled to complement what I and the university had done during the sixteen years of my leadership.

With no attempt to define Dr. Morrill's many constructive contributions, I cite two very important facilities and programs constituted and instituted during his presidency. The fine arts building, growing out of his experience at Centre College, added greatly to the university's prestige, program, and community relationship. Thus, that superb building and its program is today one of his key legacies.

Another facility that came into play at the right time under his presidency was the Jepson Alumni Center. His relationship with Bob Jepson contributed to the establishment of this facility. Rich Morrill also can be recognized for the early stages of the creation of the Jepson Leadership School.

Dr. Morrill was respected by the board and positively oriented to the community. To some extent, he stabilized the institution following my years of very dramatic change as he continued the quest to make it one of the best.

## In honor of Vice President for Advancement Chris Withers

Friends and colleagues have established a merit scholarship in honor of Chris Withers, for his three decades of service to the University. It will be used to recruit an outstanding student to Richmond.

For more information about scholarships, call 1-800-480-4774, ext 2.

Among those honoring Withers at a retirement dinner in April were the three presidents he served: Dr. William E. Cooper; Dr. Richard L. Morrill, H'96; and Dr. E. Bruce Heilman, H'86.

## Dr. William Cooper

Dr. Cooper came onto the campus running, making adjustments, reorienting, to some extent, the board and the institution to a broader constituency, more particularly orienting it to alumni in New York City. He also expanded the geographic makeup of the board from a substantially local membership to a more national one.

Not every one of the alumni or friends of the university appreciated that broadening process, which I had also faced in a way of attitudes and spirits when I broadened the board and brought people who had not, in the past, been functioning on the board. Change always makes waves, and some of the alumni of long tenure didn't appreciate some of what Dr. Cooper was doing.

Without trying to cite the many contributions of Dr. Cooper, I identify the particular contribution that sparked a strong negative reaction. My interpretation is—and I think many other educators would agree—that the University of Richmond, while a very good university and developing rapidly toward a high level of visibility throughout the state, nation, and world, had not yet taken on the image as being at the same level of some of the elite such as Vanderbilt, Wake Forest, Williams, and other elite schools throughout the country because our tuition and fees were substantially lower in comparison to the others.

Individuals of wealth tend to identify quality with cost. Therefore, Dr. Cooper's dramatic increase in fees, while not well received, has had as much to do with the image of the university today as anything he or anybody else has done in the immediate or long-range past.

In the eyes of our alumni and friends—whether they liked it or not his action placed us alongside the prestigious, elitist colleges and universities simply because if it costs this much, it must be good. I applaud Dr. Cooper, and I think most people do today for the boldness with which the action took, and the contribution he made will go down in history as one of his major contributions to the enhancement of the image of the institution.

Dr. Cooper, in his nine years at the university, implemented an ambitious tenure-strategic plan along with a comprehensive campus master plan, adding to the momentum along with the Transforming Bright Minds campaign that raised $200 million, exceeding its goal. He created the Richmond Quest, an innovative program designed to engender intellectual inquiry and cohesion, and that led to the development of unique courses, symposia, and student research projects. During Dr. Cooper's presidency, the endowment grew from $751 million to over $1 billion.

I have a letter from Dr. Cooper about the historic occasion that is the unveiling of the statue of Mr. Robins.

Many thanks for being a part of the E. Claiborne Robins statue unveiling ceremony last Friday. Your remarks were wonderful, personal, and meaningful to everyone who knew or knew of Mr. Robins. Each member of the Robins family expressed to me how personally pleased they were with the ceremony and the tributes given. They know you speak from the heart and experience, which makes your words even more meaningful. It is obvious they hold you and Betty in the highest esteem, and I am grateful for your continuing tie with this important family.

I believe this goodwill communication from Dr. Cooper represented the good spirit that has prevailed between all of us who have served together.

## Dr. Edward Ayers

University of Richmond President, Dr. and Mrs. Ayers with University Chancellor, Dr. and Mrs. E. Bruce Heilman

The next president succeeding Dr. Cooper was Dr. Edward Ayers, from Charlottesville, Virginia where he was dean of arts and sciences of the University of Virginia, one of the most respected and published academicians anywhere in the country and the world to hold the presidency with a flair. It was not a short-lived tenure, but he presented a good, strong image and confidence on the part of the public as he worked his seven years with great focus. He gained the confidence of faculty, staff, alumni, and friends with his speaking and reputation. His self-studies and directions lifted the university another rung on the ladder of prestige, visibility, and academic virtue.

As was the case in every presidential change, new facilities began to appear, and he had much to do with bringing about the new admissions facility that took over almost everything that had to do with student admissions, student aid, and the registrar's office. He brought together all the campus functions that were integral to each other. Due to his reputation at the University of Virginia, a lot of attention was directed to the University of Richmond from a local and stabilized standpoint, and he brought new visibility and respect to the university.

In his leadership position at the University of Richmond, he continued to contribute immensely to the special expertise he had developed throughout his professional career in American historical activities. He served on the board of the National Humanities Center, the American Council of Education, and a variety of other international and national higher education leadership groups. He showed the importance of American history through his pioneering work in digital scholarship and cohosting the nationally syndicated public radio program "Backstory with the American History Guys."

During his presidency, undergraduate applications grew by nearly 50 percent, and the quality of the entering class improved by every academic measure. The number of American students of color increased markedly in the entering class, and international students doubled. The university doubled the number of Pell students. The faculty of color and women numbers increased markedly during his presidency.

A comprehensive tenure campus plan was developed and academic facilities, new and improved, were an enhancement along with the business school, new residence halls, a student activities center, and athletic facilities. Fund-raising continued at a high level, and the university's endowment continued to be among the best performing in the nation, surpassing $2 billion. The university connection to the city was strengthened with community-based learning programs.

## Dr. Ronald Crutcher

This, of course, was a surprise to many. He was African American, and it was still the South. The university was created, thrived, and advanced in the South. However, his election presented evidence of a new era, a new understanding, and a broader engagement of the university with the public, the world, and society to have an African American president.

In addition to being an educator and the former president of Wheaton College, Dr. Crutcher is a professional musician. He works with the local symphony and plays his cello all over the country, highlighting a particular department of the university that would not have been, perhaps in the past, as highlighted. He brought to the university a distinguished partner with a PhD, also engaged in the life of the university.

Dr. Betty Crutcher has the qualifications to fit into any faculty role and a personality that lights up the room. At the time of this writing, they've completed two years of exciting adventures at the university because of their joint leadership, their historic past, and a new era in human relations for the university.

Of course, Dr. Crutcher has continued the advancement to new levels all dimensions of the university and represents a new era in that he is the first African American president of the university. His excellence as a cellist and association with professional groups continues to elevate the visibility of the university.

Having identified some aspects of each of the presidents who succeeded me and acknowledging that each and all brought new meaning to being one of the finest small universities in the country, I give credit for where we are today. I am proud of my own part, but once I had done my part, new leaders with new ideas picked up where the predecessors left off. They added to their best efforts and claimed the right to the acknowledgement that the University of Richmond is the totality of those who were its leadership throughout its history.

A gathering of family members who are all Spiders and whose children are also Spiders."

First Lady Betty Heilman

With friends BJ and Vickie Senior

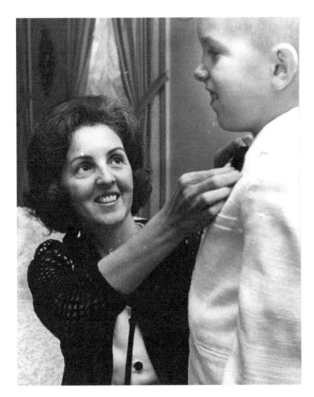

The First Lady as well as a Mother

With Son Tim, a Spider

# A tribute to
# Betty J. Heilman

First Lady of the University of Richmond
Presented by a special group of friends from the University
And from the community at a luncheon held at
The Commonwealth club, Richmond, Virginia, on November 20, 1985

In the fifteenth year of Betty Heilman's career as First Lady of the University of Richmond, it is appropriate to pause and give thanks for the example she has set through her strong dedication to her family, for her special contributions as hostess at a never-ending array of University and community social functions, and for her deep commitment to all aspects of the University's program of educational services.

Betty June Dobbins of Louisville, Kentucky, became Mrs. E. Bruce Heilman in 1948, while both were enrolled in what was then Campbellsville Junior College, in Kentucky. Sharing the same moral values and with a "Christian attitude toward the whole of life," the Heilmans have placed great emphasis on the family as a unit, on togetherness, mutual helpfulness, and love. This emphasis and her church work with children have, in Betty's words, given her "enormous satisfaction and fulfillment."

In 1971 after five years as First Lady of Meredith College, Raleigh, North Carolina, where her husband had been eminently successful as President, Betty Heilman faced the new challenges at the University of Richmond with courage, a positive attitude, flexibility, and resourcefulness, while keeping a sensitive ear to any unsettling trials of relocation that the five Heilman children might encounter. Now, four are graduates of the University of Richmond and the fifth is a degree candidate. There are seven grandchildren.

As the First Lady of the University of Richmond, Betty Heilman had the pleasant task of collaborating on the planning and furnishing of the spacious new President's Home on River Road (a task she had earlier performed at Meredith College). In characteristic manner, she kept utmost in her mind the needs of the students, faculty, administration and staff, Trustees, alumni-alumnae, and other friends of the University, as she worked out the design and furnishings for the downstairs rooms and the lower recreational area. Upstairs, she was careful to create pleasant, private living quarters for her family and special guests.

As First Lady, Betty Heilman receives all visitors with warmth, charm, and gentle dignity, making clear to all by example that the President's Home is an integral part of the total education and social programs of the University. It takes a stout heart just to contemplate the number and variety of events held in the President's Home: receptions with over a thousand guests each, dinners, luncheons, early breakfasts, and various get-togethers for all University constituencies and for special guests outside the University. With grace, composure, and good humor, Betty handles her responsibilities as hostess in a relaxed manner, totally at ease but quietly in charge. Even when the University's Catering Services are involved, Betty supervises all of the functions and performs much of the work herself.

Then there are the special holidays, with extensive tree-trimming at Christmastime, decorations in each room to give a different international flavor, and season emphases reflecting important University events, such as the football paraphernalia this fall point up Spider Spirit and the team's successes, including national rankings in Division 1-AA. Also in evidence is the well-known collection of dolls assembled by Betty from all over the world, inspired by her interest in doll collecting.

All of these efforts speak eloquently to Betty Heilman's unique contributions to all phases of University activities, reflecting high honor on the University through her devotion to her husband's remarkably fruitful career, to her family, and to the larger family of those who live and work at the University, as well as alumni and alumnae, and other friends who join in supporting the University's program of qualitative growth.

With this Tribute, we gratefully salute Betty Heilman with admiration, respect, and affection, and we express the fervent hope that the months and years ahead will bring continued joy and fulfillment in every endeavor.

SCENES OF ENTERTAINING
IN THE PRESIDENT'S HOME

## DRESSED TO ATTEND VARIOUS FUNCTIONS AS
## PRESIDENT AND FIRST LADY

# VIII

## THE FIRST LADY: MY WIFE

If I had hatred in my heart toward my fellow man,
If I were pressed to do him ill, to conjure up a plan
To wound him sorely and to rob his day of all their joy
I'd wish his wife would go away and take their little boy
I'd waste no time on curses vague, nor try to take his gold, Nor seek to shatter any plan that he might dearly hold. A crueler revenge than that for him I would bespeak;
I'd wish his wife and little one might leave him for a week
I'd wish him all the loneliness that comes with loss of those Who fill his life with laughter and contentment and repose. I'd wish him empty rooms at night and mocking stairs to squeak That neither wife nor little boy will greet him for a week.
If I despised my fellow man, I'd make my hatred known By wishing him a week or two of living all alone;
I'd let him know the torture that is mine to bear today
For Buddy and his mother now are miles and miles away.

Betty June Heilman

Until five years ago, when my wife of sixty-five years passed away, I might have read these verses passively. Living without her for almost five years—after living with her for sixty-five— makes these verses real. Fortunately, I still have my little boy even if he is now a man.

In giving appropriate credit to Betty and a special tribute following her death, I share something of her qualities as the First Lady of both Meredith College and the University of Richmond, a total of twenty-two years in that role. At the same time, she was raising our five children and engaging in the growing up of our eleven grandchildren. I can't be too effusive in conveying my recognition of her talents as they are expressed by many others—the exception to the rule in so many ways.

Betty has been given accolades over the years by almost everybody who has ever known her. That has been a result of her personality, her sweet spirit, and her goodwill toward everyone she has met. I share some of what others have written about her campus involvement, including the hosting of events for parents, alumni, visiting scholars, retiring colleagues, community leaders, and unending entertainment in the president's home and on campus. Her managing and hosting social functions and goodwill hospitality has been unending: decorating and maintaining the university residence, traveling around the country and the world, and an unending schedule of activities of unlimited functions.

How many breakfasts, luncheons, dinners, weekend parties, parents' weekends, student backyard parties, receptions, open houses—multiplied by the numbers of people involved—were her engagements in a year? Too often, she was the unsung hero. She performed real work and deserved recognition for playing a role she never avoided. Being married to the president, her responsibilities were inescapable. It affected how she dressed, the behavior of her children, and her schedule. She could not escape being a role model. Living in the president's home determined, to a large extent, her life pattern, both public and private.

While the president's house is a home, it is almost never a private place. The working day begins at seven or sooner for me. Often, for her, it began at six clock, getting ready for seven o'clock breakfast, and ended somewhere between eleven and midnight for the president, the spouse, and the family. The presidency tends to eat up all the time there is every day, every week, every month, and every year.

The First Lady's image from a public standpoint is fairly well portrayed in an article and story by Allison Griffin in *Richmond Magazine* as she shared her observance of Betty's life and role at the university.

One day in 1947, Betty June Dobbins, a student at what was then Campbellsville Junior College, in Campbellsville, Kentucky, had a conversation with Dr. John Carter, the president of this small Baptist school where everybody knew everybody.

"Betty June," Dr. Carter said, "I have already selected your future husband. He is a very fine young man who is taking my course on 'The Life and Work of a Preacher.' You two are perfect for each other."

The young man in question was named Bruce Heilman, a farmer's son who had recently enrolled at Campbellsville after returning from four years with the US marines in the Pacific.

Dr. Carter introduced the two young people. Six weeks of dating convinced them that the president's idea was an excellent one. Three months later, Dr. Carter officiated at their wedding.

Now, thirty years later, living in the president's home of the University of Richmond, blessed with five children and a fresh delight of a year-old grandson, Dr. and Mrs. E. Bruce Heilman heartily reaffirm the soundness of Dr. Carter's prediction.

"We have always shared the same moral values," Betty Heilman explains in her quiet way. "And I think we've grown more alike over the years."

Though she appears serenely at ease in her role as mistress of the spacious and handsome president's home, and as hostess at the enormous variety of social functions involved in her role as UR's First Lady, Mrs. Heilman does not come from a background of privilege. With typical lack of pretention, she will tell you that she grew up as the oldest of six daughters of a railroad (mechanic) brakeman in Louisville. While she was a college freshman, her mother died, and her father, unable to keep the family together, had to send her sisters to be raised in a children's home. Later, the Heilmans invited one of her sisters to share their home.

Those who know her well affirm that Mrs. Heilman's outstanding characteristics are her personal warmth, her enduring strength of character, her imperturbability in the face of the various crises, large and small, that inevitably crop up in a university community. One admirer recounts with respect amounting almost to awe, the tremendously effective moral support she gives the president when accompanying him on many of his in-state travels. Not only does she handle the driving, leaving the president free to work on a speech or a report or on correspondence, but she calmly and unfailing manages to get him to his scheduled destination on time, regardless of rain, snow, or any other travel hazards.

One of the things that the First Lady has been beneficial to a large extent as the hostess has been in respect to the travel abroad program, which, for some forty years, the president has hosted for two or three weeks every summer somewhere around the world with students, faculty, alumni, parents, and the extension of all of these traveling to approximately 145 countries.

The people who have traveled with Betty and Bruce Heilman have been whoever wished to be a part of those journeys all over the world with the University of Richmond president and First Lady becoming even further friends and advocates of the university. Many of them being or becoming substantial contributors not only because they were graduates and friends, but because they became better acquainted with the Heilmans.

When my family moved to Richmond to assume the role of my being president of the university in 1971, the university president's home became the chancellor's home occupied by the former president and new chancellor. That home up on a hill had only three bedrooms and its age made it a little less than easy for entertaining. I moved

Entertaining as husband and wife

Spider daughter and Husband, Mike          Betty with young children in China

Betty and E. Bruce Heilman, above, were married in August of 1948 in Louisville, Ky. The Heilmans both were attending Campbellsville Junior College in Kentucky when he proposed at the airport one night. He is the current president of the University of Richmond and they have five children.

President and Mrs. E. Bruce Heilman

Visiting a Development Officer
at the College of the Ozarks

Our children, all of whom later became Spiders

At our Alma mater

Grandson Christopher now a Spider

With Grandson Patrick and Son Tim, both Spiders

The First Lady Betty relaxing at home

Our Wedding

First Grandchildren, now all Spiders

Grown Granddaughters – both Spiders

into two adjoining townhouses making it a fourbedroom house because it had two bedrooms in each section. My family moved into that facility near Freeman High School where my children attended. For a couple of years, while the new home was being built on campus, it was relatively inconvenient for entertaining. We converted a room at the university, which would become the president's dining room, and started entertaining.

It was not until a couple of years later that we moved into a new president's home on level ground where people of whatever age could come and go and get in and out. The best of what a residence could offer with food, entertainment, and goodwill became a center for raising money and cultivating friends.

Two years after I assumed the presidency, we moved from our apartment complex onto the campus and the 8,950-square-foot house that became the social center for the university. With concrete walls and floors, it was built to be fireproof, almost like a dormitory. Betty made it soundproof and added an intercom system, and it became a pleasant residence and home for the family and friends.

Betty was given free reign for decorating and providing for what would represent the university. She always had the place looking like the season that was in vogue at the time. We had receptions for faculty, staff, students, community, friends, and alumni; whatever was central to good public relations was what we did. Three thousand people attended one reception. The house was a university place to entertain and a warm place for the growing children and personal friends.

We entertained Bob Hope, Earl Hamner, Paul Duke, Elizabeth Taylor, and President Gerald Ford, ordinary and necessary people from Washington and elsewhere, including generals and admirals who were parents of students and movie stars and politicians, most with the relationships as parents and students.

Betty had a great relationship with food service, the maintenance people, and everyone else. They loved her, and she loved them. Between the personal aspect of the president's home and the working responsibility within which it fit, she was the master of getting along and enjoying the process. When asked by Vanderbilt University to honor someone who helped me get through college, I gave the following response:

> Perhaps this will be a first, but my honoree selection is my wife, Betty, whom I married when I was a freshman in college and who helped me through all of my degrees from age twenty-one to thirty-five, including a PhD at which time she had already born six children. With all that to look after, she not only continued her college work but worked to put me through college and took classes such as French in order to help me pass my exams.

Sentiments of her passing are represented by this note from General Gray, commandant of the Marine Corps.

> Jan and I were deeply saddened to hear about Betty June's passing. We want you to know that our thoughts and our prayers are with you and the family during these difficult times. After hearing about your heartbreaking loss, I went back and read your book again. You and Betty had a wonderful life together, and she was the perfect person for you and all that you believed in. Love and Semper Fi, Al and Jan.

How could a marine buck sergeant not be proud to have preserved this letter from one of the finest commandants in the history of the Marine Corps. It is truly complimentary just by its having been written by hand by the general.

Excerpts from sketches from Ben Burroughs—entitled "My Wonderful One" fit well my feelings.

> What Joy and Happiness you have brought,
> My love, my life, my own
> What sweetness in your wondrous lips
> Just meant for me alone,
> What great and endearing tender charms
> You give to me to share
> The glory of your being and the beauty of your hair.
> What heaven you have brought to me about what you say and do.
> A heaven that is beyond compare and known by oh so few. You fill my life with ecstasy and overflowing stream. What can I say, what can I do for all that you have done, You truly are the world to me, my most wonderful one.

A resolution by the Meredith board of trustees prominently highlighted Betty as a significant participant in the successful leadership component of our five years as president and First Lady.

Further, she was made an honorary alumna of Meredith College.

The Betty Dobbins Heilman House, Campbellsville University

Granddaughters Hillary, Natalie, Whitney and Carly, all Spiders

Betty pretending to be riding

At the Berlin Wall

Young Betty

Surprise Gift

Grandson Patrick, now a Spider

All in the Family

# CHAPTER TWO

## MEREDITH COLLEGE—ANOTHER MIRACLE

# I

# INTRODUCTION

When I came to Meredith, I had to bring with me some expectations, some beliefs, and some confidence that I had to spread around because we were setting out on some challenges not before claimed at the same level. When I joined Meredith, no one warned me that Meredith trustees would not contribute substantially to their college because they never had. Had I known it, I would have been afraid to ask and would not have received the pace-setting commitments of this group.

Neither my colleagues nor I knew that it would be foolish to try to build five new buildings and remodel the whole campus in a short five years. So, we set out to do it before we found out it couldn't be done. We didn't know that increasing our charges dramatically in two years would price us out of the market and force our students to transfer, cutting our enrollment. We did it anyway and had immediate increases with more applicants than ever before. We filled the floor of the infirmary after our dormitory capacity was filled. Sometimes it is good not to know what we can't get done until we have done it.

During my early days as president at Meredith, I cited Edgar Guest's poem "It Couldn't Be Done" over and over—and then we did it.

Before we knew what we couldn't do, we had announced and put into place, our longrange plan, the construction of a new library, new student center, physical education facility with swimming pool, two new dormitories, air-conditioning of all facilities, campus lighting, dormitory remodeling, administrative building remodeling, music building soundproofing and remodeling, dining hall remodeling, telephones campus wide, a new organ, and on and on it goes. We didn't know we would succeed, but we assumed we might. Of course, we did.

All the time, our attitude was one without reservation because the cause was so valid. With a positive attitude, everything begins to happen. Enthusiasm begins to rise, confidence builds, excitement is generated, and everything changes—and that is exactly what happened.

We eliminated the fear of failing simply by not recognizing that as a possibility. We set forth our mission, and we determined to fulfill it—and we did.

***

The First Lady of Meredith College

# II

## ACCEPTING THE PRESIDENCY OF MEREDITH COLLEGE

Ladies and Gentlemen of the board of Meredith College, I would like to respond and react to the high honor that is mine on this occasion. It is certainly not trite to suggest that words fail to express my deep regard for this responsibility and the sincere humility with which it is accepted. Until now, I never thought much about the well-worn phrase "Life begins at forty," but at age thirty-nine, the challenge of the future appears so promising that truly the past is prologue and the years ahead represent the period for which I have been preparing. Viewed from this perspective, life holds many treasures for my family and me as we yoke ourselves with those already dedicated to this noble venture.

I recognize that the shoes to be filled are large and that succeeding a man like President Campbell will not be easy. He is a man of stature in the educational world, he has earned the respect of his colleagues, and he has maintained high expectations for the college. Everything I see and hear speaks well for the administration of Dr. Campbell. Even as I pledge myself to a high level of direction, I salute Dr. Campbell, his administrative team, his faculty and staff, and the trustees for a job well done. However, Meredith has always endeavored to surpass its prior accomplishments, and its future should be no different.

I am attracted to Meredith for many reasons, not the least of which is its character as a church-related liberal arts college for women. Of paramount importance to me is its commitment to perpetuate and preserve these excellent traditions that make it unique. While everyone agrees that the basic objectives will not change, the trustees, administration, and faculty speak freely of and listen intently to possible new approaches. Such open-mindedness typifies an attitude that allows for maximum adaptability to the best that education has to offer.

Already my wife and five children are as anxious to move to Raleigh as I am to get on the job. We look forward to many wonderful years with you. We expect to find maximum satisfaction and fulfillment at Meredith and will endeavor to justify your trust in us. We cannot perform miracles, but we can add our best to your best and together continue the optimistic forward march anticipated by Editor Bailey of the North Carolina Baptist paper in 1900 when he said of Meredith, "We have built this institution to last as long as Baptists have anything to do. We began it with the intention of never ceasing to give to it … We can never be done giving to a really great cause." As long as this spirit will prevail, and with God's help, we cannot fail.

\*\*\*

The Director of Public Relations

Dear Mr. President: I commend to your attentional Jack Wilberger's article in the current issue of the *Collegian*. It is an interview he conducted with the presidents of student governments of Richmond College, Westhampton College, and the business school. I was impressed with the enthusiasm of the three presidents and particularly with their cordial attitude toward the present administration. I have not known so much harmony on this campus in the past ten years.

Surely any such interview conducted at any time in the past ten years would have been devoted to a great extent to griping and, as we marines sometimes say, "bitching."

The students feel that this administration is interested in their problems. They are beginning to see the great future that extends beyond our present horizons.

Sincerely,

Joseph E. Nettles

Dear Mrs. Heilman:

As the year ends, I am increasingly grateful for all the five years that the Heilman family have been at Meredith.  What Dr. Heilman has done for the College is beyond value.  I have often tried to tell him of my appreciation but my words have been in adequate.

I am more grateful for his goodness to me personally.  His more than generous estimate of my part of the works of the college, of his encouragement in my revising of its history.

And my personal gratitude to you is equally great, your friendliness is heartwarming as his is. I am especially grateful for your kindness to my sister.  So long as she was herself at all, it meant a great deal for her – your visits, your gifts, when you have so many calls on your time and strength. I know you had a little opportunity to know her.  All these made her days and mine happier.

My best wishes go with this – I will always be yours, with my love, Mary Lynch Johnson.

Please tell Dr. Heilman I did not want to interrupt him after the luncheon to tell him how much I enjoyed it – I appreciated the honor of being asked.

Mary Lynch Johnson

President Campbell's term of service was the longest of the five; his successor's was the shortest. It is hard to realize that E. Bruce Heilman was at Meredith only five years, because so much was accomplished in that time. In a few weeks after his arrival, plans for the Advancement Program were well under way, and in the five years it made giant strides toward completion. During his presidency four buildings were erected and two more were under construction.

New buildings, greatly increased student aid, increased salaries, all necessitated increased financial resources, possible only with increased interest in the College. President Heilman was expert in this capacity. His experience in various aspects of college administration—as business manager, treasurer, controller, dean, vice president—familiarized him with the needs of colleges and possible sources of income.

His boundless energy would make a whirlwind seem a gentle summer breeze. Representing Meredith at sessions of the Baptist State Convention and of Baptist Associations, speaking all over the state and beyond to churches, service clubs and alumnae chapters, conferring with business firms, corporations, and foundations, he managed an almost incredible schedule. He was of necessity off campus a great deal; yet he quickly came to know faculty and students well, and immediately put at ease anyone who came to his office. His larger plans for the College never made him impatient with the immediate small problems near at hand, for he never lost the common touch. And he had the firm conviction that "the Christian faith is the integrative principle of the Meredith program."

On every trip he made, whether to Cary or Cairo, whatever the purpose, he always had a list of the alumnae in the vicinity and sought them out. When he talked with alumnae in these visits or at chapter meetings, his generous appreciation of Meredith's past endeared him to them as did his enthusiastic confidence in her future.

That enthusiastic confidence won friends to whom Meredith had formerly been only a name, or not even a name. Grants from foundations and corporations increased markedly during his administration, and individual donors have been most generous.

*The New Depression in Higher Education* embodied the results of a study made by the Carnegie and the Ford Foundations of universities and colleges during the years 1959-1971. Forty-one institutions were chosen as representative of different types of schools over the United States. Of the 41 studied, 29 were in financial trouble or headed for it. Meredith was one of the 12 fortunate ones. Charles G. McCurdy, executive secretary of the American Association of

# E. Bruce Heilman
# 1966-1971

Universities, visited Meredith as a representative of the Carnegie Foundation for this study. Reporting to the Foundation the result of his visit, he added:

Meredith College is one of the few institutions of higher learning I know about which disseminated good cheer and confidence for the future. . . . As one who has entertained the thought that small colleges like Meredith are in trouble and may face extinction, I am now obliged to change my thinking and just hope that other small colleges can emulate Meredith and all it stands for.

A note from the current president of Meredith College, Dr. Allen and the first graduate of Meredith to become president conveys:

> Dear, dear, dear Dr. Heilman: I tell you that I am inspired by each Meredith president in many ways, but you have set the bar highest on getting out the message about Meredith's strengths, opportunities, and future … I have so often reread Dr. Mary Lynch Johnson's history of your tenure and especially her recognition of your drive and prowess as a fund-raiser. I read and reread the history of your work on the road and in and out of homes and communities to raise money, and I gained interest, insight, and confidence. I credit you 100 percent with the fund-raising success Meredith and I have enjoyed in this campaign. Know that you have made an everlasting impact on Meredith and on me.

On the inside page of my autographed copy of *A History of Meredith College,* Mary Lynch Johnson wrote, "To E. Bruce Heilman, whose extraordinary ability, whose wholehearted devotion and boundless enthusiasm were of immeasurable value to Meredith." In the foreword, she wrote, "The swiftly moving, significant events of president Heilman's administration required a long and important new chapter as this section was virtually completed before he accepted the presidency of the University of Richmond in March of 1971, and no mention had been made of the great loss to Meredith."

"The Doors are Open Wider: 1966–1971" is a chapter on the history of Meredith:

> President Heilman came to the office with wide experience, unbounded vigor, and genuine enthusiasm for Meredith. He needs all these qualities because the presidency of a college never sinecure has become an almost impossible demanding position. … His accomplishments would do credit to a much older man. … His background and experience fitted him especially well for the presidency of Meredith.
>
> He characterized the presidency of a women's college as "the most delightful experience I've ever had." and said that "Meredith has more potential than I ever dreamed." … To developing this potential, President Heilman devoted himself without reservation. … He has an almost incredible schedule, yet the faculty members, the students, or the parent who comes to him with a problem always feel welcome and assured of his sympathetic interest. It is no wonder that the board of trustees in a resolution of appreciation adopted in September of 1968 said that "President Heilman has succeeded in doing in two years what the board of trustees had aspired to accomplish in five years or more."

His ability and experience keep him in demand in wider educational circles. Among other responsibilities, he served in 1968 as director of longrange planning studies for predominately Negro colleges for the advancement for educational development. And in the same year, he was the director of the annual workshop for the council of development of small colleges. In 1969, he took part in seminars in four countries, Britain, Austria, Russia, and Germany sponsored by the International Society of Comparative Education. In 1970, he was elected president of the Southern Association of Colleges for Women.

Before the library was complete, a new dormitory was underway. A second dormitory was completed in 1971 almost identical in plan. Completed in September 1970, the Weatherspoon building amply meeting the need and half of its cost, was given by the family of the late James Raymond Witherspoon and by his brother, Walter Herbert Weatherspoon. Two more buildings are under construction, the college center and the president's home. As the new buildings were going up, many improvements were being made in the existing buildings and on the grounds. Alumni coming back for commencement in 1970 remembering how hot and noisy the dining room had been during the alumni luncheon could hardly believe they were at Meredith as they entered the air-conditioned room. The grounds had been improved in many ways, yet the need for adequate lighting on the campus was remedied by a gift of $75,000 from the General Electric Company in 1968, providing bright lights over the entire campus.

A new board called the board of associates was created, which the history characterizes "an extension of the board of trustees in that its members will be committed to the ideals of Meredith, to its program, and to its support."

Of course, in all that was being done by me as the leader and my staff and colleagues, two powerful men—Sharon Harris and Cliff Cameron, one chairman of the board of the Carolina Power and Light and the other chairman of the board of the First Union National Bank Corporation—made a dramatic difference. Both assumed similar positions during my tenure to lead the college strongly and influence others.

Meredith's position in appealing to foundations and corporations was undoubtedly strengthened by the results of two recent studies. The New Depression in Higher Education, made by Earl Cheit, was sponsored by the Carnegie Foundation and the Ford Foundation. The Golden Years, made by Hans H. Jenny and G. Richard Winn, was published by Wooster College in Ohio. The New Depression in Higher Education was a study of forty-one colleges and universities for the years 1959–60 to 1970–71. The institutions were chosen as representative of 2,729 colleges and universities in the United States, and Meredith was one of the forty-one selected. It was only one of eight in the South and one of two in the state. The other was the University of North Carolina at Chapel Hill, and the one other women's college was Mills College. The study showed that twenty-nine of the forty-one were in financial trouble or headed for it. Of the twelve liberal arts colleges, only four were not in trouble financially or headed for it—and Meredith was one of the four.

The Golden Years, an analysis of the income and expenditures of forty-nine liberal arts colleges in the United States over a period of eight years, showed that about half of the forty-eight colleges studied were operating with a deficit. Meredith was the least expensive of all forty-nine for every year from 1962–1970 with one of the smallest endowments of the forty-eight, but in recent years, it had one of the highest levels of gift income. The expenditure per student for administration was one of the lowest, and for plant and operations and maintenance, it was the lowest of all these colleges.

> But, President Heilman warned against over confidence about Meredith's finances. If the college is to continue financially healthy, the enthusiastic support it has received must continue with our gratitude for its prosperity must go with a determination never to yield our uniqueness of a small liberal arts Christian college for women seeking to be different rather than following the footsteps of the trends financial or otherwise.

Of alumni and alumnae and their understanding of finance of higher education, one lady asked how soon we would get one hundred thousand new volumes for the library, thinking it ought to be soon. In the next breath, she expressed concern for the increasing tuition charges. The fact is, we can't have it both ways. We can't buy one hundred thousand books without money, and we can't have money without charging or investing in time, effort, and energy to raise it. So, one of my first moves was to create a development office and bring in development individuals to kick off a major campaign of $5 million.

My own study of Meredith was most comprehensive and intensive as indicated by its 370-page length. Part of the final report quoted a sentence pertinent to the situation: "Planning without action is futile, and action without planning is fatal."

While president at Meredith, I led the establishment of the cooperating Raleigh colleges where all of the colleges and universities in the area came together as a consortium formed by Meredith College, North Carolina State University, Peace College, St. Augustine College, Saint

Mary's College, and Shaw University. A cooperative venture between these state universities of North Carolina and Meredith, and the neighboring institutions, it was funded by businesses in the area so students from any one college could take courses for credit at any of the other institutions. Among many other things instituted were sabbatical leaves for the faculty and dramatic increases in faculty salaries.

Charles G. McGurdy, executive secretary of the Association of American Universities, visited Meredith in connection with the Carnegie Study of Higher Education:

> Meredith College is one of the few institutions of higher learning I know about that disseminates good cheer and confidence for the future. I have been mulling over this situation ever since my visit trying to assign reasons for it, and I believe there are many, not the least of them being the institution exudes optimism and is able to infuse it into others. One who has entertained the thought that small colleges like Meredith are in trouble and may face extinction, I am now obliged to change my thinking and just hope that other small colleges can emulate Meredith and all it stands for.

It is said that the most difficult part of any project is in getting started. It is a fact that getting started was never my problem. Because I have always stayed busy, the process of starting never entered my mind. Being action oriented solves many problems. Always staying on the move kept me ahead of my competition. I reflect with pride on our accomplishments in the five years I served as president of Meredith, one of the finest colleges in the country.

# V

## MY MOST IMPORTANT ACTIONS

Boards of trustees are no doubt much as Richard Armour describes them: "one of thirty-six members and self-perpetuating." Self-perpetuating means that most remain in office for life and some even longer.

The president, Armour reminds us, is appointed by the trustees and serves, according to the charter of the college, "at their pleasure." He tries his best to please them, and when he can't, he tries to fool them. As an administrator, he must set directions and be willing to live with directions that are set. Otherwise, he will be tossing to and from by the winds of day-to-day activity and get almost nothing done.

I remember quite well the earlier conversations I had with the trustees, faculty members, and interested patrons of Meredith before and immediately after assuming the presidency. People often said, "The college's big weakness is in its development program. Unless it has more money and a continuing attitude of financing itself, it will surely not continue to succeed." I am confident that the observations were true for the most part.

I heard on every hand that the college must find someone with courage enough to raise tuition boldly so that salaries could be increased substantially. It was suggested that there needed to be delegation of internal duties to other administrators and that there should be major authority given and organization and administration clearly defined to make this possible.

It was further suggested that the president should make himself greatly involved in translating the aims and objectives of the college in attracting interest on the part of patrons, advancing the possibilities of new physical facilities and tools, creating funds for sabbaticals, and reducing faculty loads. I believe all this, and observing the strengths from the past, spent the first year doing my utmost to quickly stimulate and initiate attention of many publics toward financial support.

I have applied similar efforts, energies, and actions at Meredith and at the University of Richmond, which have been paramount in bringing about broader successes than would have otherwise been possible. One of those has been, in both cases and to one extent or another, changing, augmenting, or adapting the effectiveness of the boards of each of the institutions in such a manner that the result was engagement, contributions, and influence.

All in all, this made the full board much more effective and caused individual members to either judge that they were unable to perform within expectations or resign out of their own choice, understanding the responsibility that would come about under my presidency. Some moved into another defined relationship called the board of associates, where their talents, commitment, and interest could still be applied. Thus, they were able to help make happen the dramatic changes that did happen.

Trustees giving of their resources and applying their influence with people who had money was the difference between what had been and what had to be. Testing out my theme because of my experience in the past, I shared with the board an exciting vision that would dramatically change Meredith in a short time. The change would be in increasing enrollments, improving and adding facilities, increasing salaries and benefits for faculties and staff, and upgrading all that had simply lagged far behind.

In laying out my ambition for the institution, after the board had generalized to me their expectations, I pressed hard the principle of having members with more financial capacity on the board. We had to develop a larger commitment to funding the college; everybody had to give at a higher level and influence others outside of the board to do the same. Most board members expressed to me their understanding that money had to be a major component in their commitment and active service.

I set out to do what I cited to the board I would do. I would find some of the most influential people of leadership, well known in the state of North Carolina, which would make such a big difference that others would want to serve with them. Thus, we would build one of the strongest boards of any institution in the state. I had the support of the board in doing this to the extent that some volunteered to serve in other capacities to make possible space for people with money and influence.

I started the process of making things happen by inviting the chairman of Carolina Power Light, Sharon Harris, to come on the board and discovered that his mother had attended

Meredith. His influence was great. His ties to such corporations as General Electric and General Motors where he served on both boards—as well as his top position at Carolina Power and Light—made a difference just by announcing his addition to the board.

Sharon Harris joined me in bringing a top banker in the person of Cliff Cameron, and after getting his commitment, the two of them were able to bring in a top builder in the state and others who were well known and greatly influential. Immediately they made their contributions and their pledges, and they committed time to help raise money and set the standard for the board members with their personal contributions. Others followed their examples of doing what they had not done in the past because it had not been expected of them.

With this kind of influence, we went national as well as local with the time and energy of board members even to the extent of using their aircraft to take me all over the state and beyond to invite support for Meredith. When new board members went with me, it was clear that we were going to succeed. We drew up our campus plan, developed our long-range vision, and defined specifically where we were going and how we were going to get there. We started marketing through people who became excited and began to influence people who had not thought of Meredith in the past or for a long time. They began to recognize that Meredith was going to be one of the exciting adventures in the future of higher education.

In a speech at Meredith College, Sharon served as trustee, he noted:

> What has gone on before constitutes a noble heritage worthy of our sincere tribute but we, here today, also must account to the founders for what goes on today. Somehow I foresee that Founders' Day in the centennial year of 1999 will celebrate the period through which we are now passing as the era in which the college made significant advancement toward its intended greatness.
>
> Dr. Heilman's dynamic leadership enriches the heritage and fortifies that prediction. The present administration has established an objective worthy of its heritage, and in my judgment, is pursuing sound plans to accomplish its aim.

With leadership like this, the institution moved forward with strength.

Mr. Cliff Cameron, the chairman of the board of trustees, made a speech at the next significant gathering:

> When we contribute to causes great such as Meredith, we are enhancing our freedom, our community, and ourselves. When we ask others to give, we are helping them with patriotism being scorned, personal ethics liberalized, and religion downgraded by so many today. It is apparent that money contributed to our gift-supported institution as the power for greater good than ever before.

These two great men made possible what I did, made the board strong, and brought to light the board's understanding of what would be required. All the board members understood what had to be done if the institution was going to thrive and burn with progress.

# CHAPTER THREE

## MARINE MOTORCYCLE MAN AND MISSION

Life is to be lived. If you have to support yourself, you had bloody well better find some way that is going to be interesting. And you don't do that by sitting around wondering about yourself.
—*Katherine Hepburn*

# I

## LIVING LIFE TO THE FULLEST

The Things That Haven't Been Done Before
*Edgar Guest*

The things that haven't been done before,
Those are the things to try;
Columbus dreamed of an unknown shore
At the rim of the far-flung sky,
And his heart was bold and his faith was strong
As he ventured in dangers new,
And he paid no heed to the jeering throng
Or the fears of the doubting crew
The many will follow the beaten track
With guideposts on the way,
They live and have lived for ages back With a chart for every day.
Someone has told them it's safe to go
On the road he has traveled o'er, And all that they ever strive to know Are the things that were known before.
A few strike out, without map or chart,
Where never a man has been,
From the beaten paths they draw apart To see what no man has seen.
There are deeds they hunger alone to do;

Though battered and bruised and sore, They blaze a path for the many, who Do nothing not done before.

The things that haven't been done before

Are the tasks worthwhile today; Are you one of the flock that follows, or Are you one that shall lead the way?

Are you one of the timid souls that quail At the jeers of a doubting crew,

Or dare you, whether you win or fail, Strike out for a goal that's new?

# BRUCE ON THE LOOSE

Chancellor E. Bruce Heilman is always on the go—promoting the University, riding his Harley, traveling abroad and living life to the fullest. By Randy Fitzgerald, R'63 and G'64

Bruce Heilman doesn't want to ride into the sunset. He wants to blow right by it—preferably on his brand new Harley-Davidson Ultra Classic Electra Glide Patriot Edition.

The bike is a gleaming beauty: chrome and black with red and blue stripes, a Marine Corps emblem permanently affixed to the gas tank and an American flag painted on the rear fender.

Heilman and his wife, Betty, recently drove to Huntington, W.Va., to pick up the motorcycle just before his 81st birthday. He rode the bike 400 miles back to Richmond with Betty following in the car.

"I know he's a good driver," she says, "but I kept my eye on him." She acknowledges with a laugh that he was leading the way, as he always has in their 59-year partnership.

The following pages represent my experience in the United States Marine Corps and my motorcycle travels and related activities.

Webster's Encyclopedic Dictionary of the English Language defines the word *adventurer* as "one who attempts or takes part in bold, novel, or extraordinary enterprises. Related definitions of adventuresome are: daring, courageous, enterprising, bold, full of hazards, attended with risks, and dangerous."

When I identify my life as *adventuresome*, I immediately establish the challenge to relate my life to extraordinary examples of unusual occurrences. I share some adventures and remembered happenings from my early life until today.

As a little boy, riding with my father on a heavy wooden structure and being pulled by a horse to break the clods before planting, I fell between the boards and under the drag. It could have been a serious mishap. Riding with my father on that contraption when only a little boy was dangerous—thus an adventure.

My next adventure happened when, as a teenager, I was riding a blind horse we called Teddy. He was very sure-footed, but for a teenage boy who would try anything once and trying to see just how sure-footed he was, I rode him near the banks of a dry creek bed. There was no firm ground, and he tumbled down into the creek bed with me on top. Landing on those hard rocks could have been serious, but as young boys often do, I escaped serious injury.

At ten years old, I was working with my father at killing hogs. While we were searching for a knife dropped on the floor of an old 1928 Chevrolet with holes in the floorboard, the car left the road at a curve, ran over a culvert, turned over, and left us both with minor injuries.

At about thirteen years of age, I began sleeping in the barn with a twelve-gauge shotgun to protect the tobacco crop that was much of the family income. I lay between bales of hay with the gun pointed toward the barn door. The idea was not so much that I expected to shoot someone but that the word always drifted out to those who might be inclined to steal that there was a shotgun inside. Another adventure for a very young boy.

I remember substantial physical damage, especially to my back, when wrecking my 1926 Model T Ford touring car, which I had purchased when I was sixteen years old for twelve dollars off a used car lot in the county seat. With only a cloth top for protection when it rolled over, everything was crushed, including me. Even today, in damp weather, the aching bit of pain brings back the risks of the teenage years. All the way through the Marine Corps, my back ached from the mishap. That accident could have killed me and two other teens, but we survived another adventure with only the Model T Ford the victim in a state of total destruction.

Things began to get more serious as I grew into my teenage years. I risked greater loss by doing little or nothing educationally speaking. I flunked out of high school by sleeping through classes. Only as I grew more mature did I realize that this was a more serious mistake than those physical encounters. My good fortune was my rectification by way of my greatest adventure, World War II, and four years in the Marine Corps.

I joined the Marine Corps, rather than the army or the navy because the marines seemed to be where the greatest danger, risk, challenge, noteworthy adventure, and an attempt at something unusual could result. It appeared to be enterprising, daring, and full of hazards, but I learned from that experience.

What did I select to be my big challenge in the Marine Corps? To be a tail gunner in dive bombers, something exciting, something novel, extraordinary, even daring, perhaps courageous, and full of hazards, but it was the life of adventure for me—bold and full of risks.

Of course, having established myself as a marine, everything from there forward presented hazards, risks, challenges, and occurrences that were stimulating whether being attacked by a Japanese submarine on a troop ship, being attacked by suicide planes, or landing on the beach, under fire. It was all super engaging, adventuresome, stimulating, and never dull, and it continued when I was flying. I crashed in an airplane, which few people have ever experienced and lived.

That was an adventure. For the rest of my life, I thought, *Well, I couldn't be at more risk than that.* I incorporated into my life motorcycling and other challenges not sought by the average person.

After the bombs were dropped, we marines changed from warriors to occupiers. Even in the transition, adventures followed me.

I moved up to Opama from Okinawa on a troopship that encountered a typhoon en route.

Most of us wished when it went down it wouldn't come up again, we were so ill. But arriving in Tokyo Bay and moving into Japan was a sobering experience. After having known the Japanese to be such vicious warriors, to find them bowing on the street corners and becoming totally submissive was a great surprise.

During the early days, we did everything to make ourselves comfortable, including running steam through the cold-water pipes to provide hotter water that either scalded us or froze us in the barracks. After arriving at the Japanese naval base on Tokyo Bay, I was assigned to the aircraft of the commander of the Fifth Fleet as radio operator. This was a R4D, which we flew all over Japan and all over the Pacific. One of the first things we did was take an intelligence group to Hiroshima, which gave our crew the opportunity to see the devastation of the bomb. We all noticed that it was hardly more devastated than Yokosuka, Yokohama, or Tokyo. They were all bombed or burned to the ground, and it was hard to tell a substantial difference. They were all destroyed.

The tank in the belly of the old R4D allowed us to fly as many as ten hours at a time. We could go from our base in Japan to Guam, Iwo Jima, Okinawa, and all over Japan proper. On one occasion, we took the plane to Guam for servicing and flew back to Japan on an Army R4D. We were "hitchhiking." We landed on the island of Iwo Jima for refueling. We took off with a heavy load and a lot of baggage in the tail section of the plane. After we were about fifty feet off the ground, a crosswind hit us. The tail section was lagging, and the plane rolled over and spun in. As we were crushing to the ground, all the high-ranking intelligence officers aboard were just as scared as me. Fortunately, the plane did not catch fire. As far as I know, we all survived. Nonetheless, we all spent a few seconds with our lives passing before us. We all thought it was ending. I was not a survivor in the Battle of Iwo Jima—where a lot of my friends were wounded or killed—but I did almost lose it there after the fact.

On occupation duty, I became convinced that I wanted to make the Marine Corps my career. Along with the crew chief and the base photographer who flew with us frequently, I reenlisted in April 1946. I flew back to the States for a sixty-day leave before engaging in another two years in the Marine Corps. After serving eighteen months and seeing a message on the bulletin board that one could be discharged at the convenience of the government to go to college, I applied and was let out in time to enter college in the middle of the year.

That moved me from the military to a career in higher education, but I have never been far from the Marine Corps. I've served as chairman of the board at the Marine Military Academy, chairman of the board at the Marine Corps University, and secretary of the board of the Marine Historical Foundation, the Marine Corps Association, and a variety of other Marine Corps activities.

Then came the adventure and challenge of acquiring a college education on the G.I. Bill and discovering my partner of sixty-five years. This proved to be a great risk but a worthy one. Pursuing a career leading to leadership positions in the field of higher education was a large challenge, ultimately leading to a PhD, making possible attaining the highest position in higher education: the presidency of a college and a university. This too proved to be a grand adventure.

Perhaps my most pervasive adventures, unlike any other, resulted from riding a motorcycle. I have a whole script on that hazard and its challenges and risks. I find joy in communicating with nature. Such a disposition is well expressed in an article from *USA Today* entitled "Five Reasons to Love a Motorcycle" by Gary McKechnie. He states "I have been riding motorcycles since I was a teenager because I knew I preferred motorcycles over automobiles.

But it would be another twenty years before it struck me why I felt this way."

The rider, when traveling some distance on his motorcycle with his wife following in her automobile, stopped to share with her what he had observed. He discovered that she had not seen much of what he had seen. In fact, she had missed it all. The car's roof blocked her view of the high cliffs, the radio drowned out the sound of the river, and with the windows up and the airconditioning on, she never scented the perfume of the pines.

The rider of the motorcycle said, "Becoming part of nature is one reason why I like motorcycle vacations." He cites five reasons why he loves his travels on his motorcycle. One is because of the adventure, which he explains in detail as I could from my experiences. He cites the well-worn cliché that traveling is the journey not the destination, and with motorcycles, that is even more true than otherwise. "Depending on where you are traveling, the farther you are from home, the more intrigued others are by your journey."

It's a different world when you are on a motorcycle. "There is," he says, "that spiritual pleasure in riding a motorcycle. You can smell the countryside and experience things that you don't get inside a car." He adds, "While a motorcycle may be just a vehicle, it is also the instrument we use to experience life, to explore, to discover new people and places, and to affirm friendships."

The following sections give attention to all the stimulation, satisfaction, excitement, and freedom that only a journey on two wheels can provide. It is not only the ride; it is the meeting of people as diverse as fish in the sea or the colors in the rainbow. We all become satisfied and fulfilled compatriots on a mission sometimes defined and sometimes without a planned purpose except to face the wind, breathe the air, and wonder about riding off into the sunset.

A motorcyclist who rode with me many miles between California and Richmond, Virginia, wrote:

> It has been a life-altering event for me. The example that you set is exemplary. Everyone that meets you walks away consumed with how they themselves can be better people, myself included. To respect you is an easy thing to do. To have your respect and friendship is surreal and beyond any expectation. I'm very grateful for the opportunity to share time on the road with you sir.

Another motorcycle rider wrote:

> It was my great fortune to have had the opportunity to escort you through Ohio and through Oldham County, Kentucky, to Louisville. Words cannot possibly begin to describe this feeling. I hope that when I am East again visiting my family, I can stop down in Richmond to see you for a few minutes. You are a great leader, marine, and friend. In the weeks following our meeting, I have been busy talking about you and sharing the importance in keeping the Spirit of '45 alive.

Flunking out of high school has given me no credibility, and my experience as a cab driver is exemplified by picking up of three ladies at two o'clock in the morning at the Top Hat in Louisville, Kentucky. When instructing me where to take them, they informed me that they were broke and would have to pay me with favors. Feeling especially generous that night, I judged that there were others who would welcome those favors more than I would. I returned to the Top Hat and deposited them there.

Almost immediately, I was informed by headquarters that another driver had been shot. The next morning, I resigned and took a job driving an ice cream truck. I was free to eat all the ice cream I wanted, and I did for three days until I couldn't stand the taste of ice cream. Then I took a job stacking lumber from 7:00 a.m. to 5:00 p.m. I soon realized that there was no future there and returned to college. It's amazing how hard work or unfulfilling circumstances can turn us toward more education.

Later in life, I discovered that riding a motorcycle gets me more attention and acclaim at an older age than all the years of serving in higher education. I have recorded some of my experiences to share the fulfillment that I derive from riding. Since age eighty-three, I have traveled about 100,000 miles. I enjoy the adventures of riding as I actively serve nonprofits, the military, and goodwill invitations. I do what others my age fail to do because it is disguised as impossible.

Traveling the periphery of the country, touching thirty-four states that border the rest of the forty-nine, reemphasizes the magnitude of the country. At the same time, it says I had put my arms around the whole country, short of Hawaii and Alaska, in a matter of days. One can travel the perimeter of the country and feel at home. There's a McDonalds almost every fifty or sixty miles—and often more frequently than that. *USA Today* can be purchased anywhere in America. Cracker Barrel restaurants are in forty-two states from Maine to Florida, from Florida to Arizona, from Idaho back to Maine, and all over the country.

There are some five thousand Dairy Queens scattered around the nation off of the interstates, and people still come in great numbers to get ice cream, banana splits, and milkshakes. All the states have different laws, yet they are so compatible that one need not study the rules beforehand. The signage when entering each state guides one quite well.

The interstate system is like a ribbon around the Lower 48 that binds everything together. As long as one stays on the interstate with many exits, it is almost like being at home. People all along the way are interesting and considerate. Some pay for my meals, invite me to stay overnight, engage me in conversation, and express regret that they quit riding their motorcycles too soon. They wish they had the courage to do what I was doing and express great respect for my wife who, while she wouldn't ride with me, wouldn't make me feel guilty for the enjoyment of riding on my own.

Neither the drivers on the highway nor the mangers of hotels, food services, roadside stops, or any business were ingenuous, unkind, or short-tempered as they went about serving my needs, disregarding the fact that I was a Virginian at a mature age circling the country.

Every morning, I couldn't wait to be on the road again to see what was over the next hill. As I mounted up my Harley, I sometimes found myself speaking as I would to my wife when we were driving in a car. I would sometimes, without thinking, ask, "Where would you like to stop for lunch?"

Calling my wife to let her know I had just passed through downtown Chicago was not a lot different from surviving Short Pump in Richmond at the busiest time in the afternoon.

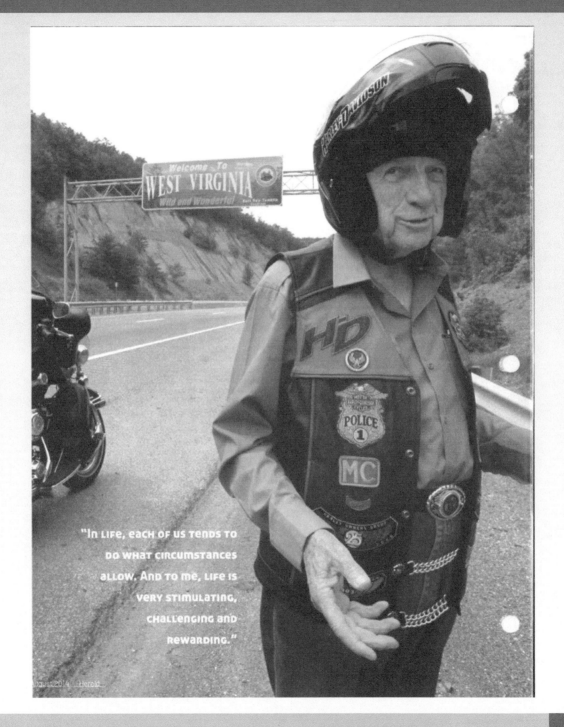

"In life, each of us tends to do what circumstances allow. And to me, life is very stimulating, challenging and rewarding."

miler from Virginia to Alaska – on June 8. As usual there were plenty of family, friends and media looking on, including fellow members of First Baptist Church in Richmond.

"They always say 'we wish you wouldn't go,'" Heilman says a couple of days before departing on his 1,200-pound Harley Davidson.

They see a man approaching his 90s heading out into a nation teeming with traffic, construction and glaciers. Heilman sees Marines struggling up Mount Surabachi, he sees radioactive Hiroshima dust on his GI boots, and he remembers the plane crash that didn't kill him.

A few solo motorcycle jaunts on (mostly) paved highways in the United States and Canada? How could that possibly rattle him?

"Sometimes you just have to do it," he says, "and that's what I'm doing."

For Heilman it's always been about doing. It's been about raising a family while earning advanced degrees and embarking upon a distinguished career. It's been about fundraising while on vacations and giving two or three speeches while riding to Alaska. It's been about nurturing relationships with the military and fellow veterans. All the while, he serves on at least a dozen boards, including ABPnews/Herald.

How does he keep doing all this at 88? Heilman answers with a question: how can he not?

"I have lived through the Great Depression and World War II – I find if I don't have a little challenge out there, life gets a little dull."

## Sheer energy

Life certainly wasn't dull immediately following the war. Heilman married and in short order there were mouths to feed – five children.

So he went to school – and with gusto. He attended schools like Peabody College, the universities of Omaha, Kentucky and Tennessee, and what is now Campbellsville University. Along the way he picked up bachelors, masters and doctorate degrees – and all without a high school diploma.

During his schooling he discovered a knack for teaching and especially for helping others teach. Those discoveries led to a career in higher education administration that culminated in university presidencies and renown as a premier fundraiser.

He was president of Meredith College in Raleigh, N.C., before becoming president of the University of Richmond in 1971 – a post he held until he became chancellor in 1986.

During his tenure as UR's president, he boosted its endowment by $200 million.

Heilman says such accomplishments were all about relationships – building and keeping them. Those who saw him at work say it was also sheer energy.

"He was all over the country raising money for the university," says David Burhans, special assistant for advancement at UR and a former university chaplain who worked under Heilman for decades.

"We almost never saw him. We just lived by phone messages and memos back and forth to each other."

## Working vacations

Nothing has really changed for Heilman. In June, he embarked on his Patriot edition Harley-Davidson Electra Glide Ultra Classic for a 5,000-mile ride from Richmond to Alaska. But he had more than sightseeing on the agenda: stops were planned in places like Louisville and Kansas City to see old friends and colleagues – and to seek contributions from University of Richmond graduates. Other stops and speaking engagements included speaking at a war museum in Canada and a civic club at the University of Alaska.

Those appointments, along with planned service stops for the motorcycle, are part of what keep Heilman going from mile to mile. It's how he has covered tens of thousands of miles and been through 48 states – Alaska will make it 49 – since he began riding again at age 71.

It's always been like that, recalls son Tim Heilman, a fundraiser at Campbellsville University.

He remembers the years when his father was president of Meredith College. The entire family jammed into the family sedan heading out for some rest and relaxation in South Carolina. But there was a catch: there were major executives, important alumni and other school supporters in most cities along the route.

So they stopped at each one of them. There was no way his father was going to miss an opportunity to raise money along the way.

"His vacations were always working vacations," says Tim. "We'd load up the car and make 10 stops from Raleigh to Myrtle Beach."

So it is that Heilman's 2014 journey follows that pattern. As long as the University of Richmond wants him to serve, he'll serve. He says he feels the same about his bike.

"And they will always ask me: 'When are you going to a retirement home?' I say as soon as I get a place to park my Harley."

## 'When I get old'

The bike, the road and even the fundraising and speaking events all keep Heilman young. Others see that youthfulness just as much as he feels it.

"He always comes back looking a heck of a lot better than when he left and feeling a lot better than when he left," Tim says of his father's annual mega rides.

In its own way, the war has kept Heilman young, too. That includes the regular trips to military hospi-

tals to visit young marines and soldiers
th shattered bodies. They are often am-
tees or even multiple-amputees with their
pe taken from them.

It's yet another role for Heilman: spokesman
the Greatest Generations Foundation, a non-
ofit group of veterans serving veterans.

Heilman leads veterans of previous wars,
me of whom are amputees. He makes the in-
oductions – using his skill as a natural rela-
nship builder to help senior citizens connect
ung and old. It isn't long before the young
n or woman feels optimism returning: if
ese old guys lived full lives with a missing leg
arm, maybe he or she can, too.

Then he steps back and watches as the old
ys are helped, as well. "They will talk to each
er and both experience healing."

Another job with the Foundation is to lead
irs of battlefields in Europe and, on Pacific
ands so that veterans of those conflicts can
perience closure from the psychological
ounds of war. He's led veterans to historic
es like Omaha Beach, Okinawa and Bastogne.

In both settings – hospitals and battlefields
participants in their 80s and 90s experience
e feeling of being much younger.

"We revert to being 18 and 19 years old,"
ilman says.

People routinely ask Heilman when he's
ing to put down the bike, take off the
ndraising hat and just slow down? But why
ould he when he's feeling like a young man?

"My bike is a two-wheeler but a lot of people
ink I'm riding a three-wheeler. I tell them I
saving that for when I get old."

## 'THAT YOUR BIKE?'

Plus he just isn't giving up life on the road – not
with the sights, smells and people to be met
along the way.

"You see more and you sense more because
you can smell" while riding a motorcycle.
"When you're in Texas, you know when you
are coming up to the next cattle ranch."

There was also the guy in Oklahoma City a
few years back who approached Heilman as he
was having a Coke and sandwich in a parking lot.

"That your bike?" the man asks, as so many
people on the road do.

"Yes, sir."

"Where you from?"

Heilman tells him.

The man then responds with the most
astonishing story of running away from home
at 13, being in prison, getting out and having
his wife divorce him. He got a job in a bakery,
liked it and eventually came to own that store
and a chain of bakeries. He also raised four
daughters.

You don't meet people like that in church,
Heilman says, adding there's something about
encountering an 80-something motorcyclist
that seems to get people to open up.

"It's amazing that people have a story to tell
and he just needed to tell me his," Heilman says.

His motorcycle odysseys and regular
exposure to college campuses and uniformed
military personnel also have helped him maintain a respect for the character and spirituality
of younger generations.

Heilman grew up regularly attending a rural

Baptist church and two- and three-week revivals
where the message was about not sinning. "I was
18 years old and in the military before I learned
religion is about what you *do* do."

And that's what he sees in youth today.
"They are good people and I enjoy being around
them."

Yet he's still regularly questioned: how
long can it last? Isn't he just fortunate to have
a sound mind and body at this stage in
life?

Heilman agrees some of it may be genetic.
But he's seen others in his family break down
and die at much younger ages. To him, just as
much of his situation is due to decisions he's
made as it is DNA or luck.

"In life, each of us tends to do what circumstances allow," he says. "And to me, life is very
stimulating, challenging and rewarding."

But Heilman says he gets it. He understands
why his children, members of his church and
folks on the road sometimes can't get their
head around the idea of an octogenarian
putting tens of thousands of miles on a
motorcycle every year.

In fact, back when his late wife gave him his
first Harley some 16 years ago, he was a little
shocked himself.

"When I started riding at 71, I thought that
was pretty old to be riding a Harley," he says.

But that was then.

"Now, 20 years later, I don't have any
problem with it at all."

*– Jeff Brumley is assistant editor of
ABPnews/Herald.*

Photo by Bob
Brown/Richmond
Times-Dispatch

# II

# NOT RELEGATED TO A LIFE VOID OF ADVENTURE

The thrill of the special adventure of motorcycle riding is renewed each time I share it with others. It begins when getting astride my Electra Glide, facing the wind, and cleansing my mind of everything mundane. The world becomes my domain as the open road is laid before me in ribbons of asphalt with panoramas on all sides that offer visions of grandeur, aromas of the area, and weather conditions as real as the openness before me. Only a motorcycle allows the wind in my face, the nature of the area, the weather conditions, my speed, and the large semi-trucks passing me by even when I set my cruise control above seventy miles per hour. Many of the western interstates allow eighty miles an hour as the routine speed limit.

So, climb aboard my comfortable back seat and enjoy the experience. Helen Keller said, "Life is either a daring adventure—or it is nothing." Well, for me, my ninety-one years have been an adventure, and these latter years have not seen a diminishing of that gratification. In many ways, it has been an acceleration.

I retraced my journey of seventy-five years ago when I hitchhiked across the country on old Route 66 after returning from World War II. In old age, I seek to broaden the perspective a bit from an age when most have long since given up their passion for motorcycle riding—if not for adventure itself. They are relegated to a life void of adventure because of age or otherwise.

It has been well advertised that I am now ninety-one years old and still riding across the country. I have received a great deal of publicity for taking several rides throughout the United States on my Harley-Davidson Electra Glide, Ultra Classic, Patriot. It's been astounding that so many have deemed this act so unusual or special or interesting or outstanding.

In a past issue of *HOG*, the national Harley-Davidson magazine under a section titled "Spotlight" is a subheading, "Bruce Heilman, Super Patriot."

So, as I engage this journey I celebrate my eighty-third birthday, my marriage to the same woman for sixty-five years, my sixty-five years as an educator, my forty years at the University of Richmond, and my seventy years as a US marine.

Following is an excerpt from a sign on my Harley in route:

"Tom Brokaw called us the Greatest Generation, so I wanted to prove that we were still pretty great." With flags representing the marines, the United States, the University of Richmond, and Harley-Davidson, Heilman was greeted all along the way by fellow marines, veterans, patriots, and Harley lovers of all stripes. He reckoned the experience to returning to Okinawa in 1993, forty-nine years after he was in combat there. It was like a dream, he recalls. "I thought, 'The world has changed so much—did I really do this? But I did.' Heilman returned to the Marine Corps base where he went through boot camp sixty-four years earlier. It was great to see firsthand that they are still training young people there to do great things for their country.

This is just one of many summaries of my travels from Richmond to San Diego from October 1 through October 10, 2008. I completed the first three thousand miles, averaging three hundred miles per day.

On my first day of travel, I arrived at the Jepson Alumni Building on the University of Richmond campus at 6:45 a.m. It was still dark, but there were lots of people with and without motorcycles awaiting me. They were there to join our campus security to escort me through the campus and on to I-64 toward Charlottesville as I began my ten-day ride to San Diego.

Along the way, they spun off little by little. When I arrived in Staunton for breakfast at the Cracker Barrel, there were twelve or fifteen who had not fallen by the wayside. Dr. Jim Sease, an eighty-one-year-old UR alumnus, had ridden on his Harley from Winchester to be my breakfast guest.

Following a hearty breakfast with all my goodwill ambassadors, I left the restaurant to greetings of others who observed our camaraderie. As I approached my motorcycle, a lady asked if I was a veteran. When I acknowledged that I was, she hugged me and said, "I just love you veterans!" I decided that I really was glad to be a veteran!

As I traveled down I-81 on to I-64 west through the countryside, I spied a welcoming McDonald's sign in Covington. Over coffee, I met a marine from the past and a variety of other veterans having their morning social gathering. Some were motorcyclists who wished they could go along, which was the case everywhere I went.

Having not had my motorcycle wet in a year and a half, I was pretty determined to keep it dry. I carried my own cover to protect it at the first raindrop, and I also had rain gear for myself. That afternoon, between Beckley and Charleston, West Virginia, with little warning, the rain suddenly came down in buckets. I parked under an overpass, so close to the highway that the trucks sprayed me with grit, dirt, and rainwater until I was really messy. When it slowed a little, I took off for Charleston in rain squalls realizing that "wet" was better than "wet and dirty."

I arrived in Charleston after encountering numerous downpours. As I looked for my hotel, the sky turned darker—and an even heavier downpour descended upon me. In the early evening traffic, the car and truck lights were blinding me, which produced about the messiest situation one could imagine.

I don't ride in the dark, and I don't ride in the rain. Well, it was night, I was in the rain, and I could hardly see. My windshield was covered, I had no wipers, and I was lost. Finally, I found my way out of that mess and had a nice dry overnight at the motel. So, much for the first day of my experience! I wondered whether it was an example of what I might encounter along the way.

The next morning, Thursday, October 2, at about seven o'clock, I set out for Huntington, West Virginia. I arrived at the Harley dealership at eight thirty. They didn't usually open until ten, but they had promised to start servicing my motorcycle at nine.

The supervisor of the repair and maintenance department dispatched a marine to take good care of me. It was after noon before everything was completed. While waiting for the repairs, I tripped on a walkway and spilled my coffee, causing me to slip on the wet concrete. I had a badly bruised hip for some time. So, swinging onto my Harley was not easy, but I survived it with a couple aspirin.

I arrived in Louisville at four that second afternoon and met a reporter from *The CourierJournal* who interviewed me as a "home-state boy" passing through on an unusual adventure. Several friends showed up to greet me, including a lady from high school, one who traveled abroad with my group several times, and a cousin and her husband. Two other couples were interested in my ride and my memoirs. At a table in the hotel, I sold half a dozen copies of my book. I was off to a good start in paying my way across the country. Because of the weight of my books, my wife and daughter were carrying them in a car not far behind me.

I was supposed to have had a GPS installed in Huntington, West Virginia, but they didn't have the proper mount. So, they called ahead to Louisville, where I would be staying that evening within two blocks of the Harley dealership. On Friday morning of my third day, my GPS was installed before I headed to Saint Louis, Missouri. Even with the leathers buttoned up tightly, at seventy miles per hour, it was chilly, but that was better than sweating.

As I traveled through Kentucky and Indiana, I found devastating drought conditions. Cornfields and pastures were completely dried up. Even though a recent hurricane had blown in from the Houston area with winds up to a hundred miles per hour, there had been not a drop of rain. With the time difference, I had an extra hour. I arrived at the Comfort Suites in Saint Louis and sent my daughter Nancy to the airport so she could fly back to Richmond on Saturday morning.

On the fourth travel day, October 4, Dede Boudinet, a 1989 graduate of UR, and I enjoyed a wonderful breakfast together. She purchased a copy of my memoirs, which she carried to the St. Louis chapter meeting of UR alumni the next week when the president, Ed Ayers, spoke.

Betty was poised in a rental car not far behind me, and I mounted my Harley at eight thirty for an all-day journey. I headed south on I-44, and the next stop was Springfield, Missouri. From there, my course drifted south for twenty miles to Branson and the College of the Ozarks. I spent the night with the president—and longtime friend—Jerry Davis. I arrived at the beautiful Keeter Center for an early dinner. Between Saint Louis and Branson, I had enjoyed the transitioning of the countryside. It was not hot or cold; it was just right. Cruising at sixty or seventy miles per hour, I enjoyed the humming of the Harley and the beauty of the day.

On the fifth day, I was up bright and early. I had breakfast in my room at the Keeter Center at six forty-five and was my way by seven thirty. Between Springfield and Tulsa, I observed hay, greener grass, and lots of cattle as I smelled the aroma that goes with them. I passed through Oklahoma, remembering one of my Marine Corps buddies from boot camp. He was from Ada, Oklahoma—and a farm boy like myself. We were great friends, making the best of the situation in wartime when all of us were preparing for serious business. I had called him three or four years earlier—about sixty years after World War II—to find that he had passed away. Thus, we never got to see each other again. His cousin told me that he had become a cattle salesman and auctioneer, had done very well financially, and was always proud to be a marine.

Because I arrived in Tulsa earlier than anticipated, I canceled my reservation there and moved on to Oklahoma City. I completed my travel on I-44 and began a long stretch on I-40 to California. Deciding to go on to Oklahoma City was a lifesaver because the rain came down the next morning. I would have been soaked and probably would not have made it to a luncheon with representatives of the Harley-Davidson Company.

Following a good night's sleep and a full morning of rest, relaxation, and planning the remaining journey, I cleaned the bugs off my windshield. Betty joined me and four Harley executives—one male and three females—for a delightful luncheon. They all engaged in grilling me regarding my reason for this long trip, how things were going, and whether I would be willing to talk to Harley owner groups in Oklahoma City the next summer at the National Harley Rally. The experience of an eighty-two-year-old representing World War II veterans and my university made the conversation engaging and enjoyable.

Almost everywhere I stopped, somebody bought a copy of my book. At the luncheon, each of them bought a copy—and one bought two because he wanted to give one to a friend. The Harley folks were the planners for the Oklahoma City National HOG Rally for June of 2009, and I would be in attendance. I had the manager of that event and three people in other positions related to that planning process for the summer rally.

Monday, October 6, was Black Monday on the stock market, but it was a good day for me. I traveled from Oklahoma City to Shamrock, Texas, through the Texas Panhandle. I saw wide-open country with beautiful clouds floating overhead—but no rain. The rain had come during the prior night. It was heavy, and the wind was strong; our motel was without power for several hours, even during breakfast.

There were lots of motorcyclists on the road. We waved at each other, tooted our horns, and enjoyed just knowing that we are somebody special because there are two kinds of people— those who ride motorcycles and those who wish they could. As I covered the miles of interstate, I kept filling up with gas and washing the bugs off my windshield. As I enjoyed the sights, sounds, and aroma of surroundings, I also enjoyed interaction with people of all kinds—jolly, jovial, friendly, and inquisitive. Along the way, I saw huge windmills producing electricity.

The highway was straight through rolling hills and periodic flatlands, but there were no large cities between Oklahoma City and Amarillo, Texas. The little town of Shamrock, where I spent the night of May 6, only had one eating place that could really be claimed as a restaurant. I had dinner there with folks from the countryside. A graduate of the University of Richmond and some others had planned to motorcycle up from Dallas and ride with me from Shamrock, but they canceled at the last moment because one of their children was ill.

On May 7, I traveled to Tucumcari, New Mexico, seeing more cattle and more plains. Depending upon circumstances, I occasionally deviated from I-40 to Route 66 for a little sightseeing. There was added time because of another time change. New Mexico provided wideopen spaces, and the roads were as straight as an arrow. Huge wind turbines produced electricity from horizon to horizon almost circling me. There were lots of cattle until I entered the desert, where it began to look like New Mexico, Arizona, and parts of California are supposed to look.

There was not much activity along the highways, but there was a good bit of wind, especially when the heavy trucks passed me. Even when I was traveling at seventy miles per hour, they passed me like I was standing still. The wind in my face produced a good bit of windburn that required a bit of lotion to save my complexion and good looks. When stopping for coffee, I received a "Semper Fi" from a Desert Storm marine.

# 34 DAYS, 6,000 MILES, 21 STATES

## A MODERN-DAY PAUL REVERE RIDES ON A HOG

### TO CELEBRATE THE 70TH ANNIVERSARY OF THE ENDING OF WORLD WAR II

*by E. Bruce Heilman*

Dr. E. Bruce Heilman, of Richmond, Va., an 89-year-old Marine veteran of World War II and a 1949 graduate of CU, traveled 6,000 miles on his Harley-Davidson across America to raise awareness of the 70th anniversary of the end of World War II.

The Spirit of 45 is a grass-roots organization dedicated to the purpose of recognizing and transmitting the sense of unity and community shared amongst the Greatest Generation when the country had to come together for a common cause.

The Spirit of 45 is about their sacrifices and sense of responsibility to country and to one another. It is about values that need to be taught to young people today. It is about young people being inspired by The Greatest Generation.

In educating the public about all of these, it was determined that a modern-day Paul Revere, travelling by Hog (Harley Owners Group) rather than a horse, would be effective in spreading the news. An 89-year-old World War II veteran was chosen for the role to travel some 6,000 miles over 34 days to 21 states on his Harley motorcycle.

As there were no other applicants for the job, I accepted the invitation to serve, which proved to be an adventure unlike any other in my lifetime.

My assignment was to highlight these attributes of the war years and to encourage celebrating our country's victorious success at forestalling the dictators who would have dominated the world. The uniqueness of my travelling by Harley, as a means of getting from point to point, brought people to see me. Once they saw, they listened.

Along my route, I met with governors, mayors, veterans, high school and college students, laid wreaths in cemeteries and spoke wherever there was someone to listen. I encountered wonderful people who were anxious to hear about the spirit of that era.

## WHEN WE DISCOVER IN LIFE VALUES WORTH DYING FOR

## WE LIKELY HAVE FOUND PURPOSES WORTH LIVING FOR

## — UNKNOWN

I reminded my audiences that WW II liberated women, that it ended the Great Depression and that the G.I. Bill was the veterans' reward. It was a grand journey, and I am happy to share it wherever I go, because it is still my message, including that on the 14th of August, we celebrated the 70th anniversary of the end of WW II.

My ride and the accompanying message proved to be popular, especially as I represented those who fought and died for freedom in the world. Thus, out of respect for the message I carried and the veterans I represented, the Mayor of Shreveport declared the day of my visit the E. Bruce Heilman Day and noted that I, as a rider throughout the country highlighting all that the Spirit represents, was serving a worthy purpose.

The mayor of Cincinnati proclaimed my visit E. Bruce Heilman Day in respect for my raising awareness for the Spirit of 45 and of the 70th anniversary of WW II.

The judge in Oldham County and the mayor of LaGrange, Ky., gave citations naming May 19th Dr. E. Bruce Heilman Day, and made me an honorary citizen. The mayor of Louisville named me an honorary citizen of Louisville for my journey in honor of the Spirit of 45 and the veterans of WW II.

I proudly accepted these acknowledgements for all those I represented and all who followed my journey. I applaud their dedication to highlighting the 70th anniversary of the end of WW II and the Spirit of 45. Together, we represent the vanguard of those all over the world who understand that freedom isn't free and stand ready to defend it at any cost.

To read Heilman's unabridged narrative, go to: www.campbellsville.edu/dr-e-bruce-heilman-on-spirit-of-45-june-2015.

During lunch, I was greeted by a Vietnam marine. I didn't run into many World War II marines since too many have judged themselves to be older than I think I am. No matter their ages, they are always proud to be marines. At the end of the seventh day, I overnighted at the airport in Albuquerque, New Mexico. My daughter Terry was scheduled to meet me the next morning and would accompany Betty.

On October 8, I added to the two thousand miles already traveled. Terry arrived at ten fifteen so she and her mother could travel together by car along the route I was taking. Balloon races were taking place in Albuquerque and Gallup, New Mexico. The winds seemed to be favorable for that particular sport. I periodically departed from the I-40 corridor, which for all practical purposes was supplanted over much of old Route 66, but I veered over the original route to observe some of the contrast of the past with the setting of today: old hotels, restaurants, and professional buildings. It brought back memories of sixty-two years ago when I was traveling that highway and venturing into some of these facilities. There were lots of MexicanAmericans in the area. In places such as Wal-Mart, those faces were the prevailing ones, and I was the more unusual.

In the countryside, small houses and mobile homes frequent the communities. The small ranches were adorned with pickup trucks and older cars. At a coffee stop, I encountered a Korean War vet—a marine of twenty-six years. My Marine Corps emblems on the motorcycle and on my jacket inspired those contacts. Around noontime, Betty and Terry joined me at a casino where we had lunch and ordered the "two-for-one." The steak was good, and gambling was prevailing in midday.

I arrived in Gallup, New Mexico, by three thirty and had a leisurely meal at a drive-in hamburger-and-milkshake place before cleaning the bugs from my windshield. I had looked forward to meeting Kenneth Reige, the manager of the Quality Inn in Gallup, where a veterans' group had volunteered to pay for my lodging. My fairly early arrival gave me some time for fellowship.

In that part of the country, the lure of Route 66 attracts lots of activity. There are visitors' centers, festivals, railroad museums, shopping options, and unique dining spots. Historic hotels and restaurants blend in with the more modern ones. Native American jewelry, carpets, and rugs of many colors can be purchased there. I was not exactly on a sightseeing tour, although I wanted to remember some of what I saw when I was hitchhiking.

At the Great Wall

With the Dillards and daughter Terry visiting David Ho in China

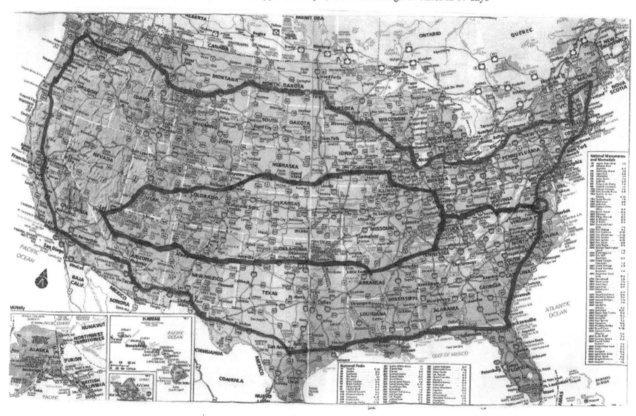

Outer route traveled 2012: 9,200 miles through 34 states in 25 days
Inner route traveled 2013: approximately 6,000 miles through 17 states in 17 days

At breakfast, I visited a gentleman who had been a navy corpsman in Korea. He manufactures commemorative coins for the Harley Company, and he sent me some. Mr. Reige purchased a copy of my book, and several weeks later, I received an e-mail:

> It's funny, but I have had hundreds of thousands of people that have passed through the doors of this hotel since I have been the manager, and you are the guest that I know that I will always remember. I have been really enjoying your book and can't wait to finish it so I can start it over again. My wife has been looking at the pictures in the book, and she wants to read it next.

On the ninth day, I had breakfast early and hit the road. I traveled to Flagstaff, Arizona, so quickly that I decided to bypass where I had intended to stay and went on to Kingman, Arizona. I traveled three hundred miles through some very windy territory! It would almost blow me off my motorcycle. I had to lean into the wind or run smack into it until I had windburns all over my face. So, the next day, I wore a full-face helmet.

Along the interstate, I saw beautifully sculptured hills, which the good Lord made from nature by way of rising mountain terrain. They broke off and dropped straight down, which is not what the Smoky Mountains provide. It is very beautiful country, rustic and brown. Kingman is a very historic place because it's right on Route 66. Leaving Kingman, I traveled across the desert.

The highway was straight, and there were fewer trucks.

On the tenth day, I headed for Barstow, California, and the Marine Corps Logistics Base. The Santa Anna winds were fierce, and I checked in at Barstow early because it was almost impossible to ride. In Barstow, I stayed at the Quality Suites near the 66 Mother Road Railroad Museum and a ghost town. I visited the Marine Corps Logistics Base for two hours in the afternoon. Staff Sergeant Houston White wrote a story about my journey for the *Barstow Log*, their base newspaper. I made the front page—motorcycle and all.

On the morning of the eleventh day, the wind had died down, but it was cold. With double jackets, double trousers, and leather gloves, I traveled the two hundred miles south to San Diego. The freeway is eight lanes wide and packed with traffic traveling above seventy miles per hour. That tested my motorcycle skills a bit, but I survived that frightening experience without fanfare, enjoying the scenery along the way.

As I settled down on the outskirts of the city near the Miramar Marine Air Base, I put my motorcycle to rest and did a little paperwork, recording my adventures. I had completed my journey to San Diego. It was ten and a half days on the road for three thousand miles, and I had not pressed hard. I averaged almost three hundred miles per day. After lunch, I took Terry to the airport. She flew to San Francisco, leaving Betty and me on our own again.

In San Diego, I spent half a day at the Marine Recruit Depot where I had graduated from boot camp. It was reflective to watch the young recruits in the swimming pavilion, jumping off towers, learning how to survive in water, trying the obstacle course, and marching precisely on the parade grounds. Remembering how much a few weeks in boot camp does to discipline and mature young men added a sense of pride in this old marine. For my visit, a captain and a sergeant DI accompanied me through all aspects of the command post.

The next day, I went to the Marine Air Deport at Miramar. A young corporal proudly showed me everything, including the Leatherneck Museum where I met a number of volunteers and the bookstore and gift shop manager who wanted to order my books for sale. My memoirs are now on sale from the East Coast to the West Coast.

On Wednesday, October 13, I attended the get-together of the San Diego chapter of the University of Richmond in competition with the televised presidential debates. We didn't have many present, but we had a nice party. I sold three more books, which made it twenty on my trip.

On October 14, I stored my motorcycle where it would remain until March 28, 2009, when I flew back to San Diego to ride it south along the Mexican border during months of favorable weather en route to Richmond by way of several places and activities as time and circumstances would allow. I drove Betty to San Francisco and then back to Richmond.

I originally anticipated having my Harley shipped back to Richmond, believing that I might be exhausted from the one-way ride, but I reconsidered. After resting over the winter, I flew to San Diego on March 29, took my motorcycle out of hock, hit the starter button, and roared off.

I flew in on a Saturday night and took I-8 on the Mexican border to El Centro, California. I was in a part of the country where I was experiencing sights that I had never encountered before. Between San Diego and El Centro—and on to Yuma, Arizona—I saw what could have been the far side of the moon. Compared to the East Coast and other parts of the United States, it was rustic, barren, and full of boulders, sand dunes, and substantial hills.

Experiencing the changing landscape was fascinating to me. In Yuma, I met a new friend who had contacted me after reading my story in *HOG*, the Harley Magazine.

> If you are coming through Yuma, I want to meet you. I'll arrange for you to have your Harley serviced at the Harley dealership. I am a Harley rider, a marine, and I am interested in what you are doing. I'll even arrange for you to sell and autograph your book at a restaurant near the Harley dealership while you are here. Some old marines and others are interested in purchasing copies.

At the Harley dealership in Yuma, Robert Gwinn, a reporter from KSWT, was waiting for me. He was looking for a story to develop for the evening news. It was around noon, and we had a two-hour engagement, including a stop for lunch. I met the proprietor, and I began autographing books while my motorcycle was being serviced. I was windblown, and I'm sure the alumni in the Yuma area who may have seen the evening news might not have recognized me with my hair uncombed. I must have looked a mess, but considering the circumstances, perhaps that was the image that was appropriate to portray.

It was three o'clock in the afternoon by the time my motorcycle service was completed, and I still had many miles to travel to Tucson, Arizona, before my day was done. The landscapes were unusual, and I had never traveled on I-8. As I intersected with I-10 at Casa Grande, I turned south toward Tucson, but it was not as early as I had hoped. It was an hour after dark before I arrived there for the overnight stay. I don't usually ride on strange highways after dark because of animals, car lights, and other risk factors.

I noted wild boars grazing along the highway, but not on the highway. I had heard about a motorcyclist who struck one and wrecked himself. I was careful of deer and wild hogs, and signs along the road told me to be careful about them as well as windstorms and dust storms. I was adjusting to the heavy wind and dust.

I arrived at about eight o'clock in the evening, and it was too late to have dinner with Charlotte Fugett. the former head of Human Resource Services for the University of Richmond, but we agreed to have breakfast the next morning. She was president of a community college, and she showed up bright, cheery, and professional. We had a hearty breakfast at the hotel and reminisced. I autographed a book and continued to sell my autobiography. I had traveled almost four hundred miles that day.

The next day, I headed for El Paso, which would be the next overnight stop. The three hundred-mile journey was a little farther from the Mexican border. Along the way, I enjoyed unusual territory. As I got closer to El Paso, I looked over into Juarez, Mexico. Texas is a long state.

My route took me through Van Horn, a small town on I-10, and Fort Stockton. I finally overnighted in Sonora. In each of the towns, I stopped at McDonald's for my breaks and refreshments. The Texans wouldn't call it that, but it felt like a no-man's-land. The highways are straight, and the speed limit is eighty. I set my cruise control on seventy and just kept going. On Tuesday, March 31, I covered another three hundred miles and reached Sonora.

On Wednesday, April 1, I was up early and on the road. I had worn two jackets and two pairs of trousers most of the way, even though it was north of the Mexican border. It was still chilly at seventy even in the late afternoon, and I never had to remove a jacket to stay comfortable. As I moved closer to San Antonio, it began to get a bit warmer. I shed some of my double clothing.

I passed through San Antonio and Corpus Christi, another 350 miles or so, and overnighted in Kingsville, Texas on Wednesday, April 1. Having traveled 1,500 miles in total, I had bugs on the windshield and other parts of the motorcycle. It was pretty dirty. On Thursday, April 2, I headed toward Harlingen. I stopped in a little community with a car wash and washed my motorcycle. I wanted to look good coming into Harlingen and the Marine Military Academy, flying the United States flag, the Richmond Spiders flag, and the Marine Corps flag.

I arrived in Harlingen at noon, checked in at the academy, and relinquished my Harley to the head of maintenance, where it would be stored until I could pick it up on Sunday, May 3. I would be riding to Houston for an alumni meeting and storing it there for another two months. I would then fly to Pensacola for a reunion of my World War II marine buddies. Two months later, on June 24, I would return to Houston and head north to arrive in Oklahoma City to attend the National Harley Rally from June 25–27.

Following the rally, I'd ride back toward Richmond, leaving my motorcycle in Kentucky until I can return there. I was due back in Richmond to lead a group to South Africa, and I didn't have time to ride all the way back to Richmond. I'd fly to Kentucky in July or August to complete my ride to Virginia.

Among the signs I saw were "Warning: Dangerous Dogs," and I was stopped more than once. On one occasion, the border patrolman looked directly at my jacket, which was adorned with the Marine Corps emblem, which was also painted on my motorcycle, and asked if I was an

American citizen. I almost responded to that. Other signs were "Possible Dust Storms: Visibility

Zero" and one I didn't quite understand: "Do Not Stop in Travel Lane."

My total miles traveled between San Diego and Harlingen was 1,641. A miracle of all miracles, I never had a drop of rain in four days. And having traveled ten days in October to get to San Diego and encountering rain only in West Virginia, I must have been doing something right. They say if you don't ride in the rain, you don't ride, but I have certainly proved that to be wrong.

It was an exciting event that enriched my life by doing something that few others of my age would have attempted—and it set an example of a continuing saga of motorcycle travels.

People ask me, "Why?" And I answer, "Why not?" I am healthy and well and have lived a life of adventure. Why would I, as a healthy eighty-three-year-old, not be seeking adventure and purpose and association and relationships and physical and mental challenges to a substantial level both now and well into the future? I am doing just that.

Life for me would be distressing without challenge. That ride was just one recent challenge, and another was the writing of my memoirs. Now I am traveling around the country speaking and autographing at several bookstores and gatherings.

What are some of the things I remember most from my ride? I learned that you meet many more people when you travel solo. When you're in a big crowd, you get crowd conversation but not a whole lot of intimacy with strangers. In my case, I was alone. My interactions were mainly with others who were alone. I look back most fondly to the times I spent with people I met along the way.

People are generous in their time and spirit with strangers. They tell them about themselves because they are not sharing secrets with someone who might use them in inappropriate ways. These are people they will probably never see again, and they get things off their chests.

Talking to total strangers was fascinating. At the rally, thousands of Harleys were gleaming in the sun. It didn't matter if it was two thousand or ten thousand—all the riders were under shade trees, at picnic tables, or in the air-conditioned pavilion. They were all interacting with friends and total strangers. With a soft drink and a granola bar, I found a bench under a shade tree. A gentleman in his forties or fifties asked where I was from. "From Richmond, Virginia," I responded.

"Oh," he said. "You've come a long way."

I said, "Well, I have—and I came here by way of San Diego." That produced an even stronger glance at me. I inquired as to his origin, and he said, "I'm from here in Oklahoma City, but I've been away for a long time."

My curiosity led to my next question: "Where have you been?" His response surprised me. "In prison," he said.

So, attempting not to appear too surprised and also to convey that which I assumed would suggest a level of comfortable comradery, I said, "Well, up to now, I managed to avoid that."

He seemed to find it comforting that maybe I hadn't missed it by too much. He warmed to more conversation and conveyed to me that he had a son who was old enough to have a Harley, but his mother wouldn't let him have it. "She tells me that if I support him getting a Harley, I want to see him get killed. Anything I want for him, she thinks just the opposite. She hates my guts."

Well, I didn't pursue that too far or push too strongly toward whether he had taken drugs, shot his neighbor, robbed a bank, or any of that. I just let it ride and treated him as if he were just another of the ten thousand Harley riders gathered for the annual rally. I was pleased he didn't press the contrast possibilities between my life and his.

In Springfield, Missouri, I stopped at a McDonald's for coffee.

A gentleman, perhaps ten years younger than I, approached me at the coffee counter and inquired whether that was my bike outside. I said, "Yes, it is."

Wearing my leather jacket made that a very good possibility.

"Well," he said. "I'm a Harley rider myself. Get your coffee and come on over and sit down."

After asking where I was from and finding out that he was from right there in Springfield, he said, "But you know something, I was homeless when I was thirteen. My father and mother disowned me, and my grandmother and I couldn't get along, so I hitchhiked to California. I took my bath in filling station restrooms and sometimes slept there. I was imprisoned as a vagrant when I was fourteen and taken by the sheriff to the edge of town and told to hit the road or I was going to be locked up in jail for more days than I had already served.

"I hit the road and hitchhiked to Milwaukee, Wisconsin, where I got a job in a bakery. I worked hard, and the owner took a liking to me, and when the bakery was not being managed well several years after and was about to go out of business, I asked the owners to give me six months to put it back in business and buy it from them, which I did. I succeeded in business, created a string of bakeries and other businesses, and while I never finished grade school, I educated my four children through college, and today, I own my own business and am comfortable riding my Harley."

I commended him for his successes. Again, I was not obliged to share my failures and successes. As in most cases, I simply listened to the others, benefitted from the conversations, and didn't give away too many of my secrets. After the fact, most of them probably wondered whether I had been in prison, was a vagrant, or was a success or failure, which suited me fine.

I learned a lot about others without them discovering too much about me. On occasion, we exchanged cards. They would look at mine and seem not to know what to think when they became aware that they were with a university chancellor—whatever that was.

Above all else, what I like about hitting the road on my Harley is that I am doing it my own way, on my own time, with my own schedule, meeting people with whom I am most comfortable, whoever that might be, without divulging too much of myself. What human interest stories I hear. And I imagine the human interest stories I have not yet heard.

\*\*\*

# III

# GOLD STAR FAMILIES RIDE NUMBER ONE

I left early on the morning of Friday, May 18, 2012, from the Westhampton Lake at the University of Richmond. Campus police and motorcycles escorted me across the James River to the Chippenham Parkway, and the motorcycles continued to I-95 and south to the Cracker Barrel restaurant to celebrate my ambition.

My first objective was to reach Jacksonville, Florida, the turning point at which I changed from traveling south to heading west on my journey through all the thirty-four border states of the Lower 48. I was unable to make it to Jacksonville that first day, but I did cover the 450 miles to Yemassee, South Carolina, where I spent the first night. It was a long ride but a good first day. It threatened rain much of the way through North and South Carolina, but because I kept moving, I managed to stay ahead of any downpours.

Early in the morning of Saturday, May 19, I found a note on my motorcycle from two ladies with whom I had conversed the evening before:

> Sorry, we know that no one should touch anyone's bike, but had to share our feeling. We just want to tell you how much of an honor and privilege it was to meet and talk with you. We are still in awe. You have an amazing story to tell especially in light of the world we are accustomed to. You are the definition of a true biker Much love and respect. May God continue to bless and watch over your journeys, Tammy and Hy.

Traffic was minimal since most folks were still sleeping, and I enjoyed having the highway to myself as I traveled from just north of Savannah, Georgia, to Jacksonville.

The Florida Visitors Center was filled with people drinking free orange juice. As I took off my full-face helmet, revealing that I was no spring chicken, a fellow marine introduced himself and asked where I was headed. Two or three others listened in wonderment as I told him of my destination. None of them could quite comprehend that I was on my way to San Francisco and beyond. Obviously, their skepticism was reinforced by their impression of my age. This perspective was to prevail throughout my adventure. I turned right on I-10 and began the long ride across the border of the Lower 48. I headed toward Tallahassee, Florida, and stopped at a town called Crestview. I had traveled six hundred miles that day, most of it on I-10 after leaving I-95 in Jacksonville.

I was on the road early on Sunday, May 20, and passed through Pensacola, Florida, and Mobile, Alabama. Because it was still early, Baton Rouge became my destination. The weather continued to be excellent, and I missed the heavy downpours that others encountered. The weather warmed up considerably, and I shed the jeans under my leathers and removed the leather vest from under my jacket. When the weather became hot enough, I changed into blue jeans and a leather vest without sleeves.

From Baton Rouge, I headed for Lafayette and beyond, finally arriving just short of Lake Charles. In Rayne, Louisiana, I stayed at the Best Western after only 380 miles, my shortest day yet. I was amazed that so much of I-10 in Louisiana was built on stilts like adult Tinker Toys.

For miles and miles, it was like a bridge built over water.

The next morning, Monday, the stage was set for moving on to Houston and San Antonio, covering another three hundred miles. It was ninety-three degrees for most of the day and ninety-five the next two days. Because of the heat, a change of everything every day was necessary—blue jeans, socks, and everything else. After a day on a motorcycle at those temperatures, a quick shower in the evening along with fresh clothing was a refreshing experience.

On the open highways at seventy miles an hour, my motorcycle absorbed a lot of fuel. I stopped about every 150 miles to fill up, providing breaks to what could be monotonous otherwise. The speed limit was seventy-five miles per hour on most of I-10, but it was eighty in Texas. I tried to flow with the traffic. My Harley performed flawlessly as if it were a good friend. As soon as I saddled up and touched the button, it was ready to go. It was as if it couldn't wait— like a bucking bronco.

I left San Antonio after breakfast on Tuesday, May 22, and covered four hundred miles to Van Horn, which was about 120 miles short of El Paso. Along the way, I stopped several places and interrupted people I perceived to be World War II veterans. One of those I met had served in World War II in the Seabees. He joined the air force, became a pilot in Korea, and served in Southeast Asia in the Vietnam War. Another one I met, a merchant marine, had his daughter with him and would not have made it on his own. All were willing to chat and have their pictures taken, which would later remind me of our conversation.

I visited with a lady in a short order booth. I said, "You were probably a little girl during World War II, but maybe your father served in the military."

She laughed and responded, "No, my father did not, but my brother did, and after he left home, we never saw him again. He is buried somewhere—we are not sure where. He was first noted as missing in action, but later, we received word that a mistake had been made, and he was killed in action."

With that sad encounter, I uncovered another perspective of World War II and the families who suffered the consequences of the losses. The lady was pleased to have her picture taken after the conversation and to be identified as a member of a Gold Star family.

On Wednesday, I went to El Paso and journeyed directly to Tucson. I went to a Harley dealership because I had jumped a curb and knocked the kickstand out from under my motorcycle. I could not get off because the motorcycle would fall over. I had to hold up that thousand-pound motorcycle until I found a friend with a little piece of plastic string to hook up the stand as I rode 150 miles to the Harley service center. As they were fixing the problem, they told me that my back tire was less than safe. I had the tire replaced as well. After the repair and tire change, I checked in at a motel next to the dealership for a restful and welcome rest.

With my Harley kickstand repaired, a new back tire, and a few other things adjusted, I was in good shape for a ride through the desert on Thursday. The heavy winds, dust storms, heat, and traffic through Phoenix presented a challenge all the way to Palm Desert, just a hundred miles from Los Angeles.

I overnighted in Cathedral City, California. The address was Date Palm Drive, and along the route, there were references to Bob Hope. After traveling for days with no green grass or trees, I looked down from the high peak coming out of the desert and thanked the good Lord for water. Palm Springs evolved water on sand like the Israelis made the desert live.

As I left the Palm Springs area on Friday morning, the wind was blowing so hard that it held my motorcycle back and kicked off the cruise control. Big electric generators located around Palm Springs and the valley picked up the wind. As I passed through, it was almost as if those big blades were going to chop me up. They appeared to be descending upon me. They were there because the wind can blow a lot of good electricity as well as blowing cars and motorcycles off the road, but I survived.

With all the travel across the country, I should have gotten soaking wet. However, the first rain I encountered was between Palm Springs and Los Angeles. I also had rain near San Francisco, but I never stopped. I was going so fast that my luggage didn't get wet. Because of the spaghetti-like interstates in and around Los Angeles, I failed to turn a couple times and had to go off into residential areas to find my way back.

On Saturday, May 26, I was up while it was still dark and headed for San Francisco with 110 miles to go. I did not go into the city the night before because it was Friday, and heavy traffic was everywhere for the Memorial Day weekend. I decided to hold off until Saturday morning when things would be quieter. It was very cold, and having traveled so far in extreme heat much of the time, it was surprising. It was as uncomfortable as the heat had been, and I was not wearing my leather trousers—just blue jeans with my leather jacket. I arrived at Terry's home by eight o'clock that morning.

I spent most of Saturday getting reorganized, parking my motorcycle, and deciding to relieve myself of some of the things I had taken that I really didn't need. I decided I would travel fewer miles per day on the next phase and have more time for social interaction with alumni, friends, donors, veterans, and anyone else with whom I might make contact. I had traveled 3,600 enjoyable miles on the first leg, meeting deadlines and averaging roughly 425 miles per day.

The stage was set to begin the second phase of my thirty-four-state circle. I would return to San Francisco on June 16. I had less baggage and would travel a couple hundred miles a day rather than 425. I would see more people and enjoy the northern route, which would be new to me. I left my motorcycle and flew back to Richmond after ten days on the road to catch up on responsibilities there.

This second phase of my travel around the perimeter of the Lower 48 would take me to Milwaukee, Wisconsin. I did begin that day, but with a problem. When checking for all the necessary items to carry with me, I realized I did not have my driver's license, which covered my motorcycle as well as my automobile. I do not know what happened to that important piece of documentation.

Forty-nine hours after that realization—and 450 miles north of San Francisco—I was traveling without a driver's license. I could not wait in Richmond until Monday to replace my driver's license. Fortunately, I was not accosted by police—and had that been the case, I might have been in jail rather than at a motel dictating this experience along with other things that transpired.

On Sunday, hoping I would not be stopped for any kind of interrogation by law officers, I set out just as daylight was peeking through. My son-in-law Dave and Terry mounted his motorcycle and led me through San Francisco to the appropriate interstates that led me to I-5. I spent that evening about sixty miles south of Eugene, Oregon, at a place called Sutherlin. I had not ridden I-5 north of San Francisco in the past even by automobile, so I was able to absorb a lot of the countryside.

North of San Francisco, a great deal of I-5 was valleys between mountain peaks with all kinds of agriculture, cattle, and fields of hay. There were colorful bushes for miles and miles between the lanes of the interstate. I saw mountains, lakes, and even snowcapped peaks.

I had a scare when I passed a truck by slightly exceeding the speed limit. In my rearview mirror, I saw a police car with lights blinking. I thought, *Here's where I go to jail.* Fortunately, he was either headed for lunch or pursuing somebody far ahead of me because he didn't slow me down or distract me from my progress in spite of the fact I had no driver's license.

On Monday, June 18, I was off early in the morning. I covered the 175 miles to Portland, Oregon. In spite of rain that would come and go, I continued on. I would pull off and fill up with gas, get something to eat, or hide under an overpass. I called alumnus, Walter Schnee, who reminisced about getting a $100,000 foundation grant during my presidency. Because he was leaving town, we could not visit, but the long chat by phone was a good contact.

I talked to Beth Jordan, class of 1974, whose daughter graduated more recently and arranged to join her for lunch. She lives in Gig Harbor, near Seattle, and the rain deferred our lunch about two hours.

After lunch, I traveled to an interesting little town called Cle Elum, Washington, population 98,922. I don't know where they put them all because it looked so small. I had dinner at the Dairy Queen over a banana split that I walked off because it must have been twelve blocks, and all uphill going back.

On Tuesday, June 19, it was cold in the mountains. The highway ran up and down hills. Gradually it warmed up as the sun was brightly shining. I moved beyond the hills with evergreens and towering peaks to flatland with agriculture, cattle, grape arbors, lots of hay, and beautiful straight roads. I made good time getting to Spokane as my first intermediate objective.

I left my hotel on Wednesday, June 20, never expecting to travel five hundred miles but ended up in Butte, Montana. With the time change, it was almost eight o'clock when I arrived. I passed through some very high mountains in several states, some very much like the Great Smokies with lots of pine trees. In other areas, there was hardly a tree anywhere. High-density agricultural areas required a lot of irrigation. From horizon to horizon, there were all kinds of crops, cattle, and haystack piles under shelters getting ready for winter.

June 21 was the longest day of the year, and it was daylight by five o'clock. I was on the road by six. Butte, Montana, was outside my second-floor window, and heavy traffic was coming and going in and out of the city.

On the night of Thursday, June 21, I arrived in Miles City, Montana. For a couple of days, I hardly knew what state I was in. When I left Washington, I went into Idaho for a short period of time before crossing over into Montana in the same day. I was in Montana for two days and headed to North Dakota. I was just minimally familiar with those states, and it was very interesting traveling through them with relatively cool weather and pleasant riding. As I rode east, it became progressively warmer.

On Friday, I found myself in North Dakota, which is very different from the South. In the wintertime, we hear about the deep snow and the cold. Riding through North Dakota in the summer is pure pleasure. The fields are green—even without much irrigation. In some parts, from horizon to horizon, there are not many trees, bushes, or shrubs. The land is covered with hay, cattle, and lots of pickup trucks.

Unlike a few years ago when you saw Toyotas and all kinds of foreign cars and trucks, today you see lots more Chevrolets. In fact, the dominant pickup is the Chevy or the GMC. The big-dude pickup trucks pass me when I'm doing seventy-five—even if they are pulling a farm implement or a trailer loaded with farm products. They hustle all summer to catch up with all they can't do in the winter.

In North Dakota, cattle pastures and fields of corn, wheat, barley were prevalent. The state is defined by its farms and ranches. I learned from conversation that it's cold country and warm people. I would like to experience more of that state in the future.

On June 23, I traveled through the dairy state of Minnesota all the way to Eau Claire, Wisconsin. There was more traffic in Minneapolis and St. Paul. Eau Claire was a little less congested, and at the Best Western, I made calls to alumni with the hope that I might visit or converse.

On Sunday, June 24, I was up early and headed for Madison, Wisconsin. I enjoyed the almost two hundred miles through open country with not much traffic and lots of crops and dairy farms.

On a stop for coffee, I asked a gentleman if he had any relatives who were World War II veterans.

He said, "Yes, my father. He died in the arms of a fellow navy friend when they were having a reunion on a golf course. He had a massive heart attack at the age of fifty-four and died in the arms of his navy buddy." He told me more about how much his dad appreciated his service and how the Greatest Generation really was the greatest. He knew that from his father and what he represented in fighting at Normandy and elsewhere as a sailor hauling troops and doing other good work.

On Monday, June 25, I was up at four. I headed to Milwaukee and the Harley headquarters. In the meantime, I had a call from Betsy and Terry Royals who live in Madison. They are graduates of the class of 1979 and 1980, and they picked me up and took me to dinner. They invited me to come to their home and spend the night, but I decided not to do that because of my schedule. Terry is associated with Direct Supply, and Betsy had just been laid off from her job. They live in Menomonee Falls, Wisconsin, about forty-five minutes north of Milwaukee. On Tuesday, June 26, I checked in early at the Clarion Hotel near the airport in Milwaukee and had dinner with the Royals. I visited the Harley headquarters the next day and had my motorcycle checked in for the twelve days until I returned to complete the journey. I met with several leaders there and went through the museum with Bill Davidson, the head of the museum. I flew back to Richmond on June 28 for twelve days after dinner with the Harley folks.

The third leg of my adventure began on Saturday, July 7. I arrived back in Milwaukee and enjoyed a great surprise. A cool breeze was blowing. When I left for my trip back to Richmond, it had been hot as blue blazes.

At the Clarion Hotel my friend Chris Urban—representing Mike McCann at the HarleyDavidson Company—had delivered my motorcycle the day before. My motorcycle was parked right outside the hotel, and I headed south to Chicago in cool, pleasant, eighty-degree weather.

I was certain that going through Chicago was going to test my capacity to handle the big city. I had tried many other big cities and had succeeded. Going through Chicago on a Saturday was a piece of cake due to the express lanes. Even on a Saturday, there are backups in downtown

Chicago. After the eighty-mile trip to Chicago, I headed east about 450 miles to Cleveland, Ohio.

I overnighted south of Albion College and then went north from the Indiana Freeway into Michigan to visit the campus. I took the Ohio Expressway, continued on I-90 all the way to Buffalo, and spent Sunday night there.

I was up early on Monday, July 9, to go to Batavia right outside Buffalo and to a Harley dealership. I arrived there at six and spent an hour and a half over a McDonald's big breakfast. I waited for them to open at nine o'clock to have my motorcycle serviced, which took all morning.

It had not been serviced for almost ten thousand miles.

While waiting for my motorcycle, I called Bob Bailey in Albany and arranged to stay overnight just north of New York City. Bob is director of the BMW Motorcyclists of Vermont. He had emailed me about my journey after reading a *Richmond Times-Dispatch* article to say he would like to meet me when I came through New York. So, he took a day off and joined me for breakfast at seven and escorted me around the city. He led me through the countryside for a twohour visit that brought me into New Hampshire. I headed north on I-85 to Brattleboro and toward Norwich, Vermont, to visit with Bob and Betty Porter, the daughter of Claiborne Robins Sr.

I arrived there about eleven thirty, parked my motorcycle, and joined them at their home for lunch. We visited Dartmouth and various parts of Norwich, Vermont, the community in which they live. At two in the afternoon, I traveled south on I-87 to Maine. From Maine, I headed south to New Hampshire, spent the night, and caught up with dictating this record of my journey.

On the night of July 10, I stayed at the Hampton Falls Inn in Hampton Falls, New Hampshire, before heading south to Boston. I traveled through Rhode Island and settled in for the night at a Comfort Inn in Guilford, Connecticut. I called a good friend Melvin Reilly from World War II and arranged to meet him in Middletown, halfway between Hartford, where he lives, and where I was staying.

I parked on Main Street in Middletown and waited for Mel Reilly. He was the crew chief with whom I flew as a crewman on the staff ship of the admiral of the Fifth Fleet. A gentleman with a cane who looked like a panhandler walked up to me.

I asked, "Are you a veteran of Vietnam?" He said, "Yes, I am of the Tet Offensive." "Thank you for your service," I said.

He thanked me for mine. All veterans seem to think that being in World War II was different than any other war. He admired my motorcycle and told me about his, and we passed the time until my friend arrived.

Mel and I had met a couple times after the war, and Betty and I had visited with them on our honeymoon. That's how close we were. His wife had Alzheimer's, and he moved into a rest home with her. Things were very different for them but when we came together, we were once again young marines.

We sat outside a café under umbrellas, drank coffee, and chatted for an hour and a half. We talked about all the things we remembered from our life in the marines. We reminisced about flying to Hiroshima and Nagasaki and all over the Pacific. We remembered having trouble with our aircraft, losing our way in the vast Pacific, and what our lives were like in another era.

After my visit with Mel, I headed south and then west and then north to Montgomery, New York, on I-97, a main route between Albany and New York City. I visited the *Choppers* headquarters, the television program that highlights the building of motorcycles. The head public relations person took me through all of their operations, and I had quite an interesting visit with the people who design and build the motorcycles.

After lunch, I started to leave.

The guy in the next booth saw a marine emblem on something I was wearing and said, "Semper Fi." He asked if I would sit and visit with him a few minutes. He was a proud marine of the Vietnam era, and he was amazed that I was a World War II marine circling the perimeter of the Lower 48.

We shared stories of our pride in our Marine Corps service. He picked up my check and wouldn't let me pay my bill. He asked whether the movies of the World War II era, particularly of the Pacific series were realistic. All of the younger marines, no matter what their combat experience might be, think theirs is secondary to marines in World War II.

Tim Davis of the Greatest Generations Foundation set up an interview with Fox News in New York City, but we concluded that, because the time was uncertain, we would bypass New York and wait for them to call me back later for some special program if they were interested. I passed through New York into Pennsylvania and finally to Philadelphia and a little bit beyond. I overnighted at the Marriott.

On the local roads, there was a stoplight every block or so. Every few hundred yards, there were residential areas. I couldn't make very good time, but it gave me an opportunity to visit Princeton University. Along the way, I visited many colleges and universities. I also discovered colleges, universities, and extensions of state schools.

At the Marriott, I covered my motorcycle because rain was predicted. On Saturday, July 14, I uncovered my motorcycle in the rain. I pulled under a shelter because I couldn't take off in the pouring rain.

I rode out of Philadelphia after waiting out the rain. It was about eleven o'clock. It would stop briefly and start again. I took off with the hope of outrunning it. I just kept moving, and once I outran the rain, I had a nice overcast sky for the rest of the day. On I-95, the cities and metropolitan areas have heavy traffic.

I found a place where I could wash my motorcycle since it was much in need of that. I wanted to get it looking decent for my ride into Richmond on Monday morning, July 16.

I was just south of Washington and relaxed a bit as I headed to Virginia. I arrived in Fredericksburg and relaxed for the rest of the day.

Monday morning was cool, and I arrived in Ashland by eight o'clock for the Cracker Barrel breakfast with my motorcycle friends. They escorted me back to Westhampton Lake at the University of Richmond by ten. The media was there for a news story and a video.

My journey ended on my eighty-sixth birthday, July 16, 2012. In twenty-five days, I rode 9,200 miles through thirty-four states around the periphery of the United States.

# IV

## A MODERN-DAY PAUL REVERE

While attending a conference of the Spirit of '45 in San Diego in 2015 concerning the recognition and celebration of the seventieth anniversary of the end of World War II, the planning of a convoy of World War II vehicles was mentioned. Someone suggested that a vintage motorcycle might escort the column. One thing led to another, until my name, my World War II ties, and my motorcycle were mentioned. That led to a suggestion that a motorcycle trip across country by a World War II veteran announcing the coming of the seventieth anniversary of World War II could be an effective means of highlighting the occasion.

Shortly thereafter, I was invited to ride my motorcycle some six thousand miles from one coast to the other, making everyone aware of the seventieth anniversary of the end of World War II. I would, in a sense, be a modern-day Paul Revere shouting, "The British are coming." This time, friends and allies would help celebrate the anniversary. While Paul Revere was on a horse, I was to be on a hog. I was carrying a message to highlight the seventieth anniversary of the end of World War II on August 14.

Seventy years ago, with millions of troops, I was poised and ready to invade Japan from Okinawa. But, as if the impossible had intervened, two atom bombs were dropped. That circumstance changed history and allowed me seventy more years to live. I was afforded the opportunity, at age eighty-eight to mount my Harley and remind all of our citizens throughout the country of that anniversary and its significance.

My message was that we should acknowledge, memorialize, and celebrate with pride our country's success at forestalling the dictators who would have dominated the world. My message was that we should recommit ourselves to the patriotic spirit that we had seventy years ago, that we should educate our young people to an understanding of what it takes to have a free country, that freedom is not free, and that we must stand ready in the face of those who would stifle our freedom to defend it at any cost.

That was the spirit in which I set out on my mission. My motorcycle was my means of getting from point A to point B, but it also had another purpose. Because I was in my eightyninth year, was riding on two wheels, and was traveling six thousand miles over a full month, people would take note and listen to my message:

1. First, I was representing the University of Richmond as it participated with the State of Virginia Legislative Commission in cooperation with the Spirit of '45, carrying a message of tribute to WW II veterans in commemoration of the seventy-fifth anniversary of the end of World War II. From Virginia and throughout the nation, a host of dignitaries and veterans would gather on December 10 at the University of Richmond to pay tribute to veterans. The Virginia Commission would sponsor the event and at least one other signature event each year in locations across Virginia involving statewide partners, leading to the seventy-fifth anniversary of the end of World War II.

2. I was carrying a flag honoring Admiral Isaac Kirk, killed in action on the USS

   *Arizona* when Japan attacked Pearl Harbor. The flag would be flown over the Capitol until given to me for transporting from coast to coast and back to Washington DC. It would be sent to Hawaii for the seventy-fifth anniversary commemoration of the attack on Pearl Harbor on December 7.

3. My ride would awaken American's awareness of the true meaning of Memorial Day and the importance of honoring the memory of those who made the ultimate sacrifice in the service of their country.

4. I would be promoting awareness of the efforts of Medal of Honor recipient, Woody Williams, to erect at least one public memorial honoring America's Gold Star families in each state by 2020. Woody is the last surviving member who received the Medal of Honor on Iwo Jima—where the largest number of any battle received the Medal of Honor.

5. I would represent the Spirit of '45 as the national spokesperson.

6. I would represent the Greatest Generations Foundation as the national spokesperson.

7. I would lead the parade in Washington DC with the American Legion Motorcycle Riders and others on Memorial Day, May 30.

8. I would engage the collaborative known as the National Parks Service to form activities related to veterans in their service to our country in the San Diego area.

9. I would be escorted throughout the country by the American Legion Riders and the Patriot Guard Motorcyclists.

10. My ride would be known as, among other things, the second Annual Memorial Day Ride for American's Gold Star Families.

11. I would be celebrating my ninetieth birthday.

My beginning date was established as April 23, 2015, through Memorial Day. The American Legion Riders would provide escorts selectively along the way to guide me to people and places throughout parts of the country that were unfamiliar to me.

On the afternoon of April 22, I met Bob Christie and his American Legion Riders to accompany me from Richmond, Virginia, to Quantico, Virginia. We overnighted at the Ramada Inn. We enjoyed the evening over dinner at the Globe and Laurel and then had a good night's rest. I was up about five on April 23, got everything in order, and rode into the Quantico Marine Base at seven. I had been stationed there seventy years earlier after the war. That was also where I had my first motorcycle, a 1943 Harley.

The Richmond Virginia American Legion Riders joined me on the morning of April 23 at the Museum of the Marines after I attended the eight o'clock flag raising at the headquarters of the Crossroads of the Marine Corps. A video taken there by the American Legion set the stage for my long ride.

I was met by the press, especially the American Legion media engaged in preparing a video and a story for *American Legion Magazine*. The Marine Corps had a reporter there who told me that his mother attended Meredith College. A colonel, the chief of staff at Quantico, joined us for the flag raising.

In the parking lot of the Museum of the Marines, I was welcomed heartily by marines from many conflicts. The Richmond Legion group escorted me as far as High Point, North Carolina, and a group from Kings Mountain escorted me into Charlotte.

The heavy traffic that afternoon would have been a disaster without the American Legions Riders. They had planned everything and led me right to where I was supposed to go. I was met by newspaper reporters and a host of others waiting to see the motorcycles.

I enjoyed a pleasant evening over dinner with Harriet Thompson, a ninety-three-year-old marathon runner, and her son, a chaplain in the navy serving the Marine Corps. My leathers, while unique to the setting, nonetheless enhanced the dinner conversations.

Harriet escorted me through traffic to the Hyatt where they had arranged an overnight stay for me. Originally, I was to stay at a retirement home. The King's Mountain American Legion Riders were supposed to meet me at nine o'clock the next morning, but I waited an hour and left without them due to a mix up. I was not able to join with the Georgia or South Carolina riders and traveled to Atlanta on my own.

I rode, stopped, ate, and rode, stopped, and looked at my maps and my written directions for how to get to the Holiday Inn. My room was provided gratis for the evening. Larry Roberts, my contact, had expected me to arrive much earlier. He informed me that he would meet me at nine thirty on Saturday morning, April 24, which gave me a good deal of satisfaction because he was going to lead me through the city.

I reorganized to a certain extent and then followed Larry to lunch. After returning to the hotel, he shared the news that I was to move back into my room for another night. The folks who led me from Richmond to Quantico and on to High Point, Bob Christie and Denis Graffum, were going to join me with a pickup truck and a trailer to take me to the other side of the bad weather and tornadoes so I could begin riding again.

Bob and Denis traveled most of the night and planned to sleep through noon. They escorted me on the next part of my agenda, and we bypassed some of it due to the weather. We visited the Museum of Coca-Cola with Ray and Ellie Williams, both World War II veterans of the navy.

Donna Garbs, the national chair of the Gold Star Organization, joined us. The museum was a delightful experience. We all went to lunch at a popular spot for college students in Atlanta.

When I was ready to check out with everything in hand, Larry Roberts explained that the hotel had extended my stay another night because the weather was threatening and dangerous. I canceled my activities for the day and stayed put. My luggage on my motorcycle and some of my clothing had become wet, and I went through a drying process.

Due to the weather, we missed having contact in Birmingham with Fran Carter, founder of the American Rosie the Riveter Association, and her daughter, Nell Brandom. On Sunday, April 26, we bypassed Birmingham and headed to Monroe, Louisiana, which was about four hundred miles. We also canceled our meeting with Nell Calloway, the daughter of General Chenault, the executive director of the Chenault Aviation Military Museum.

In Tyler, Texas, a wonderful group of enthusiastic individuals hosted me at the Atria Willow Park. It was a home for the more mature persons, but it was a delightful place. I spoke there for about an hour, answering lots of questions. I was escorted by the American Legion Riders. I moved on to the Dallas/Fort Worth Cemetery, a beautiful place where we had a wreathlaying ceremony.

From Tyler, Texas, it was spitting rain and was uncomfortably cool riding during the day on Monday, April 27. In the evening, I stopped at the Days Inn to rehabilitate myself and get rid of the chills. After a good night's sleep, I was on my way to Abilene, Texas. I had hoped to arrive by day's end, but because it was chilly and raining, I decided to stop about an hour before Abilene.

On Tuesday, April 28, I departed for Pecos, which was about 243 miles and about five hours. I stopped in Midland to visit the Commemorative Air Force, which used to be the Confederate Air Force. Next was Pecos, Texas, and Las Cruces, New Mexico. I dined with the New Mexico Honor Flight Organization and enjoyed the excitement of conversation about the veterans' monument visits.

I left for Tucson after a wonderful evening with David and Deborah Melcher, chairmen of the Honor Flight of Southern New Mexico and El Paso, Texas. We had a nice turnout, a nice dinner, and an afternoon of conversation. The road to El Paso, 450 miles, had a speed limit of eighty miles an hour, which I used to the benefit of time. A motorcycle group met me in Benson, between Las Cruces and Tucson. An American Legion group led me to the interstate toward Yuma, and I stayed overnight at the marine base.

The weather was accommodating, cool in the morning and hot during the day. Everything went well with the motorcycle, and I was enjoying the challenge, the ride, the people, and the pleasure.

The next morning, the Marines Leatherneck Motorcycle Club escorted me to their meeting place. A few hundred people and breakfast offered a pleasant period of relaxation before a hundred motorcycles led me into San Diego for a party at the Harley-Davidson dealership. I shared my mission of highlighting the seventieth anniversary of World War II and the importance of recognizing our veterans.

The next day, I visited the aircraft carrier *Midway* and spoke to other marines. We laid a wreath at the Miramar Airbase Cemetery where I was once stationed. We visited the Marine Recruit Depot, MCRD, where I was in boot camp seventy-one years earlier.

I had committed to giving the commencement address at Campbellsville University in Kentucky and flew back to Richmond for one day to check my mail and then on to Campbellsville before continuing my journey as a modern Paul Revere. My motorcycle was undergoing a fifty thousand-mile service in preparation for the 3,500-mile return to the East Coast.

Upon returning to pick up my motorcycle, a whole host of motorcyclists from the Leatherneck Motorcycle Club accompanied me to the City of Lights. In Las Vegas, we had another party with the Harley-Davidson dealership. I spoke about my mission and emphasized the Gold Star mothers. During World War II, for every son lost, there was a gold star in the window. Some had two or more gold stars.

I met with parents who had lost sons and daughters in recent wars and had gold stars in their windows. I tried to educate young people in schools and colleges about what the gold stars were all about. Occasionally, I had to give a little history lesson about Paul Revere and his ride.

After a night at the famous Bally Hotel in Las Vegas, I was up bright and early to meet another host of riders to escort me to Denver. After a five hundred-mile ride, we overnighted in Grand Junction. I had breakfast with Gold Star parents.

Everywhere I went, I met with the press, television, and radio. I spoke numerous times because people wanted to hear from me. In Denver, I had press, radio, and television for two days and met many veterans. A police escort led me out of Denver the next day.

From Denver, I traveled to Nebraska and rode through a downpour for several hours. The rain subsided as I reached Iowa. I was joined for dinner with the couple who were to accompany me to the governor's office the next morning. That meeting proved to be a delightful experience.

After meeting the governor, I moved on to Marseilles, Indiana, to meet Diane Nowak of the Dignity Memorial Organization. We had a high school band and parade, and I was able to share my story.

I went to Indianapolis and visited the American Legion Headquarters. I also visited the race track and met Juan Pablo Montoya who had won the Indy 500 race the previous year. We were free to visit cars being serviced.

I was escorted to Cincinnati for Bruce Heilman Day. I was given that recognition for what I was doing. I spoke at a dinner that evening for several alumni of the University of Richmond, and Terry joined us.

Next, I traveled to Louisville, Kentucky. As in many cities I visited, I was met by the Kentucky Highway Patrol. Motorcycles escorted me to La Grange. I grew up nearby in

Ballardsville, and the La Grange police and Kentucky Highway Patrol met me at the county line. A proclamation was read by the mayor and another from the county judge. A luncheon at the Oldham County History Society provided a speaking opportunity. I also visited the mayor of Louisville and had dinner with a group there. It was just like old home week being in Louisville and La Grange since I knew my way around and saw old friends.

The next day, I had breakfast and spoke to the residents. I headed for Richmond to unload the heavy weight from my motorcycle before going on to Washington for Rolling Thunder and the Memorial Day parade, which was to be the culmination point of my ride as a modern-day Paul Revere.

Along my journey, I met so many warm and friendly people and engaged in so many activities with receptive people and warm spirits. As a World War II veteran, and an eighty-nineyear-old man, the younger people thought I was "cool." Some of the older people thought I was "crazy," but it was a grand adventure. I am happy to share it wherever I go. It was my message to remember that we would celebrate the seventieth anniversary of the end of World War II on August 14. By its ending, we terminated the killing that was transpiring everywhere. We celebrated so much at the war's ending that we killed six of our own through the celebration of firing everything into the air and its impact on coming down.

My journey proved to be popular wherever I visited as the messenger representing those who fought and died for freedom in the world. The mayor of Shreveport declared the day of my visit E. Bruce Heilman Day and noted that I, as a veteran and rider throughout the country, was highlighting the significance of August 14, 2015, as the seventieth anniversary of the end of World War II, a worthy act on my part.

The director of Veterans Affairs at Dallas Fort Worth Cemetery gave me a certificate of appreciation for my commitment to veterans. The Illinois Department of Veterans Affairs issued a certificate of appreciation for lifting awareness and honoring Gold Star families. The Cincinnati mayor proclaimed it E. Bruce Heilman day with the purpose of identifying my service in raising awareness of the seventieth anniversary of World War II.

The county judge in Oldham County and the mayor of La Grange gave citations naming May 19 Dr. E. Bruce Heilman Day and made me an honorary citizen. The mayor of Louisville named me an honorary citizen of Louisville for my journey in honor of the Spirit of '45 and the veterans of World War II. So, accepting for the veterans and all those who escorted and followed my journey, I applaud the dedication to the purpose of highlighting the seventieth anniversary of the end of World War II and the Spirit of '45.

When I arrived back in Richmond, I was quick to get rid of the heavy weight on my Harley. I stayed overnight to catch up on my laundry and my telephone messages. I traveled with some American Legion Riders from Richmond to Washington DC. We checked in for three days of activities, including Rolling Thunder and the Memorial Day activities. I was the lead motorcycle in the Memorial Day parade, spent three days with the American Legion leadership, and rode with a lot of interesting people.

# V

# JOURNEY TO ALASKA

The bravest are surely those who have the clearest vision Of what is before them
glory and danger alike, And yet notwithstanding, go out to meet it.
*—Thucydides*

**Routing Details For The
Fairbanks, Alaska Trip of
E. Bruce Heilman
Leaving Richmond June 8, 2014
and
Returning to Richmond on or about July 16, 2014**

I leave Richmond early on June 8, a Sunday, and ride west on I-64 to Louisville, Kentucky, approximately 570 miles which I will likely complete in one day and overnight in the area. The next day, Monday June 9th I will visit in that area, friends, alumni, and the Oldham County History museum for some publicity and photographs for the Fall Veterans Gala.

Sometime on Tuesday, June 10th, I will leave Louisville on I-64 en route to St. Louis approximately 258 miles then through St. Louis on I 70 to Kansas City, another 250 miles, a total of 508 miles, where I will overnight and visit an alumni couple.

On the morning of Wednesday, June the 11th, I will travel I-29 north to Omaha, 189 miles and on to Sioux Falls South Dakota still on I-29 approximately another 181 miles a total of 370 miles to overnight.

On Thursday the 12th from Sioux Falls on 1-90 I will travel 350 miles to Rapid City, South Dakota where I will stay overnight.

On Friday the 13th of June, continuing on I-90, I will travel to Billings, Montana 376 miles where I will overnight.

From Billings, Montana, on Saturday, June 14th, I will (not interstate) take Highway 3 to Great Falls, Montana estimated to be about 250 miles where I will overnight.

I'll visit the Big Sky Harley Davidson Dealership at 4258 10th Avenue South, Great Falls, Montana 59405 to have new tires put on my motorcycle on Sunday the 15th of June. I will have e-mailed and confirmed the appointment. While there, I will visit an alumnus.

On the 16th of June, Monday, I will travel north to the Canadian border on I-15, 120 miles. I will cross the border just below Coutts and go into Highway 4 in Canada. I will follow that to Route 3 at Lethbridge then Route 2 at Fort MacLeod 96 miles and to Calgary another 105 miles, a total of 321 miles. I should be able to get there by the evening of Monday the 16th and overnight.

On Tuesday, June 17th, I leave Calgary and travel north on Route 2 to Edmonton – 181 miles and then Route 14 to Valley View 114 miles, a total of 295 miles so I will overnight there.

On Wednesday, June 18th I will travel 73 miles to Grand Prairie and another 79 miles to Dawson Creek where I enter the Alaskan Highway taking route 97 to Ft. St. Johns 47 miles a total of 199 miles where I will overnight.

On Thursday, the 19th I take Route 97 to Fort Nelson 263 miles and overnight.

On Friday the 20th, I go Route 97 330 miles to Watson Lake and overnight.

On Saturday, June 21st I take Highway 1 to Teslin 150 miles and from Teslin still on Highway 1 I continue 100 miles to White Horse a total of 250 miles where I will overnight.

On Sunday, June 22nd, from Whitehorse on Highway 1 I go 102 miles to Carmack and 221 miles to Dawson City a total of 323 miles where I will overnight on Sunday June 22nd.

On Monday, June 23, I travel route 9 for 108 miles to Chicken and another 66 miles on Route 5 and on Route 2 106 miles to Delta Junction a total of 280 miles where I will overnight on the evening of Monday, June 23rd.

On Tuesday, June 24th I will travel 96 miles to Fairbanks and settle in for 2 days getting my Motorcycle serviced and speaking and then heading south to San Francisco leaving Friday, Jun 27 with the following itinerary.

I travel south on Friday, June 27th to Delta Junction 96 miles on Route 1. Then Route 2 continuing 108 miles to TOK. Then on route 2 80 miles to Port Alcan and 20 miles to Beaver Creek for overnight after travelling 304 miles and here I will overnight.

On June 28th, I take highway 1 184 miles to Haines Junction. Then on Route 1 I travel 100 miles to Whitehorse where after 284 miles I overnight.

On June 29th, on Route 1 I ride 38 miles to Jakes Corner, then on route 1 I travel 61 miles to Teslin. I go 146 miles to just before Watson Lake and turn right (south on Route 37) toward Dease Lake 146 miles. After 391 miles I overnight at Dease Lake.

On June 30th on Route 37 I start a 602 mile ride on Cassiar and Yellow Head Highway to Prince George. I will overnight about half way or where I find an acceptable place.

On July 1st still on Route 37 I complete travel to Prince George to overnight.

On July 2nd, on route 97 I ride 149 miles to Williams Lake and 126 miles to Cache Creek, a total of 275 miles and plan to overnight.

On July 3rd on route 97 I hope to do 120 miles, then 50 miles for the US border and Route 15 and 25 miles to Bellingham and 91 miles a total of 286 miles to Seattle for overnight.

From there on July 4th I ride to I-5 807 miles and will overnight a couple of days through July 6th, leave my motorcycle and fly back to Richmond on July 7th to celebrate my 88th birthday on July 16th. Then I retrieve my motorcycle and take a route to be chosen back to Richmond.

I will have spent 28 days on the road and approximately 10,000 miles.

PASSING THORUGH THE TUNNELL AT TOP OF
MOUNTAIN ON I-70 COLORADO

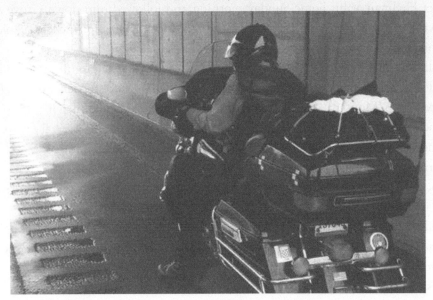

Yes, indeed. This has become an annual ritual for Heilman, who in recent years has rumbled across and around the country, setting foot (and wheels) in the Lower 48, missing only Alaska, which explains his current destination, and Hawaii, which is next on his bucket list.

Of course, Heilman is not your average eighty-seven-year-old. His body is fit, his mind is sharp, and he has an insatiable hunger to keep moving, to keep seeing unfamiliar places, to keep making new friends. He travels constantly in his role at U of R and is a member of numerous boards around the country. As an "old marine," as he put it, and as a spokesman for the Greatest Generations Foundation, Heilman goes on these motorcycle excursions as a way to honor and represent his fellow World War II veterans on the road—and to prove he can still do it.

And it gives him something to look forward to—sort of like when he enlisted in the marines as a scrawny teen to get away from 3:00 a.m.

wakeup calls to milk cows on the farm where he grew up in Kentucky.

"I joined the marines so I could sleep late," he said with a laugh.

He missed that one by a shade, but his view of needing something that "excites you and interests you" is spot on.

"Life is a series of anticipations," he said over a hearty breakfast of country ham, eggs, and baked apples at his first stop after leaving Richmond, at a Cracker Barrel in Waynesboro. "You're always looking ahead. My desire to do things is my anticipation. One of the things I don't think about anticipating is retiring."

We met Heilman at his home Sunday morning and followed him down Grove Avenue as western swing music blared from the bike's CD player, to UR's campus where he picked up a couple of bikers he knows from First Baptist Church.

We followed Heilman into the mountains as far as the West Virginia line and said our goodbyes as he headed toward Louisville and his first overnight stop. By next Sunday, he expects to be in Great Falls, Montana ("We have one Spider there!" he said), and then it's on to Canada—Calgary and Edmonton—and Alaska. He's meticulously plotted out his itinerary not only to the point of knowing where he will stay and eat each day, but also so as to avoid all gravel roads. He hopes to arrive in Fairbanks by June 24.

All along the way, he'll meet with World War II vets, UR alumni, and anyone else he happens upon. The man is the ultimate networker.

Before he left home, his daughter, Terry, had one more reminder for him: "Phone home."

"My mom always made him check in every day," she said. Her mother—and Bruce's wife of sixty-five years—Betty Dobbins Heilman died December 2013.

Bruce said he would call.

He also said his anticipation will not end with Alaska or even Hawaii.

"I anticipate trading in this motorcycle at ninety-one," he said, "and getting a new one with a twenty-five-year loan." That way, he said, he'd have to hang around that long to pay it off so as not to hurt his credit rating or reputation.

What kind of Harley would he want to ride in his tenth decade? "The newest, biggest Harley I can get," he said with a smile.

And that's the way my Alaska ride was stated by Bill Lohman. But because some of the finer aspects of the journey could not be experienced or observed by Bill, I will provide a bit of filler even with pictures actually en route and on the scene.

To Bill Lohman's version, I will add the following commentary from Facebook from Eileen Arentz and family members whose paths crossed mine in Canada at a filling station:

I met Mr. Heilman traveling to Alaska this summer with my two sons. We had stopped in Rancheria, BC for fuel and breakfast. He was there at the gas pump. I couldn't help but notice that Harley with the Marine Corps emblem on the gas tank. We introduced ourselves, and I was still hoping my hand had no permanent damage after our handshake when I quickly found out about his riding to Alaska from Virginia. I was driving from Atlantic City, New Jersey in a van with 203,000 miles and must admit to being a little concerned of our chances of success. Meeting anyone riding a motorcycle across the country and up to Alaska was amazing to me.

It casually came up that he was riding there for his birthday and when I asked him which one, I was again amazed that he was going to be eighty-eight years old. I asked him how he didn't have anyone along with him for such a long, memorable adventure, and I was told he couldn't find anyone in their eighties or a World War II veteran who would ride along. That—finally—was understandable. He allowed me to take several pictures of him and that great Harley, and he gave me his business card. He departed about twenty minutes before us, and the weather had taken a turn for the worse with steady rain falling when we got underway.

There was no shelter for miles and miles ahead, and I kept an eye out for him possibly pulled over waiting for a break from the rain. I hoped we would see him, pull over, and spend some more time talking while getting him out of the rain. It didn't happen, and I wasn't surprised as my late dad was a marine, and marines don't let some rain keep them from their mission. E. Bruce

Heilman became my inspiration for the rest of that trip when I would think of where he might be or look back at those pictures. I was checking them out today, still feeling inspired. Who wouldn't be? Happy birthday and safe travels for your eighty-ninth! Ed Arentz, Ventnor, New Jersey

\*\*\*

I have been a higher education administrator for sixty-five years in four states and in every defined senior position, including two presidencies, but I have gotten more acknowledgment for my motorcycle riding in my eighties than all the years of work in higher education. I am asked to speak more after my travel through all fifty states— totaling some seventy-five thousand miles— than my sixty-six years in higher education. I am delighted to share something from the wonderful experiences that have been mine as a result.

Each time I get astride my Electra Glide and face the wind, it cleanses my mind of the mundane. The world becomes my domain as the road opens before me and the ribbons of asphalt provide a panorama of nature, offering visions of grandeur and aromas of the area.

### June 8: Richmond, Virginia

My journey to Fairbanks, Alaska, began in the garage at 4700 Cary Street in Richmond on Sunday morning, June 8. At daybreak, I was attaching last minute add-ons and dictating equipment to record what transpires along the way. I have shirts, shoes, rain gear, and much else strapped to the back of my motorcycle. Every nook and cranny is filled; even the back seat is full of enough to last me a month. There are blankets in case I sleep out, rain cover in case it's pouring rain, and books and maps to cover all options without putting undue weight on the motorcycle.

At five thirty, daylight is breaking through. The press has joined me for a few pictures before we ride out to Waynesboro and the Cracker Barrel for breakfast. It's a beautiful day, but it's already hot. I am traveling with no leathers except a vest identifying me as a motorcyclist. I have company on the early part of what will be over five thousand miles to Fairbanks, Alaska.

Bill Lohmann, a *Richmond Times-Dispatch* writer, and Bob Brown, a *Times-Dispatch* photographer, along with David Beach, a Richmond Law School graduate, accompanied me to the West Virginia border. Journeying with me also until Charlestown, West Virginia, were Billy Buford and his grandson Dylan. The latter two joined me for Big Macs and milkshakes at McDonald's before parting. They were going north, and I was going south at Charleston, West Virginia.

It started raining beyond Virginia and did so through much of Kentucky, but that didn't slow me down. With my motorcycle's cruise control on seventy, it just blew over the windshield and nothing in the back became wet. I arrived in La Grange after completing 565 miles the first day.

**Monday, June 9: Day 2**

On my second day, I arose to a good breakfast, feeling refreshed, and was joined at nine by B. J. Senior and his wife. Vicki informed me that I was to be joined at the local Cracker Barrel at eleven by a host of supporters with whom I had enjoyed friendships over the years. They were there to welcome me and send me off on my long journey to Fairbanks. Included were high school chums, family, representatives of the Oldham County History Society, and TV, radio, and newspaper reporters. I had already been highlighted in an early morning television report as a hometown boy at age eighty-eight passing through the area en route to Alaska by motorcycle.

I spoke to the group and had lots of conversation with friends including my son, Tim, the director of Development at Campbellsville University, and the president and First Lady of my alma mater. After more interviews, lunch, and filling up with gas, I headed for St. Louis. I was in rain for a couple of hours before settling in at a Best Western for a good night's sleep.

**Tuesday, June 10: Day 3**

On Tuesday, it was still raining. Nevertheless, I headed out in what was supposed to be sporadic rain. I cruised at seventy, and the rain blew around me. I headed for Kansas City after allowing the morning traffic to slow a bit. I found my way from Route I-64 to Route I-70, traveling in the rain much of the way from St. Louis to Kansas City. Near Kansas City, I turned toward Liberty, Missouri, and to the home of Ann and Chris Sizemore, graduates of the University of Richmond, and I spent the night. He is the former president, and she the First Lady of William Jewell College in Liberty, Missouri.

## Wednesday, June 11: Day 4

On Wednesday morning, June 11, the president of William Jewell joined us for a hearty breakfast. I repacked my Harley, traveled I-29 north to Omaha, 189 miles, and on to Sioux Falls, South Dakota, still on I-29, another 181 miles, for a total of 370 miles.

I became lost coming out of Omaha and missed I-29, which also occurred when I left Liberty, Missouri. Being in heavy traffic with an overloaded motorcycle is not good. When asking for directions, one person would say, "This is the way to get back to I-29." Someone else would say something different.

A young lady saw that I was still confused, but her simple direction confused me even more.

I turned around and parked in front of a little church.

The young lady pulled in behind me and said, "Follow me." She led me right out to the interstate.

Following a young lady under other circumstances might have gotten me in trouble, but the motive was honorable. She really saved my day. I usually find somebody helpful rather than anyone who is hurtful.

## Thursday, June 12: Day 5

Quite early in the morning, I headed out through Kansas and transitioned into Nebraska. I touched a little bit of Iowa and then headed to South Dakota. I covered several states that day.

I remarked to myself—there was no one else to talk to—about the beauty of everything. Corn was coming out of the ground, and the hayfields were green. Adequate moisture made it all possible. With flatlands and straight highways at seventy-five miles per hour, people were passing me like I was standing still—they must have been doing ninety.

I met two World War II veterans—one a marine and the other army—and we drank coffee and talked about things we didn't talk to many others about. It was interesting to see them dressed in casual clothes. One was ninety-three, and the other was in his early eighties. It was hard to fathom that they once dressed in starched uniforms and fought a war. Those veterans are who I represent as I travel with University of Richmond Spiders, motorcyclists, and whoever else shows up along the way—in addition to those I have planned to meet.

The day proved to be clear with a little sprinkle here and there. After a pleasant ride, I pulled into the hotel in Sioux City, South Dakota. I had traveled a little over 1,500 miles without incident. It started raining hard, but the outer cover of my luggage dried by morning. I traveled up I-29 through Omaha to Sioux Falls and then west to Rapid City, South Dakota, about 350 miles, then I continued to Billings, Montana.

**Friday, June 13: Day 6**

At noon, I stopped at a MacDonald's. I had covered about 150 miles and needed a cup of coffee. In line, a gentleman said he was in the army and recognized that I was a World War II marine. When I said I was just stopping off for a cup of coffee, he said to the lady, "Give him a cup of coffee."

En route to Billings, I had very cool weather. I put on my full leathers and extra thermal underwear, but it was still chilly. It started to rain briefly, and the wind became fierce.

**Saturday, June 14: Day 7**

At breakfast on my seventh day, I met a couple from Taiwan. They had lived in the States for twenty years and found my travel experience amazing. After it warmed a bit, I stopped for a banana split—having almost been blown off the road.

A couple rode up on a motorcycle and sat at the table next to me. I inquired how best to get from Billings to Great Falls, Montana. They explained the best route and then mentioned that they were from Sheridan, Wyoming. They talked about their business, which they said was thriving. I remarked that I had spoken to the Rotary Club there.

"If you ever go back through or if you pass through in the future, stay with us. We have plenty of accommodations," they said.

After finishing my banana split, I decided to stay overnight before heading to Billings. I could make my motorcycle presentable for when I arrived in Great Falls to visit an alumnus.

It had been rainy, cold, and windy, but those weren't negatives. I just kept riding. I put on my leathers to keep out the cold and enjoyed the straight-as-an-arrow highway at seventy-five miles per hour. The greenery all over that part of the United States was fantastic. I was still on schedule and doing well.

**Sunday, June 15: Day 8**

I left Billings in a downpour. I could have stayed there until the rain stopped—or I could get on my motorcycle and start riding. I took a bit of advice from a lady at a coffee shop who lived near where I was headed. She put me on the right path across country rather than on the interstate to Great Falls.

I keep looking for something to prove that not all is right with the world. However, I keep discovering the opposite. For example, when checking in at the Fairfield Inn in Great Falls, I had a discount certificate with which I had hoped to save a few dollars. Looking over the coupon and conferring with a companion, the lady said, "I can reduce the price if you would like."

After discovering that her rate was sixty-nine dollars per night, almost forty dollars less than my coupon, I put my best persona in place and said, "If you ladies are so gracious as to save me almost forty dollars a night below the coupon, I will forgo the coupon and stay two nights so that Mr. Marriott will still get his $109."

It poured down rain for two solid hours, but I just kept moving. We—my luggage and I— pulled into Great Falls, found shelter, and parked next to a Dairy Queen that advertised a fivedollar lunch special. I was hungry, cold, and windblown by that time, and I ordered the fivedollar special, which proved to be a hot dog with chili, French fries, a cup of coffee, and a marshmallow ice cream sundae.

In Great Falls, I had a wonderful time with an alumnus and his family. Fred had breakfast with me at the hotel, and we took my Harley to the Big Sky Harley Repair Shop. We picked up the rest of the family and went to a buffalo jump where they used to run buffalos off the cliff to kill them for the buffalo meat. This was followed by a visit to a museum.

The weather was fine even though it had been rainy and cold. I purchased a new back tire, had the brakes serviced, and changed the oil, filter, and other things that needed to be done in preparation for crossing the border into Canada with a refreshed Harley.

## Monday, June 16: Day 9

On Monday morning, I reached customs after traveling about a hundred miles. I had enjoyed two good days in Great Falls and was rested for my journey. I continued up the road for a hundred miles or so in clear and fairly warm weather, and then it changed to rain.

Near Calgary, I visited the World War II Museum of the Lancaster Bomber. A gentleman who had visited me in Richmond had invited me to be his guest at the museum. I was shown all of the airplanes and then, with a helmet on my head, placed in the turret of one of the bombers to do what I was trained to do as a tail gunner in the marines. I managed the fifty-caliber machine gun quite well. It reminded me of my younger days in training.

For the rest of the afternoon, I traveled through heavy rain. Because the traffic on the outskirts of Calgary was so heavy and the rain and night were falling, I pulled into a service station to wait out the downpour. That was around six o'clock on June 16, and I was still there at three in the morning on June 17. I had remained there all night. After standing around for hours, an employee asked if I would like a chair.

I slept in that chair for several hours, and the employees brought food, coffee, and hot chocolate. They would not charge me. They treated me as someone needing assistance. The most important thing was having the chair because I couldn't go anywhere in the rain and in the dark of night. I just had to wait it out. Finally, there was a break in the weather about six, and I was back on the road carrying food donated by friends from my overnight station.

**Tuesday, June 17: Day 10**

I traveled north to Edmonton 181 miles to route 14 and to Valley View to overnight. I was looking forward to sleeping in a bed that night. After 3,200 miles, my Harley was still performing well. The sun was shining, and after a full day of travel, I slept well in a bed.

For the most part, I rode alone, but wherever I stopped, motorcyclists chatted with me, gave me information about how to go around a city, and told me the best routes based upon their personal experiences of having ridden to Fairbanks. Most were just generally friendly and offered helpful information and advice.

**Wednesday, June 18: Day 11**

The roads became gravel after they were torn up. Particularly after rain, they become slippery mud wallows that tested even the most skilled riders. I had the most comfortable motorcycle anywhere on the road—even if it wasn't made for that kind of road service.

The Alaska Highway is 1,520 miles in length and stretches from Dawson Creek to Fairbanks. Travelers are advised that on a narrow bridge to yield to trucks for they will not yield to you. I yielded. Dawson Creek, British Columbia, is supposed to be where it all starts. Since I was traveling from Richmond, Virginia, almost four thousand miles away, I had started much sooner.

While all that I experienced is available by automobile or tour bus, it could not be as spectacular or as challenging as taking the tour on two wheels—even though the latter certainly carries more risk. The people along the way were hospitable, and so were the conditions, generally speaking. Even the adventuresome risks are hazards that stimulate the mind, palpitate the heart, and alert the rider to the reality of serious consequences of failure to remain fully alert. Riders must stop while wild animals cross the highway—and stop some distance away from the animals.

If I get lost and can't find my way back on my own, I'm usually found. On my way to Dawson Creek, I was traveling nicely on Route 2, a four-lane highway, at seventy miles per hour or more when I saw a sign that said Dawson with an arrow to the left. I immediately went that route because Dawson Creek was where I was headed. With my usual literalism, I followed precisely what was there on the sign. That usually got me into trouble—and it did again. I went onto the wrong road, which was a serious error.

I thought I was being trained for the Alcan Highway, and that it would make it easier to transition. The farther I traveled, the less I was assured that it was the right road. The sign had clearly said "Dawson." Finally, after seven or eight miles, I came to a two-way stop where there were no directions. I went to the right, but it was becoming more country with more farms. The road still had blacktop but just barely. After ten or fifteen miles, I knew I had made a mistake somewhere.

I was lost. I pulled off onto a little patch of blacktop, got off my motorcycle, and pulled out a map to reassure myself of where I was.

A pickup truck came out of an intersection, and I waved it down. "Sir, I'm looking for Dawson Creek, and this is not Dawson Creek." He didn't understand me at first.

I asked about the Alcan Highway.

He said, "Well, you go up here so far, and you turn left, then you go so far, and you turn right." After a few more attempts to direct me, he said, "Follow me. I'll take you to the road leading to where you want to go." We must have traveled fifteen miles or more when he stopped, got out of his pickup, and came back to my motorcycle. He told me to follow the road to Dawson Creek. There is no one more reassuring than a farmer in a pickup truck.

Still straddled on my Harley, I could only reach out to shake his hand and tell him that he did me a great favor that was deeply appreciated. I said, "If I could dismount the motorcycle without it falling over, I would give you a hug."

As he turned away, he seemed to feel that he could get along quite well without the hug.

The day before, I had left a key card from my checked-out motel room on a table as if it had been forgotten. I was preparing to ride out of the parking lot when a man rushed out to tell me that I had left my key on the table next to his. I keep finding that I am the beneficiary of a lot of goodwill.

I saw my first moose grazing the highway. I also experienced lots of mosquitos. The roads were good compared to what I had anticipated. I had two or three short bursts of rain and lots of sunshine. All in all, it was a good day. I would be in Watson that night. I was about four thousand miles from Richmond and getting closer to my destination.

**Thursday, June 19: Day 12**

I spent the night at Walton Lake. The town was quaint, and the hotel was pretty archaic, but it was fine and the best thing there. It was the biggest town within miles. The next town would probably be similar. The folks were nice, the food was acceptable, and my dirty Harley was humming right along.

I had breakfast at five after spending the night at Valley View and headed to Grand Prairie and Dawson Creek. I took the Alaskan Highway to St. Johns. I was ahead of schedule, but I was getting closer areas where the roads were a bit wavy and a little rough.

The day was as bright and cheery as the past several days had been gloomy. That was not true of myself; it was just the weather being cold and rainy or sunny and warm. I anticipated wet weather in Alaska and Canada, but it looked to be not quite as bad as I thought.

While the Alaskan Highway has been reworked, graded, straightened, and paved, in isolated populations, there remained some very wild sections that were tamed only to a certain degree. It was still an uncivilized part of the continent. The romance and challenge that adventurers look for can still be found. It's not the getting there that is the objective; the process of going is the experience. Anyone who has actually traveled the Alaskan Highway will never forget the journey—and will be a member of the "I Did It Club."

From Richmond to Fairbanks was about five thousand miles, much of it consumed by eight states. The long and enlightening adventure is only an opener for the real thing—an experience of a lifetime. One must risk the little anxieties that come with any unusual adventure.

Mine were not the best kind of tires to venture on a muddy, slick, rocky road. Most of the other motorcycles I encountered had rubber-cleated tires. While most of the literature told me that the road was paved with the qualifying sentence "except where they are rebuilding and repairing," it should have declared "much of it is unpaved while rebuilding and repairing."

I rode 350 miles through curves that went around in circles up the mountains, and it was a slow day. Toward the end of the day, the road straightened out. I came into the only populated place with amenities that allowed me to get through on my phone. I tried to call Joy, my assistant, a number of times, but I couldn't get a connection. In a more metropolitan area, I was able to use the phone to update Joy on my travels.

I saw Father Bear, Momma Bear, and Baby Bear on the side of the road and saw bears twice more. None of them were in the way, but the mountain sheep, also known as rams, the animals with the big curly antlers, tended to get onto the middle of the road. I had to stop twice. I also saw a groundhog and a few antelope.

The countryside was beautiful but isolated. I took few photos of the animals because I don't want to pull my Harley onto the shoulder, which was made up of loose gravel.

That day, perhaps above all others, reflected the Alcan Highway experience. It typified much of what the literature personified and experienced travelers to Fairbanks had expressed to me. The road was everything all in one from rather good to very bad—from seventy-five miles per hour to creeping along just enough to have the momentum to hold the motorcycle on its two wheels.

From White Horse to Haines Junction, I made relatively good time with little to deter me from constant progress. However, from there to Beaver Creek, there was a continuing story of permafrost swells, which, without flag markers to warn of the next hazard, the pothole or valley or normal repair could lead to despair in a sudden dip or peak. On one such swell, while on a straightaway, which were few and far between, I came upon a swell at seventy miles per hour. It lifted me airborne, and I came down so hard that the shock absorber dented the tailpipe.

The real challenge was the many miles of road repairs with delays and disruptions. A four-wheeled vehicle could navigate the muddy mixture of gravel and filler, to keep down the dust, when sprayed with water. A motorcycle with deep-routed cleats was nominally safe from losing traction. For those like me with turnpike tires, it was hazardous all the way. Only the heavy weight of my bike and all its contents kept the traction adequate to prevent it from sliding out from under me.

While AAA assured me that I would be traveling on hard-surface road, much of it was under repair. Between the repair areas, it was a roller-coaster ride. When I wasn't riding on high alert, a dip would sometimes lift me from my seat along with my heavy load of luggage, which was both an asset and a liability. In fact, I lost two bolts out of three holding my windshield in place from the vibrations that it withstood.

So, as I fretted, my Harley just took it all in stride. On one occasion, it seemed to say, "Boss, I took you successfully through the entire Lower 48, and I'll get you through this. Just remember that compared to getting to Hawaii for your fiftieth state, this is a piece of cake."

Through forty-nine states, my Harley had been my close companion with no failures of any kind along the way. I'd come to trust it as my home away from home. As long as I kept its tank filled with fuel, I'd move from one grand experience to another. I trusted that marvelous machine.

The ride was almost like the dangerous ice I encountered in Colorado. The bikes with cleated tries could go almost anywhere and wouldn't slip so much.

The rain gave me an opportunity for a two-hour visit on the front porch of a quaint restaurant. My motorcycle was uncovered and soaked, but I took the opportunity to cover my luggage to keep it from getting thoroughly wet.

I was the only Harley parked there. The rest of the bikes were dirt bikes with big cleats for the backwoods and elsewhere. My Harley is not really made for muddy and treacherous roads. I was in some hazardous situations, and I really needed tires with cleats. It was a tough road while it was being worked on, especially when it was raining. There was mud, loose rock, and gravel. My motorcycle and leathers were a mess.

While the rain held me up for two hours, I was blessed to sit on the front porch of that restaurant and converse with two French loggers. They were riding dirt bikes from Canada to South America. I had the most interesting conversations.

My hotel in Whitehorse, the Elite, was not as elite as the name suggested. It was a bustling city. I arrived in the late afternoon—with traffic that was going home. It was really hard to get around, but I enjoyed the evening and had a good night's rest. I didn't see any animals. It was raining, and I guess they stayed home.

**Friday, June 20: Day 13**

The sun was shining at two o'clock in the morning as I prepared to cross back into American territory. Customs was nineteen miles from Beaver Creek, and I spent the night there. My thirteenth day would take me through most of the remaining territory in Canada. I had traveled 4,500 miles to get to Whitehorse, and I had six hundred miles to go.

I was adopted by a busload of American tourists who seemed to show up at the same overnight and eating places as me. I definitely was not traveling alone. There were motorcycles everywhere, but most were fit for the condition of that part of the world and not the turnpike. I decided to stick to the Lower 48 where I had accumulated forty-six thousand miles over the past four years.

**Saturday, June 21: Day 14**

I'm on my way to Port Allen and back in the United States for breakfast. I have difficulty using my iPhone in this part of the world since Wi-Fi is unavailable along the way. I've learned above all else to keep fuel in the tank since it may be a long walk alone with the animals. Today, I encountered a brown bear and photographed a herd of wild horses roaming the highway.

In Alaska, it is daylight for most of the night, which takes getting used to. My bike and leathers are caked with mud from the road repairs, but it will all wash away upon the completion of this grand experience, which I will remember for all of my days. I stayed overnight in a room just opened in Beaver Creek. It didn't have a phone or TV, but I enjoyed the quaint little room and bed.

**Sunday, June 22: Day 15**

In my many travels over forty years, totaling 144 countries, I have found that I am always happy to return to the good old USA. Not even our warm and cordial neighbor Canada could change that, especially after the tribulations of managing my Harley over the massive road repairs. So, with twenty-two-hour daylight fast approaching in Alaska and a good night's rest, I was wondering if it was day or night as I prepared to hit the road.

No one was awake except me, and nothing was open. No coffee, much less breakfast, was to be had. With the cover off my Harley and everything tied down to offset the permafrost swells and dips, I took off in broad daylight for the border crossing, which was only nineteen miles away. I only discovered, after upping my speed to about sixty miles per hour, that it was cold even though the midnight sun was shining.

**Monday, June 23: Day 16**

When I arrived at the American side, I was informed there was no coffee or breakfast for ninety miles. My hands were already cold, and there was no warm invitation to come inside. It was business as usual from the warm side of the window. After a few miles and a cold road ahead, I stopped on the side of the road to get the blood flowing back into my fingers. There was absolutely no one on the highway as I warmed my gloves with the engine heat.

I finally came upon a grand restaurant and a full American-style pancake, egg, and ham treat. Beyond the meal, sitting by a sunny window to defeat the chill, I was happy that there was Wi-Fi. I called family, which I had been unable to do the prior day.

Once in my home country, I realized that not much of the Alcan Highway is in Alaska. After a couple hundred miles, I would be in Fairbanks. The road was an improvement, and it was warmer, but the permafrost swells guaranteed that I would continue the roller-coaster ride. The miles of chuckholes and gravel and unpaved conditions were so severe that only one of the bolts for my windshield was still holding. One more would leave me with the wind in my face— literally. Heaven forbid.

**Tuesday, June 24: Day 17**

With 5,100 miles completed and prayers answered from all those who shared their concerns for my safe journey, I was thankful to plant my flag in Fairbanks. I read stories in the local paper about celebrating the twenty-two-hour daylight. I rode through the city, which was larger than I expected it to be, and I found a lovely Best Western just across from the Harley-Davidson dealership. I would have everything serviced and the cakes of mud removed after dealing with the unloading and cleaning all the luggage strapped to every available support area.

Packing to go on any journey, while exciting, is never as satisfying as settling in after a strenuous effort at getting the most out of an adventure, and that I did. So, restored and alert to options that evolved over many hours of contemplation while riding, I realized that it is two o'clock in the morning. It could just as well have been two o'clock in the afternoon.

On June 25, I lunched with a University of Richmond alumna, Dr. Annemarie Billingsley, in Fairbanks. I serviced my bike and arranged to ship it back to Richmond rather than repeating the long ride back. I decided to ship my motorcycle and save the travel time for riding back on the East Coast with friends.

The difference in the cost of shipping and airfare, motels, fuel, and food was minimal. I had not considered the unexpected experiences of the Canadian road repairs and the challenges of negotiating a heavy-duty turnpike bike over such treacherous roads.

**Wednesday, June 25: Day 18**

My agenda, which many were following, had me arriving in Fairbanks on Tuesday, June 24. With lots of daylight and persistent riding, I managed to arrive on Sunday, June 22. I enjoyed some relaxing time to visit, rest, clean off the mud, and arrange for the return of me and my bike to the East Coast.

I confirmed plans to leave Fairbanks on Tuesday evening, June 24, at 8:30 p.m., and arrive in Richmond at 10:10 a.m. on Wednesday, June 25. One of my many children and grandchildren would be there to meet me. My motorcycle would travel separately. The bike and I would be reunited later.

It took eighteen days to complete the adventure of adding the forty-ninth state to my accomplishment from age eighty-three to age eight-eight. The challenge has been met, the claim has been filed, and the flag has been planted.

Perhaps this is small compared to landing on the beach of Okinawa at age eighteen, but for a marine of seventy-one years, it defines the principle that it's not over till it's over. The Marine Corps has an adage, collectively, selectively, or individually: "Don't quit until the mission has been achieved." Alaska was not handed to me on a silver platter. Perhaps a better analogy was that I fought a good fight and finished the course. I rode into town on a muddy Harley, proud and unbending, ready for the next encounter on my bucket list.

Without my faithful friends following me every day, the journey would have been much less interesting. I may travel alone, but I was actually accompanied by a host of well-wishers. I would do it all over again at age eighty-nine if it were left to do. It is one hill not left for me to climb—and one more city is now taken. The magic of goodwill has prevailed. After I called three trucking companies to arrange to ship my motorcycle—finding bureaucratic delays with all three places—I fired up my Harley and rode to the Harley dealership.

While waiting through a line for servicing, I was confronted by a clerk, a highly tattooed codger, who asked my problem.

I said, "I need to have that mud removed from that thing and see whether there is a Harley underneath. Then, within the time I am in town—with a plane to catch tomorrow night—I need to have a contract for shipping it to Harley-Davidson in Richmond, Virginia."

"No problem." He started to sing as he tackled the thing that couldn't be done, and he did it. He drove me back to my hotel and told me to call him the next day to be picked up and transported back to Harley. After that, he would drive me to the airport.

I ended my adventure in broad daylight at 12:30 a.m. on Tuesday, June 25, and prepared to reenter the world as it was supposed to be—half light and half dark—so that I can tell when to lie down and when to rise up. As I signed off from the Alaskan adventure to face my accumulated stack of mail and the resulting world of work, I remembered the words of Edwin Markham: "There is a destiny that makes us brothers, none goes his way alone, all that we send into the life of others, comes back into our own."

\*\*\*

# VI

# THE RISKS OF LIVING AN ADVENTURESOME LIFE

*Do the things you fear, and the death of fear is certain.*
*—Ralph Waldo Emerson*

We can never go back and correct our mistakes. In almost one hundred thousand miles of riding my Harley over twenty years, I have experienced several mishaps that could have been fatal. Fortunately, none have been. Each has provided a lesson in how not to engage in risks of similar kinds in the future.

My first lesson leading to my safety record over the years took place at age fourteen as a farm boy in Kentucky. Believing that a motorcycle was simply a large bicycle, I mounted a Harley of an older friend without his knowing that I had never ridden a motorcycle. I twisted the throttle and let off the clutch, and the motorcycle suddenly reared up on its back wheel and took off through a board fence. I was petrified but survived to ride again, never anticipating that motorcycling would extend into my ninety-third year and beyond. I would always remember the power—and the danger if uncontrolled—in the hands of the rider.

My second experience at riding a motorcycle was five years later as a marine home from combat in the South Pacific and the occupation of Japan following World War II. That ride resulted from an automobile mishap following a sixty-day furlough from Louisville, Kentucky, to Quantico, Virginia, with a fellow marine. We were on a mountainous, curvy road in West Virginia when we had to slow down for road work. The flagman was frantically waving us on as a truck bore down behind us with little evidence of stopping.

Before we could respond, he plowed into the back of our car, which sent us careening off the mountain road and into an almost bottomless crevice. We rolled and tumbled until a big tree stopped our descent. From my back in the upturned car, I watched as the truck cascaded over the same path and directly toward our car. Having remained alert and alive up until then, I wondered whether the coming collision could be survived. As it tumbled, a door of the truck flew open and ejected a body that landed on our car just ahead of the truck. When the crashing of metal ceased, gas fumes entered my nostrils. After a momentary silence, I realized that the front and back doors of our four-door sedan were blocked. Any minute the whole wreck could burst into flames. Looking for a safe option, I saw a light from the trunk, which had been ripped open. With all my strength, I was able to move my buddy toward the opening and out of the car. Others lifted him up the mountain to arriving vehicles.

The road crew and others descended to the wreck and gathered two dead bodies from inside and under the truck. With the assistance of others, I was able to get my buddy up the hill and to an emergency vehicle for his ride to the hospital. While I was bruised and bloody, I chose not to be conveyed to the hospital. Instead, I hitchhiked on to the marine base at Quantico. Two weeks later, my friend arrived on base with no serious injuries. His insurance paid in full for the car, and we went to Washington and purchased two Harley-Davidsons. We concluded that motorcycles were less dangerous than automobiles and easier to exit in an emergency.

During the remainder of my enlistment, I enjoyed the freedom of having that motorcycle. After I enrolled in college and got married as a freshman, it became clear that I could not afford both a wife and a motorcycle. That feeling of loss was offset fifty years later when I was a father of six, grandfather to eleven, recipient of a PhD, and a university president. My wife gave me a brand-new red Harley-Davidson Road King. She told me I was now old enough to have one. I was seventy-one years old.

Twenty-one years later, I am ninety-one years old. I rode the red Road King for ten years, accumulating twenty thousand miles, purchased an Electra Glide Ultra Classic Harley in 1981, and added eighty-five thousand miles. After a hundred thousand miles, I am healthy and well, but I still recall each minor accident or serious mishap.

My first mishap happened when I stopped at an intersection too near to the edge of a high blacktop curb. I lifted my right foot from the brake and reached for solid ground, which was about six inches lower than anticipated. As I leaned to reach solid ground, my foot went beyond the high curb—and my motorcycle followed me to the ground. Unhurt, I could not have prevented its falling or lift it from its prone position. Fortunately, two women at the other side of the intersection saw it all and came to my rescue by helping me lift my motorcycle. No harm was done to me or my motorcycle, but as pride usually goeth before a fall, mine went with the fall.

Not long after learning that lesson, I was at a red light in heavy traffic. I was in front of a very eager truck driver. When the light changed, he accelerated and plowed into the back of my motorcycle, pushing me into the middle of the intersection and nearly ejecting me from my seat.

Fortunately, I was unhurt. The three thousand dollars in damages was covered by his insurance, and I was whole again. It was another lesson learned.

Following thousands of miles all over the United States, coast to coast, and just three days before leaving on a five thousand-mile ride to Fairbanks, Alaska, I was at an intersection within two miles of my home in Richmond. After looking both ways—but blinded on the left by a parked car—I accelerated quickly. Just as I was into the street, a car from that blind spot suddenly appeared. With front and back brakes at maximum, I was thrown off balance and was grounded by the back fender of the car. The motorcycle and I were on the ground. As assistance emerged to upright both me and the motorcycle, I prepared an accident and damage report for the police. I had my bike dispatched for repairs.

My great concern was for my scheduled ride to Fairbanks in only three days. I asked the Harley mechanics how rapidly the damage could be corrected in order to preserve my schedule. I was told that parts such as the front fender could not be procured in time to meet my schedule. Pressed for a way to preserve my plans, I was told they could temporarily straighten the out-ofline parts so that I could meet my deadline. So, with a covering of mud hiding the scratches, I managed to ride five thousand miles with no recognizable damage to those unaware. Thus, my Harley served me well until it was repaired when I returned. On my hazardous journey to Fairbanks, it was covered with so much mud that no damage could be seen.

On a cross-country ride, a deep hole was almost my undoing. Pulling into a filling station on a rainy day with several other riders, I rode directly into what I perceived to be a mud puddle. It hid a large hole that almost swallowed my motorcycle. At fifteen or eighteen miles per hour, the jolt almost threw me off my seat. Only with great effort did I come out of the huge cavity still astride my upright motorcycle. A month later, I still felt the muscle pain caused when that hole jerked my front wheel. The handlebar twisted so quickly that the muscles in my left arm were twisted. Surprisingly, it wasn't broken. I was lucky not to end up in the hospital.

As I continued to learn from my experiences, I faced a totally unanticipated circumstance between Laramie and Cheyanne, Wyoming. It was a rainy, foggy, cold morning with heavy clouds below the mountaintops. I can still sense the feeling of uncertainty during the fifty-mile ride. I was afraid it would be my last one if a stopped vehicle or a wandering animal appeared out of the mist. The white line was my only guide and my only assurance that I was on the blacktop. It was a miracle that I survived that fifty miles without losing my motorcycle, myself, or both. The eighteen-wheeler trucks with fog lights passed me so fast they almost blew me away.

On May 8 and 9, 2013, I dealt with my most frightening experience on a motorcycle en route to Denver. Coloradoans say, "If you don't like the weather, just wait a while—and it will change to something else." I witnessed that fact several times on I-15 in Utah and I-70 in Denver. It was supposed to be spring, but on a summit of six thousand feet in Utah, I encountered snow all around me. The interstate was wet, and the temperature was near thirty-two degrees. I worried that ice would make traveling at any speed on a two-wheeler unsafe, and I was exceedingly careful.

In Denver, I was planning to meet some veterans and some media people. I was expected to travel almost six hundred miles on May 8. However, two hundred miles short of that, a heavy rain came down. I pulled off the interstate at three in the afternoon and parked under the shelter of a filling station in a town called Parachute. This was an appropriate name because I dropped in since it was the only available place to get out of the rain. After waiting three hours, filling up with gas, and seeing no break in the weather, I checked into a motel to wait overnight for a change in the weather.

At six o'clock on Tuesday morning, there was no rain. I set out for the two hundred-mile trek to Denver. By seven, I was within 115 miles of Denver. In Georgetown, I decided not to risk my life and that of my motorcycle any further.

After leaving the safety of Parachute, the interstate trended upward—and the temperature moved downward. My hands were getting very cold, and I could see a great deal of snow ahead on the upper levels of the mountains. The temperature was below forty, and it was getting colder even with a thermal shirt, a leather jacket, heavy jeans covered with leather pants, socks in leather boots, a completely closed helmet, and a heavy scarf.

In Vail, Colorado, only the median strip and the ski trails were clearly visible. I was where I never wanted to be—in snow country. The plows had pushed it over to the side of the highway so I could not pull off even if circumstance suggested that I should.

After passing through Vail and assuming that things would improve, I was going higher and higher. I did not see any other motorcycles on the interstate. Each mile suggested to me that it could not get any worse, but it did. My windshield was being sprayed by all the cars and trucks that passed me by. I realized, by reading the signs, that I had only wished things would get better: "Put On Chains When Flashing." I had no chains, and I had never heard of using them on a two-wheeled motorcycle. If I could have turned around, I would have. I knew the hazards of where I had come from and hoped they had not gotten worse.

The sleet mixed with slush, and I had to practically stand to see ahead. The sleet accumulated on my helmet. When I lifted it, the slush covered my glasses. I knew I was in trouble, and the road kept trending upward. The snow continued to get deeper, and the signs got worse: "Icy Road Ahead" and "Ice In The Tunnel Ahead." I was losing traction. When I saw a slice of asphalt just before the tunnel, I risked stopping without using my brake. I was afraid of having my wheels slide right into the mound of snow on the side. I used paper towels to clean off the frozen windshield, my helmet, and my glasses.

The vehicles with four or more wheels sailed by. Even at reduced speeds, they covered me with more slush. Snowplows were in place alongside the highway, and the signs told me to reduce my speed even more. I was already down to ten miles per hour or less, mostly in second and third gear.

I was riding a two-wheeler on ice in a tunnel—with heavy vehicles all around—and feeling the insecurity of lack of traction. I was scared. In the marines, we said, "Courage is not the lack of fear but being in control of fear." I was in control as I tested the limits of the balancing act on that motorcycle. I was fearful all the way through. I was concerned about sliding against the wall with no control on the ice. When I emerged, I saw another sign: "Slow Down, Ice Buildup." A patrol car by a fallen motorcycle was clear evidence that a motorcyclist ahead of me had hit the wall. Why not me? Perhaps it was because of my longer and heavier motorcycle and my ability to keep it upright.

As I was going down the other side, the slush was frozen. The interstate was frozen ice, but I had no choice but to keep moving. I was almost certain that I would slip off and land in the drifts or between the heavy trucks.

It became a challenge to sit forward and lift myself so that I could see over the frozen windshield. It reduced my control of the bike to the point that I seemed to bounce from one ice patch to the next. The other vehicles had their own control challenges in a strong downhill pull against the snow and ice. I wished that I knew how to extricate myself from the most hazardous situation I had ever encountered on my motorcycle. However, as the old adage says, "Things are a lot easier to get into than out of."

As I headed downhill, conditions improved. The worst was over. I was moving more and more below the snow line. My fingers and hands were numb. I needed to get off the road, warm up, and judge what to do next.

I exited in Georgetown and called my contact in Denver. He told me to stay where I was since they were having a heavy weather warning and rain. I settled in until the next day.

The next morning, the rain had stopped. Since snow was falling heavily, I waited three hours before taking off. After a while, a few hailstones fell. When it began to drizzle, I stopped, cleared my vision, and drank some coffee. I wanted to be alert. I arrived in Denver around noon, and I found out that all my plans had been canceled.

I had never been so packed with road dirt, and my motorcycle had never been so dirty.

Even my leathers were covered with road debris. My muscles ached from fighting to keep that Harley on the road. Even touching the brake would have sent me into a slide. Instead, I controlled my Harley by shifting up and down.

I checked into a hotel to recover. I was so relieved to be free from a hazard that could not have been anticipated by one unfamiliar with the area. It was not at all what I perceived to be a possibility in the spring. The lesson I learned would prevent me from getting into a similar dilemma until I traveled to Fairbanks to celebrate my eighty-eighth birthday. Helen Keller said, "Life is a grand adventure—or it's nothing." We don't quit doing things because we get old—we get old because we quit doing things. But none of that matches my ride to Alaska or my airplane crash on Iwo Jima.

The greatest risk to motorcycles and motorcyclists is automobiles. Auto drivers often treat motorcycles as if they didn't exist. Further, coupled with alcohol, the combination makes them the greatest enemy of motorcycles. I have been fortunate because I have observed how vulnerable motorcyclists are, especially if coupled with alcohol. At a minimum, it is four wheels against two and a cover of steel around one and open space around the other. I observed firsthand the consequence of a contest between alcohol and automobile that I shall never forget. I can still see the cloud of dust and the following silence except for the one still living, but dying, of the three persons involved.

I was at an intersection of two busy highways in Lexington, Kentucky. About a full block from the intersection, a car passed me at a high rate of speed. *Reckless driver*, I thought. To the left, coming perpendicular to the automobile's trajectory, a motorcycle appeared with a man and a woman—with the right of way. They entered the intersection, perhaps not even seeing the speeding car entering the midpoint without slowing down. The car ran broadside into the middle of the motorcycle—sending the motorcycle and two bodies into the air. The car rolled through a fence and into a weedy pasture.

I was so close, and it was almost as if it were a movie. I was the only one to observe the impact and reach the bloody scene. From under the upside-down car, I heard moans and cries and immediately smelled alcohol. I turned to the weeds and found the two motorcyclists. The man was dead. The woman's body was grotesquely mangled, and parts were separated by the impact.

Finding both deceased, I went back to the upturned car. With the help of others, we rolled the car over. The trapped driver was sobering up to the reality of his dilemma. As I lifted his head, he said, "I don't want to die. Get a priest." An ambulance took him to the hospital.

The next day's newspaper noted that three people were killed in the accident. After the funeral, I visited the family and shared my conversation with him in his last hours. No wonder I never fail to give the automobile and driver the benefit of the doubt. In fact, on motorcycles and in automobiles, alcohol is frequently present, creating the most serious hazard on the road.

A very unusual accident took place when I was traveling with the individual responsible for the American Legion Riders group in Virginia. A man who had perhaps as much experience riding a motorcycle as anybody in Virginia had ridden for years without an accident. He was escorting me from Indianapolis to Richmond. After a veteran's activity in Louisville, he accompanied me to Cincinnati for another meeting. From Charleston, West Virginia, to Beckley, West Virginia, was about fifty miles.

That section of I-64 is mountainous, and it is popular with trucks. Seventy miles per hour is the maximum. About halfway to Beckley, I was leading my escort. At about seventy miles an hour, I went around a truck and came back into the lane in front of the truck. I kept my eye on the rearview mirror, looking for my escort to show up—but that didn't happen. After a few miles, I began to be concerned. On that busy highway, there was no good place to pull off. I couldn't imagine why he would pull off unless he was forced off or had an accident.

I was waiting on the side of the road when a lady pulled over and asked whether I was riding with the person who just had an accident. "I probably am," I said. "I was not aware he had had an accident."

She said, "He was lying on the road, and his motorcycle was up against the concrete divider."

If he had an accident at seventy miles per hour, he probably couldn't have survived.

She called 911 because my phone was not working at that time.

Another couple pulled off and wanted to know whether I was riding with a person who had an accident. The guy said, "He is standing up back there."

I was immediately relieved that he was standing up. I was certain he must at least be badly hurt. I couldn't go back because I couldn't get to the other side. It was a madhouse. The ambulance took him to the hospital in Charleston, and I went on to Beckley.

Even though it was only four o'clock, I decided that I couldn't go much farther. I was so shaken. I checked into a motel, and in the process of parking on a hill, my motorcycle fell over. I incurred $3,600 in damage. I had to get help to set it up. The next morning, I rode to Richmond. My friend called and told me the only thing they could find wrong with him was a sprained little finger—and they were discharging him.

A couple of days later, on the way to his home on the coast, he called and said he had his trailer and his motorcycle, and he was doing fine. I went from believing that he couldn't have survived to realizing that only destiny holds the outcome when you are riding a motorcycle. I was relieved, and I had learned another lesson.

In 1945, we were refueling on Iwo Jima in a R4D twin-engine transport. We boarded an army transport R4D and hitched a ride back to Tokyo. As the radio operator on my plane, I was responsible for the loading and making sure the plane was balanced. Some intelligence officers were hitching rides back to Japan. The plane was filled, and I was in the back. The officers were piling heavy gear in the back of the plane, and no one checked it's weight or balance. As the loader on my plane, I used a slide rule to be sure the plane was balanced. I was a corporal, and I assumed the high-ranking officers knew better than I did.

So, with my seatbelt tight and the engines revved, we started down the runway. We were at full speed for takeoff, and the airplane lifted into the air over the ocean. At about fifty feet in the air, the tail began to lag. The pilot revved up the engines. All of a sudden, the plane was hit by a crosswind on the right. The pilot realized that it was nosing over, and he cut the engines. It crashed into the left wing, bending it straight up as the plan nosed into the ground propellers, twisted like spigots from digging into the runway, and the whole front end crashed.

The plane, because it was full of fuel, would have exploded ninety-nine times out of a hundred. The young pilot, a second lieutenant, cut the engines so that it did not immediately burst into flames and incinerate us all. It just twisted the aircraft like a tin can. My memory does not reflect precisely the condition of the people aboard the plane, but I got out of there quickly. As a low-ranking soldier, I didn't stand around asking questions and debating why we had crashed. I was fuzzy about how many were taken to the hospital or if any died.

Even though the aircraft was severely damaged, most of us got out of the plane with minimum physical damage. We overnighted again, hitched a ride on another aircraft, and took off for Japan.

In Iwo Jima, I picked up a Christmas card: "Merry Christmas, 1945, Iwo Jima." I still have it. I wrote a letter to my mother to convey my experience, but I tried not to scare her. I just said, "I had an accident."

I am now on record at the Iwo Jima Foundation as an Iwo Jima survivor. I did not land on the beach where many were killed, but I did escape the risk of dying there.

# CHAPTER FOUR
## FAMILY

"All my Family"

"My grandson Christopher and his wife with Betty"

Nothing in life is more influential than home and family. In our society, most everything is centered in this time-honored arrangement. What we witness in our early years affects our lives for as long as we live—whether we like it or not. A father reprimanding his five-year-old son for cramming down his food intended to set him straight. He remarked, "Son, you're a regular pig." The father was reminded of his own responsibility when the little boy asked, "Daddy, does that mean that I'm a hog's little boy?"

The fact is, a pig is a hog's little boy—and neither the pig nor the hog can ever outlive the fact. In spite of what we have done in college or what college has done for us or to us, what we are is more likely the result of our home and family background than because of anything that happened in college. Through education, students may amplify and complement that which they are, but they will seldom become something else.

Students should be honored when they take what they have or start where they are and progress in an excellent fashion, but we should recognize those who have played significant parts in laying the foundations. We must acknowledge the probability that this honor comes because the family and home background that provided the incentive and nurtured the aspiration essential to success.

If we don't know where we've been, how confident can we be about where we are heading? Nothing starts from nowhere. Everything is built upon the past. How can we confidently determine our futures unless we have evidence of our pasts? That is the foundation upon which we build our future. Knowing where we came from gives evidence of where we are going and the direction we will likely take. Only then can our ultimate destination be predicted.

My Family

If suddenly we were lost and in a mental lapse, having forgotten where we were going, people would ask, "Where did you come from?" The road leading out of any community is tied to the road leading in.

History preserved is knowledge perpetuated and projected into the hearts and minds of descendants. By knowing past mistakes, they have the option of selectively planning their future. Those who forget the past are destined to repeat it. This mostly has to do with family, which is the root of our being, our beginning, and our end.

When the stock market crashed in 1929, I was three years old. I was just old enough where my memory was beginning to emerge. Today, things appear serious if unemployment approaches 8 percent. In the early 1930s, it was about 25 percent. In those days, the government had no safety nets such as unemployment compensation to break the fall of people in that circumstance.

However, if I thought the Depression was over for me in the 1930s, I was mistaken. It arrived again after World War II when I married as a college freshman and had five children before finishing graduate school. My wife and I both worked. Her work was interrupted only by frequent pregnancies and looking after the children.

We actually budgeted one dollar a day for food during our early college years. While she worked for ten cents an hour at the five-and-dime store, I worked for about twelve cents an hour at the woodworking shop. I also worked for the A & P as a butcher, from six on Saturday morning until eleven thirty at night and most afternoons while carrying a full course load. This was a godsend because, at the end of a Saturday night, almost everything was marked down because meats, vegetables, and most fruits would not keep until Monday morning. So, we would have a veritable feast on Sundays with our Saturday-night purchases that cost little or nothing.

Much that I experienced in the Depression was also a fact in my early marriage. Betty was a good seamstress. When a dress shirt had a frayed collar, she would remove it, turn it inside out, and sew it back on to hide the wear. From the markdown store, we bought day-old bread, bakery products, and anything else we could get for half price or less.

In the Depression, rather than paying to have shoes resoled, we bought rubber half-soles at the dime store and glued them on the shoes. I remember how important it was to buy boxes of oatmeal that had dishes stored in the oats. That was how we managed to keep glasses, cups, and saucers available. Most people used outdated catalogs and telephone books in the outhouse to save money on toilet paper.

It is often said that the older we get, the poorer we once were as children. So many of the things we can tell are so far removed from the experience of my grandchildren that they find the stories hard to believe. The long underwear we wore on the farm and the knickers we didn't like to wear to school were just two things that embarrassed us then and would make us laughingstocks now. To some, the experience may sound adventurous. We didn't want any part of it, but our grandchildren might be sorry they missed the Depression.

One of the major marketing ploys during the Depression for feed and seed was to put commodities into feed sacks manufactured from brightly colored fabrics. While it was not fine and elegant, it certainly was acceptable to wear for a farmer's family. Polka dot, striped, or flowered, it all added up to beautiful dresses for girls or shirts for boys. In addition to clothing, the sacks and the cloth from them were used for dish towels, tablecloths, napkins, doilies, doll clothes, curtains, and even spreads, pillowcases, and sheets.

A successful entrepreneur shared advice for how to be rich: "Be bold, work hard, marry carefully. You have to be bold in the market but careful when you come down the aisle." While I am sometimes bold and have always worked hard, I should be rich. I did not marry carefully, but I married well. My life has been a joy most of the time.

As a youth, in addition to doing what was essential to help my father with the milking, raising tobacco and corn, and whatever else he assigned, I would earn a little money on the side by helping neighbors. I will never forget the day I worked for five hours at about a nickel an hour. It was hot as blue blazes that afternoon, and my neighbor brought me an Orange Crush, which caused me to think that he was just about next to God. When he paid me my quarter for my five hours of work, he took back a nickel for the Orange Crush. I was crushed, and I have never forgotten it.

Even though I grew up in the Depression, it was not a disgrace to be poor in those days. Sometimes we even took pride in our condition.

We had a great family life, we were active in our church, we were loved by our parents, and above all else, our family was respected in the community because of the integrity of our parents. While working hard was a virtue passed on to the children, studying hard and getting an education was not something that was drilled into us as much as maintaining high moral standards. Measuring up to the rigors of our work schedules was most important of all. Even though I never anticipated going to college or realized what that could mean, I had a vision of getting off the farm. I did just that with the intervention of World War II.

We never had much time off from work, but when we did, we went to the creek that ran through the farm down below the open fields. We would seine for fish, swim to our hearts' content, and sometimes, even with our Dad—though he did not often take off from work for anything—fish over the old stump. That was our Disneyland when we had time to indulge.

On the Fourth of July, we would go to the Kentucky River for a picnic. One year, my older brother almost drowned after being carried too far with the current. Just before disappearing under the water, my father was able to reclaim his oldest child. I believe deeply that poverty breeds ambition—and success breeds success. Thus, a bit of both shows up in recording these pages about family.

# I

# THE MOTHER, GRANDMOTHER AND GREAT GRANDMOTHER

There is but one and only one, Whose love will fail you never. One who lives from sun to sun With constant fond endeavor. There is but one and only one, On earth there is no other. In heaven, a noble work was done, When God gave man a mother.

Our daughter Sandy is a German teacher, and she sent her mother a birthday card to answer the question: "What is a mother?" The card did not cite the author.

A mother is our first touch of tenderness, our first breath of warmth, and our first discovery of devotion. A mother is someone who can find sunshine in every cloudy day. She knows the best songs to sing, the greatest games to play, and all the stories children like. A mother is someone who knows how to put love between a little child and a big world. Her touch can mend our hurts, give us strength, and warm our hearts. A mother is someone who helps without being asked, understands without questioning, and gives without expecting anything in return … But above all, a mother is someone who loves without end. A mother's love and guidance go far beyond childhood … she's a silent partner in whatever we try to achieve, whatever we want to become. Her love is a quiet, constant companion in our walk through life.

At the end, Sandy wrote, "Love, Sandy—and thank you for being the wonderful mother you are."

Yes, the mother of my children and the grandmother of my grandchildren was all of this and more. While living up to all these expectations, she was as good a wife as she was a mother.

\*\*\*

# II

## CHILDREN, GRANDCHILDREN, AND GREAT-GRANDCHILDREN

The following verse from "THE FINEST AGE" by Edgar Guest represents each one of the twentyfive:

And at every age, We can't go back and foul up the things we did right either!
The finest age
When he was only nine months old,
And plump and round and pink of cheek,
A joy to tickle and to hold Before he'd even learned to speak, His gentle mother used to say:
"It is too bad the he must grow.
If I could only have my way
His baby ways we'd always know."
And then the year was turned, and he
Began to toddle round the floor
And name the things that he could see And soil the dresses that he wore Then many a night she whispered low:
"Our baby now is such a joy
I hate to think that he must grow
To be a wild and heedless boy."
But on he went and sweeter grew,
And then his mother, I recall,

Wished she could always keep him two, For that's the finest age of all.

She thought the selfsame thing at three.

And now that he is four, she sighs

To think he cannot always be The youngster with the laughing eyes. Oh, little boy, my wish is not Always to keep you four years old.

Each night I stand beside your cot

And think of what the years may hold;

And looking down on you I pray

That when we've lost our baby small, The mother of our man will say "This is the finest age of all.

Love all whom we hold dear, and precious is the time you share,

So, don't wait for tomorrow—as tomorrow may not be there."

I can't imagine what life would be like without a family. I was a member of a family of seven until age seventeen when I left that experience and amalgamated with and into the United States Marine Corps. For four years, I was in a family that will always claim me even though I was discharged into a college community of veterans on the G.I. Bill seventy-five years ago.

Up to then, I simply moved with the currents of circumstances and had relatively little to do with where I fit in. There was always something or somebody to which I was attached so that there was an identity beyond myself.

As nature took over and presented me with the option of finding my next identity, I fell in love with a coed whose charms and other attributes fostered feelings unlike any other family relationships of the past. So, setting aside the uncertainties—and confident of the ultimate outcome—we married while I was still a freshman in college. Within ten months, we became a family of three. Before finishing graduate school, I had fathered six children and laid the groundwork for what became eleven grandchildren and eleven great-grandchildren. As marriages of our children and grandchildren took place, we expanded to forty members.

When I write about family, I am writing about something that has been a serious part of my life and my partner's life. Every day for the sixty-five years of our married life, the family has been the core of her existence, and joining that family circle each evening was the highlight of my day. Thus, to leave out the family in this extension to my memoirs would be to leave not only a blank space in the book but also a hole in my heart. As the ninety-one-year-old senior member of my clan, it is with great pride and satisfaction that I rank my family as my first priority.

Edgar Guest's verse speaks for me to those of every age in my family circle. Each and all make me proud and represent to me all that they reflect of Betty after sixty-five years of family togetherness.

With such a large and diverse family, living in many places throughout the world, life offers many lifestyle options. With love and appreciation for our families, we hope for the best for each member and wish that our children and their children will follow practices that represent the best of what they learned from us. We use what influence we have to maintain family ties, hopeful that we might set some examples that are worthy of emulation. Much of what they select will no doubt evolve from those who become their day-to-day companions.

Because no one is perfect, it is presumptuous to think of ourselves as exemplary models—even for members of our own families. However, age and experience provide knowledge worthy of passing on to those whom we love. The years teach much that the days never know.

Posted in my datebook is a verse that has, in many ways, set the direction of my life's journey. I pass it on to those following in my footsteps: "Do not follow where the path may lead. Do not follow the crowd or flow with the currents. Go instead where there is no path and leave a trail."

In taking the road less traveled, I have found that the opportunities are greater, the competition less pervasive, and the distractions less disruptive. Certainly, the temptation to fall back into the crowd, take the easy route, and satisfy short-term appetites is always prevalent.

However, the rewards of not yielding are great in the long run.

As I complete four score and eleven years, I can testify that life does not end at eighteen, twenty-eight, forty, fifty, or any other age—including ninety-one. If we prepare ourselves well and seek to live a life directed by purpose, there is no time more satisfying, more fulfilling, more exciting, and more reflective than the here and now. I want to share this—and much else I have learned—with my many offspring. One of the most satisfying days in my life was July 16, 2016—my ninetieth birthday! That is true for no other reason than it connected my past with future ambitions. I shared that occasion with all my children.

At ninety-one, I have good health, have enjoyed a sixty-five-year marriage to a wonderful woman, and have fathered a host of offspring, which is gold for my golden years, contributing to a fruitful life. For me, life is not an empty dream. It continues to offer the satisfactions that are essential to self-fulfillment and personal well-being.

I realize with a sense of resignation that I am within a few years of moving on, as conveyed in words from the poem Thanatopsis, to "that mysterious realm where each shall take his chambers in the silent halls of death." Having had a rewarding life through all the years past, I need not acquiesce to go "like the quarry slave at night, scourged to his dungeon, but, sustained and soothed, by an unfaltering trust, approach thy grave, like one who wraps the drapery of his couch about him, and lies down to pleasant dreams." Following the afterlife speculations of Thanatopsis, I will await my offspring, knowing that, in the meantime, they are loving, living, learning, getting, giving, and seeking as they fill themselves from whatever fountain they seek to drink.

While my own children may have set their pattern and likely will be influenced very little by these admonitions, I offer some guidelines for living to all my grandchildren and greatgrandchildren:

1. Take the road less traveled for that will make all the difference.

2. Dare to be different. The world will respect you more and will recognize you as outstanding because you will stand out. It is difficult to be identified in a crowd.

3. Take time from what you already know about yourself to learn more about your spiritual self. There is a spirit within us whether it has surfaced or whether it is recognized as important. Learn from the Bible all the history that it contains, its social message, its sound advice, from love thy neighbor to the eternal verities of life. Even if you choose not to respond to all the admonitions in the Holy Scriptures, you are ignorant if you are unware of their relevance.

4. Be educated to the fullest. I was and am a simple country boy with little possibility for making an impact beyond tilling the soil. But, with hard work, determination, selfconfidence, and opportunity based upon all of these—and a mate who supported me rather than distracted me—I have been able to reach levels of success not dreamed of prior to building an educational base. Most of my offspring have a much greater opportunity to be lawyers, doctors, ministers, presidents, or tops at whatever they undertake. I know they will not disappoint me and—more than that—themselves.

5. "Never despair" said Edwin Burk. "But if you do, work on in despair." Always look upon the bright side—and you will find your way.

Henry Wadsworth Longfellow was in a state of depression. He was feeling sorry for himself and doubting the worth of life in general. Out of his misery—with an enlightened spirit of belief and resolve from his deeper recesses—came his guiding light, which he shared with the world:

The Psalm of Life

> Tell me not, in mournful numbers, Life is but an empty dream!
> For the soul is dead that slumbers,
> And things are not what they seem.
> Life is real! Life is earnest!
> And the grave is not its goal;
> Dust thou art, to dust returnest, Was not spoken of the soul.
> Not enjoyment, and not sorrow,
> Is our destined end or way;

But to act, that each to-morrow Find us farther than to-day.

Art is long, and Time is fleeting,

And our hearts, though stout and brave, Still, like muffled drums, are beating Funeral marches to the grave.

In the world's broad field of battle, In the bivouac of Life,

Be not like dumb, driven cattle!

Be a hero in the strife!

Trust no Future, howe'er pleasant!

Let the dead Past bury its dead!

Act— act in the living Present!

Heart within, and God o'erhead! Lives of great men all remind us

We can make our lives sublime,

And, departing, leave behind us

Footprints on the sands of time;

Footprints, that perhaps another,

Sailing o'er life's solemn main,

A forlorn and shipwrecked brother, Seeing, shall take heart again.

Let us, then, be up and doing,

With a heart for any fate;

Still achieving, still pursuing, Learn to labor and to wait.

ALL THE FAMILY

We don't have children in selfish anticipation of what they can do for us; we look forward to what we can do for them. That's what family is all about. Nothing is as rewarding as knowing that those we love, love us back. Nothing means more to me personally than the notes I have received from family members that, unsolicited, only children and grandchildren young and older are willing to share. They write what they feel, and they make those to whom the notes are directed feel better because their simple words mean so much.

I have preserved some warm and thoughtful messages from my children and grandchildren to their parents and grandparents over the years. I will never forget how the writer felt about a particular situation at the time. And as I reread them, I also remember the words from Edgar Guest's "The Living Beauties."

The Living Beauties

I never knew, until they went, How much their laughter really meant.
I never knew how much the place
Depended on each little face;
How barren home could be and drear
Without its living beauties here I never knew that chairs and books Could wear such sad and solemn looks! That rooms and halls could be at night So, still and drained of all delight. This home is now but brick and board Where bits of furniture are stored.
I used to think I loved each shelf
And room for what it was itself
And once I thought each picture fine Because I proudly called it mine. But now I know they mean no more Than art works hanging in a store. Until they went away to roam I never knew what made it home.
But I have learned that all is base,
However wonderful the place
And decked with costly treasure rare Unless the living joys are there.

I have tried each year to bring my whole family together although that has become a large order as the numbers have increased. There are so many of them. Five children, eleven grandchildren, and eleven great-grandchildren—plus all the in-laws, husbands, and wives. But when I do bring them together, the responses from them justify every cost and every effort.

The most important communication of all that I received just a few weeks before Betty became unable to write and could hardly communicate. Just a few months before she passed away, I went on an Honor Flight to

Washington, and she wrote a note to me: "I love my marine of sixty-four-plus years. Love Betty." It was in an envelope with another card: "Sometimes good things happen to good people—like when you happened to me. Thanks for the wonderful memories. Love, Betty."

Grandchild

> I love you so much, Pawpaw, and I am so appreciative of everything you and Mawmaw have done for me over the years. There have been so many memories in my life that you have created for me. I hope you know how special that is for me.

A granddaughter, student at U of R:

> I just dropped by your office to see how you are doing and say hello. I hope all is well. Do you want to go with me for breakfast or lunch one day? Call me. I love you.

> Thank you for coming out for Christmas. It is so nice to be lounging in front of the fire with two people I love so much. One thing I cannot thank you enough for is your generosity. You know how much I love to travel and your taking me year after year on your fantastic vacations. It's unbelievable. I am so lucky to have such wonderful grandparents who think I am special enough to join them. You are the best role models and heroes that I could ever have. Thanks for a fantastic Christmas.

> The two of you are the most special and influential people in my life, and I can't tell you how much you mean to me. Because of you I have the most wonderful mother. You have instilled in her morals that she has instilled in me.

> I thought of you and Mawmaw this weekend on your wedding anniversary. I hope one day to have built a marriage and family such as you all have. I could not imagine a better way to live. I love you, and I will see you soon.

From a granddaughter, one of nine students at the University of Richmond:

Dear Mawmaw and Pawpaw, thank you so much for the birthday check. I have loved getting to spend more time with you recently. I am loving Richmond so much. I love getting to go out to dinner with you or just hanging out.

Children

You hid eggs in the yard at Easter, and you bought us little green and blue dyed chickens and white rabbits. You led us whispering as we slowly crept down the stairs at Christmas to see our stockings filled with candy and nuts and fruit and little cereals. You drove all night to get to Grandma and Grandpa's where we would dress the cats in doll's clothes, and you took us fishing so we could catch fish to eat for dinner. You took us on your business trips to faraway places and to the state fair and the drive-in movies. And Christmas parades and the park for cookouts and around the city to see the Christmas lights. These were a few of our favorite things.

Words can never convey our appreciation for all that you do and the generosity that you share not to mention the example of giving back. The compliments, accolades, words of respect, and appreciation for you continue to amaze me as I meet with alumni all over the country. You have no idea of the impression you have made and that have impacted so many lives. You and Mom were a formidable team and created such goodwill within the university family. It is such an honor to be your daughter. Thank you for being my biggest cheerleader and loving us all so unconditionally.

Today you enter your tenth decade of your life. Wow, so many memories, so many good times, so many fabulous trips and adventures as a family. You have accomplished so much—former Marine Corps veteran, educator, fund-raiser, tree farmer, author, motorcycle enthusiast, which makes you a gang member according to the FBI, and, most of all, my dad.

Your character has always spoken volumes, you are someone others can trust, you are a man of your word, and you treat people with respect. You are looked upon, up to, and admired not just by your family but by everyone who knows you. You taught us the values of being honest, loyal, conscientious, and persistent. So, happy birthday, Dad, I admire you, I am proud of you, and I am proud to be your daughter, and I love you so much.

From a daughter with children of her own, from the ending of a three-page letter and something that every one of my children has said in one way or another over time:

> You are a terrific father, and I am blessed to be your daughter. You're my hero and my life would not be the same without you. With love, admiration, and appreciation. Happy Father's Day.

> Dad, Thank you for your unconditional love for each one of us in being purposeful and being intentional about getting the family together. I think I speak for us all that there is not another family we would rather have.

> You've touched so many people in extraordinary ways and will leave a legacy that will continue to do so. You never tried to be anyone else. You were never easily influenced by others. Not many people have the ability to do that. Second, you worked hard every single day of your life regardless of who or what challenged you. Hard work always trumps talent and smarts. Third, money has never been your ultimate motivation. And finally, you were committed to your marriage and someone who believed in the same things you did and supported you every step of the way.

### Success

You can use any measure
When you're speaking of success You can measure it in fancy home, Expensive car or dress. But the measure of your real success Is the one you cannot spend. It's the way your kids describe you When they're talking to a friend.
Each generation must take nourishment
From the other and give knowledge to the One that comes after.
    —*Author unknown*

Grandchild

My youngest daughter taught in Germany for more than twenty years and in Japan for five. She married a German native and had a son. After serving twenty-five years abroad, they moved back to the States. After growing up to age fifteen in Germany and Japan, Nick wrote the following for the college admissions officer:

> I consider myself a global nomad, but most importantly, a citizen of the world. I was born abroad, and until age fifteen, lived abroad, absorbing the customs, cultures, and languages of the world. My mother is a US citizen, while my dad is a German national. However, I also fell in love with the warmth of the people and culture of Japan, which thus makes me feel truly Japanese-German-American. The world to me has no borders, and I believe that people are people no matter where you may find them, with wonderful differences and opinions that make us all unique and special.
>
> Experiencing Darwin's vision of the Galapagos Islands through my own eyes, crawling into the Great Pyramids of Luxor to see the tombs of the pharaohs, swimming in the Amazon River while visiting indigenous tribes who continue to live the same way they did hundreds of years ago are all experiences with which few American students are able to identify. Walking on the Great Wall of China, envisioning the emperor's life locked within the Forbidden City in Beijing, strolling the streets of the great capitals of Europe where the crowned heads reigned until their empires collapsed through revolutions were all experiences that moved and changed me. I crossed the vast savannah of Kenya, watching survival of the fittest in its bloodiest form, while hours later, viewing the incredible beauty and splendor of the snowy peak of Mount Kilimanjaro in a golden sunset with the Masai people. The kindness of the Fijian people, the friendly greeting of New Zealand's shepherds, the splendors of the clear and protected waters of the Great Barrier Reef, the warm nose nuzzle of greeting from the Maori people, all have made me a better person open to new ideas, wanting to experience even more while sharing my own beliefs and cultures as well. Through my travels, I received the best education of all through the school of life.

Almost all of my grandchildren could say this—perhaps not as vividly since they didn't live abroad— because they studied abroad in college. They all traveled the same world with me and their grandmother. He refers to the wonderful education I realize I helped give them. Could anyone have expressed it better? I am proud of him, and I am proud to know that all my grandchildren had this opportunity—and their worlds were widened as a result.

My peers seem to me to be absorbed into much of the pop culture that dominates the MTV generation. Watching TV and movies as opposed to reading a classic book appears to be the pastime of choice for most. Wearing designer clothes, buying the most expensive gadgets, and being in the most popular clique seemed to be their priority at first glance. Some seem to view world events as irrelevant to them, simply new facts to be added to a history book rather than events that will alter and affect our generation's future.

I will continue to see the world as my home, not settling for just one particular place. I am a world citizen. Mark Twain once said that travel is fatal to prejudice, bigotry, and narrow-mindedness. "Broad, wholesome, charitable views of men and things cannot be acquired by vegetating in one corner of the earth all one's lifetime." I couldn't have said it better myself.

# CHAPTER FIVE
## LEADERSHIP

The two most important days in your life are the day you are born and the day you find out why.
—*Mark Twain*

Good leadership requires commitment to the cause, to the organization, and to what it represents. That representation should be consistent with one's goals and objectives as a human being. If that is the case, then every problem becomes an opportunity.

Great leaders love what they do. American soccer player Mia Hamm says, "If you don't love what you do, you won't do it with much conviction or passion." People act as a result of being inspired. And great leaders inspire others to action.

Leaders are at the heart of change. Thus, leadership never was, never is, and never will be in a vacuum. Leaders have to adjust to change at whatever level, depending upon circumstances at a given time in history.

We often think of leaders as aggressive, strong, and loud. This may be appropriate for some, but others may be quiet, persuasive, and unintimidating. Being effective requires years of experience, continuing study and learning, and the application of the best that others have proven valid over time.

One who permits himself or herself to capture the potential of what an organization or institution might become will not think of the problems or of what might not be possible. That leader will be committed to what is essential at the highest level of ambition.

Excitement, enthusiasm, and inspiration alone will not provide the momentum essential to overcoming obstacles that engulf leaders every day. In addition to vision, they have a plan of action pursued in an organized fashion.

For a leader, action must be the password. Knowledge is not power by itself. It becomes power only when it is applied. Delegation is important, but that, in and of itself, is not enough. There must be colleagues capable of accepting and acting on that delegation. Such people are at a premium and require good pay and benefits and the support and confidence of the team leader. It is not easy to take the self out of success, yet leaders do not succeed alone. If we cannot share credit, we soon learn there will be no credit to share.

Leadership Characteristics for Administrators
Of College and Universities
Bruce Heilman

1. Leadership and People – the ability to select, employ, and retain good people; to delegate and maintain a team spirit and while helping colleagues to grow and develop by way of the old "give them some rope" technique.

2. Being the best – a leadership spirit and attitude.

3. Commitment – passionately pursuing the ambitions of the institution within its purpose

4. Personal stimulation, excitement and inspiration.

5. The facility for instilling and inspiring confidence

6. A sense of vision – seeing the future being pursued

7. The capacity to codify vision into a plan

8. Enhanced with energy and salesmanship – essential to attracting resources

9. Flexibility of mind, heart, and spirit

10. The courage to act on the application of the plan

Nothing comes to fruition by accident. There must be a precisely defined objective espoused by strong leadership and supported by dedicated followers. In *Good to Great and the Social Sectors*, Jim Collins says,

> People want to feel the excitement of being involved in something that just flat out works. When they begin to see tangible results, when they can feel the flywheel begin to build speed, that's when most people line up to press their shoulders against the wheel and push. But it all happens from strong leadership that creates the momentum.

Success breeds success, which breeds even greater success, which breeds support and commitment because people like to be winners. I have been in leadership positions all my life, and wherever I observed great results, it was the leader who made the difference irrespective of the size of the organization, its location, or its purpose. No organization or institution can rise above its leadership, but there is no height to which it cannot rise with the right leader.

When it comes to valid, strong, and effective leadership, integrity cannot be stressed too often. Values are many, and they mean many things to different people. Among those accepted by most as essential at the top leadership level is ambition, which reinforces determination, which is fueled by commitment. Ethics is fundamental for the leader, and with honesty and integrity as natural ingredients, the leader is worthy of respect and being emulated.

These values often are reinforced by belief in oneself or self-confidence. In *Hamlet,* we read, "Assume a virtue though you have it not, knowing that the dynamic power of habit will bring it into your character." If we don't already have self-confidence, we must filter it into our mind's eye and apply the assumption of that virtue. By habit, we will go far beyond our imagined capability. It is said that the world steps aside to let those pass who know where they are going. If we appear to know what we are doing, the world gives us the benefit of the doubt.

I have assumed the virtue of selecting good people and having the innate sense of doing that well. Much of my success has resulted from good judgment in identifying, employing, and retaining good people.

Without strong leadership, many organizations continue to survive—but they have relatively little potential for doing better. But those influenced by strong leaders can, like cream, rise to the top. There is always the choice of being good, better, or best. The world recognizes leaders who stand out by standing up and making a difference. Greater human, financial, and physical resources come to those who boldly and confidently exploit these virtues.

A few organizations have been great in poverty, but not many. Many have been great because they had great resources, but not all. Most have been great because someone believed in them in such a way that confidence spread to others, making greater and greater achievement possible.

Julius Caesar said, "There is a time in the affairs of men when taken at the flood, leads to fortune." An organization can find itself moving with a strong tide, which can lead to a flood with commitment for overcoming a lot of obstacles and meeting the charge for a more certain future than some may believe possible.

> Life's battles don't always go To the stronger or faster man. But sooner or later, the one who wins
> Is the one who thinks he can.
> —*Edgar Guest*

We must believe in our cause, in ourselves, and in the fact that our cause can make believers of the world at large. Ours will be the future as planned and recognized as reality. If we always do what we've always done, we'll always get what we always got.

\*\*\*

# I

# VISION AND OTHER PRINCIPLES
# APPLIED TO LEADERSHIP

*Where there is no vision, the people perish. —Proverbs 29:19*

Leaders can accomplish little unless they possess a vision ordinarily growing out of a dream. The transformation of the dream into a definable vision represents a conversion of the vague and surreal into practical and workable ideas that can be converted into concrete accomplishments by way of a plan. Vision is a first mental draft of a set of expectations formulated to convey ambitions beyond today, tomorrow, next week, next month, or next year. Trivialities of the moment are less apt to intervene when there is concentration on the broader vision. Einstein said, "Imagination is more important than knowledge." Focusing on the distant horizon rather than on the nearest mountains is the essence of vision.

Vision is the key to outstanding leadership success. Being bold without clarity of where one wants to go or knowledge of the action one will be required to take is fallacious to the utmost. Vision allows the leader to project action within the mission beyond that which is clear to most. A strong leader moves the organization or institution toward results to which the mission subscribes and the vision anticipates. The coalition of vision and leadership results in momentum, and the greatest impetus to good leadership is motivation, which inspires confidence.

A bulletin from Jerold Panas, Linzy, & Partners states, "Momentum in an organization doesn't just happen. There must exist the invincible force of the leader, stubbornly devoted to unswerving in the pursuit of an objective with an ardor and zeal that accepts no limits."

With visionary leadership, what would have seemed impossible otherwise proves plausible and doable—and desirable and noble. Those who would otherwise settle for small success no longer fear bold action to accomplish greater things. Vision in a vacuum is of no acclaim. Vision must be acted upon, and action comes from ambitious leadership.

## The Impact of the Marine Corps on My Leadership Ability

Ronald Reagan said, "Some people live an entire lifetime and wonder if they have ever made a difference in the world. Marines don't have that problem." General H. K. Johnson, United States Army, declared, "I can never again see a United States Marine without experiencing a feeling of reverence." While watching the US Marine drill team at a ball game, a little girl asked her mother how the marines learned to do the things they just did at halftime. Her mother replied, "They practice long and hard, and they are marines—they are the best.

After failing to complete the necessary credits in high school to enter college, I studied through the Marine Corps Institute. It was hard work. It was extra work. It was above and beyond the call of duty, but some of what I have and what I am results from that effort. During those years, as I stood in the chow line for many hours, I noticed that some individuals were always reading books. At the time, I was not aware of the importance of using such time for productive learning.

Today, however, when waiting in airports or offices, when traveling with someone else driving, when traveling by airplane, or even on cruise ships or buses or on vacation, I always carry a briefcase with something to read, something to write, and something to do. I always have something that will keep my mind occupied productively.

## Leadership Opportunities in Higher Education

In my career, I have never been without a job or without a prospect for one—even for a day. Having a job, doing it well, serving professionally, and maintaining a positive outlook as I have faced the challenges before me has kept me too busy to look for another job. The job opportunities have always come to me, and I have responded to possibilities only when I felt the time and place was right. Each move has led to better things professionally and personally. My good fortune is that my family supported me when I made each decision, and they reinforced me after the fact.

I have kept a file over the years of the many job opportunities that have come my way. Even before I finished my undergraduate work, I was invited to teach at my alma mater. That experience continued while I pursued a master's degree. Immediately after completing college, I considered three job offers. None of them appeared to provide for my further education in my major field of accounting, except with a public accounting firm, which offered me the lowest salary of the three.

From there, I moved progressively to the various positions that are elaborated throughout my book. Among those I chose *not* to accept in my earlier years were assistant treasurer at the University of Buffalo—I decided the weather was too cold—treasurer of Berea College, and assistant director of business and finance and executive accountant at the University of Maryland.

Later, I was offered the job of treasurer of Furman University and business manager of New Orleans Baptist Seminary, Mississippi State College for Women, and Davidson College. I was offered the job of executive vice president of the Southern Baptist Theological Seminary in Louisville and vice president for administration and nonacademic affairs at New Orleans Baptist Seminary.

Further along in my career, I was offered the presidency of Union University in Jackson, Tennessee. Other invitations included a senior position at Oklahoma College of Liberal Arts, president of the University of Tennessee in Nashville, president of a new Baptist college in Maryland, and vice president and business manager at Macalester College in Minnesota.

As I moved further into more visible positions, I was asked to consider college presidencies such as Oklahoma Baptist University, Carson Newman College, and Stetson University, the third of which I was actually offered the presidency. I was asked to consider the presidency of William Jewell College in Missouri and Campbellsville College in Kentucky, my alma mater.

Shortly before accepting the presidency of the University of Richmond, I was asked to consider the position of Alabama commissioner of higher education. After I became president of the University of Richmond, opportunities were presented to me as president of Memphis State University, president of the University of Louisville, and as the executive director of the Council of Higher Education in Kentucky.

Others, over time, invited my consideration for their presidency: Virginia Polytechnic Institute (also known as Virginia Tech), Tennessee Tech, Furman University, University of Texas at Arlington, Georgetown College in Kentucky, East Carolina University, Western Kentucky University, the University of North Carolina at Charlotte, the University of Texas at Austin, the University of Miami, Dartmouth College, and Salem College. These were not all offers of the presidency, but they were serious invitations to become a candidate. I was also asked to consider being the chancellor of the University of Alabama system. In most of these that I declined and where I gave consideration, I was either offered the position or was a finalist.

I always sought to leave with the goodwill of those for whom I worked. In that way, I could carry to the new job the goodwill I had built up at the old one. It is my belief that hard work, deep commitment, and good human relations laid the foundation for continuing strong recommendations, which kept job offers coming my way over the years.

The job opportunities never stopped coming—even when I stepped down from the presidency at age sixty and became chancellor of the University of Richmond. I have remained uninterested in moving from the university or from Richmond, and I expect to spend the remaining years of my life there.

Beyond job offers, consulting and speaking engagements have taken me throughout the country. They continue—even at age ninety-three—to be a steady part of my activities. I have consulted and spoken at more than a hundred colleges and universities as well as a variety of institutions and organizations all over the country.

## Opportunities in Political Leadership

While I never personally pursued a political career, I was contacted a couple of times about running for governor of Virginia by some very influential political leaders in the state. Also, during the administration of President Nixon, I was contacted about a position in the federal government. A letter received from President Nixon when he was president-elect stated, "As you may know, I have pledged to bring into this administration men and women who by their qualities of youthfulness, judgment, intelligence, and creativity can make significant contributions to our country." And after having been recommended by several, I judged that this was not something of interest to me.

## Communication in Leadership

If you ever wonder if you should say something, don't say it. In any field or endeavor, especially as a senior leader, being articulate and being able to communicate ideas clearly is of utmost importance. In our society, power comes first and foremost with proficiency in public speaking and discourse. Effective communication is a formidable tool and a vital skill. Words can be more effective than weapons.

I continue to apply the basic tenets of speechmaking I have learned over the years. Most of all, public speaking—which is marketing—is just another form of persuasion. The speaker is marketing himself or herself as well as the product at hand. In my case, that product usually has been quality higher education. William Jennings Bryan, who was considered a great orator, used the following formula:

1. Choose a text.
2. Tell something from your own experience.

3. Quote a great man.

4. Use an epigram or aphorism.

5. Tell a story.

6. Recite a poem.

While I am no Bryan, I do tend to utilize aspects of his formula.

It has often been suggested to me that I should write a guide to speechmaking, and though I have never compiled a handbook, I have offered a few guidelines to those who question me on the subject. In my efforts to be as effective as possible, I used the following principles:

1. Speak from the heart. If you don't believe in what you are saying, your audience will realize before you are on your third sentence that your presence at the podium is ideal time to drowse. You can't persuade unless you are convinced. It has always been easy for me to speak about institutions I have served because I feel passionately about my subject. On the other hand, I have spoken on many subjects over the years, some of which I could hardly be considered qualified as an expert. A keynote address I made at the Virginia Governor's Conference on Gerontology comes to mind. At the last minute, I was asked to speak to this group when the planned presenter could not attend. With the help of a professor who did know the subject, I was able to put together a credible address—maybe a bit light in substance, but based in truth. Most importantly, I could deliver the address with conviction and justify its publication by the state for permanent reference.

2. Dress for success. No matter how informal the audience, I wear a dark suit and a tie. Right away, I look important and command attention. I'm taken seriously.

3. Speak boldly and confidently with a positive, affirming attitude. Hopefully, one can feel that way when speaking, but even if not, how the talk is delivered is nearly as important as what is being said. An audience expects to glean something of merit from the address, and if spoken with confidence, certain gems will be there. Boldly attack your subject and dare your audience to think you are nervous, although a little nervousness means that you are taking your audience seriously.

4. Know your subject well and let the situation lead you into what you are comfortable saying. For important speeches, plan and prepare ahead. Then refer to your draft again and again and make adjustments until the last moment. My draft is never complete until it is delivered.

5. Choose a title that sets the stage for the message. My convocation addresses bear names like "Making the Most of Yourselves" and "Opening Doors to the Future." Speaking to the Association

of Presidents of Independent Colleges and Universities, I used "Keeping Your Head: Use it or Lose it." "You're Never Too Old to Learn" was an address that became an article, and so did "Challenges and Opportunities for Church-Related Colleges." Suggest in your title that your address will include important information for the audience to garner.

6. Speak at a pace that can hold the audience's attention. Most individuals can listen to 450 words a minute, while the average adult speaking rate in conversation is 125 words per minute. Unfortunately, speakers usually slow their pace to a mere hundred words per minute, and the audience drifts into a bored stupor.

7. Closely related to the pace of your speech is your length. Keep your audience in mind when planning the length of your delivery—and remember that brevity can be an effective tool in communicating what really needs to be said. Someone said, "The longer the spoke, the greater the tire."

8. A written speech should be typed boldly enough to be clearly visible when you stand before your audience and make the delivery. This is not the place to skimp on paper. Use fourteen-to-sixteen-point bold type.

9. Don't allow a dry mouth to confound your efforts. Put a small mint in your mouth to take care of that problem until it naturally diminishes during the course of your speech.

10. Practice. The more you become accustomed to speaking before audiences, large or small, the easier the craft becomes. A few compliments will ease the process, and success will breed success. Accomplished public speaking and rhetoric—speaking with propriety, elegance, and force— opens more doors to opportunity than any other skill.

Some values were absolute, others were by implication, and some were left to be learned in other places and in other ways. Values are many, and they mean different things to different people, but among those accepted by most as essential to fulfillment and success in life is *ambition,* which reinforces determination, which is fueled by commitment. These values often are fulfilled by still another value, which is belief in oneself or self-confidence.

## My Faith Disposition

He, who from zone to zone,
Guides through the boundless sky thy certain flight, In the long way that I must tread along
Will lead my steps aright.
　　—*William Cullen Bryant*

My faith, like the faith of most, results from the teachings of my family, my church, and a continuing interaction with people of that faith. Through all my years, the nature of my faith has been altered. The basis for it has remained substantially the same. Setting aside the theological foundations of what I believe, a few verses of scripture are the essence of how I explain what I believe.

Paul had about the best definition of my faith as any other: "Faith is the substance of things hoped for and the evidence of things not seen." "Faith without works is dead," is another guideline for the continuing application of my faith. And a third, "Love they neighbor," rounds out rather well the obligation I must accept within my faith. Theologically, these may not satisfy many who spend time delving into the details, but these are my guidelines for living a life within the discipline of what I believe—while remembering to treat my fellow humans is if I were in their shoes.

> Success in life is determined by the character of your journey. It is your testament to impeccable and rigid standards, an unwillingness to settle for anything less than enduring and unshakable principles.
> —*Jerry Panas*

I believe that our faith should be played out in such a fashion that at the end of life, one can be confident of the eternal reward prescribed for those who have practiced that faith to the fullest, while loving his neighbor as himself.

In *Thanatopsis,* William Cullen Bryant provided a simple guideline for living out one's faith:

> So, live, that when thy summons comes to join The innumerable caravan which moves
> To that mysterious realm where each shall take
> His chamber in the silent hall of death,
> Thou go not, like the quarry slave at night,
> Scourged to his dungeon, but, sustained and soothed
> By an unfaltering trust, approach thy grave Like one who wraps the drapery of his couch About
> him and lies down to pleasant dreams.

In my memoir, I cited that an interruption changed everything about me. After four years in the marines, the question became where, when, and how my life would continue to unfold as my vision reached out to the ends of the earth for success allowed by time, capability, health, and opportunity. Much of what happened over time was based upon the principles cited in this chapter about ideas, actions, and experiences. "These are most effective when ethics is at the heart of any and all actions and when honesty and integrity are natural ingredients added to the mix."

General George Sylvester defines as his last will and testament a number of principles, values, and experiences that he cherishes and wishes to share, hoping to enrich the lives of his grandchildren and children.

1. Integrity first. Service before self-excellence in everything you do. These are the core values of the United States Air Force in which he had succeeded to a three-star level. They are appropriate for everyone in and out of uniform.

2. Integrity is such a precious quality. Its cousins are trust and honor. You will be tempted to violate your integrity on numerous occasions. Once lost, integrity is exceedingly difficult to regain. Take the high road—and choose the hardest right rather than the easiest wrong.

3. Morality. Since an early age, we have known the difference between right and wrong. There are lots of temptations, and it sometimes takes strong will, self-discipline and faith to resist them. In the final analysis, there can be no compromise.

4. Character. Your thoughts become your words, your words become your actions, your actions become your habits, your habits become your character, and your character becomes your legacy.

5. Humility. He defines this as the opposite of arrogance, which is one of the least attractive of human traits. As you climb life's success ladder, it is important to maintain a healthy measure of humility. It helps to always remember where your success came from and give some extra attention to the little people—those who toil in anonymity and rarely get any recognition.

6. Respect. We all like to be respected by those we know, especially if we are in a leadership position. Respect has to be earned, usually over an extended period of time. Living the core value of integrity and service before self and excellence in everything you do is a pretty good recipe for gaining respect of your subordinates, superiors, and clients.

7. Leadership. Some people are so-called natural leaders. Others have to learn how to lead. Early in life, you discover whether you want to be a leader, and that sets the stage for the rest of your life. Leadership takes hard work, sound principles, and—above all—being a people person.

8. Attitude is something within everyone's capacity to control. You can't control the color of your skin, how tall you are, your IQ, or who your parents were, but a positive attitude is within everyone's reach.

These attributes, embodied in the consciousness of a good leader, can lift one to a position of greatness. With the characteristics in the following chapter, they will give credence to the person and the organization to which that one is related.

\*\*\*

# II

## THE BODY FOLLOWS THE MIND

The person who knows *how* will always have a job. The person who knows *why* will always be his boss.
—*Diane Ravitch*

Promotion

Promotion comes to him who sticks
Unto his work and never kicks,
Who watches neither clock nor sun
To tell him when his task is done;
Who toils not by a stated chart,
Defining to a jot his part,
But gladly does a little more Than he's remunerated for.
The man, in factory or shop,
Who rises quickly to the top,
Is he who gives what can't get bought: Intelligent and careful thought.
No one can say just when begins
The service that promotion wins,
Or when it ends, 'tis not defined
By certain hours or any kind
Of system that has been devised; Merit cannot be systemized.
It is at work when it's at play;

It serves each minute of the day;

'Tis always at its post, to see New ways of help and use to be. Merit from duty never slinks, Its cardinal virtue is—it thinks!

Promotion comes to him who tries Not solely for a selfish prize,

But day by day and year by year Holds his employer's interests dear.

Who measures not by what he earns

The sum of labor he returns,

Nor counts his day of toiling through

Till he's done all that he can do. His strength is not of muscle bred, But of the heart and of the head. The man who would the top attain Must demonstrate he has a brain.

There is not today, and there never has been in my sixty-five-year tenure as an educational administrator, an end to the ifs, ands, and buts. Thus, in order to set some of these aside rather than facing them head-on, we allow them to become our crutches, our excuses for failure, or our justification for a lack of success.

Not many would believe that I know more about solving the specific dilemmas of finance, enrollments, and other conditions and circumstances facing higher education than do many others. However, if I concentrate on the broader aspects of leadership, perhaps they may take notice.

As I expose my expertise, or lack of it, in dealing with challenge and change, I find myself projecting the same message that has been valid in my own experience through nine years as a chief financial officer in three colleges, two years as a coordinator of a state system of higher education, three years as an arts and sciences dean, three years as an administrative vice president, and more than fifty years as a college and university president and chancellor in two institutions.

There are many sides to leadership. I am presenting only one of many in dealing with the idea of successful results by leaders. My approach may appear unusual and even narrow and simplistic in the whole scope of considerations affecting the subject, but I believe it is a controlling factor.

Some who are sophisticated and learned in the language and philosophy of leadership education may look upon my approach as shallow or trite. If so, then they indulge in that perspective at their own peril. In fact, they may have failed to measure up to their best potential due to a lack of understanding of the reality of my simple message.

The body follows the mind, and the flesh is less weak when the spirit is willing. The level of our energy and the extent of our action are substantially affected by mental and emotional factors. Explicit activity is brought to fruition as the result of motivation from within.

Energy and action must be triggered by some significant spark to ignite the maximum force of power within us. The fire that is ignited is the spirit that controls our minds and energizes our bodies.

We all experience weariness to the point of feeling that we can't rise from a chair or the bed. We come home tired from a hard day's work, overwhelmed by stress to the point that we project a sense of uselessness. As a result, our minds are dulled. We are in low gear. We want to set aside anything and everything that even reminds us of active involvement. We want to close ourselves off from the world, distance ourselves from reality, and hide from the challenges and charges around us.

In that state, the mind becomes the thermometer of the body. That overpowering control mechanism leads us right down to the chair, the bed, or—for some—the depths of depression.

We have all, at some time or other, experienced the stimulation and exhilaration of being suddenly awakened from our lethargy and our morbid drowsiness by virtue of a happening that sparked a transition from passive to active and from inert to alert. Adrenaline starts to flow, and the mind shifts quickly to a new gear.

Our posture changes as we prepare to follow our minds and deal with a crisis, take advantage of an exciting opportunity, respond to an important telephone message, a loud and commanding knock on the door, or a scream from one of the children, or engaging in whatever called our minds to heightened stimulation.

The body follows the mind. Any exhaustion is immediately washed away and forced aside. All of our inclinations to close our minds and turn off our bodies are overpowered by the spirit, which is sparked by the incident that calls forth our full interest. We go to a movie with an old friend, join somebody in a golf game, or rush to the scene of the accident. The mind responds to the spirit, and the body follows without question. There is no debate, there is no delay, and there is no measure or restraint; when the mind speaks in a commanding way, the body follows.

We have all demonstrated this kind of energy at some point in our lives. It may have been a moment when we knew we were communicating effectively because we absolutely believed in what we were saying. Remember how it feels? We are enthusiastic, our posture is good, and we are determined. In short, we have the right kind of energy.

What does all of this have to do with leadership? A great deal more than most recognize. The compelling fact that the body follows the mind should be kept in the forefront of our thinking as we deal with leadership. The considerations involved go well beyond the mood of the moment. Personality is involved. Attitude is involved. One's general outlook on life is involved, and one's background and experience are involved. Leadership cannot be separated from the reality that the body follows the mind. Some leaders make great progress in spite of the obstacles placed in their way, and others never build enough momentum to lift themselves and their instructions over the peaks following the inevitable dips that confront them.

The hands, eyes, mouth, and nose are only instruments of the mind. We smell when the mind recognizes an aroma. We look when the mind visualizes or fantasizes something worthy of that look. We listen when the mind is alert to the prospects of hearing something worthwhile. We touch when the mind tells us that good results will occur. We hold back when the mind senses the danger of a hot stove or a sharp instrument.

Leadership is not a physical thing; it is a mental thing. We act and react without a sense of mental concentration to many things and in many ways. The control center sends the message that is inspired by the emotions of the moment. Controlled though they may be, they are based upon the deeper beliefs, convictions, and experiences of the leader.

To a large extent, leadership boils down to disposition. One's disposition leads either to action or the lack of action. Disposition is the spirit that affects the mind, which activates the body. The whole matter of disposition is affected by satisfaction or lack of it in our place of service and the roles we play as leaders. An otherwise good leader can be a superb leader if the mind can shift from a low gear or neutral to a higher gear.

In that state of momentum, one can maintain a high level of excitement. The mental and emotional juices are stimulated regularly, and the mind and emotions set the pace so that the body seldom gets tired. In this spirit, one can work from early morning until late at night. One can even labor throughout the night if necessary. In fact, one can do whatever he or she must do to accomplish that which the mind truly believes and conceives with minimum loss of energy, physically speaking.

Henry Wadsworth Longfellow discussed the rewards in "The Ladder of St. Augustine."

The heights by great men reached and kept Were not attained by sudden flight.
But they, while their companions slept, Were toiling upward in the night.

The right attitude and state of mind has a lot to do with why some far outpace others. It can make a vast difference in how we deal with the problems and opportunities that face us in higher education today. In fact, the spirit with which we face the challenges may be more important than our techniques and know-how.

We can be excited and stimulated and inspired so that the body is motivated by the mind and spirit, but adrenaline does not always flow at the same pace. Being engaged in activities that are of minor or of no interest leaves the mind bored. This brings disaffection rather than excitement; the body and mind are turned off. Adrenaline flows more slowly, legs get tired, the bed is harder to leave, and life can be a problem rather than an opportunity.

To bridge the dips and peaks in the long road of life, we need discipline. This is a mental exercise that involves determination and focus. Goals keep us keep moving, and dealing only in larger objectives can exhaust our optimism. Chopping down a large forest may seem an impossibility to a woodsman, but taking out the trees one at a time can provide great satisfaction on a day-to-day basis.

In whatever we commit ourselves to, we should be certain that it is in keeping with what is important to our short-range and the long-term interests. What we do should be in keeping with our values, our religious and spiritual motivations, and all else that gives life meaning and gives us a positive mind-set.

With these broad admonitions before us, I want to focus on specific approaches to leadership that best enhance the prospects for utilizing the benefits of the relationship between the mind, body, and spirit. We can extend it beyond ourselves even as we utilize it more personally. We can maximize our leadership competencies and exploit them to the fullest by doing our best in that which holds our interest.

This extension of my life story grows out of an opportunity given to only a select few. Only about one in ten men reach the age of ninety-one. As an exception to the rule, I have attempted to translate the results of this privilege into examples that others may want to emulate.

As I have transitioned to life beyond eighty, I have continued my productive life. These thirteen years have been like a gift of time that allow me to enjoy a lifestyle I never anticipated, some of which served me well in my first eighty years. Though many of my reminiscences were recorded in my earlier memoirs, the extended years have allowed reflections on the fullness of my life before and after eighty.

### Purpose, Passion, Priorities, Performance, and Perseverance

Much of the driving force in my first eighty years can now be conveyed as reflections because time has confirmed concrete results that prove my successes were real and my efforts were based upon sound principles. Purpose, passion, priorities, performance, and perseverance sum up the spirit and character of why these have been years of progress for me and my colleagues at the University of Richmond.

A young marine corporal in Iraq had his hands blown off and was left with a serious wound in his leg, but he continued to lead his men. When asked why he didn't pass out, he said, "I couldn't pass out. I was in charge." That marine embodied responsibility, strength of character, and commitment to purpose. Somewhere—at home, at school, in his church, or in the Marine Corps—this value was developed. When called upon, his mind and body responded automatically to the responsibility at hand. Because the situation asked for the impossible, the result was to get the best possible.

My sixty-six years in senior leadership positions in higher education are based upon clear purposes that I have passionately pursued day and night. The level of energy and the resulting action has been, to a large extent, determined by the degree of passion for my committed purpose. A purposeful state of mind by many has had much to do with why we at the University of Richmond have outpaced most other colleges and universities.

The flesh may be weak, but it is stronger if the spirit is willing. Thus, the spirit with which we have faced our challenges at the university has often been more significant than professional know-how. Rick Warren of the Saddleback Church in California says that purpose is the driving force in our lives. Most people, he says, are meandering through life without a purpose. Their whole goal is getting more of everything with the misconception that having more will make them happier.

One of five things suggested in Warren's *Purpose Driven Life* is that knowing our purpose gives meaning to our lives. Knowing our purpose, he says, simplifies life. Purpose, he says, produces passion, which motivates action. Without purpose, he says meaningless activity wears us down, zaps our strength and robs us of joy. According to George Bernard Shaw,

> The true joy of life is being used for a purpose recognized by yourself as a mighty one, being a
> force of nature instead of a feverish selfish little clot of ailments and grievances complaining that
> the world will not devote itself to making us happy.

Someone said, "If we have our own *why* in life, we can bear almost any *how*." With purpose, the collective energy of body, mind, and spirit tends to instill and inspire confidence and excitement in those around us. It is a leadership characteristic more important than most.

While an organization cannot rise above its leadership, there is no height to which it can rise with the right leadership. And with the right leadership, an organization knows no obstacles that can forestall the march toward that which "those whom the dream hath possessed" have established as their goal. It is said that if you've done it, it ain't bragging. I suggest Edgar Guest's verse as a worthy suggestion:

> Think big and your deeds will grow;
> Think small and you'll fall behind;
> Think that you can and you will— It's all in the state of mind.

Most of us likely do not sense the extent to which we have progressed by virtue of others lifting us to each new rung of the ladder. We are often inclined to give ourselves the credit for our accomplishments to the point of believing that we can lift ourselves by our own bootstraps. I have sought to keep in mind that no leader succeeds alone. Each new leader stands on the shoulders of those who have gone before, so that he or she can see farther and dream bolder because of the tides created by those who have served before.

But to understand why leaders, and I include myself, succeed in life, certain attributes enhance the level of that success. The following characteristics have been instrumental in my success at the University of Richmond and elsewhere during my professional life.

## Values

Each of us succeed or fail within a value structure. Whatever one commits to do should be in keeping with strongly held values. For many, this extends to the tenets of religious faith and fulfilling a mission. John Gardner calls this individual fulfillment within a moral framework. It represents what is meant when we allude to the right person, in the right place, at the right time. It is living for a purpose. The courage of one's convictions can be strong enough to sail upstream even against strong currents.

An essential value for success as a leader is ambition, which reinforces determination, which is fueled by commitment. These values are fulfilled by another value, which is belief in oneself or self-confidence.

## Disposition, Spirit and Attitude

Throughout my life, I have realized that success boils down to disposition, which leads to action or the lack of action. That inclination affects the mind, which activates the body. A controlling factor in success undergirding disposition is attitude. If it is positive, then challenges can be met head-on with the kind of determination and confidence that produces outstanding results. The human organism loves a challenge. With the right attitude, almost every problem is an opportunity.

The nineteenth-century author and publisher Elbert Hubbard said, "The greatest mistake you can make in life is to continually fear you will make one." If you think you can, you can, and if you think you can't, you can't. Over the years, I have embraced Shakespeare's admonition: "Assume a virtue though you have it not, knowing that the dynamic power of habit will build it into your character." Positive thoughts energize to the extent that strength overcomes risks in whatever we do.

An old saying suggests that the mediocre are always at their best because they never let us down. They are constant in their satisfaction with the level of their accomplishments. On the other hand, those who fit the classification of excellent tend to have found a purpose that inspires a passion, resulting in a dynamic spirit that drives them to excel at an even higher level. For them, "the rung of the ladder was never meant to rest upon, but only to hold one's foot long enough to lift the other higher."

Such have been the kind of senior leaders brought to the University of Richmond during my presidency. They have been filled with this and the other attributes listed in these pages. It is no surprise that more than a dozen moved on to become presidents of other colleges and universities:

- Dr. Gresham Riley, president, Colorado College
- Dr. Melvin L. Vulgamore, president, Albion College
- Dr. Thomas L. Reuschling, president, St. Andrews Presbyterian College and Florida Southern
- Dr. Sheldon F. Wettack, Wabash College
- Dr. Russell G. Warren, president, Northeast Missouri State University
- Dr. William E. Walker, president, Tarkio College
- Dr. Charles E. Gassick, president of Gettysburg College
- Dr. Stephanie Bennett, president Centenary College
- Dr. John Rousch, president, Centre College Action

An important thing to understand about any institution or social system is that it doesn't move unless it's pushed. What is generally needed is not a mild push but a solid jolt. If the push is not administered by a vigorous and purposeful leader, it will be administered eventually by an aroused citizenry or by a crisis.
—*John Gardner, Recovery of Confidence*

Carlyle suggests that it is not what lies dimly in the future that is important but what lies clearly at hand. There are people who inspire others, are themselves inspired, have vision, and may even plan toward the goal visualized—but never act out of any of these. David George said, "The finest eloquence is that which gets things done." Knowledge cannot be power without the action through which it is applied.

### Resiliency

No matter how positive the mind, strong the spirit, or confident we may be, we face good days and bad days, victory and defeat, give and take. Thus, it is important that we not let success affect us unduly or defeat to get us down. We must bounce back from every set back.

The warrior in the old Scotch ballad is the example. "I'm hurt," Sir Andrew Barton said,

"I'm hurt but I'm not slain; I'll lay me down to bleed awhile, and then I'll fight again."

## Courage

No leader will travel the superhighway of life without courage. "Touch a thistle timidly, and it pricks you; grasp it boldly, and its spines crumble," said William S. Halsey. Problems will make us suffer most when we try to dodge them, and they will be less frustrating when directly confronted. Problems are the making of success—not the destruction of it. Bob Jones said, "The doors to success swing on the hinges of opposition."

"Never despair," said Edmund Burke, "but if you do, work on in despair."

## Character

When leaders are to be trusted in positions of responsibility, it is important to know what they will do under normal conditions and what they will do under pressure. It is important to know what they will do when they are being watched and what they will do when they feel sure they are not being watched.

"Character," wrote Emerson, "is higher than intellect."

Dying, Horace Greeley exclaimed, "Fame is a vapor, personality an accident, riches take wings, those who cheer today will curse tomorrow, only one thing endures—character."

## Generosity

The spirit of generosity is an admirable quality for a leader. An unknown author said,

He is dead whose hand is not open wide to help the need of a human brother; he doubles the length of his lifelong ride who of his fortune gives to another; and a thousand million lives are his who carries the world in his sympathies; to give is to live; to deny is to die.

Generosity should go beyond the material, which is ably expressed by Ella Wheeler Wilcox in a poem:

> I gave a beggar from my little store
> Of well-earned gold. He spent the shining ore And came again, and yet again, still cold And hungry, as before.
> I gave a thought, and through that thought of mine He found himself, the man, supreme, divine!

Fed, clothed, and crowned with blessings manifold.
And now he begs no more.

The greatest gift we can give is that which helps others to help themselves. The effects of our actions and our attitudes can be our greatest gifts to our fellow humans.

**Boldness**

In many years of leadership, I often have been accused of being bold, and I take that as a compliment. Charles Moore said,

> Make no little plans. They have no magic with which to stir men's blood and probably they themselves will not be realized. Make big plans; aim high. Remember that our sons and our grandsons will do things that would stagger us. Remember that when you create a situation that captures the imagination, you capture life, reason, everything.

As I look back over the sixty-five years of administrative experience, I do not have to defend myself against arrogance when I say that I have been successful. In every aspect of my success, I appropriately and correctly acknowledge that I did not climb to the heights. I was raised or lifted—and in some cases, I was pushed and shoved—by good people. Along the way, I occasionally slipped and sometimes fell, but I always landed in the arms of those who were a part of my support system.

Some things never change as expectations and guidelines continue over the years. I, along with a host of successful people, have applied the following guidelines expressed in a variety of ways to enhance our successes:

- Show dedication to the organization.
- Show loyalty to the people to whom we are responsible.
- Show consideration of those junior to us.
- Give the benefit of the doubt to all with whom we have contact.
- Praise those who represent us publicly and scorn only in private.
- Show mutual respect for each other within our spheres of influence.
- Continue growing and developing, always learning and encouraging others to do likewise.

- Keep a positive attitude, always seeing the glass as half full when dealing with the public and our colleagues.
- Do more than that which is defined in our job description.
- Love what we do so that we will never have to work a day in our lives, remembering that only we can make our jobs worthy of that love.
- Never complain in public—excuse ourselves and complain in private.
- Never argue in anger with a customer, a staff member, or a senior or equal partner; vent any frustration in private.
- Try to direct our efforts toward the upper side of possibilities so that the future and the organization will benefit.
- Speak well of your organization.
- Never criticize your boss. If such is often justified, look for another job where such criticism is not necessary. Self-criticism and self-evaluation may cure your concerns.
- Assume a larger responsibility than assigned.
- Think of yourself as more important than you are—and prove it. I was always the second-highest-paid employee—even though much younger—but I was worth it.
- Always find something to like about your boss—even if it's difficult. Pay compliments and volunteer often enough to be recognized as rising above the crowd. Stay out in front to avoid choking on the dust of others.
- Go out on a limb where the choicest fruits are found.
- Be helpful to those who are new or in lesser positions, and they will be helpful to you when it is least expected.
- Learn the art of communication and practice speaking to individuals and groups. Your future may depend upon it. The next level up demands it. My best jobs— including presidencies—have all resulted from good interviews.

In sharing the characteristics I have sought to embody, I risk appearing a bit arrogant, but everything that has happened during and after my leadership justifies my confidence. I have built permanent foundations on which towers have been erected. I now proudly affirm that I, and my excellent colleagues at the time, can be appropriately acknowledged as outstanding leaders.

***

# III

## AXIOMS FOR LEADERSHIP

Charisma is defined as the ability to inspire, and it is the most important leadership characteristic. As a successful leader, I believe that I left each position with a sense of regret on the part of my colleagues due to the obvious progress made at each institution as a result of my service. I consider my leadership to represent guidelines for effective results.

I have identified certain qualities that distinguish successful leaders. The following principles and practices exemplify leaders who succeed beyond the ordinary:

1. The secret to getting things done is in getting things started. I am always surprised at the number of people who cannot get a project underway. Yet, starting is 90 percent of completion. Those who start have a good record of completing what they start.

2. Leaders are action oriented. They speak when they must, and they do that well, but their actions speak even louder than their words.

3. Leaders are willing to assume responsibility and involve others in bringing their action to successful fruition. They function as team leaders without selfish intent or claiming all the credit as personal.

4. Leaders have a sense of anticipation. This embodies vision, fueled by dreams of what might be, clothed in the garments of practical application of energy, and related to plans of how something can be taken from where it is to where it ought to be.

5. Leaders think big and act boldly. They agree with Charles Moore and "make no little plans that have no magic to stir men's blood and they themselves will likely not be realized. Make big plans, and aim high."

6. Leaders have courage that is based upon commitment and conviction. Thomas Jefferson said to General George Rogers Clark when he was being viciously slandered, "If you meant to escape malice, you should have confined yourself to the sleepy life of regular duty." The passive life of a follower can be much more placid than the sometimes-turbulent waters of leadership.

7. Leaders have a strong sense of purpose. They believe in something and act on that belief. Someone said, "He who has a *why* to live for can bear almost any *how*." An old Spanish proverb says, "If you would be pope, you must think of nothing else."

8. Leaders tend to have positive attitudes. In fact, leadership is probably 99 percent attitude. There is a tendency on the part of leaders to be optimistic, full of hope, and capable of instilling others with a similar spirit. Leaders believe that the world steps aside to let those pass who know where they are going.

9. Leaders tend to assume capabilities and develop competencies that might not have been realized from past experience and preparation. They accept Shakespeare's admonition of assuming a virtue though you do not have it—and it will become yours.

In a nutshell, leadership requires the courage to dream, the ability to organize, and the strength to execute. If we believe that our job cannot be done, then someone else should assume the leadership of our organization. If we possess the axioms as presented and to the extent that our organization is willing to invest in good leadership, it will likely be able to afford the investment it makes.

Leaders face up to problems. They possess the courage of their convictions, and they are inspired, optimistic, and enthusiastic. Leaders have knowledge of planning, the capacity to delegate, and the ability to judge their colleagues. They understand management and finance, have good communication skills, and embody the spirit of anticipation. Leaders set goals and play a strong role in their implementation.

And finally, leaders dig in their heels, set their sights on the future, and believe they can become what they are determined to be.

Leadership embodies being prepared to face any problem and taking advantage of every opportunity to be most effective in service to their constituents.

This opportunity and accomplishment of success is the reward that is a part of what leadership opportunity has to offer.

# IV

## MY OLDEST GRANDSON: CHRISTOPHER

I have written a great deal about leadership, but it has mostly been about institutional or corporate responsibilities. Little has been said about leadership of the family. I have chosen to share that aspect of my life and responsibility through some excellent papers prepared as school assignments by two of my grandsons who were certainly more objective than I could have been.

First is a paper prepared by my oldest grandson, Christopher Hudgins, when required to do an interview project during his freshman year of high school. First is a personal statement dated November 10, 1995. Following that, in his words after interviewing me, is the story of my life as he recorded it from his interview.

There are only a few things in life that seem to affect the way one directs his or her future. Frequently, these episodes require choices that can change one's life forever. Age is not a factor, as it could occur when someone is seventeen or seventy. It has happened to me in my senior year.

My grandfather, Bruce Heilman, was telling me about his educational experiences as a youth in Kentucky. He was not an exceptional student. In fact, he finished his high school education in the Marine Corps. After his military service, which he says, turned a naïve teenager into a mature young man, he quickly began to understand the importance of education. It was then that he began to apply himself to his educational pursuits.

My grandfather chose education as a way of life and earned his master's and doctorate degrees. He later found himself in Richmond as the president of the University of Richmond. After working in this position for sixteen years, he retired and became chancellor. He continues to support and speak highly of the university and the local community.

I have heard this story many times, and while extremely proud of my grandfather, I never gave it much thought until recently. I have also talked to my mom, who was not an exceptional undergraduate student. But in her graduate work, she made a 4.0 in all her courses but one. She made a 3.0 in that course. She says she wishes she had worked harder in high school and college because she knows now that she could have been a much better student. Nevertheless, she is now an excellent and much-requested teacher in her school because she loves what she does and has worked hard for it. She continues to take courses that help her with her job.

I have realized that I am much like my mom and grandfather. I am not a student with a 4.0 average, and I may never accomplish this feat, but I also do not want to look back and wish I had done better or tried harder. I am beginning to realize the value of a good education, and I am building more confidence in myself. I am committed to apply myself, as my grandfather did, and make the most out of my college years. I have been involved with the university since I was a baby because of my grandfather, my mom, and my dad. I have seen the community involvement of the UR family and am beginning to understand the excellent education opportunities provided at Richmond. I look forward to the lifetime relationships that I will develop during this period of my life.

There seems to be a perception that teenagers have trouble taking advice from their parents, grandparents, and other family members. Most of my family, however, attended the university and consider it in a class all its own. I have always valued their opinions, and so I began to think that if I received the same advice from all these people who cared about me, it must be beneficial.

The effect of my grandfather's life, as well as other family members especially as they pertain to the university, have convinced me to pursue an education there. I look forward to completing my education at UR if given the opportunity and giving back to the university proudly as an alumnus and member of the Spider family.


Interview Project
Chris Hudgins
Fourth Period ACD


\*\*\*

On October 24, 1992, I interviewed my grandfather, Dr. Bruce Heilman. He is the retired president of the University of Richmond and still works there in other capacities. He was born in Ballardsville, Kentucky, on July 16, 1926. He now lives in Richmond, Virginia.

## Early Life

Bruce Heilman was the third out of four children. He enjoyed his position because he was not quite as obvious as the first or last child. "I could be more independent and individual. What I did wasn't so recognized, and I liked that." As a child, he and his family enjoyed going to church together, playing croquet, sitting on the front porch swing, visiting relatives and neighbors, and playing with other children. Because he lived on a farm in the country, he had many chores. He would begin early in the morning helping to milk forty cows. During tobacco-harvesting season, he would weed, worm, cut, strip, and house tobacco. He cut wood for the fireplace and stove, brought in water from the well for bathing and washing, beat the dust from the carpets, and mowed the lawn with a push mower. He had many hardships compared to today. His family was poor and had little money. But they had what they needed—food, friends, and clean clothes. He walked several miles to school every morning. Another hardship was not having the modern-day conveniences we have today. Childhood was very different from the way it is now. He had no electricity, and so he was not aware of current world events because of no TV or radio. They had a lantern instead of lights, so the whole family stayed in one room at night.

They didn't travel because they didn't have a car until later years.

What he remembers most about his mother: "She was a good cook— the best until I trained your grandmother and your mom. She kept us clean and always was concerned that we looked good and behaved in public. She switched us when we didn't behave. I think of her as a good mother." What he remembers of his father: "He was a highly disciplined individual, a strong believer in values and in church. He was a community leader even though he wasn't a well-educated man. He was very honest, and we respected and minded him. Parents then were not overtly loving—they did not hug and kiss as much. But they were good to us and provided a good home even though they couldn't afford to give us much."

## Schooling

Bruce Heilman's first school was a square building with four classes in one room. There was a potbellied stove to heat and a cistern outside to pump water. They all drank from one cup that hung on the cistern. There was a stable for kids who rode their horses to school. "We used to go behind the stables and smoke mullen, a plant we crumbled up and rolled in paper like tobacco. I remember jumping out of the classroom window and entering the school several times to trick my teacher. I didn't like school; in fact, I hated it." He enjoyed playing marbles for keeps, which was against the rules because it was considered gambling. He liked recess, the noon hour, before and after school. His favorite part was first thing in the morning when the teacher read from the Billy Whiskers book (*Misadventures of a Goat*). Algebra was the subject hardest for him. He failed it. He took it again in the Marine Corps and passed. He didn't like school, so he didn't study. His parents didn't push school. Neither was well educated and didn't expect their children to go to college. He especially remembers "my algebra teacher because he flunked me. He never helped me. He thought I wasn't a good student, so he didn't bother with me."

He remembers a first grade teacher because she did help him. "She took us on picnics, had parties for us, and treated us like she really liked us. She made us proud of ourselves." The proudest thing he accomplished in school was graduating eighth grade. He was the only one in his class to graduate from high school and college. He finished his high school diploma in the Marine Corps. He enjoyed playing fast-pitch softball. "We played in the cow pasture across from school, and sometimes the ball would get dirty!"

They also played "mumlety-peg," a knife-throwing game. His favorite thing to do with school friends was go sleigh riding in the winter. "Everyone would come to the hill behind our house. There was this girl I liked, and the greatest thing to me was sledding down the hill with her on my back. I tried to scare her." They also hunted, fished, and stayed all night with each other. "One friend was an only child, so his mom would give me a banana to take to school. My family couldn't afford bananas." His best friend was Jimmy Olsen. He still is. "When we were about thirteen, he got shot in the back of the leg and almost died. I remember feeling like I was dying with him."

## Career

He didn't really choose a career. He went into the marines at seventeen as a possible career during World War II. He went to college because the government paid for it. In his junior year, he chose accounting. "By accident, I got into college accounting, which led me into educational administration. It all happened more than it was planned. If you don't have a specific career in mind, just walk through doors that are open to you, do your best, always be ready for anything, and you find what you're meant to do." He prepared by doing the very best at whatever he did, by serving well the people he worked for, by being positive, never doubting he could get the job done, being committed, believing in what he did, and working hard. "Over my life of working on the farm and doing what was required in the marines—radio, radar, gunman in an airplane, war, mustering the courage to face death, working with people, in college through earning a PhD to prepare for life, and today in writing and giving speeches—a life filled with love, appreciation and interaction with family and preparation for all I do. This all gives confidence and a feeling of importance."

"As a university president, challenges were dealing with human problems that arise, dealing with students and with parents when you expel their child for drinking, drugs, or bad grades, telling parents when their child is killed in a car accident or a student whose parent dies or commits suicide." (Also when the public wants something he knows is wrong for the institution.) He learned to face realities and that there are happy and sad aspects of life. He would advise young people to consider his occupation. "It is the most fulfilling, satisfying, stimulating, exciting work I can imagine. It is never boring." He thinks working with young people in a college/university setting keeps him forever young. An occupation in higher education as a teacher or administrator means you can do so many things. "It's a world that encompasses the spirit, ambition, and anticipation of young people. It keeps you from growing old."

## Day-to-Day Living

One of his recent days went like this: breakfast with two community leaders, a representative of the Office of Education, and lunch with an associate justice of the Supreme Court. Then he attended the dedication of the new law school building. Then back to his office to collect a fax for a speech he'll make to the Fellowship of Christian Athletes. Next, he met with major donors to the university and later spent time making and receiving calls in his office, working on speeches, and fund-raising. His favorite time of the day is 7:00–7:30 in the morning when he is most alert. He reads the paper to see what's been going on.

He appreciates the telephone most of all so he can talk to his family, and it's a part of his work. He also appreciates a nice car and airplanes because he spends so much time in them. "Transportation, communication, and personal comforts like heat and air-conditioning are what I appreciate most." He reads a lot of professional literature, journals, newspapers, and books on leadership, education, and current literature. "Lately I've read Ross Perot's book and Norman Schwarzkopf's book." He's traveled to 150 countries. He's been on every continent and in most major cities. "I've been on the bullet train in Japan, the Trans-Siberian Railroad, the Blue Train in South Africa, the Orient Express, the Gohn Train in Australia, European trains, and the Red Air Express from Moscow to Leningrad. I'm probably in the top 9 percent of people who travel." He most enjoys spending time with family and friends. "I enjoy interacting with my family, reflecting on the past, and looking ahead. It's my most enjoyable activity."

## Personal Philosophy

His advice for getting along with others is to not take himself too seriously. He has strong beliefs but says his perspective is not necessarily always right. "If I don't know someone, and I criticize them, I'm being unfair. I have to be tolerant of other people's beliefs." He says it's important to get to know people and communicate. He named several people as his idea of the greatest people of this century. He says, "Anwar Sadat is the epitome of getting along. He was willing to get to know Menachem Begin and Israel so they could live together and not die together." He also named General Norman Schwarzkopf because of his "demeanor, spirit, and success in battle, even though he didn't like war." He also says Gorbachev and Reagan allowed our countries to talk and get to know each other, which prevented war. He feels the most significant discovery of the twentieth century is the harnessing of atomic power. "Some may say it's the reason for many deaths, but it terminated World War II. One of the most important discoveries is the polio vaccine." He also feels that the automobile, air travel, TV, and the telephone are important because they "opened the world to interaction and communication."

Schools today he says are "sorely lacking in positive impact because many parents are lacking in positive impact." He says there's too little time for parents and children today, and family units don't share responsibilities. "Schools have become too technical and legal to encourage individuality." He feels schools like my high school, Farragut, are an exception because of strong parental support. "In the past, the family and church made up for what schools lacked. No one knows today what to teach as far as values. There should be values we teach for the good of society." His philosophy of education is that education goes from cradle to grave. "We need to recognize that we deal with students from the day they are born. The government can be involved in seeing that mothers have the ability and time to love and nurture children. How we are loved, fed, and clothed has to do with our effectiveness in learning—who our teachers are, physical setting, and who are our families and peers are all important." He also feels we need smaller classes, that uneducated or unqualified teachers should not be allowed to teach, and that there should be less interference in learning.

I enjoyed interviewing Bruce Heilman. I feel I now know more about him and the environment he grew up in.

\*\*\*

# V

## FROM RAISING COWS TO RAISING MONEY: MORGAN DAVIS

Who would believe that a boy so poor that he had to milk cows at five o'clock in the morning could grow up to be the president of a university? Bruce Heilman is that boy. Today, he spends his time raising money for universities and colleges. When he was a little boy, he spent his time raising corn and cows. Today, he goes around the world on airplanes. He used to go around the farm on an old tractor. Today, he teaches other people how to be successful. When he was a little boy, he was successful at driving his teachers crazy because he snuck out of the classroom window. I know this because Bruce Heilman is my grandfather.

My grandfather had a very hard childhood. He was born in Oldham County, Kentucky, in the 1920s on Moody Lane. He said it should be called Muddy Lane because it was always muddy. He had two brothers and a sister. He always worked on the farm. His family was very poor. Even though cars and electricity had been invented, he had none. His family dreamed and wished they had these things. They had to go outside to the bathroom and use the privy. They got all their food from the animals and the garden. The chicken feed came in cloth bags, and his mother sewed the cloth together and made their clothes. They used the well as a refrigerator. They put food in a bucket and lowered it down over the water. In the summer, they swam in the creek and had picnics. In the winter, they sat by the stove in the kitchen. They had one oil lamp. That was the only thing they had to light up the house, but it was better than the coal lamp they used to have. His family's idea of a good time was going to church because he got to get away from the farm. They also saw their friends and caught up on news. The only other way they heard about news was through the mail.

At age nine, my grandfather woke up at four in the morning, walked a mile to a barn, milked cows, and walked home three hours later to eat breakfast. His brothers and father did that too. My grandfather did not have much education. There was very little time for school. His family only went to school about once or twice a week. When they did go, they did not have time to do homework or study. Their father thought they should be working on the farm and not spending time studying. In the winter, the family worked from four in the morning until eight at night when they went to bed because it was dark and cold.

When he was a few years older, they moved to the little town of Ballardsville. His father worked on a farm that was four miles away and made thirty dollars a month and got a free house to live in. The family received a gallon of milk a day free and had a garden. When the Great Depression hit, and the rest of the world was hungry and poor, they had hearty meals and were happy. They always had plenty of milk, and to this day, my grandfather still drinks chocolate milk for every meal. He will go in the most fancy restaurant and still ask for chocolate milk.

When he did go to school, the school had only four rooms. He and his brothers and sister walked half a mile. They enjoyed school, but my grandfather thought it was funny to jump out the window and play hooky and annoy the teacher. He remembers being in the Future Farmers of America Club, which he enjoyed. In the club, they took field trips to farms and learned about trees and livestock. Today, that has helped him because he owns a tree farm in Kentucky, and on the farm, he has cows. The club had a band, and my grandfather played the harmonica. He still plays that harmonica today.

His aunt and uncle died in a car accident when he was around twelve and left his father some money. The family bought some cows and started a farm with a neighbor. While his family was working this farm, the war started. His older brother had joined the marines, and he decided to follow in his footsteps. He left high school and spent four years in the marines and got enough high school credits to go to college. A little college in Campbellsville, Kentucky, was willing to give him a chance. Today, he is on the board of trustees of that same college. The college also took a chance on a poor girl named Betty Dobbins from Louisville, Kentucky. My grandfather was still poor in college. He loved pie, so Betty snuck him a few pieces of free pie. Soon they were married and ended up with five children: four girls and a boy.

After my grandfather finished college, he worked at many jobs while he got his master's degree and his PhD. After he did this, he was Vice president of Peabody College in Nashville, Tennessee, and then president of Meredith College in Raleigh, North Carolina, and finally, he went to the University of Richmond in Virginia. He went there to help raise money so the school wouldn't have to be shut down due to not having enough money to take care of the school. The people on his team for raising money were his staff, his vice presidents, his board of trustees, the faculty, and his administrative team who helped find the people who have money to give.

They also helped my grandfather convince the people to give their money. They keep the records, and they keep track of who donated money. Mr. Claiborne Robins who had given $50 million to the university, was one of my grandfather's greatest helpers, friends, and influences. My grandmother, Betty Heilman, helps my grandfather remember the many people's names he meets. She also helps him keep track of his schedule and gives dinners and luncheons and entertains the wives of the men who help him. She even packs his suitcase for the many trips he takes to raise money all over the United States and even the world.

His main accomplishments in leading this team were that he taught his team that you can accomplish any goals if you believe in yourself and you believe in the purpose of your goal. He taught them to be on time, to look nice, to be positive and friendly, and to listen to other members of the team. He learned to surround himself with people who had the skills and the education and the belief in themselves to help him lead the team. The team's goals were to raise as much money as possible for the University of Richmond so that it could become the best small private school in the country.

They wanted to raise another $50 million. The team had to overcome the problem that some people did not believe they could reach the goal. But my grandfather convinced them to keep trying and try new methods and be positive about the task and the goal. As he convinced more and more people that they could complete the task, they continued to raise the money. Overall, he, with the help of his team, has raised over half a billion dollars in the twenty-seven years he has been associated with the University of Richmond.

The world is better because of his accomplishments. Now many colleges and universities all over the United States have succeeded in raising money because of my grandfather. He has helped raise much money for many different colleges. He has taught other fund-raisers how to believe in themselves and how to convince others to believe and give money. One of the special things he did to make the University of Richmond better was to start the first school of leadership at a university in the United States. One of the people he convinced to believe in that school was General Norman Schwarzkopf, who is a member of the board. My grandfather tries to convince very important people to help him make the university a better school. He was listed in a book as one of the ten best fund-raisers in the country.

One of my grandfather's strengths is that he can convince people to believe in themselves. He does this by helping people figure out how to turn their weaknesses into strengths. Another strength is that he surrounds himself with people who can help him succeed because he realizes that he cannot do everything by himself. One more of his strengths is that he appreciates work, and he realizes that it is important to set goals and complete tasks. His very strong faith helps him find a purpose in accomplishing tasks. He loves his family very much too, and that helps him want to succeed. He is a very good father and a very good grandfather. He believes that your faith comes first and then your family. He realizes though that to be successful in a job, your family doesn't always have enough of your time.

This could be his main weakness. He wishes that he could have had more time with his family. He is making up for it as a wonderful grandfather. Another one of his weaknesses has always been his feeling that his early education was poor. But he overcame that because he believes in himself. He also thought it was a weakness that he couldn't do everything. All in all, he has done very well in being successful at his job.

He learned early that he could succeed in life. He learned that working every day pays off in the future. He learned that you can work better if you believe in yourself. He learned that many good things can come from bad things if you have the right attitude. When my grandfather talks about his growing up, he says there's no better way to build a foundation for being your best than the simple things like tilling soil, raising animals, growing crops, working hard and late, and giving up something for something even more valuable like helping your parents make a living.

# CHAPTER SIX
## TRAVEL

# I

## TRAVEL - SUMMER ADVENTURES

Travel agent boosting economy tour to client: "You land in four countries and fly low over another six."
Harry Mace, *The Christian Science Monitor*

# II

## UNUSUAL EXPERIENCES WHILE TRAVELING

In my travels to 145 countries over forty years, there are many highlights. Some were unanticipated incidents that come with the frequency and extent of my journeys. Some unusual happenings proved to be favorably disposed with little negative effects besides some anxiety in the process.

I can remember many incidents while traveling that might sound frightening, disturbing, disconcerting, or discouraging to others. However, all the tragedies and discomforts are overridden by the joys, pleasures, and enlightenment of travel.

I was traveling around the world with about thirty students, faculty, staff, alumni, and others, and we were going through American Samoa. Our flight was either completed or was in process when the travel agency decided to cancel that option and schedule another flight. That flight, a fully loaded jet, crashed on takeoff or landing in American Samoa, and everyone aboard was killed. That's about as serious as it can get. It was not really the traveling itself, but circumstances that are incidental to airline travel—such as accidents in cars or motorcycles—that are dangerous. It is all part of living with the various comforts that life has to offer.

On another occasion, we were flying back from Sydney, Australia. We had been in the air for about thirty minutes when the pilot announced, "If you can see out the right window, you will note that a piece of our wing has just peeled back. We are returning after jettisoning some fuel because we are fully loaded to get another airplane."

A piece of the airplane wing wouldn't affect our landing, but I'm sure the pilot felt that it would not be appropriate to continue for six hours with a piece of our wing fluttering in the wind.

In Africa we were supposed to have been in a jet, but Haile Selassie, the ruler of Addis Ababa, had priority—and he had the jet. A four-engine roaring transport plane carried us to Addis Ababa. We were supposed to stay for three or four days. As we were landing, an engine burst into flames. A Japanese tourist ran down the aisle, banged on the cockpit door, and shouted, "Engine on the fire!"

We landed with an engine flaming and discovered that they weren't going to let us get off the plane because they were at war with another country. Where we were supposed to stay? Our itinerary was for three or four days in the city. I finally persuaded them to let us go into the terminal and have a sandwich because we hadn't had anything to eat and didn't know where we were going. We went inside, and I worked things out, which is what a tour leader is supposed to do.

On several occasions, our flights were changed, which disrupted the itinerary. If you miss one flight, you've messed up all the other flights—and the airlines put somebody else in your place.

We took a boat down the Amazon River to Venezuela, and when it was time to catch our flight, I was notified that it had been canceled because the plane was already full. I did what a tour leader does and said, "We will be at the airport and we will board the plane because we have reservations." We went to the airport. I guess they understood clearly what I said because we had no competition. We got on the plane, went to Venezuela, and had our visit there. As a result, our several weeks of flights would not be messed up.

On a visit to the Galapagos Islands, we were flying in two or three small planes. At the time, there were tires being burned on the streets. There was a lot of negativism around. A lot of our travelers were uncomfortable about the safety of the airplanes and the rebellion.

My travels began long before I was taking people abroad as a university and college president. I was the crew member of the staff ship of the admiral of the Fifth Fleet when we were on occupation duty. We were flying out of a base near Tokyo, and our equipment sometimes did not provide full protection from Mount Fujiyama even though we had a ground-control approach. We really didn't know where we were. If we were flying into Tokyo, we had to be pretty darn sure where we were coming in. If we didn't have good guidance, we were also over Tokyo Bay. The cliffs surrounding the water were higher than the space between the water and the clouds. We would try to get down over the water and follow the cliffs into Tokyo Bay and our landing strip.

We were flying in without any real knowledge of where we were, and we kept letting down, hoping that we were over the water and not heading down to the cliffs. We came out below the clouds, and the cliffs extended up into the clouds. We found our way by following the cliffs to the airstrip in Tokyo Bay. The weather closed in before we touched the ground, and we could see nothing.

We actually hit the ground before we could see it. There was snow on the ground, and the fog looked like the snow. Even after the wheels were on the ground, we couldn't see where we were. I stood behind the pilot, putting different earphones with different beeps and sounds, and communication of one sort or another over each ear, advising and counseling on distance and the ground control unit. Sweat was running down our necks. We were not sure if we had touched the runway with our wheels or hit the ground on a wing or an engine and were heading off the runway.

On another occasion, as we were traveling to Okinawa, we were low on fuel—and our electrical system went out. We had no guidance. We had to use the age-old approach to squaring our flight until we luckily squared into the island without any real direction finder or navigator.

We landed with an empty tank.

Our airstrip was a short strip that ended over a concrete barrier that was right against the water. We had an engine change, and as we managed to lift up just enough to clear the wall, one engine went out. We dropped below the wall—right above the water—and the pilot gave the one engine everything it had. It hovered like a bird landing for an interminable period of time. We had every bit of engine effort, and after hovering for some time, it began to lift itself up. We got high enough to circle, come back, and land, but it was a close call. There was a carburetor interchange missing a bolt or some such thing, which almost made us spin into the water. That could have been fatal. There is a fine line between life and death.

A positive part of traveling were the trains. The Orient Express was delightful, and we had a wonderful experience. The Gohn Train across Australia was another wonderful experience. In South Africa, we flew from Johannesburg to Cape Town and spent two or three days on the Blue Train.

On another occasion, we took the Chinese Express and the Russian Trans-Siberian Railroad to Outer Mongolia. We left from Leningrad through Moscow to Noversberks to Lake Michael. The three- or four-day ride was challenging and unusual.

While they might not have always been as comfortable as trains in Canada or America, the Trans-Siberian Railroad was a very interesting experience. We took it all the way to Irkutsk in Outer Mongolia. We had three days with no place to eat. There was no food on the train, and we would stop at stations. The available food was full of flies and dirty. We ate peanuts or anything that didn't attract flies.

Six of us slept in a sleeper car on the train. People from Outer Mongolia mounted the train as it went along. They would stop along the way for people who were waiting on the side of the tracks. Two of them slept in our little room. One of them became very ill and messed up the whole room. I threw him out, and he kept banging on our door to get back in.

\*\*\*

Travel for me began when I left home on a train for the first time on a four-day trip from Kentucky to California. It was the beginning of the transformation of who I was, what I knew, and where I had been. It changed my life completely by changing my mind, my habits, my activities, my disposition, my culture, my environment, my sense of who I was, my potential, and every word I can imagine to say about myself.

It was a new departure, and travel began a large part of that. When life opened the door to travel, I was the guide, the leader, and the one who had to learn to deal with all the opportunities, problems, circumstances, and personalities. I was the teacher as well as the student, and I learned that travel served me well in my fund-raising and expanding relationships with alumni, students, faculty, and the rest.

When I became a college president, I was as untraveled as some others were traveled. Most of our college community had been everywhere. Within the community of a college, somebody had been here, somebody had been there, and in total, we had covered the world. As the new president, I could not claim that I had traveled extensively. I had expanded beyond the farm. I had been in combat in the Pacific, and I had been in Japan on occupation duty. However, I had not gone in an academic sense—teaching and learning and interacting with other people. It was my chance to get educated, to learn how to deal with travel, and realize that if you take a group with you, you can get your way paid, which was a big incentive.

In the long run, you could even have the extra privilege of bringing your spouse and some of your family. Therefore, it became one of the real sources of family relationships, broadening of education, learning what happens in the world, and seeing that other people are not that different from those of us who have been in a cocoon for much of our lives.

I did not just go to Paris and London—where many go because that is the realm of enlightenment. They are places we know about. We even have friends there, and everybody else has been there. We need to have been there too. Most people find themselves restricted to just those kinds of places. Perhaps they have been to the Taj Mahal and can claim that. I began my journey, and I indulged myself every summer in the learning, teaching, and the conveying of information and knowledge. Those were the things to speak about at colleges and universities where I served during that forty-year period when I was traveling the most.

## BACK TO OKINAWA

# University President Doubles As Tour Chief

Dr. E. Bruce Heilman Rides Camel in Cairo in June

**Richmond Times-Dispatch**
Sunday, November 26, 1972

Reprinted From
Page 1, Section J

By JAMES P. BERRY

If Dr. E. Bruce Heilman were to set up a travel agency he'd likely do a land office business. Who could resist globe trotting with a handsome, urbane Southerner who just happens to be president of a major university as tour director?

The fact that Dr. Heilman is a university president precludes such a commercial venture, but he does direct tours. He has seen a good portion of the world in the past few years and not solely for the ordinary tourist's reasons.

When he became president of Meredith College at Raleigh, N.C., Dr. Heilman discovered he was less widely traveled than many of the faculty and students. "I was supposed to be the leader and they were talking about things I had not experienced in many cases." He decided he would set aside some time every year to go abroad "and be as knowledgeable as those I was trying to lead."

The idea came at a time of stress between students and administrations. It wasn't long before Dr. Heilman, three of his daughters and 25 Meredith students headed for Europe and a tour of 10 countries. Traveling and eating at student rates, Dr. Heilman lived off hamburgers for three weeks, grew a splendid beard and got very close to 28 students.

"You're a different person on campus after you've taken 28 of your students abroad for three weeks. You're no longer that isolated person up in the ivory tower, and it spreads around. It gives you a little better understanding and appreciation for your students and it makes them see you more as a human being."

Dr. Heilman also recognized that many world travelers would be representative of many off-campus constituencies that a college or university relates to, such as alumni and trustees.

He organized a tour of the Orient in 1970 and led another group to Europe, the Mediterranean, the Middle East, Africa and South America this year. He's planning a trip to Australia next summer and is hoping to assemble an around the world trip, including a stop in China, the year after.

**Plenty of Travelers**

"I have professional travel people working with me but I decide where we are going." The travel groups draw up the details such as air flights and accommodations.

A Heilman-directed tour is marked by the number of points on the globe touched. He never has had difficulty getting a group together. "Travelers get impatient if you stay put. Three days is about all you want." He views the policy as a question of "how many places do you identify with so you have an interest in learning about them."

After that trip to the Orient, tour members were already getting in line for the next one. "I simply say to the group who have traveled before, we're going to go here, and I get 15 or 20 of those and their friends and we've got a crowd. It's that simple really."

**Director Kept Hopping**

When the tour is under way there is enough activity to keep the tour director hopping. In Ethiopia, a cancelled flight caused a sequence of problems with transportation and accommodations that kept Dr. Heilman busy for several hours.

In one African country, the tour members nearly lost their personal cash when border officials decided that the money couldn't be taken out of the country since it hadn't been registered upon arrival.

"We had a very serious problem for about an hour." He ironed it out successfully. Another time in Africa, the worldwide pilot strike cancelled another flight. "What you do is just sit there, and we did."

Dr. Heilman's main reason for traveling is education and he gets that. "I learn three times as much as anybody else because I'm dealing with the natives of whatever the land. I may not speak the language but I've got to get through to them and they to me. I'm forever reading the maps. I learn a lot more about the country than anybody who's just along for the ride. They relax, I don't."

**Exciting Moments**

It is sometimes pretty exciting. He recalls vividly barreling down a mountain road in Japan in fog so thick he couldn't see beyond the window. The aircraft which flew Dr. Heilman and a tour group to Ethiopia landed with one engine on fire. "That's part of the excitement of traveling, anything can happen."

Such incidents are rare, however, and hardly discouraging. Planning for the trip to Australia is already in full swing.

"Most of us think we're so blamed busy that this is an impossible task. But I made a judgment that if I really was going to provide some sense of leadership and have a perspective that's world wide that I simply had to build this time in. Then when summer comes I'm so busy I can't go but I've already got people lined up and can't fail to go. So I go.

"If you didn't do it that way you wouldn't do it. Now I've discovered it's so valuable in every way, very meaningful to the institution and to me and to those I work with, I do it as a matter of course.

---

There were many experiences associated with these travels, but even a thumbnail sketch will contribute much to the interest of those who did not travel with me. I will try not to go into full detail by year so that it becomes boring, but I will at least do a thumbnail sketch about where I have been, what I have learned, and what the experiences have meant.

I have traveled abroad, and I have traveled within the United States on river cruises and special programs and activities. I have been a speaker, and I have been involved in professional programs. With the benefit of my Harley-Davidson, I have covered all fifty states. In many circumstances, I was either speaking or serving veterans programs or traveling in other ways. I have contributed a valuable service.

Beyond my activities in America, I have covered the world for the privilege and benefit of myself and the institutions I have served—as well as the staff, faculty, alumni, and students who joined us on these occasions.

I have been to China four times. The last time was a cruise on the Yang-Tze River in

2002. I was there for fifteen days with a wonderful group of people. It was just before the YangTze River was closed to the tours because the new dam was being built. We were privileged to make the cruise just before the interruption of the dam.

An unusual, wonderful journey was on a coast-to-coast Canadian rail adventure. There was an around-the-world-in-fifteen-days trip with a delightful group of people. We toured Munich, Delhi, Katmandu, Lajsa, Chengdu, and Hong Kong.

We did a Mediterranean cruise, a Panama Canal cruise, and an enchanting Galapagos Island, Kato, and the Amazon cruise in one fell swoop. I have taken a very popular cruise to Alaska three times.

A South Africa journey included Namibia, Botswana, Zimbabwe, Swazi Land, Ciskei, and Transkei. We traveled by bus. Another unique trip was a tour to Siberia. We rode the TransSiberian Railroad to Outer Mongolia. We stayed at the capital city of Ulaanbaatar on the sixtieth anniversary celebration of their communist government.

We had a South Pacific tour that was different from the one we had taken before, but it was interrupted by the testing of an atom bomb by France. We traveled to Cairo and enjoyed riding camels.

We went to Iceland for the 350th anniversary of the Passion Play and back to China for a Far East tour. We have taken two or three trips for the highlights of Europe with students and our own children.

Another journey was to the Ivory Coast, Egypt, and a Nile cruise to Tunis and Sousse.

Another Mediterranean cruise covered Italy, Turkey, and Greece.

A pleasant and restful cruise was on the *American Queen*. In Australia, we took the Gohn

Train and visited the Great Barrier Reefs. Another journey took us to Germany, Poland, Hungry, Czechoslovakia, and Rumania. Another one went to Scandinavia, Russia, Eastern Europe, Kenya, Egypt, and the South Pacific.

Another tour was to Southeast Asia, and many family members joined us on a Kenya safari. A special cruise to eleven countries on the Orient Express was followed by Russia, Bulgaria, Turkey, Greece, Yugoslavia, Italy, San Marino, Austria, Switzerland, France, and Great Britain.

We rode the Blue Train from Johannesburg to Cape Town, South Africa. Another tour was the best of Scandinavia, Copenhagen, Anders, Oslo, Fjord Country, Bergan, and Stockholm.

All of these lasted two or three weeks. I attended the Baptist World Alliance and introduced Billy Graham in Europe.

We cruised to Oahu, Kauai, Mali, and the Big Island aboard the Norwegian Cruise Lines' *Pride of Aloha*. In Tibet, the lack of oxygen gave us headaches as we climbed into the Potala Palace. We also visited Katmandu, Nepal, Vietnam, Cambodia, and Thailand. We cruised on the Baltic Sea to Denmark, Russia, Finland, Sweden, Estonia, and

Germany. A tour of the highlights of Europe included London, Amsterdam, Brussels, Paris, Venice, and Vienna. A Kenyan safari took us to Egypt, Nairobi, Ambos Eli, Mount Kilimanjaro, Lake Nauru, Masaimara, Cairo, and Luxor. We also visited Eastern Europe, Prague, Warsaw, Istanbul, Vienna, Budapest, Lucerne, Hong Kong, China, Tibet, Burma, Thailand, Singapore, Malaysia, and Taiwan. We went through the Panama Canal and took a Caribbean cruise. We took an Iberian holiday on Air Portugal. We were in Germany when the Berlin Wall came down. All of these were exemplary experiences.

\*\*\*

# III

## THROUGH SIBERIA BY TRAIN TO OUTER MONGOLIA

In my travels, I have spoken to groups and found a lot of interest. This one represents Russia or the Soviet Union in a unique way. For those who are much younger, it is a little bit of history, and I hope it will be of interest to most people.

It was a long time ago, and many things have changed. I was with the presidents of fifty other colleges. There were two of us from each state, and most were college presidents. We were being educated, and it was part of the process. This history is based upon the way things have changed, and I wrote it in 1968.

The following paragraphs are just a small part of a paper I prepared on the journey to the Soviet Union to put a historic context on my trip.

\*\*\*

Galapagos Islands
Two roads diverged in a yellow wood and I—I took the road
less traveled by and that has made all the difference.
——*Robert Frost*

Cairo
Good company on a journey is worth a coach.
—*Scottish Proverb*

Moscow is a quiet city. Drivers are forbidden to use horns except in cases of emergency. There are no sirens shrieking or ambulances. No aircraft pass over the city, and children seldom yell in the streets; in fact, they are seldom seen there. Silence is strange because it is a city of great crowds, and normally you would expect noise. Men and women—short, square, and squat— make up the masses, and there seems to be no such person as a Russian alone. And yet, Russia seems to be a lonely world in spite of the masses. There is very little juvenile delinquency in Moscow compared to other large cities and very little crime, although windshield wipers are removed and stored inside the car.

Imagine being in a world where you can't get a coke and being out of communication with the Western world. The radio at the hotel had one switch—on and off—and only Russian programs. Could you believe that a country could survive with a policy of no tipping and that the gesture would actually be refused—or elevators being shut down for repairs in a major hotel so that for a week everyone walked to the fifth, sixth, or seventh floor, carrying their luggage and with no complaints, at least not audible?

In Russia, I ate less—and I liked it even less. There were many courses, and one never knew which was the beginning and the end. Ice cream was the nearest thing to American food, and we looked forward to it. There was no such treat as cereal and milk. The eggs were always boiled and somehow didn't get the job done.

We visited the largest pioneer palace in Moscow. A pioneer palace is where selected youngsters go to do all kinds of things after school hours. It is a kind of combination YMCA, Boy Scouts, and Sunday school. But of course, its goal is the Young Communist League rather than a haven or some other comparable place. The age range for pioneers is from six to eighteen. Here they do their thing, but clearly that thing is what they are expected to do.

The soil of much of Siberia is permanently frozen, and only the surface melts in summer, so the crops are difficult to grow. In Siberia, it can get as cold as ninety degrees below zero.

Average summer temperatures are between fifty and sixty-five degrees Fahrenheit.

I saw only a few peasants riding in horse-drawn sleds. Most were plodding through the snow in huge felt boots. Men wore fur caps with big flaps covering their ears, while women were wrapped in woolen scarves—so many woolen scarves that they seemed to have no necks. Everybody looked rotund to the extent that some appeared that they might roll more easily than they walked. Steam rose from their mouths as they trudged along.

Siberia is to the Soviet Union what the West was to the United States over a hundred years ago. This is the great pioneer land. With much mining and with new dams and resulting power, much industry has developed. Great forests exist, and timber is plentiful as are bears and other game. Outside the cities, small villages have unpaved streets and a rough pioneer appearance. For hundreds of years, it has been a place to send exiles and criminals. Many have helped develop the area.

One of the wonderful aspects of visiting Russia is in returning to the Western world. The cold citadel of communism is changing on the surface, but it still has a personality that's hard to define and hard to accept. It is clearly the other world. Moscow is the epitome of Soviet determination. It also embodies the limitations of the Soviet system. The system is in the hotels, in the airlines, in the streets, in the tourist attractions, in the educational system. It is everywhere. There is no question that it is durable, it is vital, and that there is an inhuman drive, an almost ruthless determination in that which takes place in the day-to-day activities of the Soviet Union.

Carribbean Cruise
The supreme happiness of life is
the conviction that we are loved.
—*Victor Hugo*

President and Mrs. E. Bruce Heilman with alumna Carol Green at the Taj Mahal.

Venice
Better to have a friend on the road
than gold and silver in your purse.
*-French Proverb*

Disney World
Give a little love to a child
and you get a great deal back.
*-John Ruskin*

Bangkok, Thailand
God shares with the person who is generous.
-Irish Proverb

**June 27–July 18, 1981**

Last summer, when being introduced as one who had recently journeyed to Outer Mongolia, there was a studied gaze in my direction and then a somewhat awe-inspired response: "I've never before seen anyone who's been to that planet before." This typifies the reaction to and the mystery surrounding the name and the place that had captured my interest over the years and finally inspired my decision to lead a group of thirty-eight well-traveled tourists to this faraway place with its strange-sounding name.

Certainly, all of us have a feeling of studied excitement for the unknown. We fantasize about the history of the people who are in worlds apart from ourselves. Especially are we intrigued by those places in the world where habits and philosophies are strange to us, where creations of nature are unusual, and where circumstances of impositions brought about by government, by war, by economic circumstances, or by something else are in contrast to our own.

Outer Mongolia fits the bill in many ways when characterized by the above. So does the Soviet Union, particularly that part called Siberia. The latter became a pathway on a journey to Outer Mongolia for a group of people who had literally been everywhere else and who longed for adventure rather than comfort, for new perspectives rather than old habits, and for the possibility of risks rather than guarantees of security. No one was disappointed whose views followed this pattern.

Although our itinerary took us from New York to Helsinki, Finland, to Leningrad, Russia, and by Red Arrow Express to Moscow with much to do and see along the way, our most unusual experience had its beginnings on a train called the *Russia*, headed east out of Moscow on the Trans-Siberian Railroad.

The great Siberian Express plunges east through one of the world's richest and least populated areas. It clicks over barren but beautiful terrain, through forests and steppes, through ninety-three towns and villages. The railroad, which was built to protect the Great Russian outpost beyond the Urals from China, Japan, or some other invader, is continually under construction, giving evidence that it is regularly upgraded and still unfinished and likely will never know completion.

Signs of the old Trans-Siberian track could be seen in various stages of its earlier construction, having deteriorated on the mounds that still existed. The newer railroad is certainly a grand improvement, due to bridge construction and improved roadbeds.

As the line moves eastward, on its southern side lies China, and to the north are the unmarked regions of frozen tundra from which, during the long winters, ice, snow, and charging winds sweep down. Between the two are fortunes of much promise of a new national destiny for the Soviet Nation.

One old legend has it that in the beginning when God was distributing resources around the world, his hands froze as he passed over Siberia so that he dropped all of the rich resources he was carrying. Hence, Siberia's wealth of oil, minerals, timbers, gold, and much else.

Siberia is a large part of the land mass of the Soviet Union, which composes one-sixth of the inhabitable land area of the world and extends over almost one-half of Eurasia, and Siberia holds only a small part of its population of over 250 million.

Siberia, with its limited population was a center of world political power during the twelfth and thirteenth centuries when Genghis Khan's Golden Horde thundered across it to conquer most of Asia, Europe up to the Danube, and Asia Minor up to the Suez.

The people of Siberia say with tongue in cheek that winter lasts twelve months and the rest of the year is summer. This is almost more truth than fiction; there is an extremely short growing season for corps. Rivers turn to ice in winter temperatures of forty degrees below zero, and the permafrost soil can swallow buildings, highways, and even airfields if it finally thaws.

The czars tried to develop Siberia's gold mines with political exiles, Stalin used his famous slave-labor camp approach, while today workers are offered high wages, bonuses, paid vacations, and even the right to buy new cars when they return home if they will work in Siberia for a stated period of time.

Novelist Maxim Gorki describes Siberia as a "land of death and chains," but the Soviet government insists that all problems can be whipped if everyone would work harder.

## The Train

Each of us had our own impression of the Trans-Siberian train. But for most of us, it proved to be not so different from trains we had experienced in other parts of the world. It was not as clean as some, but it was cleaner than others. It was not as new as some, but it was newer than others. There was one first-class coach on the train (only two to a compartment). Our group of thirtyeight could not be accommodated there, so thirty-six were put in one car that contained four to a compartment. Our oldest member (eighty-six) had a top bunk so that she could jump out and jog every morning. My wife and I were placed in a different coach with some very delightful Swedes and a number of Russians. In our immediate compartment were a girl from Switzerland and our Russian tourist guide, Nastasha.

A little old lady looked after the coach and acted as if she were a hen caring for her chicks. She swept the aisle regularly and periodically used a small vacuum. She locked and unlocked our compartments, closed and opened windows, made tea, herded us on and off at the various stops, and admonished us not to miss the train, suggesting that when the whistle blows, it is already too late. Two members of the group from Sweden did manage to miss the train at one stop and caught up with us two and a half days later.

Along the way, we passed large and small hayfields. We saw a variety of equipment, including scythes being used by old ladies and old men cutting the hay along the railroad tracks. They were stacking it with pitchforks. These plots, we were told, were rented from the government for a few rubles, and the hay was stacked in the barns beside the houses to feed the cattle during the cold, bitter winters.

One could see a variety of fences made from long white birch trees and other kinds of wood that grows in abundance. On one occasion, we saw a train carrying prisoners in cells within the train. We could not, of course, take pictures.

In the distance, we could see Siberian cowboys rounding up cattle, and at the stations, we observed affection between mothers and children, and husbands and wives, and no doubt, sweethearts and lovers, all of which has an international appeal.

Outside the cities, tucked away in narrow valleys, could be seen the traditional greenhued, single-story wood houses with triple-thick glass windows to keep out the winter cold. Some looked like shacks, but cozy nonetheless. Pipelines winding through the countryside reminded us of Alaska.

When it rained, it poured, but it cooled the un-air-conditioned train, even in Siberia.

There were woodworker communities along the way with logs stacked high and sawmills visible. Sawdust was being spread on bare ground for road surfaces.

We moved through cities with populations that ran into the hundreds of thousands. Some of these were centers for gold mining, ultra-modern hydroelectric power stations, or paper mills. In Omsk, population three hundred thousand, farm products, dairy, and cattle-raising predominate. Greenhouses and irrigation along with fields of cabbage and potatoes, are evidence of the significance of agricultural activity. The potatoes were being harvested by machinery, while the gardens growing right against the houses throughout Siberia were being tended by individuals who, in the early morning, were clothed with wraps to offset the cool air.

As we traveled, we almost became dizzy from the frequency of trains passing from the other direction. The Siberian railroad is a busy one.

Metropolitan and educational and cultural centers such as Novosibirsk appeared as we sped east. We could see Aeroflot aircraft overhead and other business that goes with a major city. The population of Novosibirsk, the capital city of Siberia, is more than one million. It is a city of science and culture. It hosts the Siberian branch of the USSR Academy of Sciences and has brought world renown to the Soviet Union.

At the station at Novosibirsk, one could buy sweetbreads, brown bread, fish, pickles, and cigarettes. In every city, we could see the apartment houses springing up because more people need more apartments, and relatively few people live in houses. We saw goats at one main thoroughfare in Novosibirsk. Seldom did we see paved roads outside the city, and just a few cars except in the city.

The scenery is much the same throughout the Trans-Siberian journey. Green fields, birch and conifer forests, scattered villages, rivers, and marshes with wildflowers can be seen all along the way. The weather was rather warm, and we usually slept without sheets or blankets. When it rained, it poured and when it became chilly, it penetrated. As we moved in and out of cities and through the countryside, we saw Russian military men and equipment as well as numbers of police personnel. They were not always distinguishable, but they were on the watch and on the prowl as we were to discover after several days on the train when, at Irkutsk, I was summoned and told that it was reported to officials that we were taking pictures that were uncomplimentary to the Soviet Union and inconsistent with rules of our travel. I was told forthrightly that if this continued as we headed south toward China, not only would the film of the one guilty be taken away, but the film of everyone in the group would be destroyed. I transmitted the message and cameras disappeared for much of the rest of the journey through Russia. They never totally reappeared—even in Mongolia.

No pictures were to be taken in or near tunnels, water, bridges, entrances to railroad stations, trains, railroad junctions, airports, or of anything or anywhere that would not present the best of Russia and its efforts toward peace and cooperation of the people—or involving its security. They said to me, "Do not get in unpleasant situations because Intourist (Soviet Travel agency) can do nothing about it" (someone else would take over). "Have a good time," they remarked, "and remember that if the police see one taking such pictures, he will be compelled to act."

## Irkutsk

We were privileged to spend several days in Irkutsk, a modern city north of the Mongolian border and deep into Siberia. The history and art museums are cultural attractions in this city where it sometimes snows as late as the middle of May. The Angara River divides the city, and when swimmers brave its cold waters, they are called walruses. Most of the people in the city are old, and those who are young suffer the consequences of the deep cold. Children stay home from school when the temperature drops forty degrees below zero.

A frost-free period exits for only ninety-three days on the average, providing a very short growing season. In fact, it frosted at the end of June just before our arrival.

Because of the cold weather, apple trees do not grow tall. They grow along the ground like snakes. Plums come out in September before the snow. There are watermelons, even though they are small in size. The seasons are winter and summer. Winter lasts nine months, and summer last three. Average temperatures in January are minus twenty degrees Celsius.

In the marketplace in Irkutsk, flowers, fruit, and berries are sold in much the same fashion as in the free market enterprise situation we have in our country. Individuals rent government space, bring their overage from rented government land, and make a little profit. We saw everything from cucumbers to strawberries to potatoes to beans, radishes, apples, seeds of all kinds, and flowers of every description, many of them familiar to us. Some of our ladies received flowers in exchange for their chewing gum.

Department stores were comparable in size to our major shopping centers, but the quality and variety were very different. Many of the same items would be found in different departments.

As we strolled the city, we were dodging automobiles because the pedestrian is on his own and therefore is at risk. He must watch out for the cars.

There are fifty thousand students in Irkutsk, mostly studying engineering, mineralogy, and other skills that are so greatly needed by the Russians in Siberian country.

At the Russian Museum of History in Irkutsk, we saw the development of the Siberian area from prehistoric days to the current year.

Outside the city of Irkutsk is one of the real attractions of Siberia and one of the real wonders of the world, Lake Baikal, which contains 10 percent of the world's fresh water. The lake is lovely, dressed in its deep blue and trimmed in green. In the area of this great body of water can be found the highly valued Siberian sable whose pelt is highly prized. These and other animals, including mink, ermine, chipmunk, muskrat, wolverines, and Siberian squirrel are found near the lake because it never freezes over due to its warm currents.

Lake Baikal is twenty million years old and is thought to be the oldest lake in the world. It was formed by earthquakes. It would take an hour's flight to get from the southern to the northern end of the lake, a distance of almost four hundred miles.

Baikal has more water than all the Great Lakes of America put together.

Wild azaleas bloom there, but the most spectacular flowers are the wild, bright peonies. Orange *Trollius assiaticus*, which looks like ranunculus, also bloom there. The Russians call them fire flowers.

There are grassy hills but no birch forests along the fringes of the Gobi Desert near Lake Baikal. The only high, snowcapped peaks of the entire trip could be seen there.

## Mongolian Train

After our stay in Irkutsk, we discovered that we had been displaced by diplomats on their way to celebrate the sixtieth anniversary of the Mongolian revolution on the Peking Express. We were relegated to a slow train, which would be better defined as a Mongolian cattle train—in the best sense of the word. For two nights and a day, without a dinner or any means for food except what we carried with us, we would plow southward without bath or even water safe for cleaning teeth. But on our way to Ulan Bator, the capital city of Outer Mongolia, not all was lost in disillusionment and disappointment. We were learning firsthand how Mongolians travel and live. That was, after all, the reason for our journey.

In our first evening aboard the Mongolian train, we visited Russian and Mongolian students traveling home for vacation. We exchanged not only conversation, but gifts as well; one of our group receiving an ashtray in the likeness of a little bear catching a fish, and I received a small crock Mongolian face mask. One of the students who was an English major translated as we discovered who was Mongolian and who was Russian. It was not too difficult to tell, but confirmation was helpful nonetheless. Some were studying economics; others were at institutions of various kinds.

They were interested in everything imaginable—even our school systems. Vala indicated it was difficult for her to understand the different opportunities we have in America and hoped, she said, she could come to America someday, but it was so far away and very difficult.

By the time we arrived at Naushki (Nowski), the border town of Russia on the way to Outer Mongolia, we were hungry enough to eat almost anything, almost anywhere, and did so in a dining room that was crowded with flies. The soup was good, the juice was wet, and the salad was green. Most indulged; some did not. A few attempted to eat meat and bread, but not many. It was at least a break in the routine. We enjoyed about an hour and a half of our four-hour layover in the dining room.

The balance of the time was spent under the shade tree watching soldiers from a nearby airbase. As you can guess, no cameras and no pictures were allowed, which is pretty understandable because it was a border area.

We left Naushki at 7:25 p.m. after a six-hour delay and very shortly came to the border town between Russian and Mongolia. There, going into a satellite country, there was a Russian guard tower, barbed wire fences strung high, and dogs. It would be futile for anyone to try to leave or enter as elsewhere in the Russian empire.

Though we were out of Russia, we were not sure who was in charge of the train at that point. Part was Mongolian, part was Russian, so we took no chances in taking pictures. Russian guards continued on the train beyond the border. Perhaps it was a neutral zone of some sort.

We entered Outer Mongolia at the border town of Suki Bator. We could see gers (yurts in Russia) along the highways, often surrounded by horses and cattle. This was a very different kind of scenery from that we left behind in Siberia.

Colorful banners flew in communities and at the railroad stations we passed. This was evidence of the great celebration that was taking place in the country—the sixtieth anniversary of the revolution.

As we traveled south, potatoes were still to be seen beside the train, and there were mountains in the background. Under a bridge, mountain goats congregated, and along the way, there were snow breaks and wind breaks of pines.

In Outer Mongolia, horses are the main means of transportation locally. People catch the train almost like they would mount a horse. The train stops almost anywhere. It stops not only at the stations but in the countryside. People rush to get on, and others jump off. An old lady was running across a field at full speed, and the train waited until she made it, but just barely. Everyone was applauding and rooting for her as she made her way through the barbed wire and onto the train just as it lurched forward. Where they come from and where they are going is hard to know because the area is pretty desolate.

Yurts and horses dot the countryside. The mail is picked up and deposited in a place that looks like a depot, but it could have been a post office. Cattle roam the hillsides. It is an isolated and primitive countryside.

When soldiers are seen in uniform, they are dirty and certainly not very military in the rural areas. Signalmen ride horses up to the side of the train holding flags.

At about two in the morning, one of our roommates disembarked and was replaced by a Mongolian who was very drunk. He awakened the other three of us, trying to get to an upper bunk. He was very loud, and we could understand nothing of his shouting. Soon, he became ill, and the result was disaster to our compartment. After trying to clean up, we found him no better. He leaned over the top again and fell out; I caught him on the way down and ushered him out.

With some help from the compartment team, we managed to pull his hands away from the door and routed him to the hall where we tried to get him to lie down. He fought his way back into the room. He was as strong as he was drunk. Finally, we managed to pull him out, and the door was locked from within, but I was still outside where he tried to fight but couldn't find me. He went up and down the hall, opening other compartments, until finally he went into a Mongolianoccupied cabin where he could be understood. I went back in my cabin, and we locked him out. During the night, he returned periodically, sometimes with reinforcements, but we never yielded.

When I went to the back of the car trying to settle the drunk, I looked at the car behind us at about three o'clock in the morning, the people were like sardines packed and standing. They banged on the door, motioning for me to unlock it, so they could come to our car and spread out.

I did not dare do that, being afraid they would take over the whole place.

When we arrived in Ulan Bator, we were greeted by the Intourist of Outer Mongolia, an organization called Hzuulchlin. We soon discovered that there was a substantial lack of efficiency and not a great deal of concern for whether we were satisfied, but a lot of regimentation and routine.

Immediately upon arrival, we were taken to our hotel, only to be told that we could not stay there because of the great holiday crowds occupying the rooms because we were a day late in our arrival. Our rooms had been canceled. We were soon back on the road to the airport with our guide, Mr. Batsu, to catch a Mongolian airline headed for the Gobi Desert where we could be accommodated for the evening.

We drove our tour bus right to the aircraft and filled it with our thirty-eight members and our handbags. We could not accommodate our large luggage.

As we flew over the land from the airport, we almost immediately found ourselves in what looked like desert country. There was green along a stream, but otherwise, it was desert of a sort. But we knew we were in the "Country of the Blue Sky."

We landed on an unbelievable runway. It was simply the floor of the desert. The dust and sand were heavy, and it was very bumpy. One felt like he was taking off rather than landing. In fact, we did both several times on the way down. The gravel and dirt and sand were anything but smooth. Such would be our mode of transportation and the source of our highways through the sand dunes to Iolt (Yolt) Valley, in "the Land of the Blue Sky."

The gers in which we resided were of white felt on the exterior and were a sort of conical tent in which Mongols still live while tending their herds. Each tent was equipped with four beds, a stove, a table, a dresser, and all other necessary equipment. The floor was carpeted, and the arrangement was attractive.

These collapsible gers had served the nomadic herdsmen for centuries as warm, portable shelters against snow and blizzards, where the temperature can drop to fifty degrees below zero. The protection is a felt-covered cocoon. The ger, which stands twenty to thirty feet in diameter, has a lower wall formed by a lattice of wooden lathes a little more than four feet high. The side walls collapse like an accordion for packing on animals or in carts. Curved poles fasten to the circular walls, like the ribs of an umbrella, holding up the domed room. The rib ends are socketed at the top into a wooden ring about three feet in diameter. A flap of felt can be drawn across this hole by rope to control the light and keep out rain and keep in heat. Layers of felt cover the ger, over which lies white canvas. The doors close, and when the roof flap is drawn, the ger is as snug and windproof as any house.

Early in the morning, we traveled to Iolt Valley, sometimes called Bald Eagle Valley (*"Iolt"* means mountain eagle in Mongolian). At six o'clock, we watched a beautiful sunrise, partially obscured by clouds. Herds of camels roamed the desert on both sides of the highways.

Gers nestled in the valleys and stood out on the hillsides. Horses and rams, with mountains in the background, added to the scenic setting. Ground squirrels darted in front of us, and butterflies and a variety of birds fluttered about. Now and then, we could see a desert rat.

Streams of water provided refreshment in the desert for the two-humped camels and the famous Prejevalsky horses. We had the pleasure, or displeasure, depending on one's point of view, of sampling some kumiss, a brothy brew of mare's milk.

Following that exciting experience, we flew back to the capital city where manufacturing plants, apparently for petrochemicals, household goods, and steel construction components, were numerous. If it takes place in Outer Mongolia, it takes place in Ulan Bator—whether business, social, cultural, or governmental.

A huge storage area outside the city along the railroad tracks seemed to be the warehouse of Mongolia, completely open to the elements. There was not a great deal of traffic on the streets except for the public transportation system composed of buses and trucks.

In Ulan Bator, many buildings were new and modern. A huddle of one-story shacks not too many decades old, the city had broad avenues and squares lined with government buildings and apartments. But outside the city, most of Mongolia was served by dirt roads.

Universities and colleges, opera houses, ballet performances, and much else of education and culture exist alongside the primitive arena called Outer Mongolia.

Mongolia's only contact with America has been by the Voice of America from Okinawa over many years or English broadcasts from China. As Justice Douglas once said after a visit to Mongolia, "The Mongolians are so far removed from Western culture, so distanced from the influence of Judeo-Christian civilization, so unaware of the West's great books and humane letters, that if they long remain in an isolated pocket between the Soviet Union and China, they may evolve into ideological puppets."

A wedge between the USSR and China, Mongolia once bred nomadic warriors who burst from their land like fire from a volcano, but for three hundred years, the nation has been in a slumber. She became a member of the United Nations in 1951, entering the current of world affairs for the first time in centuries. Genghis Khan and his sons and grandsons put together an empire extending from Peking to the Danube and touching Egypt in the south. Traveling on horseback, these men captured Moscow in the dead of winter. The daring of the Mongol raiders was only exceeded by their ruthlessness. The Great Wall of China was built to keep these northern barbarians from China's back door. When China finally conquered Mongolia in 1691, she locked it up and closed the frontiers to foreigners. In the meantime, there has been a long intervening period of mystery. Since 1921 when she won her independence from China, which held most of the wealth, she has had little contact with the outside world. The revolution was also against the monasteries, which China had used to hold the country in a feudal vise.

In their struggle for domination, Russia and China have made Mongolia a pawn. Since Mongolian warriors sacked Peking and Moscow years ago, both Russia and China have held sway over the "Land of the Blue Sky" in their time, but their interests today evidently meet in Mongolia where the Gobi forms a natural barrier between Inner and Outer Mongolia. Mongolia covers about five hundred thousand square miles, roughly equal in size to Great Britain, Germany, France, Italy, and Portugal combined, but the population is less than two million.

With black hair and golden skin, high cheekbones and straight, prominent noses, Mongolians look something like American Indians. Some have round faces with ruddy cheeks and button-like noses. Many are short and wiry, though some are a rangy six feet or more. They are precise in dress, even formal, and look with disfavor on the informal sportswear of the Russians. Marco Polo wrote, "The diet of Mongols has long been flesh and milk." Perhaps as a result, their teeth are beautiful.

The milk is fermented in goatskin bags where it is stirred to hasten its forming a potent brew. This beverage, which has the kick of beer, tickles like ginger ale and tastes like buttermilk and champagne.

Frequently, one is offered a drink of Khuruud, a curd made from milk and thickened in the sun. It dries into a hard, gray substance. We had some in the form of hard cake and found it difficult to enjoy.

Mongolians milk all of their animals—sheep, goats, cows, camels, yaks, and mares—and convert the yield into yogurt, cakes, cheese, and alcoholic beverages as described above.

A flight from Ulan Bator on a Russian-made Llushian-14 took us to the countryside again. We traveled by bus to Karakorum, the buried capital city of Genghis Khan. As before, we landed on the hard, turf-covered flatlands.

In the 1200s, it was a bustling market town, and Persian traders and craftsmen thronged Karakorum's busy streets. But the great Khan's warriors disdainfully pitched their gers outside the mudbrick walls. In 1382, a conquering Chinese army ground Karakorum into dust, and men forgot where the city had stood. Excavators only verified its identity in 1946.

The only monument to Genghis Khan, who founded the Mongolian nation and launched its conquest of most of the known world seven centuries ago, is the remote northeast village where he was born. There, he received ambassadors from China, Europe, Persia, and India and fathered the campaigns that eventually took the Mongols to the gates of Vienna. His name and that of his people became synonymous with cruelty, and it is this reputation that the Mongols of today—gentle, pacific, hospitable people—feel they must live down.

As Genghis Khan's capital from 1220, and that of his successors until Kublai Khan, his famous grandson who set out to rule all China, Karakorum was both the center of Mongol power and the crossroads between East and West.

From Outer Mongolia, we returned to Irkutsk, Siberia, by way of Mongolian Airlines. It was almost like coming home. The Outer Mongolian life was more unusual for Americans than that in Siberia and Russia, and the crossing of the border seemed like a step toward home. From Irkutsk, we continued our journey to Moscow. As we were running a bit late on the way to the airport, our tour guide, Tonya, said, in a bit of reverse humor, "You don't have to worry about catching the plane. Our planes have never been known to take off early."

That bit of Russian humor leads me to some other human-interest aspects of our journey. At the very beginning of the journey, while preparing for the train ride in Moscow, it was my responsibility to visit the Mongolian embassy to procure our visas for Outer Mongolia. The procedure for travel to Outer Mongolia is as follows: "Wait until the last minute, try Moscow, and if it doesn't work there, try Irkutsk, and hope you get the visa one place or another, but never before you leave the United States." That would make the journey too simple and would eliminate the risk-reward factor that is so important. It's also a fact that you don't pay the bill before you leave the United States, but you pay it after you are in Outer Mongolia, which means that one carried nearly twenty-five thousand dollars in travelers checks to be prepared to pay for airfare, hotel costs, food, and everything else while in the country. By dealing in tugriks instead of dollars, one is not allowed to get soft and lazy, and he justifies his existence as a train leader.

As I traveled to the Mongolian embassy in a distant part of Moscow, I was confident that there would be no difficulty in acquiring the visas. I was soon to discover that there would be great difficulty. No one spoke English, the Russian guide was not allowed to go inside, and I could not communicate with the old gentleman at the desk—or anyone else to whom I was referred although the place was buzzing with activity, and there were many people around.

Finally, after about half an hour, I found a Mongolian student from the University of Kiev who said he could speak a little English, and a little English was a lot in that situation. He was from Umnigobi, near Ulan Bator, where our journey would take us later.

Through this new friend, I was told that I could not get the visas on that day or the next, even if we were leaving on the train the next day. Finally, at about two o'clock, I was told I could have them by six if I would wait. I had no choice since I had already been separated from thirty-eight passports and would not risk leaving them there.

As we waited for our visas, we visited a park across the street where Soviet citizens chatted together. The benches were run-down, the weeds were not mowed, and there were lots of trees and pigeons. I could not take many pictures because I was so obvious a stranger in the midst of all these folks. I sat next to an old Russian lady who looked like Khrushchev, and she viewed me with some suspicion even as I talked into my tape recorder. Fate was on my side, and at six o'clock, the visas were completed, having been typed by one clerk on one old, manual typewriter.

I could not have gotten the visas without the help of the cordial young Mongolian student who said no to my overtures to pay him. He said he liked me, but he did not like for me to offer him money.

Nastasha and our Russian driver could not wait as long as required, and I had to catch a taxi back to my hotel. My friend from Umn Gobi, Mr. Zorigt, hailed a cab and headed me in the right direction with a note in Russian concerning my destination. When I asked Mr. Zorigt again if I could give him anything for his substantial help, he said, "No, it is my duty to help you."

As I traveled by cab through the heavy traffic and hundred-degree temperatures, I realized there were no air-conditioned cars or buses in Moscow except for tourists.

Not to discuss politics while in the Soviet Union is difficult, especially when traveling with an English-speaking Russian guide in the same compartment for four days and four nights. One could not breathe without breathing on the other, or open your mouth without being heard by the four people in the room. In spite of admonitions to do otherwise, we did have some long conversations with Nastasha about the politics of our countries. She was in her late twenties, and was the mother of a four-year-old son. Her husband was an architect.

While we were in Moscow, the Supreme Soviet was in session to approve its next fiveyear plan. Nastasha and others were very up to date on what was transpiring there and what Brezhnev was projecting. They had answers for most things.

She was rather anti-military and believed that all the people in Russia do not want war with the United States. They want only peace, but she said the United States was the problem. The Russian leaders wanted disarmament and had proved it with the recent Supreme Soviet's decision to reduce arms. Only the United States stood in the way. She believed Reagan's increase in arms came at the expense of poor people. She noted that the Chinese were the big question and reminded me that we had just decided to sell arms to the Chinese. That was their real fear, and they had a right to fear the people from whom they had taken land in the past. I gave her some material about the Marine Military Academy in Texas, where I served on the board of directors. She returned it and said she did not want to read about the military. I showed her a picture of the president's home of the university, and she wanted to know if we kept most of the rooms locked. She did not understand entertaining for the university or the private sector of education per se. The world *alumni* stumped her. Even though she studied English all the time, she kept finding words she did not know.

Throughout Russia, we picked up little books in airports, on the train, and at hotels— propaganda pieces— that were printed for the Olympic year. There were all kinds of questions with given answers: "Do Communists have any privileges? Do you have no class differences in the Soviet Union? Do you have a free press?" The provided answers did not make a great deal of sense to Westerners, but they were just right for the Soviets. There were books about China with such titles as "The Dragon Gains Strength." It was clear that the Russians were more fearful of China than the United States, but they were propagandizing everyone concerning both.

Many people asked about the food in Siberia and Outer Mongolia. How would one describe milk skin dessert? Only if you have had it could you know what it is. It is almost impossible to describe. It is the skin of milk built up and hardened, sliced into squares, and served for dessert. One man's junk is another man's treasure, and I suppose one man's delicacy is another man's poison.

In Moscow, the food was good. We enjoyed everything from chicken to cake. We had instant coffee—not the powdery kind but a mix that is sticky, like taffy, and a drink that was something like apple cider.

The food on the Trans-Siberian train was good, but it was not quite the same as Moscow. We had drinks that resembled Coke or Pepsi—not tasting quite like either but getting better all the time. Cucumber salad and soup containing everything but the kitchen sink—from bologna to wieners—was good. Eggs over some kind of steak with peas, followed by chocolate bars and tea, was not bad. If we were worried about eating, we were sometimes on the side of overeating. Bacon, potatoes, cold peas, cucumbers, eggs, cookies, chocolate, and various kinds of drinks worked out very well for most of us. Some places in Outer Mongolia were not able to furnish that which was good for Western tastes.

Beef Stroganoff and fried potatoes came almost every dinner on the train. We frequently had a glass of thin yogurt, sour cream, or buttermilk. The ice cream was creamy and delicious in Moscow and Irkutsk.

There are ice cream stands everywhere in Moscow and in every Russian city. There are stands that disperse a milky soft drink with ice. One puts in five kopeks or so and washes the glass in a swish of water with disinfectant because everyone uses the same glass. Persons patronizing beer wagons also use the same glass.

We saw many young men and some women smoking in Russia. This was not apparent to me when I was in Russia thirteen years before. With the fact that many Russians do smoke, it was intriguing that no smoking was allowed in the subway—and no smoking was done in the subway. It was clean, fresh, and attractive.

Many Siberians own dachas (summer cottages) outside of town. To get a dacha, a worker must go to his senior work boss and request a piece of land. He may use it for a garden or a house. The houses range from log cabins to pretentious small palaces. The garden and house— but not the land—belong to the resident, and the former may be sold or willed to his family.

A farmer who gets a few chicks or piglets at no cost is expected to resell them to the state farm organization. He then earns some profit, and the government obtains more meat to sell at the empty food counters.

Farmers in Siberia don't have much to do during the winter. As a result, there is a high incidence of alcoholism—and the birth rate is proportionately much greater per family than in European Russia.

On our way back from Mongolia through Moscow, we had another interesting and unusual experience. There was no Intourist guide to meet us at the airport. I hadn't had that happen before. Procuring a bus and getting back to the hotel in Moscow wasn't easy. Still no one met us there. Working with the hotel personnel, we placed everyone in their rooms overnight, assuming someone would show up, but by morning, no one had showed up. We were supposed to go on another tour of the city, and until almost ten o'clock, I could find no one to provide that service.

Finally, at about ten, an Intourist guide did show up. She was quite upset and told me she had a problem with her little boy the evening before. He had run away from Young Pioneers Camp, and the official had brought him home in an ambulance after they found him. She was, she said, in shock, and I believed it. She said she didn't want to go into all the details, but she was asking our forgiveness for her absence and tardiness. Intourist was also giving her a fit. Her little boy was six years old and had earlier escaped from kindergarten. That sounded like an unlikely infraction to us Americans, but if they broke the rules, they couldn't go back. It was a very serious offense. She was so shocked that she couldn't do her job, and the Russian authorities wouldn't let her leave until they worked the matter out with her son. The other authorities at Intourist wouldn't forgive her for not having come.

After Outer Mongolia, Siberia, and the Soviet Union, everyone breathed a sigh of relief when the Finnair plane took off from Moscow and headed for Helsinki. Someone said, "That is the last time I will go there." Another said, "It is not worth the hassle." She had her diamond ring practically taken away by customs because she failed to declare it on entering. Such things were enough to make folks glad to be going home.

As we landed in Helsinki, the hills, green hayfields, and houses all blended with red roofs, making our joy even greater. As we saw Finlandia Hall—the setting of the big conference on security and cooperation in Europe—we remembered that the Helsinki Pact resulted from that meeting.

When I returned, I tried to reflect upon my comparison of the present Soviet Union with the one I saw during my visit there thirteen years ago. The capital was busier, and the traffic was heavier. Hotels were more up to date and newer. Girls dressed in a more Western style. There were many more jeans. There was color, and there was style. People seemed to be more conversational and not quite as aloof or as stiff-shirted as before.

But! East is East, and West is West—and I am convinced that "never the twain shall meet."

# Campbellsville
## UNIVERSITY

Presents

The 2017

# Kentucky Veterans of the Year Banquet
## *A Tribute to WWII Veterans*

Monday, November 6th, 6 pm—8:30 pm

Brown & Williamson Club

(at the Papa John's Stadium)

2800 S Floyd St

Louisville, KY 40209

Tickets: $65 per person

For more information visit

KentuckyVeteransoftheYear.org

Featured Speaker

Dr. E. Bruce Heilman

WWII Veteran

Special Guest

Woody Williams

WWII Medal of Honor

Emcee

Pat Waters

Patton's Grandson

Parade of Nominees

BG (Ret.) Norman Arflack

KDVA Commissioner

Entertainment

Ladies For Liberty

# CHAPTER SEVEN

## THE MILITARY

It ain't the individual, or the army as a whole, but the everlastin' teamwork of every blooming soul.
—*Rudyard Kipling*

# I

# INTRODUCTION

Christie Burkhart was a student on the *Collegian* staff at the University of Richmond during my presidency. She wrote about returning with veterans to the war zones where they fought years before. This experience was impacting for both the students and the veterans. "Returning to Iwo Jima and Okinawa," an article from the *Religious Herald*, provides a unique perspective from those sharing impressions firsthand.

The "Greatest Generation" is a complimentary title bestowed upon all who engaged WWII's successful end. The return to Okinawa and Iwo Jima provided a look at the personal side of those who fought and returned seventy years later to learn that it really happened.

"When the Lights Come on Again All Over the World" as a story has been told by me many times in speeches, but I include it here because it is a transition from the world at war to a peaceful nation with those who, having fought, returned home to turn the lights back on and to enjoy the freedom they had fought to preserve. They married, raised families, and took advantage of educational opportunities through the G.I. Bill. It is a message the uninformed will want to discover, and those who are old enough to know what really happened will find it worthy of review.

Remembering my fellow Marines who didn't make it off Iwo Jima and Okinawa

World War II veteran Bruce Heilman joined other American Legion Family members at Arlington National Cemetery to lay a wreath at the Civil War Unknowns Monument during the American Legion Riders Run To The Thunder on Saturday, May 26, 2018. Photo by Cheryl Diaz Meyer / The American Legion

# World War II survivor, Legion Rider talks about an evanescent generation

The World War II generation — and the stories these veterans hold — is quickly succumbing to time. Dying at a rate of nearly 400 each day, barely half a million of the 16 million Americans who served in World War II are alive today.

"In five years, we won't be able to tell our stories. We'll all be dead," said Dr. Bruce Heilman.

When Heilman talks about World War II, this is the first thing he says — a sharp reminder that time is fast running out to share stories from the Greatest Generation. His generation is reluctant to talk about the war, something he says is oft attributed to an air of bravado. But, according to Heilman, this isn't true.

"I'm going to tell you why we never talked about it," he says.

Marines of Past Service and a bride to be

The address I gave commemorating the sixty-sixth anniversary of the end of the war in the Pacific was a high honor. As the national spokesperson for the Greatest Generations Foundation, I was asked to be the keynote speaker. That position is held each year by someone selected for solid reasons. Mine was serving during World War II, being spokesperson for the Greatest Generations Foundation, as my engagements in the occupation of Japan.

As I spoke, I faced twelve World War II veterans and hundreds of people from all over the Hawaiian Islands and the world, including politicians, military personnel, young navy and marine active-duty personnel, air force generals, army, navy, and Marine Corps senior officers. However, none had served in World War II. It gave me a chance to stand where McArthur stood to end the war with his few words of closure.

I acknowledged the honor of being invited, and it was recorded in more than two hundred newspapers throughout the world. The speech I made to the National Symposium on Homeland Security is presented because of the significance of that organization. Because of my identity in higher education and my military experience, my ideas and thoughts fit in the section on the military and life after eighty.

\*\*\*

# Marine Corps University
# Board of Visitors

# Dr. Heilman

During World War II, many of my fellow marines were in life-and-death situations with all of the gore and little of the glory, living in foxholes for days, weeks, or even months on the front lines of Iwo Jima, Okinawa, and elsewhere. I was in a better circumstance than some because I was in a mud tent serving with a marine air group on the same island at the same time with a little better circumstance for keeping dry than a foxhole. In all combat situations, there are several aspects of the war going on at the same time. In our case, on the island of Okinawa, most of us were expecting to be a part of the invasion of Japan, which would come immediately after the securing of Okinawa. That was reality until the dropping of the atom bomb killed tens of thousands but brought the war to an end and saved the lives of millions. That included tens, if not hundreds, of thousands of those of us who were on Okinawa standing by to reassert our power, concentrating on the mainland rather than an offshore or outlying part of the mainland.

The chances of any of us being alive at this point in life seemed rather slim from our perspective then. William Manchester, in *Goodbye Darkness*, predicted, "The enemy would sacrifice every available man to drive us off of it." Fate intervened, and the bomb canceled our plans for that invasion. Years after the war, while president of the University of Richmond, I invited William Manchester to give a commencement address and receive an honorary degree.

We spent an afternoon together before his speech, and the reminiscing was substantial.

Twice wounded and the winner of the Navy Cross and the Silver Star, he refused to accept either for himself but rather in honor and recognition of the men who fell in battle around him, mortally wounded. As a sergeant, he boldly stormed ashore on his twenty-third birthday with 4,812 men, of which 3,512 or 80 percent were killed or wounded, and he was one of the latter. I followed his landing at Okinawa at the young age of eighteen, but unlike Bill Manchester, I was not destined to fall wounded in battle. He said, "One was almost apologetic in those days for having lived while others died, for having been free of wounds while others were wounded."

Like Bill Manchester, I was destined to spend my life in the academic arena—and both of us have survived that. When I told him that, by way of Kentucky windage, I was number two out of six hundred men as an expert rifleman in boot camp, he reminded me that he was number one and from Connecticut.

# II

# THE GREATEST GENERATIONS FOUNDATION DEFINED

The Greatest Generations Foundation is represented by those born in the early part of the twentieth century. We lived through the Great Depression and then the greatest world conflict of all time. From these and other maturing experiences, we developed confidence, determination, and leadership potential that were essential to advancing the nation beyond anything thought possible before that time. Thomas Carlyle said, "Our main business is not to see what lies dimly at a distance but to do what lies clearly at hand."

What I convey about members of the Greatest Generation is based upon long years of association, observation, close personal friendships, confessions, declarations of beliefs, convictions, and lifestyles. They all depict character, commitment, patriotism, and belief in personal responsibility. I have sought to assign these characteristics by their level of significance.

All, however, represent something special since they identify with time, place, and circumstance.

Members of the Greatest Generation were in their young lives—and remain today— individually and collectively, men of character, positive attitudes, and spirit and believers in themselves, their country, and their fellow citizens. These men were, and have remained, highly motivated, self-confident, hardworking, and family-oriented men. They have been formally and self-educated to a level that has fostered high success in their chosen fields. As a group, after fighting to preserve freedom for all humankind, they took over and ran their country for nearly fifty years during a period of its most outstanding progress in history.

While sacrifice and heroism may appropriately call to mind periods of suffering and distress, for most veterans, the pride of having served and the return on their investment in preserving freedom for themselves and their fellow humans overrides the darkness of the experiences and embraces the words of Edwin Marcum: "There is a destiny which makes us brothers; none goes his way alone. All that we send into the lives of others comes back into our own."

Wherever they go en route to past battle scenes or through cities in this country, they are touched by the hundreds of people eager to shake their hands. Many high school and grade school students, even small children, ask for autographs, requests that are accommodated with pride. To all of these, World War II veterans are ancient warriors.

At age 20, Cherry Point, North Carolina

# THE GREATEST GENERATIONS FOUNDATION

January 18, 2011

Dr. E. Bruce Heilman
4700 Cary Street
Richmond, VA 23226

Dr. Heilman,

On behalf of The Greatest Generations Foundation, I want to personally extend my sincerest gratitude to you for your great and heroic service to our country in defense of liberty. Through your timeless duty, valor, and sacrifice, you have ensured the freedoms that we enjoy today and for this, we are forever grateful. Truly, you are a great American hero and a fine representation of the 'greatest generation.'

We are honored to have your presence on the upcoming program to the Pacific to commemorate the historic battles of Guam, Saipan, Tinian, and Iwo Jima. These monumental events in history shaped the lives of the American people, and the many lives lost should never be forgotten nor the value of their deeds be allowed to disappear into the annals of history. Your participation in this program ensures that your dedication and bravery is carried to the next generation to continue educating youth about the extraordinary history of war-time sacrifice and the importance of defending our precious liberty.

Our journey to the Pacific will begin on March 10 and conclude on March 18. In the coming weeks and months ahead, we will mail you your flight information, hotel, contacts, and any other details relevant to the program.

Throughout the journey, you will be paired with a student from the Ohio State University's military studies program who will escort and assist you while listening to your story and learning from your legacy to deepen their understanding of history and of the true meaning of sacrifice. Through this partnership, your story will be recorded and passed along to ensure that your legacy is never forgotten.

Please find enclosed a Release & Waiver form as well as a Medical Release form for you to complete and return. Also enclosed is a tentative overview of our daily itinerary. Please note this is subject to change.

If you have any questions or concerns about the program, please feel free to contact Alicia Harms, Vice President of Communications, at 303-331-1944.

Again, it is an absolute honor to have you on the program and to be in the presence of a hero. I am greatly anticipating meeting you and sharing this experience together.

Kind regards,

Timothy Davis
*President & CEO*
*The Greatest Generations Foundation*

Military service gave purpose to everything else in the lives of this generation. Character, love of country, leadership, courage, duty, and honor were characteristics of the generation. Many have, over the years, attended homecomings to see their comrades from the past. Now, most of those homecomings have ceased because most of the veterans are unable to travel.

Most World War II veterans agree that their service was a liberating experience. They were blessed to be given an opportunity to fight for the preservation of freedom. While the Greatest Generation gave what some would define as the best years of their lives, their sacrifices during those years provided a foundation for more fulfilling lives during the balance of their lifetimes.

These veterans, like those since, "whether on active duty, retired, served one hitch, guard or reserve, deployed multiple times or never, at one point in their lives wrote a blank check made payable to the government of the United States of American for an amount up to and including their lives."

It was a long time ago from the perspective of succeeding generations, but it was only yesterday to those whose lives were permanently influenced by the era known as World War II. Now, to the younger generations, it is ancient history. But to those who were caught up in the intensity of the times, it was the making of history.

When those of the Greatest Generation were in their late teens and early twenties, military service was generally accepted as a patriotic duty for all. Although, for some, it was an interruption faced reluctantly as they left college, home, family, job, and profession, most left willingly. They expected to be gone for a year, but for many, that year extended to three, four, and even five. Some served two or three years of those abroad.

Most of the Greatest Generation returned from their experiences alive. Some died in combat, and others, wounded physically or emotionally, returned proud as a country full of appreciation gave loud applause for their sacrifice. Though all served under the risk of death or dismemberment, the experience fostered a can-do attitude that allowed them to provide outstanding leadership of the country over the years that followed.

Speaking at the sixty-sixth anniversary of the end of World War II on the *Missouri*, I commented that it was a sobering occasion that highlighted the lives of the twenty World War II veterans who sat in the front row representing the sixteen million who served. I acknowledged the importance of remembering the sacrifices and acts of heroism that were emblematic of their service. In five years, it would be too late for many of them. Ten years later, there would be few exceptions. What was to be said to them—and for them—should be said before it was too late.

The Greatest Generations Foundation, by returning veterans to the battlefields of their youth or reflecting upon their service, has been a part of bringing closure for the shadows that remain in the crevices of their minds. Because of their ultimate pride in having served, they never seek total closure because they recognize the significance of what they did.

Existing in mud, wind, rain, almost unbearable heat, or unbelievable cold and always being on the alert was surreal, but they learned from it. They bathed in barrels cut in half and improvised to make conditions as bearable as could be realized. They learned to be patient waiting for letters from home, which came by ship sometimes months en route, but they were the windows to their world left behind. They learned from each other—the younger from the old and the other way around. They learned that the Japanese posted on their fortifications: "Each man will make it his duty to kill ten of the enemy before dying." Finally, they learned that a big bomb had been dropped and that the war would end, eliminating the necessity only six weeks away from invading the homeland where they would likely all have been killed. They learned that they were going to survive.

As they arrived at the top of Mt. Suribachi on Iwo Jima, one veteran was crying.

Another veteran said, "I thought I wanted to do this before I passed on. and now I have. The experience has passed, but the memories are forever embedded in my mind. I'll never forget this mountain."

Another veteran said, "I swore I'd never go back again, but now I am convinced that this trip is going to help guys like me have a better life for the few years we have left."

As they climbed their mountains of the past, some shed tears or fought back emotions, but they reflected on the many success they enjoyed, the children they had fathered, and the lives they had extended while buddies had long ago given up their future on these beaches.

These men were in the conflict for the long term. Until it was over, they never could see the end, but they persevered. Toward the end of the last major battle at Okinawa, they began to anticipate the next move, which they expected to be their last battle—whether or not it ended the war. The dropping of the atom bombs and the surrender of Japan were so sudden and abrupt that—on the Okinawa and all over the Pacific—the celebrations were wild. On Okinawa, six were killed celebrating peace when celebratory bullets, fired into the air, came down and struck them on the ground. After all, most expected to die in the invasion, and to have that destiny canceled was so exciting that it was difficult to contain.

Wilbur D. Jones Jr. wrote about much of what represents the ordinary veteran of World War II:

> What did buddies endure together? E. Bruce Heilman summed it up. "We suffered together, we dreamed of the future together, we were homesick together, and if one of us received a dear John Letter, which I did, we cried on each other's shoulder in a fashion of trying to pretend that it was her loss and not ours."

Because only an estimated two hundred thousand of the original sixteen million remain, and they are dying at the rate of eight thousand per month, within the decade, there will be few of the Greatest Generation remaining soon. No one living will have personal knowledge of the warmth of president Franklin Roosevelt's fireside chats.

No one will remember firsthand the Great Depression, and no one will be around to share the stories reflecting the years of war. The torch will have been passed, and soon thereafter will come the final roll call answered with silence, indicating that their "rendezvous with destiny" as described by president Roosevelt will have been fulfilled.

***

# III

# BACK TO IWO JIMA, OKINAWA, AND HIROSHIMA

*Dr. Heilman as a young Marine in 1945. In uniform: "once a Marine, always a Marine." With a "Rosie the Riveter" lookalike at the National WWII Memorial during the youth wreath laying ceremony in Washington, DC in 2015. Below, on his beloved Harley.*

Enjoying the fruits of my journey.

# 2018 HEILMAN AMERICAN PATRIOTS TOUR

### MARCH 13-25, 2018

*Dr. Heilman, WWII veteran, in front of Mount Suribachi. The peak of Suribachi is where the famous picture was taken of the raising of the flag at Iwo Jima in February 1945.*

Walk in the footsteps of American history. Visit Jamestown, Colonial Williamsburg, and learn about the American Revolution at Yorktown. Tour the presidential estates of Jefferson's Monticello and Washington's Mount Vernon. Tour the Marine Barracks at 8th and I. Visit the Vietnam Veterans Memorial, World War II Memorial, Korean War Memorial and Arlington National Cemetery in our nation's capital. Walk the Civil War battlefields of Antietam and Gettysburg. See the Liberty Bell and tour Independence Hall in Philadelphia before traveling to New York City by Amtrak to visit the Statue of Liberty, Freedom Tower, 9/11 Memorial and Museum, Empire State Building, and a Broadway show.

All of this has been made possible by a generous gift from Dr. E. Bruce Heilman of Richmond, Virginia. Dr. Heilman serves as Chancellor at the University of Richmond. Having failed to pass enough courses to meet high school graduation requirements, he joined the Marine Corps during World War II, after which he was educated under the GI Bill at Campbellsville College and Vanderbilt University. Dr. Heilman was born in a small Kentucky town, much like the towns from which many College of the Ozarks students come. His military background and career as a professional educator have inspired his support of patriotic travel experiences for college students.

# How did war relic survive mission?

## *Veteran's flag of Japanese kamikaze pilot resurfaces*

**BY STEVE CLARK**
TIMES-DISPATCH STAFF WRITER

For the life of him, Dr. E. Bruce Heilman cannot recall how he came to possess the flag of a Japanese kamikaze pilot.

All he knows is that he had the flag with him when he came home from serving in the Pacific in World War II.

"I brought it home, but I really don't remember how I came to have it," Heilman said.

Heilman, former president of the University of Richmond who is now the university's chancellor, dropped out of high school in Ballardsville, Ky., in the spring of 1944 to join the Marines.

A year later, he took part in the invasion of the Japanese-held island of Okinawa. He was 18 years old.

After Japan surrendered, Heilman was stationed at a naval base in Japan, where he was part of the occupation force helping Japan in the transition from war to peace.

"I've always been thankful that I had the opportunity to take part in the occupation of Japan," he said. "I got to know a number of Japanese people, and it changed my view of them. They went from vicious, evil people to being good, decent human beings."

The kamikaze pilot's flag was out of sight, out of mind for years — stashed in a drawer with other war relics and mementos of bygone years. It resurfaced several weeks ago while Heilman was hunting for items that might stir a memory or two, and thus help him in the writing of a book about his life.

The silk flag with a faded rising sun in the center has many Japanese characters written on it in ink, so Heilman decided it was time to find out what the writing says.

"I had never had it translated."

He asked UR faculty member Akira Suzuki, director of Japanese language studies, to translate the writing.

"I was glad to do so, because I've never seen a flag like this," said Suzuki, a 55-year-old native of Japan.

Suzuki's father, now deceased, was a Japanese soldier in WWII. Some years ago, Suzuki invited his father to visit his family in America. His father said he did not want to visit the country of the enemy.

"I think he was half-joking, half-serious," Suzuki said. "But he never came to visit because I think he would have been uncomfortable. But my mother came six times."

Suzuki's translation turned up mainly names, including the name of the kamikaze pilot, Hideo Ogawa, and the name of an officer, Admiral Nagasawa. A dozen other names probably are the signatures of other pilots in Ogawa's unit.

"They probably would have signed the flag to wish him success in his mission," Suzuki said.

Kamikaze pilots were mainly teenagers who went on suicide missions. Their mission was to crash their fighter planes into American ships or into American military facilities on land.

In addition to personal names, Heilman's flag also has four large Japanese characters. Suzuki translated those characters as being four words — devotion, loyal, repay, nation.

"To that young pilot," Heilman said, "this flag was like Old Glory was to me."

Since this flag was a kamikaze pilot's flag, how did it survive a suicide mission?

That mystery will never be solved.

"Maybe it washed up on shore," Heilman said. "But there's really no way of knowing why this flag survived the war."

Heilman would like to see the story of this flag printed in Japanese newspapers in hopes that a family member of the kamikaze pilot or the general would read about it.

FAMILY PHOTO

E. Bruce Heilman poses with a Japanese boy during the American occupation of Okinawa after World War II.

"I would like to find a family member, maybe some grandchildren of the [admiral], and present the flag to them," he said.

That is a longshot. His other option is to donate the flag to the new National Museum of the Marine Corps to be built over the next three years near Quantico.

# Richmond Times-Dispatch

RICHMOND, VIRGINIA     *VIRGINIA'S NEWS LEADER*     THURSDAY, DECEMBER 26, 2002
A MEDIA GENERAL NEWSPAPER

## AFTER ALL THESE YEARS

BRUCE PARKER/TIMES-DISPATCH

E. Bruce Heilman, chancellor of the University of Richmond (left), and UR professor Akira Suzuki show a flag Heilman acquired as a Marine in Japan during or after World War II. The large Japanese characters on the right, read from top to bottom, represent devotion, loyalty, repayment of debt and the nation. The column of characters second from right gives the kamikaze pilot's name, and the next column gives the name of the admiral under whom he served.

TV Personality Greg McQuade

These reflections flooded back into my mind on a snowy day in February 1993. I left Portland, Oregon, on Delta Airlines and headed west. After fourteen and a half hours with a stopover in Seoul, Korea, we landed in Taipei, Taiwan. Following an overnight rest, we boarded China Airlines for a two-hour flight to the Japanese island of Okinawa. I was returning to my wartime roots some sixty-five years after the fact.

Seventy-two years ago, I landed on the beach as an eighteen-year-old private in the US Marines. It was a part of a four-year hitch that also included occupation duty in the Japanese mainland and a variety of other assignments that added up to a truly defining experience that culminated in my discharge as a buck sergeant ready to tackle the world.

In late May 1945, I began a journey from San Diego to the South Pacific battle zone of World War II. Circumstances were very different for me then. I was, in many ways, just barely dry behind the ears. I was one of 1,500 marines aboard a troop ship attached to a convoy bound for points unknown. At least, the destination was unknown to the hundreds of marines in the bowels of the troop ships in the convoy. The more recent destination for similar convoys and battle groups of that era had names like Tarawa, Guadalcanal, and Iwo Jima. Each of these bloody campaigns had led American forces closer to the main island of Japan.

I had been spared the more recent battle of Iwo Jima. While others of my platoon were killed or wounded there as the dug-in Japanese literally mowed them down on the beaches and in the coral leading to the summit of Mount Suribachi.

Being on special assignment for specific training had delayed my entry into the war. The time had come to test my resolve and confirm my patriotism along with the others who would have the opportunity to prove their determination and courage.

We settled into our small world, which was composed of a steel bunk allowing no more than six or eight inches from the bottom of the one above, stacked six deep in rows that covered the whole of the ship's compartment. Our earthly belongings were organized around us in that small space. These included M1 rifles with bayonets, toilet articles, a Bible if we were so inclined as I was, and other small things, which for me, included a Horner harmonica. This was well received in the quiet of the evening when troops had no other substitute for lullabies to keep their minds from concentrating on the probabilities that lay ahead.

A journey to the same destination in 2015, seventy-two years later, would require no long period of adjustment. There would be no sweltering nights in a hot compartment where the mere impression of air movement brought pleasure. I would, in this later visit, have a grand meal in flight, see two movies, relax in a pleasant environment, and arrive in only fifteen hours.

My earlier trip had involved fifty-six days and nights of uncertainty. Occasionally, the uncertainty was interrupted by reality. When a Japanese submarine was found tracking the convoy, action was initiated to reduce, to a minimum, the risk of losing a ship and hundreds of marines. After that encounter, the zigzagging became even more constant.

Little things—having showers available for only short periods because of fresh water limitations, no mail for almost two months, food that became progressively less palatable, and the uncertainty of not knowing when or where our journey would take us—contributed to our anxiety. Yet, because we were determined to show our best selves to each other and because we were committed to taking part in the action, the spirit and attitude of the troops was basically positive.

George Feifer's *Tennozan* quoted a marine who landed on Okinawa after managing to enlist despite being a husband and father of four: "Kids today would probably call me a sucker or something, but that is the way I am. I love the Corps and my country." Most of us in that day felt that way.

The news being picked up by the convoy and passed along in daily bulletins was not positive for the troops or for the sailors who were permanent shipboard personnel. More and more Japanese suicide squadrons were seriously damaging our ships off the island of Okinawa, the final stepping-stone to the Japanese homeland. We wondered whether we were sailing directly into that situation, which promised to be even more frightening than the anticipated landing itself. If Okinawa were our destination, we might not survive long enough to become replacements and reinforcements for outfits that had landed and initiated the battle for Okinawa several weeks before.

We would become the fresh troops that would bolster the forces in Okinawa, and we would serve as a part of the foundation for the upcoming invasion of the Japanese homeland. The latter date was already set. It was to be November 15, 1945, and for many, if not most of us, it was to be a do-or-die situation. It might require the latter in order to ensure the former.

As the Americans began a pre-invasion bombardment of Okinawa in March 1945, 250 Japanese suicide planes were launched to attack the ships. American troops joked about "the Golden Gate in '48." That was the year they hoped to be home after Japan's full defeat, three years after the Okinawan battle. To the minds of those fighting, the atom bomb cut the war short by that amount of time. It was a lifetime to some—and enough time to lose their lives for others.

No fewer than 1,457 ships and half a million men participated in the Okinawan landing. One would often find his ship a part of a smaller group and then overnight would join a larger convoy, still a fraction of the whole. Sometimes ships could be seen as far as the horizon in awesome numbers. Who would believe that so many ships existed in the world? In the first convoy of the early landing, 430 troopships came from Seattle and Pearl Harbor to Ulithi "an atoll 3,700 miles west of Hawaii that provided a fine anchorage and base for forward operations."

I was coming in at Ulithi with a replacement group. I remember it as a sandy island of Mogmog where we could enjoy an afternoon of swimming, baseball, and—for those who wished—an indulgence in beer. It seemed like luxury after being on a troop ship for many days and nights.

Feifer concluded that the armada sailing to Okinawa covered thirty square miles of ocean. It was the largest assembly in naval history, including more than forty aircraft carriers, eighteen battleships, and 380 combat vessels in the initial phase.

The main force of the invasion landed on the beaches of Okinawa on April 1, 1945, Easter Sunday. The landing had been relatively unopposed, which was contrary to what had happened during the invasion of most of the Pacific Islands prior to this time.

The Japanese commanders had decided to allow the American troops to disembark and come ashore as a part of a strategy that, in theory, was a good one. Once the troops were ashore, the Japanese surmised that the ships that had brought them would remain to supply them and that the aircraft that were on the carriers to protect them would not leave them unsupported. Thus, these planes, along with their ships, would be sitting ducks for the 1,465 plus suicide planes that had already been designated to sink the fleet.

Once the fleet had been sunk, thought the Japanese, the American troops would be isolated, unsupplied, and without recourse of any kind. Therefore, the Japanese army would be in position to completely annihilate them. And the sobering fact is that the strategy might have worked. It has been speculated that if only one out of five Japanese suicide planes in action had hit their targets, the objective would have been achieved.

As it was, only a few ships were actually sunk. Many were damaged, and many lives were lost. Many of the Japanese planes were shot down by American planes before they were able to get near the ships. Many more were eliminated by antiaircraft fire from the ships themselves. So, rather than achieving a great victory by registering the three hundred hits that might have made the strategy work, comparatively few did the damage anticipated by their Japanese commanders.

By the time the kamikazes were raining fire on our ships and sustaining the resulting losses, our troops had moved inland and were battling the dug-in Japanese on every hillside and under every foot of ground. They were making their stand, prepared to die an honorable death for the emperor.

Such had been the circumstance on and around Okinawa when I arrived in 1945. Upon my recent arrival, things were different. I was given a welcome guidebook with a page entitled "Surviving Okinawa." It contained much of the advice we had been given as troops landing on Okinawa. The one difference was that the Japanese troops were no longer hostile.

The survival suggestions highlighted the hazards of typhoons. In 1945, I experienced two of them. One blew away practically everything, sinking our planes on the water, damaging ships, and leaving us living in mud and water. At about two o'clock in the morning, my tent lifted from its moorings—tent poles and all—and left me homeless and subject to the elements for several days.

My second typhoon experience was aboard a ship, going from Okinawa to Japan after the war ended. It was so vicious that we all became ill, including the sailors. Damage was done even to some of the larger ships. Even the small boats carried for survival were blown away by the typhoon.

Another warning was about the habu snakes. When we landed in 1945, we thought we might be in as much jeopardy from the snakes as from the Japanese. This poisonous snake is most often found in vegetation, in secluded places, and in caves and rocks, and was to be feared. The Okinawa habu snake is not unlike the American rattlesnake, copperhead, and cottonmouth. It can grow to seven and a half feet long. The survival kit warned, "If you think you see one, don't investigate."

A very strong impression of the nature of change struck me as I entered a Marine Corps base and observed the American and the Japanese flags flying together. This was land where fellow marines had died to take down one of those flags. The Japanese had died by the thousands to prevent our raising the other. Such contradictions, no matter how confusing and disconcerting, are the result of the continuing shifting of the sands of time. That was not the only contradiction I would discover as I sought to retrace my steps from the past.

I was escorted to the offices of Major General Don Gardner, and he welcomed me as a warrior from out of history. Even he, the senior officer, was a youngster to one who had been a part of the "Old Corps." He briefed me on current Marine Corps activities on the island. I was escorted to "the" guesthouse, and I changed into appropriate clothing for taking a boat ride to the landing beaches where I and most other marines came ashore in 1945.

The water was choppy as I tried to get pictures of the beaches. When I landed there seventy years ago from a troop ship in a landing craft, the water was also choppy.

The marines stationed there today were not even aware that an air base existed there seventy years earlier. How would I identify the location of my tent? Where was the communication shack? The mess tent? The remembered surroundings of the past? These things were fuzzy in my memory after so long, but my pictures would not lie. I had only these possibilities for discovering the hallowed grounds on which I had walked as a young marine.

One of my pictures had preserved for me the evidence I needed to confirm that my tent, until it blew away in a typhoon, was next to a Buddhist temple. Nearby, on hot nights, we would set up an outdoor movie screen. If anything had been preserved, perhaps the temple would have survived. It was not to be found on the base, and no one seemed to be aware that there had ever been a Buddhist temple there.

Finally, after discussions with a marine whose wife was a native Okinawan in the community near the base, we were reminded that there was such a temple on the edge of the small city of Kin on the periphery of the current base. Assuming that the temple might have been moved, and that this might match my picture, we went to the site. It matched my picture exactly. Although it was not a part of the current base—and none of the old surroundings of the past could be seen—it was clearly the temple.

We contacted the Buddhist priest who lived in another facility nearby, which had been built long after the war, and asked for his help. He looked at the photo, and through an interpreter, he indicated it was the same temple and that it had not been moved. It was 470 years old, and it was one of only a few structures not destroyed during the war.

In a battle zone, there are no legal boundaries. We had located our tents and other facilities wherever we chose. When parameters had been established, the temple was outside the parameters. My picture showed that we had put a fence around the temple to protect it during the war years. It was clear that all the nearby construction had taken place since 1945.

I had some pictures of the airfield, showing mountains surrounding a valley where the airfield had been constructed. With some help of the marines, the pictures were analyzed and compared with the lay of the mountains. The outlines were precisely those of my pictures. Thus, we had fixed the mountains on one side, the temple on the other, and the field in between.

The field was completely overlaid with facilities for a different kind of marine base. There was no evidence of the airfield. The main street through the base had been the coral strip of the airfield of the past. No one would have known that it had been a fighter and dive bomber runway during World War II. Several marines, including an interpreter, a photographer, a historian, and some local people, fully agreed that we had dredged up history from the foundation of their base.

Another picture showed me standing with four marines by a communications center near a stone memorial. I didn't think it would have vanished completely. The Buddhist monk was familiar with it and took us to the exact spot where we stood for that picture. With it as a point of reference—along with the Buddhist temple and the horizon—I could almost see the Corsairs coming and going for close air support and the dive bombers warming up for their missions in the main islands of Japan.

Another picture showed me standing in my flight jacket next to the tent area. That, more than any other thing, convinced the marines and town fathers that it had been an airfield. By that time, the local leaders were excited to have copies of my pictures and hear my story. They were deeply interested in the person who—at eighteen then and eighty-eight now—had survived the years in the interim to return to the area and share the activities of those days from the past.

We journeyed to the seat of government of the city of Kin. I showed the city fathers several pictures that I had taken of bathhouses, bombed-out schools, rubble from the war, and other scenes from those bleak and desolate times. Some had lived in the area during that time, but they had been young children or teenagers. They had been living in the countryside, in caves, or wherever they could find shelter and safety.

They were aware of the landmarks I had photographed so many years earlier. The community had been so devastated during the war that their recording history had preserved very little from that period. They were anxious to have copies of my photographs, unprofessional as they were. The marines agreed to make copies of the photos for their use in a history that is now being prepared.

As we visited over tea, new friendships evolved over common interests. I was given a souvenir book. The reflections, though faded, were partially restored and made more vivid by the conversations taking place. One man—whom I believed to be much my senior—looked at a picture of me at eighteen with a small Okinawan boy of about ten or twelve by my side. He remarked, "This could have been me. I was about that age then."

From Kin, we traveled to beaches that were not far from the airfield where I had spent time in recreation and rest. Looking out over the water and into the distance beyond, I could remember the world of another time. Much had changed, and construction was closing in the open areas that made the island so different in those days.

From the beaches near the airfield, we drove near the city of Naha and the beaches where I had actually landed. I had taken pictures from the ocean looking in the day before, and now I was standing on the beaches where I landed during the war. That was where we had come ashore in landing boats. I had slept on the beach in a sleeping bag, fearing the sounds of aircraft and shelling in the distance, unaware of how dangerous they might be.

In the morning, I had observed the tombs that were before us. Some were unusual in their artistic style. Others were more practical and less lavish. They all fit the requirements of the culture of the past. The surroundings today were overrun with facilities of differing kinds, and the destructive violence of the past was no longer evident.

We paid a visit to the commander of the First Marine Air Wing, Brigadier General William A. Forney. I sat in on a lecture concerning the history of Okinawa from before World War II until today, which was for a group of marines who had recently arrived from the States. As the honored guest, I helped set the stage for historic deliberation. I was the only one who had any experience with that part of history on Okinawa and one of the few who had returned in recent years. I was the object of conversation and interest for the young marines.

I was taken to the airfield at Kadena and given a briefing on the IFF (Identification Friend or Foe) and the GCA (Ground Control Approach) systems, which were both permanent and portable. Because I was an operator of the IFF radar during my days on Okinawa and an operator of the GCA radar in the States, it was appropriate that I should see the nature of the equipment forty-nine years later. Only the operational aspects and the sophistication of the equipment had changed.

I learned firsthand how forcefully the sands of time overlay history. Old commitments have been set aside, old facilities have been replaced, old comrades had moved on, and memories are of things that matter very little to the leadership of today.

In retrospect, it is clear that what was important in the past—even if earthshaking and worth dying for—is of little consequence in the minds of those who live in a different world because they had no part in that earlier world. The flow of time distorts the worth of one's action in earlier times. My recent visit to Okinawa reinforced that fact for me.

History as it was lived then was very different from how it is perceived today. What was, to those involved, worthy of dying for becomes something subject to question, if not disdain and ridicule, by some who have no concept of that time.

According to Peter Mallet, a marine taking part in the battle of Okinawa, "Okinawa was a killing field." History recorded that, "in the eighty-two days of battle for that island, an average of about 2,500 people died every day."

Approximately 90 percent of all the Japanese in combat on the island (91,000) perished, along with 23,000 Americans and 150,000 Okinawan civilians, totaling 250,000 causalities. That was more than Nagasaki and Hiroshima combined. As the battle progressed, it became clear that the battle for the homeland would be many more times vicious and much costlier than Okinawa. In *Tennozan* George Feifer makes the point that Truman was justified in dropping the atomic bomb.

> The atom bomb and its aftermath and the public lack of appreciation for that action clearly establishes the fact that one must know the context of the times in order to justify the actions of those times. Those who have not lived history are not in the best position to applaud or condemn the actions taking place within the parameters of that history.

Today, young people—and some not-so-young people—protest the act of our having used the atomic bomb. Yet, they have no knowledge of the realities of the time. Like the disaster resulting from "the charge of the light brigade" (resulting from action being ordered by an officer who was not on the scene), those who are protected by time and circumstances from the consequences of action—or no action—should not presume to second-guess those who were on the scene.

When questioned some months ago by a young man writing a paper on the subject of the atomic bomb as to my disposition concerning its use, I responded by presenting the scenario that if the bomb had not been used, not only would many millions more have died, but many others would not have lived. For example, based upon my firm belief that I—and many of my friends— would have died in the battle for the Japanese homeland, had the bomb not been dropped, my children, my eleven grandchildren, and my nine great-grandchildren would never have been born. My wife would have been destined to find another mate, and my mother would have lost one or two—and perhaps all three—sons who served in the armed forces. The probable reality of having forestalled the use of the bomb can be multiplied by hundreds of thousands.

While there are many other possibilities that can be played out in the minds of Mondaymorning quarterbacks, I believe mine can stand the test of logic from the perspective of those living and involved in that day. The "kill-or-be-killed" tenacity of the Japanese helped justify the decision to drop the atomic bomb on both Hiroshima and Nagasaki. A few months later, I would be one of many walking through the rubble, totally unaware that the radiation might one day jeopardize my health.

By virtue of its designation as a major component of the marine forces that would be engaged in the invasion of Japan, it was not surprising that all of us who were a part of the Okinawan command were supportive of Truman's decision to drop the atomic bomb. We believe that it saved our lives.

I was only nineteen when I walked into Hiroshima, not many days after the atom bomb had been dropped on the city. It was unbelievable what I observed, but it was no more unbelievable than what I observed in Tokyo and Yokohama. The difference was that a few shells of buildings were standing in Tokyo and Yokohama, and little—if anything—was standing in Hiroshima and Nagasaki.

As to radiation and fallout, it was unknown by those of us on the scene as being harmful as we know it today. We walked the ashes of Hiroshima and Nagasaki while the ground was at its hottest, early after the occupation. Had I known what I know now, I would not have dared. I recently attended a funeral of a fellow marine with whom I walked those grounds soon after occupying Japan. He died of liver cancer at age sixty-six. His wife asked me whether I thought his cancer might have evolved as a result of that experience years ago.

I don't know. I can't know. I would hope that such is not a danger for me. But who knows? Yet to have been given a long life, which likely would not have been spared, short of forcing the Japanese surrender by using the bomb, one can only be grateful. Certainly, it is not for the second-guessers who have no roots in the times to speculate at the expense of possible loss of life for those who were.

For those who think the atom bomb must have been a painful experience, just imagine residents being roasted in the streets of Tokyo, in their homes, and in entire city blocks by B-29 raids as if they had been "shoveled into an oven." The horror was above anything one could imagine, and charred corpses were piled high where they tried to escape. It is said that the fire raced like a tidal wave "sucking city sections in the fiery vortex; a quarter of a million buildings were consumed; before daylight a fifth of Tokyo's industrial area and 63 percent of its commercial district disappeared; the heat turned bodies to ash in an instant like some industrial furnace disposing of autumn leaves; it ignited hoards at a distance with people running from the flames as fast as they could, those who seemed to be escaping, burst into balls of fire, others jumped into canals and were cooked alive in boiling water; scores of thousands died of suffocation as the flames extracted all oxygen from the air."

According to George Feifer, "This was probably the greatest one-night disaster and the largest sum of suffering endured by any city in world history." Could those at Hiroshima and Nagasaki have suffered more? I doubt it—so why was the bomb more inhumane than the thousands before?

Today, as we celebrate the seventy-second anniversary of the end of World War II, those of us who had our part are more conscious of the realities of that time. We are more inclined with this span of time between who we are and who we were to want to reflect and share these reflections. Most of those of the age we were then who are our grandchildren will never know a time like ours. Perhaps that is all a plus. But we who were changed forever by having known a commitment worth dying for, wish for them, not war but challenge, opportunity, a cause, a purpose, or a personal objective that overshadows all the unworthy diversions that for many distort life and its meaning completely.

During the eighty-two days in battle on Okinawa, there was death everywhere. Okinawa's final toll of American casualties were the highest experienced in any campaign against the Japanese. Sugar Loaf Hill would cause more killed and wounded than any other Pacific battle on Iwo Jima or elsewhere.

When the battle was finally over, there were piles of Japanese bodies that had been collecting for many days. The marines had bodies that had been dead for several days. The stench was indescribable. The mud was so bad, and it rained so hard the troops were up to their waists in water. Sometimes they slept standing up in their foxholes. Jungle rot, typhoid, and ringworms were not uncommon.

By digging a foxhole, E. B. Sledge, whom I came to know, encountered a mass of wiggling maggots that came welling up as those beneath them were pushing them out. Minutes later, his spade hit a rotting corpse. Such was an experience of mine on mopping-up operations in the hills. I dug into a cave, reached inside, and came up with a handful of rotting hair of a corpse with the face still attached.

Fourteen percent of all the marines killed in World War II were on Okinawa, and sixteen thousand were wounded. The Japanese had been told not to be afraid of combat and wouldn't go home alive. The Japanese had such hatred of the marines and thought that qualifying for the Marine Corps required murdering his parents and that marines got their laughs from castrating prisoners and running them over with bulldozers. If the Americans won, the Japanese thought life would not be worth living. They would consider anything besides surrender.

The American marines wouldn't surrender either. They believed, and it was true, that raising their hands would be almost certain death. They would be shot in the back and beheaded. Most of the marines I associated with on Okinawa are deceased. I recently gave the eulogy for one with whom I served there.

\*\*\*

# III

# WHEN THE LIGHTS GO ON AGAIN
# ALL OVER THE WORLD

If you are ninety years of age and are living today, you are an exception to the rule in many ways. First and foremost, you are, if a male, one in ten who have lived to the age of ninety and beyond. So, there are proportionately relatively few who represent a time in history dating back to the depth of the Great Depression followed by World War II. Channeled in to that later conflict, many entered a period of time earning a college education under the G.I. Bill.

For those who had received no college prior to the military and the many who never intended to pursue that course before their military service, circumstances changed by way of the broadening of their perspectives as they matured in the military. Thus, with the G.I. Bill, the door to their pursuit of education and the benefit of its results was made available.

This followed the lights coming on all over the world—a song title of verses composed for a World War II melody as follows:

> When the lights come on again all over the world,
> And the boys are home again all over the world,
> And rain or snow is all that may fall from the skies above
> A kiss won't mean good bye but hello to love
> When the lights go on again all over the world,
> And the ships will sail again all over the world,
> Then we'll have time for things like wedding rings,
> And sweet hearts will sing,

When the lights go on again all over the world.

And when the lights did come on for the sixteen million veterans, many moved from the military to educational institutions or jobs and professions. In a few years, they assumed the leadership of the country in every area. In government, in business, in social circles, in financial centers, and in all other leadership relationships at home and abroad, they prevailed and succeeded for more than fifty years.

Politics had one of the most rational and hospitable periods where Democrats and Republicans who fought in the same foxholes and served as shipmates were able to advance the country in good spirit and respect for each other. Marriages flourished, and children came in numbers to swell the population.

So, to share something of that time in history, I recalled the song "When the Lights Go on Again All Over the World."

Approximately 99 percent of the sixteen million who served in World War II have moved on, and the 1 percent remaining, about 200,000, are dying at a fast pace in that they are now all in their nineties. Five years from now, substantially all will be deceased—and there will be no storytelling from those who were actually in the battles that settled the contest.

While we of my generation are not prehistoric, we are to some, ancient. Having lived through the Great Depression as well as World War II, we carry with us impacting experiences that are unique in history. The spirit of the war years cannot be understood without the context of the trauma of the years of the Great Depression before the war. It was the war that finally extricated the country from that nightmare. The hardships suffered by those who endured the years of the Depression in many ways prepared them for facing the challenges of the World War.

At its height, 273,000 families were evicted from their homes. Without any income at all, they were unable to pay their mortgages or rent. Ten thousand banks closed, and 175,000 schools systems failed to open. And while the stock market crash caused those losing their wealth to jump out of tall buildings in New York, it didn't stop there. My own grandfather—with a wife and four children, one being my father—lost the farm to creditors and committed suicide. My father, at age twelve, quit school to help his mother support his three younger siblings.

I grew up in a tenant house on a farm where my father who never finished grade school was a sharecropper. The supporting timbers were placed on rocks, leaving openings for the winds of winter to wind their way through cracks in the floor to keep the house air-conditioned. Because education was secondary to farmwork, I failed high school and, by way of the G.I. Bill, I later corrected my lack of learning.

**The University Student Commons spans University Lake. It's one of the University's most used facilities.**

At the early age of fifteen, I slept in the tobacco barn between bales of hay with a twelvegauge shotgun at my shoulder awaiting any intruder coming to steal the tobacco that produced much of the family income for the year. At age seventeen, I traded that shotgun for an M-1 rifle that I carried onto the beach in combat on Okinawa at age eighteen.

Like many others of my generation, my future was determined more by circumstance than by design. Life became a process of walking through doors as they opened and discovering pathways incidental to conditions dictated by the realities of history.

I was fifteen years old, carrying a bucket of milk from the barn to the milk house, when the farm owner approached and said, "The Japanese have attacked Pearl Harbor." *Well*, I thought to myself, *at least that's another country*. I didn't have the slightest idea where Pearl Harbor was or the implications of that act of war.

So, when the attack on Pearl Harbor came, we were already chastened by lives of hardships from which the challenges of war lifted our spirit of adventure. A fever of patriotism united the entire country as young and old alike resolved to make whatever sacrifices were required.

Our backs were against the wall as we faced those who would put the world in chains.

We were the only power sufficient to carry the keys to unlock those chains. President Franklin Roosevelt, who I had the privilege of meeting, convinced us that "the only thing we had to fear was fear itself."

We proclaimed with feeling the prospects of success by singing songs such as "When the Lights Go On Again All Over the World." That goal was our inspiration.

During the 1940s, some sixteen million men entered the military. They put their personal lives on hold and kissed their sweethearts goodbye. Resolute but worried parents, brothers, and sisters lingered over train station goodbyes. For most new draftees and volunteers, the separation lasted far longer than suggested by the popular song of the time that began "Goodbye, Dear, I'll be Back in a Year." Before it was over, the year had extended to two, three, and four years—with many serving two or three years abroad.

The spirit of the day was "we will win." Each one of us, believing in ourselves, our country, freedom, and in the organizations of which we were a part, were willing to accept whatever responsibility and hard work was necessary. It was tough, but it was also exciting, stimulating and uplifting. Pride prevailed in all of us.

Uncle Sam considered me too young for the draft at age seventeen, but catching the fever of patriotism, I joined the marines. Like most young men of the time, I preferred to live long, but I was willing to die for my country. We were so emboldened by the audacity of the Japanese that—rather than thinking negatively about the challenge ahead—we took it as an inspiring responsibility that called forth our best, and it became an exciting adventure.

We met people we never dreamed of meeting and learned things we would not have learned anywhere else. A positive spirit prevailed irrespective of the statistics that pervaded the headlines for all to see. On one raid over Germany, of 376 planes, sixty were shot down, leaving six hundred empty bunks in England that night. An average of 220 deaths per day was recorded in World War II.

The news of marines dying by the thousands as they landed on Pacific islands braced me for the demanding discipline that I would need to endure. They sought to take away our civilian identity and make us function automatically in response to any command. The recruiting sergeant asked whether we had any scars, birthmarks, or other unusual features. When asked why such a question was necessary, the sergeant replied, "So they can identify you on some Pacific beach after the Japs blast off your dog tags." That was our introduction to the stark realism that not only characterized the Marine Corps but our personal determination to respond to the challenge.

The strength of the army was in its huge size and power. It made our successes as a nation possible. The navy carried us to the ends of the earth, and for the marines, it was our mode of transportation. Each in its own way, including the Army Air Corps, played its role in leading the world out of darkness.

The spirit of every young man was expressed by an unknown author who stated, "When we discover values in life worth dying for, we likely have found purposes worth living for." Pericles Funeral Orations stated, "The bravest are surely those who have the clearest vision of what is before them, glory and danger alike, and yet notwithstanding go out to meet it." These were the sentiments that drove us to our ultimate successes.

We celebrated some of the best days of our country's history and our lives. When the lights did come back on, the reality of our success gave us the confidence to build the nation to its maximum capacity. That confidence prevailed for the next fifty years when those who fought in the war ran the country, and it has never been more successful economically, socially, and politically. We did it because we believed deeply in what we fought to preserve.

As a country boy growing up in a very rural setting, I never dreamed of going to college. Learning was so far down my list of priorities that I literally slept through high school and was, four years afterward, rejected by a liberal arts college. I later became the chief financial officer and was invited to be its president twice.

Following four years of maturing in the Marine Corps and thanks to the G.I. Bill, I entered Campbellsville Junior College and was housed in a wooden army barracks with fifteen other veterans on probation. It burned down before the year was over, taking with it everything we had accumulated. I graduated with a 3.9 average.

Married when I was a freshman, I taught in college before completing my undergraduate degree and had six children before finishing graduate school.

In many ways, the transition from a rural farm orientation and the circumstances of history expanded my introduction to new places, new faces, broader knowledge, and tougher challenges. My opportunities socially, physically, and intellectually were greatly extended.

Even today, as the numbers of the Greatest Generation are diminished to less than two hundred thousand, there is no greater satisfaction to veterans of that conflict than that we rose when the nation called us to stand. We still stand strong for our country, believing that our sons and grandsons would do the same under similar circumstances.

As our lives play out, we acknowledge those activities that highlight our proudest days. Sherman Helms said, "The last plaintive bugle note drifts off across the valley with a soul astride." Though we are reduced to a few, we remain proud as we reflect upon who we are and what we did. Irrespective of our service branch, we salute each other for having laid our lives on the line in order to bring to fruition the greatest military success in history.

At my age, I spend more and more time giving eulogies. Most of my contemporaries from the Marine Corps, from college, and from my profession are deceased—some of them long ago. As I attend these funerals, I remember that Yogi Berra said, "If you don't go to theirs, they won't come to yours." I'm expecting a large turnout.

\*\*\*

# IV

## COMMENORATION CEREMONY – 66TH ANNIVERSARY OF THE END OF WWII IN THE PACIFIC BATTLE SHIP MISSOURI

**Confronting the Realities of Youth**
**February 27–March 9, 2010**

When invited by Tim Davis, president of the Greatest Generations Foundation, to journey back to where they had engaged in World War II combat, the decision of the eleven marine veterans was not as easy as it might appear on the surface. After all, their battles in the South Pacific had been unbelievably traumatic encounters. Several had been wounded, and all had witnessed the killing and wounding of thousands of their fellow marines while defeating the enemy in a grueling person-to-person conflict.

Would a return to scenes of the past bring back disturbing memories? Would it open old wounds of hatred of the Japanese? Would this be a journey of sadness and sorrow? Could they, after all these years, find solace from deeply ingrained emotional scars? Could there be a healing effect by revisiting those remembered places now overlaid with nature's cover and utilized for constructive purposes? These and other questions had to be answered by each of the marines, now sixty-five years older than when they endured these experiences on those long-ago, "gone but not forgotten" battlegrounds.

Finally, with an affirming and even longing spirit of anticipation, ten marine survivors of the Battle for Iwo Jima and I—the only one who did not land on the beaches there—decided to make the journey.

I was not alien to the island of Iwo Jima because many of my buddies fought there. Some were wounded, and others died there while I completed training for the Battle for Okinawa. I am, however, an Iwo Jima survivor due to a quirk of circumstances following the battle.

Thus, over the years I have been accepted by marines from that battle as a survivor. My engagement was swift and sudden, and theirs was slow, prolonged, and hostile. My respect for their grueling ordeal demands this clarification of how I too became an Iwo Jima Survivor.

We eleven, dubbed by Tom Brokaw as part of the "Greatest Generation," were blessed to be given an opportunity to return to the scenes that had laid the foundation for who we had become. We were further blessed by being accompanied by students from the College of the Ozarks.

# HEILMAN, ROLAND BENNETT

Section: 54

Grave: 1737

Branch of Service: US MARINE CORPS

Birth Date: 10/01/1923

Death Date: 11/17/2011

Interment Date: 02/08/2012

The presence of this group was afforded by a special alliance between the college and the Greatest Generations Foundation's patriotic education travel program for descendants of veterans who had served in the Pacific Theatre during World War II. Its purpose is to provide a lifechanging experience for students by learning firsthand about the dedication and commitment of World War II veterans as they engaged in defending their country. Also traveling with the group were two senior administrators of that college and Tim Davis, the head of the Greatest Generations Foundation. Accompanying the group were photographers and media specialists to record the experience.

Our student companions proved to be a positive catalyst for bridging the gap between the past and present. Because of our differences, they gave us special attention and the respect usually reserved for grandparents. The students stood a bit in awe of what had transpired in our lives. They listened and learned through the stories we told about our experiences. Sometimes they shed tears—sometimes alone and sometimes with the marine they accompanied. As college juniors and seniors, most were older than we veterans were when in combat. No doubt this fact was a bit difficult for them to comprehend.

A student reflected, "We were able to sit around with our veterans and hear some of their experiences. There was a great bonding between the students and veterans as they shared stories they hadn't told since they left the island of Iwo Jima."

In expressing her expectation, one student exclaimed, "The next eight or nine days are going to be the most physical, emotional, and spiritually challenging times I've ever experienced, but I also know they will be the most rewarding."

Each of the marines developed a deep affection for the student who was his escort. Mine held my hand when she thought I might slip and fall in the mud as we visited a cave on Okinawa. I did fall, failing to remember as she did, that I was no longer the eighteen-year-old marine who climbed those ridges so long ago.

In speaking of her veteran, another student remarked, "What a sweetheart. I have loved our time together so far and feel like we've always been family. He's lively and full of advice mixed with memories—something that seems to speak of all these marine veterans' character." Because of our common background, we marines were able to interact with each other seriously or with a bit of disarming humor. We could shed tears or be filled with anticipation as we observed, remembered, reflected, and wondered whether it had all really been true. After all, while many things were the same, much had changed.

These long-ago experiences and the resulting reflections flooded our minds as we journeyed toward places to which we had no expectation of ever returning. In early 1945, I began a journey from San Diego to the South Pacific. I had joined the marines as a seventeen-year-old. In my mother's mind's eye, I was just barely dry behind the ears. A few months later, at eighteen, I was joining a host of other marines aboard a troop ship attached to a convoy bound for points unknown to the hundreds of marines in the bowels of the ship.

From Tokyo, we flew to Okinawa, now a prefecture of Japan. Immediately upon landing, a strong impression of the nature of change struck me. The immense overlay of buildings, roadways, airport facilities, massive traffic, and swarms of people was almost overpowering in contrast to the destruction I remembered.

As we entered a Marine Corps base, I observed the American and the Japanese flags flying together and remembered that this was land where many marines had died to take down one of those flags, while Japanese had died by the thousands to prevent the raising of the other. Such contradictions, no matter how confusing and disconcerting, result from the continuous shifting of the sands of time.

The marines stationed on Okinawa today are not even aware that this was the air base from which I operated existed sixty-five years ago. How could I identify the location of my tent? Where were the remembered surroundings of the past? These things were fuzzy in my memory after so long, but my pictures would not lie. I had only that evidence for discovering the hallowed grounds on which I had walked those past years as a young marine.

In a battle zone, there are no legal boundaries. We had planted our tents and other facilities wherever we chose. In the meantime, parameters have been established—and the past has been replaced or overridden.

# Former president Heilman revisits war zone

> Kristy Burkhardt
Collegian Staff

"If something happens today, do you want to us to resuscitate?"

That was the question posed to almost a dozen World War II veterans as they boarded a cargo plane to revisit the black-sand beaches where they had landed under fire from Japanese forces 65 years ago.

University of Richmond Chancellor E. Bruce Heilman sat among the group of veterans as the plane left Okinawa, Japan – the base where he had been stationed as a Marine when he was 18 years old. In three hours, they would land in Iwo Jima, Japan, where the other 10 veterans who accompanied Heilman had fought to capture the island during a 36-day battle.

Heilman, 86, is the national spokesman for The Greatest Generations Foundation, the organization that sponsored the veterans' trip to revisit the beach.

The veterans' trip to the remote, pacific island was the product of three years of planning by the foundation, an organization dedicated to honoring veterans.

On previous trips, veterans collapsed and died from the intensely emotional experience of returning to where they fought, according to a documentary about the trip by the foundation.

In the documentary, a college student looked on solemnly as Tim Davis, the head of the foundation, kneeled to ask the veteran sitting beside him whether he would like to be resuscitated if anything were to happen when they returned to the island.

"Resuscitate," the veteran said after a moment of hesitation.

The young man sitting next to the veteran nodded and his wrinkled forehead eased. He was one of the 11 student-companions from the School of the Ozarks in Point Lookout, Mo., that accompanied the veterans on the trip last March. After traveling to the islands of Okinawa and Iwo Jima, the group flew to mainland Japan to visit Hiroshima and Osaka.

The foundation invited students to accompany the veterans to promote recognition and respect for U.S. and allied war veterans and enhance their historical education – a learning experience Heilman called "intergenerational education."

The 10 veterans who revisited Iwo

Photo courtesy of E. Bruce Heilman

E. Bruce Heilman, along with his student companion Kathleen Porter from the School of the Ozarks, traveled throughout the islands of Okinawa.

Jima beside Heilman were survivors of one of the bloodiest battles in World War II. As they walked along the island's black, volcanic sand, the veterans told the students and group of young marines about the scene they remembered, where 6,000 American troops died and 18,000 were wounded.

"As I watched these men bow their heads, I realized that specific faces and names were running through their minds, faces and names that were real people to them," said Rebecca Wright, a student from the School of the Ozarks. "Real buddies, real friends.

"Nothing in a history book can fully communicate the sense of loss that I am sure each of these men were feeling."

The group traveled to the summit of Mount Suribachi, where the famous picture of American troops raising the flag was taken after they defeated Japanese troops . The photograph – the most widely distributed in military history – represented a pivotal time in the war, boosting morale on the island and back home.

"I want to tell their stories," Tim Davis, head of the foundation, said in an interview with HistoryNet.com. "We feel that going back, seeing what they actually fought for, meeting the new generation of the people they liberated is closure for these veterans."

Unlike the ten others, Heilman did not land on the beaches of Iwo Jima – at the time he was still completing train-

ing for the Battle of Okinawa. But, like the others, he wore a hat that said "Iwo Jima Survivor" because of what he calls a "quirk of circumstances."

After the battle, Heilman survived a plane crash on the shores of Iwo Jima when he was an air crewman on a transport plane carrying a load of intelligence officers to the island.

Heilman, who was named national spokesman in July, will help to promote the organization at a pivotal time. The foundation will select 30 colleges and universities, plus military academies, to invite to participate in its student-veteran companion program, Heilman said.

Heilman said the organization had not made plans to partner with Richmond, but that Richmond had not been ruled out and its renowned international center positioned the university as an excellent candidate for the program.

The foundation also plans to purchase a $16.5 million chateau in Normandy, France, that will serve as a permanent educational facility for remaining and future generations of veterans.

The name of the foundation originated from the expression coined by Tom Brokaw, "The Greatest Generation," to describe the generation who grew up during the Depression and went on to fight in World War II. But, the title of the organization pluralized Brokaw's expression because it honors and supports generations of veterans beyond World War II, as well.

We drove near the city of Naha to the beaches where I had actually landed during the war. I had dug in and slept on the beach the first night after landing. Hearing the sounds of aircraft and shelling in the distance made me aware of the serious nature of our engagement. Today, that landing beach is overlaid with progress. Comrades have moved on or passed on, and memories affect very little the things that matter today. What was important in the past, even if earthshaking then and seemingly worth dying for, is of little consequence in the minds of those who now live there.

According to the record of one marine who took part in combat on Okinawa, "In the eighty-two days of battle, an average of some 2,500 people died every day." This included American marines, soldiers, sailors, Japanese warriors, and tens of thousands of Okinawans. The Okinawans were begged to come out of their caves, but they were fearful that their women would be raped and all of them would be tortured. Those who refused were treated as combatants. The caves were destroyed by flamethrowers, dynamite, and bulldozers. It was that kind of war.

Ninety percent (91,000) of all of the Japanese died in combat on the island along with 23,000 Americans and 150,000 Okinawan civilians, totaling more than 250,000 casualties, more than those of Nagasaki and Hiroshima combined. As the conflict progressed, it became an increasing assumption that the battle for the homeland would be many times more vicious and much costlier than Okinawa.

We visited Kakazu Ridge, one of the major battle sites, and ascended into one of the many caves. At one time, one thousand Okinawans had spent eighty days in that cave, hiding from the hell of the world outside. An Okinawan told us that he had lived in that cave at three years of age. At that time, I had been engaged in helping free people from those caves. When I began to sing a song I had learned from natives there, he immediately joined me. I realized that the past had not been a dream. I suppose, by remembering that song, I had confirmed the past had really existed.

My college student companion wrote about it in her blog: "My veteran said that it's hard for him to connect the Okinawa he is seeing right now with the Okinawa he fought on." Further, she observed, "As we looked out on an idyllic scene of pristine sand, green grass, and beautiful blue water, it was hard to envision the vast number of ships and landing craft once riding those waves." (It was the largest assembly in naval history. No fewer than 1,457 ships and half a million men participated in the Okinawa campaign.) "The men landing on this beach expected that 80 percent of them would die before getting off the beach. As we looked over the beach, my marine described what it was like to land and dig foxholes, and how it felt to be engaged in combat."

Because the commandant of the Marine Corps, the Marine Corps Drum and Bugle Corps, and the Silent Rifle Team were on the island, we were invited to attend a Marine Corps Battle Colors Ceremony at Camp Foster. At the stadium, we were given front-row seats and introduced by the commanding general as honored guests for the evening.

One student recalled,

> The crowd stood to their feet and applauded as the veterans took off their red caps and waved them proudly. I felt tears rolling down my cheeks. It was indescribable to see these men honored by so many people who admired them for their bravery. A line formed that stretched for probably sixty yards. People were taking pictures and thanking each veteran personally.
>
> I cannot even describe seeing the veterans being praised and honored like that, but I am struck by their humility as each one would say they didn't want to be praised for their heroism. For them, the real praise goes to those who died on the island.

We marines were touched as well by the hundreds of people standing in line just to shake our hands. Many were high school and grade school students. Even small children wanted autographs, a request that we marines accommodated with pride. To them, we were ancient warriors.

Many incidents occurred along the way, mostly positive. However, when it was discovered that our air transportation from Okinawa to Iwo Jima was in jeopardy, Tim Davis worked relentlessly with others of the accompanying group, political leaders, and the Marine Corps until finally a C-130 troop carrier was dispatched to ferry our group of fifty or sixty individuals to Iwo Jima.

En route, the excitement was at a high level. We interacted with the crewmen and each other, and some of us were invited to sit in the copilot's seat. I had often sat in that seat in an R4D as an air crewman. Feeling the movement of that huge airliner with my hand on the controls brought back memories.

Our group in front of a building on Hiroshima that barely survived and is now a monument

Once we arrived over the island, the pilot circled. We veterans looked out, took pictures, shed tears, and broke down emotionally at seeing it for the first time since being extracted from it alive. Some 6,800 of our fellow marines died there, and twenty thousand were wounded.

Eighteen thousand Japanese troops died there as well. One student observed,

> When the plane came within viewing distance of the island, the veterans began flocking to the windows. They watched closely and anxiously. The small windows became precious viewpoints for these men. They viewed the island with great anticipation and some began to look nervous.

Upon landing, another student observed,

A flamethrower man during his time on Iwo bowed silently to the ground. When he rose, there were tears streaming from his unusually mischievous eyes. The others continued to walk down the ramp and they gazed in amazement as our group took form on the runway. They were all watching so intently looking for something recognizable, something they remembered. The memories were flooding their minds and emotions were passing through their eyes."

Another student commented,

> As I looked up to Mount Suribachi, I wondered at the bravery of the men who had died there.
> "I just don't know how we did it," said one marine.
> "I don't either," another replied. "It was over these beaches he had packed water, bodies, and fuel for the flamethrowers and a great many other things."
> As we arrived at the top of Mount Suribachi, sighs of anticipation were released from each veteran. Pride surged in each of them and each student as we stood on the top of the mountain, knowing that each man had had a part in securing the victory sixty-five years earlier.

Another student observed,

> One veteran was crying. He knew what he went through. I felt so insignificant standing there
> with those men, having faced the situation that tore at their very souls. I put my arms in offering,
> and we embraced in a hug for several moments. I had only known them for a few hours, but it
> felt like an eternity. The veteran said, "I thought I wanted to do this before I passed on, and now
> I have. The experience is past, but the memories are forever embedded in my mind. I'll never
> forget that mountain."

As I remembered that barren place from sixty-five years ago, I could appreciate the cover that has emerged over time. Nature was aided by seed spread from the air by the American forces prior to the return of the islands to Japan.

The landscape of Iwo Jima could not have been forgotten. The black sand was still there. The visions of fellow marines dying in battle reminded the survivors of their good fortune of having enjoyed these long years of life since. In remembering raising the flag from their positions on the island, they swelled with pride in the evidence of a successful mission accomplished. Seeing that flag added anticipation to the hope that an end to the long war might finally be in sight.

As I stood atop Mount Suribachi with the ten marines who had landed on the beaches under fire, I could, along with them, embrace their good fortune in having survived the conflict against all odds. As they shed tears or fought their emotions, they must have reflected on the many successes they had enjoyed, the children they had fathered, and the lives that had been extended for them while buddies had long ago given up their future on those beaches. Following the visit to Iwo Jima, a student commented,

> We watched a five-minute segment on *ABC World News Tonight* that portrayed the veterans'
> journey back to Iwo. One of the veterans watching the news segment began to sob. Tears ran
> down his face, and his hands covered his eyes. His body began to shake, and his eyes filled with
> tears. It was heart-wrenching to see these men break down as the memories from the past and
> the trip yesterday flooded their thoughts.

As the only one of the group who had been engaged in the Battle of Okinawa, yet the only one who hadn't hit the beaches of Iwo Jima, I grew even more respectful of those who had endured and survived. I, along with the rest, wore the red cap with the clarifying words on the front in black: "Iwo Jima Survivor."

The divisions participating in the Battle for Iwo Jima had been so greatly depleted by death and injury that those remaining were sent back to other islands to rehabilitate and replenish their ranks in anticipation of their participation in the invasion of Japan.

From Iwo Jima, we flew back to Okinawa and then Osaka, Japan, where I had spent some time on occupation duty and attended the 1971 World's Fair. We boarded the bullet train to Hiroshima. I and a couple of the others had experienced the awesome destruction of the atom bombs while on occupation duty in Japan. One other veteran and I had experienced Nagasaki and Hiroshima shortly after the bomb was dropped. We had walked in the radioactive dirt, dust, ashes, and destruction of those cities and viewed remnants of the skeletons following the bomb.

In Hiroshima, one of those old buildings is still standing, representative of that awful destruction. Now, sixty-five and a half years later, I had returned to see that city as a thriving metropolis. There appeared to be little time for busy residents to reflect on what happened in 1945. Only we who came back had time to reminisce in any significant way.

As we sat in a rebuilt cathedral, I was asked to share my thoughts concerning the bombing of the city. My first response was that we marines whose lives were spared could never apologize for the bomb having been dropped. We would be apologizing for having married our wives, fathering our children, grandfathering our grandchildren, and for all the years since of enjoying the fullness of life. Without the bomb, we would have died in the battle for the Japanese mainland, either by Japanese suicide planes diving into our troop ships or by machine guns as we went up the beaches or by the poison spears that the women and children would have forced into us.

We know now the realities that awaited us had the bomb not been dropped. We also know that while some two hundred thousand died as a result of the two bombs, many more died on Okinawa in the prior four months of combat. What could we anticipate but that this would be multiplied many times over had the bombs not been dropped.

I acknowledged that it was a wonderful revelation to see the rebirth and renewal of the city, which had risen from the ashes like the sphinx, and what man had totally destroyed had been reborn. I alluded to the joy of seeing children playing in colorful attire, observing busy streets, chaotic traffic, the many impressive facilities, and thriving commercial activity. I noted that "what man can destroy, man and nature can restore" and that out of the past dictatorial government had come freedom and democracy.

One of the group wrote to me later sharing that one of her favorite remembrances was when we sat quietly in the chapel and I spoke about rebirth and renewal. She said she would never forget that time, which calls to mind that we all seek the positive outcome. Another student reflected,

We entered the chapel and sat down as a group in a small stone-walled room in silent contemplation. Veterans recalled the destruction they had seen, and students attempted to imagine it all. With voices shaking, the men sat in that little chapel and solemnly considered the price paid by the people of Japan for their freedom.

A student's blog conveyed,

> One of the men made an interesting remark as we sat in the chapel. "Thank God for Truman. If it wasn't for him, we wouldn't be alive today. It was that decision that ended the war." I grew up in a free land because of the price these heroes paid. The Japanese died a horrific death while the men who witnessed it came back from the war to continue their lives and make some attempt at normality. We owe them all our deepest gratitude and respect.

It was not surprising that all of us who were a part of the South Pacific battles like Iwo Jima and Okinawa were supportive of Truman's decision to drop the atomic bomb. We believe that his action saved our lives.

We visited the Peace Museum, now headed by an American, and listened as a Japanese citizen, who was seventeen years old and in the city when the bomb was dropped, told his story.

His family had died, but by luck of location he survived. A student blogged,

> While visiting the Peace Museum, tears swelled in my eyes at seeing display after display of suffering, horrific images of burns, tumors, and children dying from leukemia, and a mother holding the corpse of her stillborn infant. I couldn't help but be amazed that the government was willing to allow their people to endure such pain and still refuse to relinquish control.

Today, some protest the act of our having used the atomic bomb. Yet, most have little knowledge of the realities of that time. Some months ago, when a young man writing a paper asked my opinion about the use of the atomic bomb, I responded that if the bomb had not been used, my children would not have been born. My wife would have been destined to find another mate, and my mother would have lost one or two—or perhaps all three—of her sons who served in the armed forces.

To me and my fellow marines, the "kill-or-be-killed" tenacity of the Japanese could not have been overcome without the climatic impact of the atomic bombs on both Hiroshima and Nagasaki. We walked in the ashes of Hiroshima and Nagasaki while the ground was at its hottest, early after the occupation. The harmful effects were unknown by those of us on the scene. Had we known then what we know now, we would not have been so cavalier with our curiosity.

Some years ago, I attended the funeral of a fellow marine with whom I walked those grounds. He died of liver cancer at age sixty-six. His wife asked me whether I thought his cancer might have been a result of walking in those ashes years ago. I don't know. I can't know. As of now, it appears not to have had a negative effect on me—unless my prostate cancer of some years ago was partially a result.

When I walked into Hiroshima, not many days after the bomb had been dropped, what I saw was unbelievable—but no more unbelievable than what I saw in Tokyo and Yokohama. The difference was that a few shells of buildings were standing in Tokyo and Yokohama, but little, if anything, was standing in Hiroshima and Nagasaki.

For those who think the atom bomb must have been a painful experience, just imagine residents being roasted in the streets of Tokyo, in their homes, and in entire city blocks by B-29 raids as if they had been "shoveled into an oven." The horror was above anything one could imagine; charred corpses were piled high where they tried to escape. It is said that "the fire raced like a tidal wave, sucking city sections in the fiery vortex." A quarter of a million buildings were consumed.

During one raid, a fifth of Tokyo's industrial area and 63 percent of its commercial district disappeared. "The heat turned bodies to ashes in an instant like some industrial furnace disposing of autumn leaves. People ran from the flames as fast as they could, but many simply burst into balls of fire, while others jumped into canals and were cooked alive in boiling water.

Thousands died of suffocation as the flames extracted all oxygen from the air."

That has been termed as probably the greatest one-night disaster and the largest sum of suffering endured by any city in world history. Could those at Hiroshima and Nagasaki have suffered more? I doubt it—so why was this bomb more inhumane than the thousands before?

As we celebrated in reflection of the sixty-fifth anniversary of the Battle for Iwo Jima and revisited the experiences of that era, those who were engaged became even more conscious of the realities of that time. We were all young as we participated in one or more battles, and each served honorably and beyond the call of duty. Some were wounded, and all had buddies killed or wounded as they advanced with flamethrowers, rifles, bayonets, mortars, machine guns, or Browning automatic rifles. All struggled against unbelievable odds to take fortresses that now are serene and peaceful. Tears and cracking voices carried the pain of those hours of mortal conflict.

All marines on the journey had been fortunate to live long lives. Even though, along with millions of other young men of that era, we had accepted death as a real possibility and had no reservations about the cause justifying the means. Such a commitment and the prevailing potential consequences gave all of us a unique perspective for the rest of our lives. This journey was reinforcement of that perspective.

We had done what we did in response to the circumstance of the time. We had grown up in the Depression, many of us in rural parts of the country. Many would never have been as well educated as we became except that we laid our lives on the line for our country. We were rewarded with the G.I. Bill, which provided educational opportunities we never anticipated. We could buy a house on the G.I. Bill and live in a free country because we fought for that privilege.

The young people on this journey with us understood and respected all of that and didn't question our commitments, motives, or convictions. I believe they came to understand why a common culture evolved from the experiences of the sixteen million World War II veterans, which made for a better country.

One student, commenting on her impression of the veterans, concluded:

> I cannot begin to explain how powerful their stories truly were. The thing that most amazes me
> is that they do not desire any attention or praise. Instead, they want the focus to be on those who
> gave the ultimate sacrifice.

We salute Tim Davis and the Greatest Generations Foundation for a job well done. We are honored by the name of the foundation that pays tribute to all World War II veterans. This organization and what it represents instill pride in the veterans who served, especially to the less than two million yet surviving.

This journey back restored in our minds and drew from our memories a vivid part of what had faded from the past. We will forever be indebted for this privilege, which will long remain in our memories. Those who returned to reflect and share reflections carry renewed hope that their grandchildren and great-grandchildren will never know a time like theirs.

We further acknowledge the partnership of the College of the Ozarks for making possible the relationship of these students, which made the experience more vital and stimulating. Their warm friendships and youthful exuberance overrode what could have been a somber event for the old warriors themselves.

And while this journey may have brought closure for the veterans from demons in the crevices of their minds, there is neither a good place nor a grand phrase to bring closure to this commentary of our days of renewal and remembrance.

So, to all, we say a sincere Semper Fi.

\*\*\*

# IV

## THE SIXTY-SIXTH ANNIVERSARY OF THE END OF THE WAR IN THE PACIFIC PART TWO

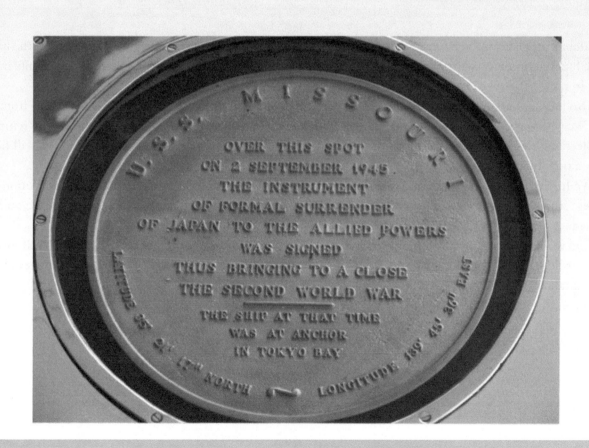

SEPTEMBER 21, 2011


DR. E. BRUCE HEILMAN:
CHANCELLOR, UNIVERSITY OF RICHMOND
28 WESTHAMPTON WAY
UNIVERSITY OF RICHMOND, VA 23173

DEAR DR. HEILMAN:

THANK YOU FOR WRITING TO ME REF THE PEARL HARBOR ARTICLE.  IF
I MAY WAX PERSONAL, WE MAY NEVER MEET SO I WANT YOU TO KNOW,
AS I READ YOUR SPEECH AT THE COMMEMORATION CEREMONY, A TEAR
SLOWLY MADE WAY DOWN MY CHEEK.  WORDS, WORDS FROM THE HEART
MEAN SO MUCH TO SO MANY PEOPLE AND YOUR WORDS ARE SO MEANINGFUL
AND HELPFUL.  DO YOU KNOW HOW MANY THOUSANDS AND THOUSANDS OF
MEN AND WOMEN HAVE LISTENED TO AND READ YOUR WORDS AND FELT
"BETTER" AFTERWARDS?  A WONDERFUL GIFT.

THE SOLE PURPOSE OF MY LETTER IS TO ONCE AGAIN, SAY "THANKS"
TO YOU BUT PLEASE ALLOW ME TO SAY I SERVED IN THE US ARMY AND
MY YOUNGEST SON SERVED WITH THE 82ND AIRBORNE, SERVED TWICE
IN IRAQ WITH THE NATIONAL GUARD AND IS NOW BACK FULLTIME AS
AN E-8.  HE WAS DISCHARGED FOR A VERY SHORT PERIOD OF TIME AND
WE WERE HAVING LUNCH AT A LOCAL RESTAURANT AND ALL AT ONCE,
HE PUSHED HIS PLATE FORWARD, SAT SILENTLY FOR A MOMENT, LOOKED
AT ME AND SAID, "DAD, I DON'T WANT YOU TO BE UPSET WITH ME BUT
I LOVE MY COUNTRY AND I LOVE BEING A SOLDIER AND I'M GOING BACK."
I KNOW HE WAS THINKING ABOUT HOW WE WORRIED WHILE HE WAS AWAY
IN IRAQ BUT I PUSHED BACK MY CHAIR, STOOD UP AND, RIGHT IN THE
MIDDLE OF A CROWDED RESTAURANT, HUGGED THE HECK OUT OF 'IM AND
KISSED HIM ON HIS FOREHEAD.

AS PREVIOUSLY MENTIONED, WE MAY NEVER MEET BUT IF EVER I'M IN
THE AREA, I WOULD LIKE TO SAY HELLO AND SHAKE YOUR HAND

I WILL SEE FRIEND BROCK SMITH THIS WEEK AND IF YOU DON'T MIND,
I'D LIKE TO SHARE WITH HIM, YOUR LETTER AND SPEECH, I KNOW HE
WILL GREATLY APPRECIATE AND ENJOY IT.  A SIDE NOTE--BROCK LOST
ALL THE TOES ON HIS RIGHT FOOT TO THE WINTER AT THE BULGE.

SINCERELY,

HAROLD M. CHILTON

Battleship Missouri Memorial
Battleship Row ~ Pearl Harbor, Hawaii

Certificate of Flag Presentation
To

## Dr. E. Bruce Heilman

## On occasion of the 66th Anniversary of the End of WWII

*In tribute to American veterans of all branches of service, the national ensign is
flown daily, 8 a.m. to sunset, on board the USS Missouri (BB 63).*

USS Missouri played a crucial and unforgettable role in defense of America in three wars spanning
more than four decades. The battleship's support of America's military forces was just as vital in the
Gulf War of 1991, as it was in the Pacific Theatre 46 years earlier. The USS Missouri's place in
America's history was forever immortalized as the site of the September 2, 1945 signing of the
Instrument of Surrender ending World War II.

The United States flag accompanying this certificate was raised and lowered
from the Fantail on 02 September 2011 at 0725.

Signed and authenticated this date 02 September 2011.

Michael A. Carr
President and
Chief Operating Officer

Robert K. V. Kihune
Vice Admiral, USN (Retired)
Chairman of the Board

USS Missouri Memorial Association, Inc.

Battleship Missouri Memorial
Battleship Row ~ Pearl Harbor, Hawaii

Certificate of Flag Presentation to

## Dr. Bruce Heilman

Of Virginia
In honor and commemoration of
your heroic and dedicated service in the United States Marine Corps
During World War II.

The United States flag accompanying this certificate is presented on
behalf of the grateful citizens of the states of Hawaii, Virginia,
and the United States of America, in honor and remembrance of
your service in the United States Marine Corps
during World War II.

The United States flag that accompanies this certificate
was flown aboard USS Missouri (BB-63) on

2 December 2011

Signed and authenticated this date, 2 December 2011.

Michael A. Carr
President and
Chief Operating Officer

Robert K. U. Kihune
Vice Admiral, USN (Retired)
Chairman of the Board

USS Missouri Memorial Association, Inc.

9/3/2011

# Ending of WWII celebrated

## Honor veterans while they're alive, Heilman urges

**The Associated Press**

PEARL HARBOR, Hawaii — A Marine who fought in the Battle of Okinawa urged Americans on Friday to honor those who served in World War II now, while veterans from that conflict are still alive.

E. Bruce Heilman, speaking at a ceremony marking the 66th year since the end of the war, noted fewer than 2 million of the 16 million men and women who served in the war are alive. They are dying at a rate of 30,000 a month, he said.

Some 20 World War II veterans boarded the decommissioned battleship Missouri, the ship where Japan signed surrender documents formally ending the war, to participate in this year's ceremony in Pearl Harbor.

Heilman, who is a spokesman for the Greatest Generations Foundation and chancellor of the University of Richmond, predicted not many would be able to come back in a decade's time.

"Most of those remaining, including those in the front row, will have passed on, so that few, if any, will be present for the ceremony of the 76th anniversary of the end of the Pacific War. Those of us still here will be of age 95 to 101," Heilman said. "Therefore the importance of remembering now the sacrifices and acts of heroism representative of their service cannot be overstated."

Some 300 people — including active duty sailors, Marines, airmen and soldiers — joined the ceremony aboard the Missouri's teak deck.

SATURDAY 9/3/11 >> HONOLULU STAR-ADVERTISER >>

PHOTOS BY CRAIG T. KOJIMA / CKOJIMA@STARADVERTISER.COM

A crowd jammed the foredeck of the USS Missouri on Friday at Pearl Harbor for a ceremony marking the 66th anniversary of the end of World War II.

# WWII veterans board ship for anniversary of war's end

## Battleship Missouri Memorial, Pearl Harbor
### Friday, September 2, 2011

President Carr, Madam Becker, Admiral Girrier, Captain James, fellow veterans, and distinguished guests engaged in this important commemorative ceremony … our presence here calls to mind an even more significant occasion in the life of this battleship. What transpired on its deck sixty-six years ago represents to hundreds of thousands who served in World War II an extension of their lives even to this day.

Nothing said or done on this deck since will rise to the momentous impact of the signing of the final surrender of the Japanese Empire to the United States under the auspices of General Douglas MacArthur.

I was among those in 1995 commemorating the fiftieth anniversary of the ending of the War in the Pacific at the Punchbowl Crater ("Hill of Sacrifice"). Among others attending were senior officers of the military who led the various services to the successful conclusion of the conflict. Bob Hope, World War II entertainer, Medal of Honor winners, and those from the political arena engaged in resolving the outcome of the war were highlighted by President Clinton. In the sixteen years since, almost all of those senior leaders during the war, the Medal of Honor recipients, and the known entertainer have passed on.

Today, we primarily have remaining enlisted and junior-level officers to tell the stories of how we won World War II. There are no generals or admirals to represent the sixteen million who served and the fewer than two million who survive. They are dying at the rate of thirty thousand a month. Ten years from now, most of those remaining will have passed on so. Few, if any, will be present for this ceremony on the seventy-sixth anniversary of the end of the Pacific War.

Therefore, the importance of remembering now the sacrifices and acts of heroism representative of their service cannot be overstated. As their spokesperson, I do not presume to characterize the best or the least of the significance of what they did. I share my reflections and experiences as one of the many who willingly committed to endure whatever hardships or injuries or risks were required. In that spirit, my comments are intended to be more generic than personal.

Last year, eleven marines with as many college students—under the auspices of the Greatest Generations Foundation and the College of the Ozarks—returned to battlefields they never expected to see again. Upon landing on Iwo Jima, one in the group bowed silently to the ground. When he rose, there were tears streaming from his eyes. "I just don't know how we did it," he said.

"I don't either," another replied.

As they climbed Mount Suribachi, they remembered the sacrifice of some seven thousand marines dead along with twenty thousand wounded. "The experience is past," said one, "but the memories are forever embedded in my mind. I'll never forget this mountain."

# E. Bruce Heilman.

Sargent.

**Resides:** Richmond, Virginia | **Age:** 90
**United States Navy:** The Fifth Fleet
**Battles:** Okinawa

E. Bruce Heilman was born in Smithfield, Kentucky, in 1926. He completed Radio Gunnery School at the Naval Air Training Center in Memphis, Tennessee. From there, Bruce was sent to San Diego, California, and subsequently traveled to Okinawa, having missed the Battle of Iwo Jima where many of his platoon buddies fought and some were killed.

He arrived in Okinawa amid suicide bombing raids on the fleet. Bruce's outfit captured Chimu Field from the Japanese, an airstrip which helped launch the bombing campaign of Japan. Heilman used his knowledge in radio gunnery to help defend the air base's perimeter from Japanese bombers and fighters.

Later, Bruce helped evacuate the wounded, and deliver supplies to service the Occupation troops. Part of the US occupation force in Japan, Bruce flew as radio operator on the staff of the Commander of the Fifth Fleet, taking intelligence personnel to Hiroshima, Nagasaki, and all over the Pacific. He survived an airplane crash on Iwo Jima and was one of the first American GI's in Nagasaki after the A-bomb.

# Jack Holder.

### Naval Flight Engineer.

**Resides:** Phoenix, Arizona **| Age:** 97
**United States Navy:** Pacific and European Theater of Operations
**Battles:** Pearl Harbor, Midway Islands, Guadalcanal, Atlantic Ocean and English Channel

Born December 13, 1921 in Gunter, Texas, Jack Holder grew up during the Depression in a shack with no electricity or running water.

In 1941, Jack was a Naval Flight Engineer stationed on the Island of Oahu, Hawaii and remembers December 6 as a lazy day of recreation like any other. The next morning, Jack assembled for muster and heard a loud crash. It was the first bomb dropped on Ford Island, which initiated the Japanese attacks on Pearl Harbor. After Pearl Harbor, Holder went on to fly missions all over the Pacific theater, including 34 missions over the Solomon Islands and Guadalcanal, where he, from 6,000 feet, witnessed Japanese Commanding General Yamamoto's plane being shot down. Holder also fought in a crucial victory at the Battle of Midway."

The landscape of Iwo Jima could not have been forgotten. The black sand was still there to remind them of the reality of their experience and of their good fortune in having lived through it all.

I became a survivor of Iwo Jima following combat on Okinawa. As an air crewman flying throughout the Pacific during the occupation of Japan, I landed there periodically. On one such occasion, our plane was buffeted by heavy crosswinds as we lifted off the runway, causing it to tilt to the left so suddenly and abruptly that the wing hit the ground.

We endured a few seconds of sheer terror, hearing the sounds of crushing metal and whirling propellers digging furrows into the earth. A miracle of miracles occurred as there was no fireball eruption. We exited the aircraft through whatever opening presented itself with our hearts pounding at full pace and with expressions either audible or in silence. Thank the Lord— we survived.

From Iwo Jima, we traveled to Okinawa where Americans died by the thousands to take down the Japanese flag, and Japanese died by the thousands to prevent the raising of the American flag. Now we observed the American and Japanese flags flying together. Such contradictions, no matter how confusing and disconcerting, result from the continuous shifting of the sands of time.

We drove near the city of Naha to the beaches where we dug in and slept the first night after landing. Today, that beach is overlaid with buildings, roadways, airport facilities, massive traffic, and swarms of people. It is almost overpowering in contrast with the destruction I remembered. What was important in the past, even if earthshaking then and seemingly worth dying for, is of little consequence in the minds of those who now live there.

In the eighty-two days of battle on Okinawa an average of 2,500 people died every day. The Okinawans were begged to come out of their caves, but fearful their women would be raped and tortured, they refused and were thus treated as combatants, destroyed by flamethrowers, dynamite, and bulldozers.

Like tens of thousands of soldiers, sailors, airmen, and marines, my journey abroad began on a troop ship. I had joined the marines as a seventeen-year-old, and a few months later, at age eighteen, I was joining a host of other marines bound for points unknown in the bowels of the ship.

Following the initial seasickness and coming to grips with the reality of it all, we progressed beyond Hawaii and into the deep Pacific where potentialities of serious consequences lay ahead. When a Japanese submarine was observed tracking our convoy, action was initiated to reduce to a minimum the risk of losing a ship and hundreds of marines.

The greatest concern was of being torpedoed on a dark night while deep in the hold of the ship. Getting out would be the first priority. Surviving in oily and burning water was the next challenge. A high school classmate of mine was on the USS *Indianapolis* when she went down with casualties of 1,200 out of 1,500. He and most others failed to survive the sharks.

The news being picked up by the convoy and passed along in daily bulletins was neither positive for the marines nor for the sailors aboard ship. More and more Japanese suicide squadrons were rendering disastrous damage to our ships off the island of Okinawa. If that was our destination, then we might not survive the suicide planes long enough to bolster the forces already there.

But land we did, and along with joining the battle, we became a part of the forward force for the coming invasion of the Japanese homeland. That battle, projected to take place on November 15, 1945, was to be a do-or-die situation—with the latter appearing to be the most probable result. We were in agreement that our chances of survival were small. The act of using the bombs was assurance that the lives we have lived in the meantime were gifts of president Truman.

I walked in the radioactive dirt, dust, ashes, and destruction of Nagasaki and Hiroshima shortly after the bombs were dropped and viewed skeletons of the few structures remaining.

Sixty-five and a half years later, I returned to see that city as a thriving metropolis.

When asked to share my thoughts concerning the bombing of the city I acknowledged that it was a wonderful revelation to see the rebirth and renewal, which had risen from the ashes, and that out of the dictatorial government had come freedom and democracy.

We whose lives were spared could never apologize for the bomb having been dropped. Doing so would be expressing regrets for having married our wives, fathered our children, and grandfathered our grandchildren. Without the bomb, we would have died in the battle for the Japanese mainland by suicide planes diving into our troop ships, by machine guns as we stormed the beaches, or by poison spears that the women and children would have forced into us.

Today, some protest the act of our having used the atomic bombs. Yet, most have little knowledge of the realities of that time. Without those bombs, my mother would have lost one or two—or perhaps all three—of her sons who served in the armed forces.

The "kill-or-be-killed" tenacity of the Japanese likely could not have been overcome without the climatic impact of the atomic bombs on both Hiroshima and Nagasaki.

We veterans here today have been fortunate to live long lives even though, along with millions of other young men of that era, all accepted death as a real possibility. The prevailing potential consequences gave all of us a unique perspective for the rest of our lives.

Whether returning to the battlefields of our youth or reflecting upon our service wherever it might have been, this celebration is a part of bringing closure from whatever shadows remain in the crevices of our minds.

Because of the ultimate pride in having served, we never seek total closure. Thus, to end this commentary of renewal and remembrance, I cite some select lines from Tennyson's *Ulysses*, representative of the aging of all the airmen, soldiers, sailors, and marines who served in World War II:

… Old age hath yet his honour and his toil;

… Some work of noble note, may yet be done,

… Come, my friends,

'Tis not too late to seek a newer world.

Push off, and sitting well in order smite

The sounding furrows; for my purpose holds To sail beyond the sunset, and the baths Of all the western stars, until I die.

It may be that the gulfs will wash us down; It may be we shall touch the Happy Isles, And see the great Achilles, whom we knew.

Tho' much is taken, much abides; and though

We are not now that strength which in old days

Moved earth and heaven; that which we are, we are;

One equal temper of heroic hearts, Made weak by time and fate, but strong in will To strive, to seek, to find, and not to yield.

And while sacrifice and heroism may appropriately call to mind periods of suffering and distress, for most veterans, the pride of having served and the return on their investment in preserving freedom for themselves and their fellow man overrides the darkness of the experience and embraces the words of Edwin Markham: "There is a destiny that makes us brothers. None goes his way alone. All that we send into the lives of others comes back into our own."

Finally, to the USS *Missouri* Memorial Association, we express our gratitude for being a part of the commemoration ceremony.

\*\*\*

# V

# NATIONAL SYMPOSIUM ON HOMELAND SECURITY AND NATIONAL SECURITY

*The quality of our American fighting men is not all a matter of training or equipment or organization. It is essentially a matter of spirit. That spirit is expressive in their faith in America.*
—*President Franklin D. Roosevelt*

Mr. Chairman and distinguished members of organizations involved in the National Homeland Defense Symposium, hell is a relative term, and today, I use it to contrast the experiences many of our World War II veterans and those of every war have suffered.

It is indeed an honor and a privilege for me, as national spokesman for the Greatest Generations Foundation, to address you on the subject, "A Presentation of Heroes," as we acknowledge what for some of them hell was really like.

A veteran—whether active duty, retired, served one hitch, guard or reserve, deployed multiple times, or never—is someone who, at one point in his life, wrote a blank check made payable to the "government of the United States of America for an amount up to and including his life."

This afternoon, I represent a special segment of the veterans' population identified by Tom Brokaw as "the Greatest Generation." As national spokesman for the Greatest Generations Foundation, I speak not for myself but as the voice of the original sixteen million who served in World War II, especially for the fewer than two million remaining and dying at the rate of thirty thousand a month.

On September 2 of this year, the sixty-sixth anniversary of the end of World War II with the Japanese, I stood on the deck of the Battleship *Missouri* in the same place that MacArthur stood when he accepted the final surrender of the Japanese empire. It was a sobering occasion, yet it represented a highlight in the life of the twenty World War II veterans who sat on the front row with a thousand or more mostly current servicemen and women from privates and seamen to admirals and generals. We were commemorating the great act that took place sixty-six years earlier after the dropping of two atomic bombs convinced the Japanese that their only choice was to surrender or be obliterated. Likely nothing short of those two bombs would have convinced them to give up the fight.

Some of what I will share with you today I shared with those on the USS *Missouri*. That occasion—and others like it—are representative of how we acknowledge the significance of the service to their country of those we classify as "heroes."

It is not my purpose to extol the unusual or outstanding actions or heroic engagements of anyone behind me or before me today, but to acknowledge these and especially those whose lives were lost in combat during the conflicts of World War II.

They are the true heroes, but others, some still living, can be applauded for the wonderful examples they set in the days of their youth when they fought on the shores of Europe and on the islands of the Pacific.

For example, one of my friends and a fellow marine, Jim Blane, landed as a marine on four hostile islands, including Iwo Jima, and lived to tell about it after being severely wounded. Another, Al Jennings, also fought on Iwo as a marine. Sergeant Major Rocky Marquez, from World War II through the next thirty years, was engaged in many major conflicts.

In the meantime, having lived their lives building a great country within the framework of the freedoms they helped preserve, they have had little time to reflect on the combat scenes of the past and to which they never expected to return. Finally, because of the Greatest Generations Foundations making it possible, they are able to rekindle their memories in the company of college students who learn that we were younger in combat than they are as juniors and seniors in college.

I was among those commemorating the fiftieth anniversary of the ending of the War in the Pacific at the Punchbowl Crater in Honolulu. Among others attending were senior officers of the military who led the various services to the successful conclusion of the conflict. Bob Hope, World War II entertainer, Medal of Honor winners, and those from the political arena engaged in resolving the outcome of the war were highlighted by President Clinton. In the sixteen years since, all of those senior wartime leaders, the Medal of Honor recipients, and the known entertainer have passed on.

Today, we primarily have remaining enlisted and junior-level officers to tell the stories of how we won World War II. There are no generals or admirals to represent the sixteen million who served and the fewer than two million who survive. They are dying at the rate of thirty thousand a month. Ten years from now, most of those remaining will have passed on so. Few, if any, will be present for this ceremony on the seventy-sixth anniversary of the end of the Pacific War.

Therefore, the importance of remembering now the sacrifices and acts of heroism representative of their service cannot be overstated. As their spokesperson, I do not presume to characterize the best or the least of the significance of what they did. I share my reflections and experiences as one of the many who willingly committed to endure whatever hardships or injuries or risks were required. In that spirit, my comments are intended to be more generic than personal.

Last year, eleven marines with as many college students—under the auspices of the Greatest Generations Foundation and the College of the Ozarks—returned to battlefields they never expected to see again. Upon landing on Iwo Jima, one in the group bowed silently to the ground. When he rose, there were tears streaming from his eyes. "I just don't know how we did it," he said.

"I don't either," another replied.

As they climbed Mount Suribachi, they remembered the sacrifice of some seven thousand marines dead along with twenty thousand wounded. "The experience is past," said one, "but the memories are forever embedded in my mind. I'll never forget this mountain."

The landscape of Iwo Jima could not have been forgotten. The black sand was still there to remind them of the reality of their experience and of their good fortune in having lived through it all.

I became a survivor of Iwo Jima following combat on Okinawa. As an air crewman flying throughout the Pacific during the occupation of Japan, I landed there periodically. On one such occasion, our plane was buffeted by heavy crosswinds as we lifted off the runway, causing it to tilt to the left so suddenly and abruptly that the wing hit the ground.

We endured a few seconds of sheer terror, hearing the sounds of crushing metal and whirling propellers digging furrows into the earth. A miracle of miracles occurred as there was no fireball eruption. We exited the aircraft through whatever opening presented itself with our hearts pounding at full pace and with expressions either audible or in silence. Thank the Lord— we survived.

From Iwo Jima, we traveled to Okinawa where Americans died by the thousands to take down the Japanese flag, and Japanese died by the thousands to prevent the raising of the American flag. Now we observed the American and Japanese flags flying together. Such contradictions, no matter how confusing and disconcerting, result from the continuous shifting of the sands of time.

We drove near the city of Naha to the beaches where we dug in and slept the first night after landing. Today, that beach is overlaid with buildings, roadways, airport facilities, massive traffic, and swarms of people. It is almost overpowering in contrast with the destruction I remembered. What was important in the past, even if earthshaking then and seemingly worth dying for, is of little consequence in the minds of those who now live there.

In the eighty-two days of battle on Okinawa an average of 2,500 people died every day. The Okinawans were begged to come out of their caves, but fearful their women would be raped and tortured, they refused and were thus treated as combatants, destroyed by flamethrowers, dynamite, and bulldozers.

Like tens of thousands of soldiers, sailors, airmen, and marines, my journey abroad began on a troop ship. I had joined the marines as a seventeen-year-old, and a few months later, at age eighteen, I was joining a host of other marines bound for points unknown in the bowels of the ship.

Following the initial seasickness and coming to grips with the reality of it all, we progressed beyond Hawaii and into the deep Pacific where potentialities of serious consequences lay ahead. When a Japanese submarine was observed tracking our convoy, action was initiated to reduce to a minimum the risk of losing a ship and hundreds of marines.

The news being picked up by the convoy and passed along in daily bulletins was neither positive for the marines nor for the sailors aboard ship. More and more Japanese suicide squadrons were rendering disastrous damage to our ships off the island of Okinawa. If that was our destination, then we speculated that we might not survive the suicide planes long enough to bolster the forces already there.

But land we did and along with joining the battle we became a part of the forward force for the coming invasion of the Japanese homeland. That battle, projected to take place on November 15, 1945, was to be a do-or-die situation with the latter appearing to be the most probable result. We were in agreement that our chances of survival were small. The act of using the bombs was assurance that the lives we have lived in the meantime were gifts of president Truman.

I walked in the radioactive dirt, dust, ashes and destruction of Nagasaki and Hiroshima shortly after the bombs were dropped and viewed skeletons of the few structures remaining. Now sixty-five 1/2 years later, I had returned to see that city as a thriving metropolis.

When asked to share my thoughts concerning the bombing of the city I acknowledged that it was a wonderful revelation to see the rebirth and renewal which like the phoenix had risen from the ashes and that out of the dictatorial government had come freedom and democracy.

We whose lives were spared could never apologize for the bomb having been dropped. Doing so would be expressing regrets for having married our wives, fathered our children, and grandfathered our grandchildren. Without the bomb we would have died in the battle for the Japanese mainland, suicide planes diving into our troop ships, by machine guns as we stormed the beaches or by poison spears that the women and children would have forced into us.

Today some protest the act of our having used the atomic bomb. Yet, most have little knowledge of the realities of that time. Without those bombs my mother would have lost one or two or perhaps all three of her sons who served in the armed forces.

The "kill-or-be-killed" tenacity of the Japanese could not have been overcome without the climatic impact of the atomic bombs on both Hiroshima and Nagasaki.

We veterans here today have been fortunate to live long lives even though, along with millions of other young men of that era, all accepted death as a real possibility. The prevailing potential consequences gave all of us a unique perspective for the rest of our lives.

Whether returning to the battlefields of our youth or reflecting upon our service wherever it might have been, all became a part of bringing closure to the shadows that remain in the crevices of our minds.

Because of the ultimate pride in having served, we never seek total closure.

And while sacrifice and heroism may appropriately call to minds periods of suffering and distress, for most veterans the pride of having served and the return on their investment in preserving freedom for themselves and their fellow man overrides the darkness of the experience and embraces the words of Edwin Markham: "There is a destiny that makes us brothers. None goes his way alone. All that we send into the lives of others comes back into our own."

And now as we reflect on "Connecting Generations," the journeys the Air Force Academy cadets with World War II vets to Normandy, I believe that you will sense the significance of such opportunities as these, both for the veterans and the younger generation, as together they experience an unusual coalescence of spirit as they learn from each other. This is just one of many such generational interactions made possible by the Greatest Generations Foundation.

And finally, I could not speak of heroes without a brief commentary on our "Common Grounds" program. Recently, a group of veterans composed of several from World War II plus six wounded but healed Iraqi veterans visited fifteen recently wounded Afghanistan vets in the army and navy hospitals in Washington.

This was to be a sharing of common experiences, which in the end might give encouragement to these recently wounded vets by their observing that, over time, such wounds would heal—and life would return to at least a semblance of normality.

The unanticipated result was that these young and severely wounded men were so positive and confident of recovery that the benefits of these visits were to us the visitors as great as to those being visited. We could not have anticipated the courage and the determination and the attitude exhibited on the part of each of those we met. Without exception, they expressed the hope that no one should feel sorry for them or mourn their condition. They were proud to have served even with the serious results, and they expected to overcome the problems created by the loss of legs or arms or other serious wounds.

Some only wished they could return to serve again. Posted on the door of one was the following:

> Attention: To All Who Enter Here
> If you are coming into this room with sorrow or to feel sorry for my wounds, go elsewhere. The wounds I received, I got in a job I love, doing it for people I love, supporting the freedom of a country I deeply love. I am incredibly touched and will make a full recovery. What is full? That

is the absolute utmost physically my body has the ability to recover. Then I will push that about 20 percent further through sheer mental tenacity. This room you are about to enter is a room of fun, optimism, and intense rapid regrowth. If you are not prepared for that, go elsewhere!

---

Whoever doubted that we still make them like we used to would have all doubt removed by one such experience as this. Yes, it's true. There were heroes in the past who set the example, and that example is being exemplified by young warriors in Afghanistan every day.

\*\*\*

# VI

## GOLD STAR FAMILIES AND WHAT IT IS REALLY LIKE TO DIE FOR YOUR COUNTRY

Because I have spent so much time traveling so many thousands of miles speaking to and associating with Gold Star families, it behooves me to convey here some of what veterans never shared with their families.

Years ago, the Greatest Generations Foundation made possible the return of many veterans to the places they served in combat seventy years before as young men of eighteen, nineteen, and twenty years of age. Great numbers were wounded, and hundreds died in battles throughout the Pacific.

Others, like myself, survived even the anticipated battle of mainland Japan although ready, willing, and able to continue the fight into Japan. The atomic bomb saved all that, saving the lives of hundreds or thousands who would have met our deaths had the bomb not been used.

So, as a result, I and others like me are still living in our nineties. Many are incapacitated as a result of having been wounded or affected by the progression of age, but they are still living with hope, pride, and as examples to the whole society that they fulfilled—their commitments to freedom during World War II.

I spoke recently by phone to a ninety-five-year-old World War II marine friend from Salt Lake City, Utah. I told him I wanted to share some of the vivid commentary he shared with me following the Battle of Iwo Jima when he and I went back sixty years later to commemorate the last battle between the Americans and Japanese.

> I will be proud because I think the world needs to know, particularly young people, what war is all about and the price of preserving freedom and about commitment to our country and about the willingness to die for it.

Irrespective of where veterans fought, when they fought, how they fought, and the intensity of their fighting, their descriptions hardly rose to the level expressed by Kenneth. If it did, there was no one who could put it in the words he did to represent what few individuals have heard from their fathers, their brothers, and their uncles when they say, "My father never told me about it." Perhaps this will show you why.

For many, the truth would be a burden too heavy for family members to bear. They kept it to themselves, assuming that was the proper thing to do. But my friend, in this commentary to me, and then through me to friends and families, has been received with appreciation for understanding better what their son may have suffered so they have an even greater respect for what they did under the circumstances. Kenneth shares this with the following words:

"I got my first taste of blood and dying," Kenneth said, "while still on the troop ship waiting for my wave of marines to go ashore on D-Day plus one. The wounded were being brought on board our troop ship because we had a doctor and a small sick bay. The chaplain and I stood by to help bring these boys up the side of the ship and hoist the stretchers on deck.

It was a hellish task because they couldn't help being bounced around. The morphine had worn off, and they were screaming in unbelievable pain. Many died before the doctor could get to them. Knowing that they couldn't live long, some wanted to leave messages for loved ones. I copied what they had to say and later, the chaplain, and I carried out their wishes by getting these messages to their families.

As we were landing on the beach, shells from navy ships were flying overhead. It seemed that the terrible bombardment from over five hundred ships would certainly have wiped out the enemy, but it didn't. They were all underground. There were plenty of the twenty-two thousand crack Japanese troops waiting for the boats bringing marines ashore.

As we were being pulled toward the black sand, the boat next to us took a direct hit. Men were floundering and being sucked under by their heavy packs. We marines yelled at our cocksman to turn back and let us help save whom we could. He didn't pay attention, saying only that his orders were to get us ashore without delay. I felt bad about leaving those men to die but also hoped the mortar shell wouldn't get us.

When I stepped ashore, I thought that the marines had lost the battle and that everyone had been killed because the Japanese had zeroed in on every inch of the beach and systematically covered it with machine gun and mortar fire. Those who had survived from the day before had tried to dig foxholes but found little escape from the murderous fire.

Our ship had been loaded with medical bags that were badly needed by our corpsmen. Since I was carrying one, a medical corpsman yelled for me to give them assistance with a wounded man who had taken a mortar shell in the chest. I crawled in the foxhole of the corpsman, took out the morphine, and helped as best I could.

I could actually see the mortar shells coming in and soon learned to distinguish their shells from ours being fired over our heads from batteries barely on shore. As a shell would land, the corpsman would move to the crater as quickly as possible trying to separate the dead from the living and then help the wounded.

They needed stretcher bearers to take those badly injured either to the beach to be evacuated or to the battalion aid station for emergency treatment. I spent my first day trying to dodge the mortar shells as I helped give plasma and carry stretchers. I was never quite able to forget the faces of those men they carried on the stretchers. They had looked to be about sixteen. While on this detail, I learned that a lot of blood can leak out of a body that had been half cut in two by machine gun fire.

The dead were everywhere and were left where they had fallen. The corpsman had frantically tried to get the badly wounded to the shoreline where they could be evacuated to designated ships

There are a number of things associated with battle that writers, correspondents, and moviemakers simply find impossible to convey or communicate to those who haven't experienced war firsthand. … The first is sound or noise. In this area, I am not referring to the usual sounds of gunfire, bombs, explosions, etc., which can be easily described or duplicated. These sounds are horrible and frightening enough, but the sounds that have hunted me from the beginning—and I still haven't wiped away from my memory—were the screams and moans, the outlandish cries of the wounded and dying.

Because our battlefield was so small (eight square miles) there was no such thing as a rear area, and so we were always on the front lines. Casualties were so high (one out of three) and corpsmen so short that the wounded could only cry out their agony. The stoic Japanese wounded were also not able to suppress their screams of pain—no matter how hard they tried. To those of us who were listeners, these shouts, curses, screams, and groans were constant day and night, and were indistinguishable as to enemy, comrades, or outfits.

Another indescribable, everywhere present, aspect of combat was the smell. Again, I do not refer to the smells usually associated with battle such as gunpowder, bombs, shellfire, and rockets that might come to mind. These smells were certainly abundant in Iwo Jima and were evidence of a ferocious battle. A fog of smoke hung over the entire island, which made breathing difficult and irritated the eyes. However, these smells were tolerable. The smells I refer to as indescribable were those of rotting, decaying, and sometimes burning human flesh. These smells were intolerable but inescapable and wholly nauseous. There simply is nothing so offensive to the senses as that of dead bodies ripening in the sun … I had ample opportunity to reawaken that remembrance when I was sent to Nagasaki, Japan, a few days after the bomb.

The graves registration people did a heroic job on Iwo trying to take care of the dead as soon as possible, but it was too overwhelming. The dead Japanese were hastily thrown into caves and crevices and bulldozed over. The Americans, as soon as it was safe to do so, were carefully carried to division cemeteries and buried in separate graves in long trenches that had been bulldozed out. Prayers were said, and markers were placed. At the end of the battle, appropriate dedications of the cemeteries took place. Because of the violence of the battle, many bodies were simply beyond recovery and so pieces and bits continued to smell up the island for a long time after it was declared secure.

The last thing I shall mention, which has not been properly portrayed in writing or on film, has to do with the process of dying from battle wounds … Dying on the battlefield is most often a long and drawn out affair. The marines on Iwo were well conditioned and in perfect health and had much to live for. I was surprised to learn how much it took to kill one of them. I have seen them with the whole lower part of their bodies blown away, still able to talk coherently for a time. The legs of a man could be gone, and he would still ask for a cigarette. I could not see how many of those men who were shot up so badly could live, but they did. God made the human body to take a lot of punishment. Too bad Iwo Jima had to subject so many strong young men to an impossible level of recovery.

At night, the enemy crept across the airfield and rolled grenades at us. The mortar fire never ceased.

Kenneth Brown trained, as I did, with the expectation of hand-to-hand combat with bayonets. We were told that, unless we learned to hate the enemy, we could not thrust the blade through his body.

We were aware that we were hated by the enemy. We went off to war knowing somebody wouldn't come back. One of my high school classmates went down on the *Indianapolis*, and another was killed on Iwo Jima. Most of my buddies of the Marine Corps today are deceased, and many were killed in battle.

Kenneth wrestles, as I have over the years, with the thoughts years later of why the boat next to mine was sunk and ours was left floating. Why did the mortar shells on the black beach land on all four sides of my foxhole instead of hitting mine dead center? Why did I later step over the mine that took out the fellow walking behind me? Why was I spared from the machine gun and rifle fire that wiped out most of the replacement company I was assigned to? And during those last days, when I was on jeep patrol bringing back the dead to the cemetery, why didn't the enemy howitzer zero in on me instead of the vehicles both in front and behind? The answer to these and similar questions were not to be found in the sands and volcanic ridges of Iwo Jima fifty-six years later.

*Nta History Society*

# The Oldham County Historical Society

Meet & Greet with Bruce Heilman          Funding sought for statue to honor WWII veteran          Monday,
May 1, 2017, Noon

Oldham County History Center

At almost age 91, Bruce Heilman never backs down from a good challenge. He also looks for special ways to celebrate his birthday, especially if it involves his Harley and bringing awareness to the contributions of WWII veterans to our nation. As national spokesperson for the Greatest Generation Foundation, Heilman rides his motorcycle across the country in honor of these special veterans.

When he turned 85, Heilman travelled to Sturgis, South Dakota with the president, chairman and senior officers of the Harley-Davidson Co. To mark his 86th birthday, he spent approximately 25 days traveling 9,200 miles among 34 states. On turning 88 he traveled to Alaska and on his 90th birthday, he rode from Richmond, VA to the west coast and back, celebrating Gold Star Families. So what's left for a 91st birthday celebration? Why, another road trip on the Harley, of course.

This time around, Heilman will make a stop in La Grange, Ky at the Oldham County History Center for a Meet & Greet on Monday, May 1 at Noon. A light lunch will follow a brief talk by Heilman. This program is free and open to the public. As with previous rides, Heilman will be saluting the 16,000,000 WWII veterans, living and dead, who fostered the designation, "The Greatest Generation."

In addition, "We are honoring the Greatest Generation at the Oldham County History Center by raising funds to create a statue of Oldham County native and WWII veteran, E. Bruce Heilman," said Dr. Nancy Stearns Theiss, Executive Director of the History Center. As a Thank You to Heilman, his Harley-Davidson and the public awareness he draws to the sacrifices made by those who fought in WWII, plans are in the works for a statue to be erected on the History Center campus so that Oldham County will never forget these brave men and women. "This statue will invite visitors to "hop on and ride with Bruce" as a tribute to the Greatest Generation." She sees it as "a fun and creative way to honor the 16,000,000 veterans who gave so much to our country."

This statue project is part of the $2 million renovation of the Oldham County History Center campus. Since 2015, $1.5 million has been raised to completely renovate the History Center's museum. As fundraising continues, additional plans call for accessibility updates for all four historic buildings and construction of a barn that will be used for demonstrations and hands-on programing, and include a colonial fireplace. Earl Bruce Heilman is originally from Smithfield, Ky. He joined the United States Marine Corp in 1944 and was stationed in the South Pacific and Japan. Since then he has traveled extensively, covering more than 145 countries, escorting travel groups annually for over forty years.

Heilman is a founding member of the National Museum of the Marine Corps at Quantico, a member and former Chairman of the Board of the Marine Military Academy in Texas, Member and Chairman of the Board of the Marine Corps University at Quantico, member of the Board of Directors of the Virginia War

Memorial Educational Foundation, board member of the Oldham County Historical Society and served for many years on the Board of the Marine Corps Heritage Foundation, and is an emeritus board member of The Families of the Wounded Fund.

Heilman has served as president of several American colleges and universities and currently holds the position of Chancellor at the University of Richmond. During his long career, Heilman has held teaching and administrative positions at Belmont University, Kentucky Wesleyan College, Georgetown College, Peabody College and Kentucky Southern College (now a part of the University of Louisville). He served as president of Meredith College from 1966 to 1971. From 1971 to 1986, he assumed the presidency of the University of Richmond.

On May 2, 2017, Bruce visited students at Oldham County High School and talked about his life experiences.

# Oldham represented at Ky. Veterans of the Year

## WWII Veteran Bruce Heilman was the featured speaker

JANE ASHLEY PACE/THE OLDHAM ERA

Oldham County was well represented at the 2017 Kentucky Veterans of the Year Banquet on Nov. 6. Dr. E. Bruce Heilman, a WWII Veteran was the featured speaker of the night. This years event honored WWII Veterans.

Pictured left to right, Dr. E. Bruce Heilman, U. S. Marines, WWII; Fred Balke, Navy Seabees, WWII; County Judge David Voegele and his daughter, Dr. Laura Voegele.

Ken and I went back together to Iwo Jima sixty years later to commemorate the dead Japanese and the dead marines as friends after we had fought with hatred for each other to get it out of our systems, but we never did get it out of our minds. Ken said, "Although I had a feeling of appreciation for having been an Iwo Jima survivor, I could not help but think of all the young men who had died there who never had a chance to get married, have children, or live a full life. I left in tears."

Many of my friends died more than seventy years ago on one of those islands. Here I am with thirty-seven descendants including my sons-in-law and daughters-in-law. I've had a full life, I've enjoyed an education, and I've had a fruitful experience. Why me? Why am I still living?

Many times, I have asked that question. I could have been killed on an island along with my fellow marines. Today, I live because the atom bomb saved my life, having expected to die invading Japan.

As spokesperson of the Greatest Generations Foundation, I speak often to and for veterans. I try to speak for all the veterans who gave their lives as well those who survived. And as one who also survived Iwo Jima from a crash on a transport plane on which I was a passenger, I am pleased to be an Iwo Jima survivor rather than one of the hundreds killed fighting that battle.

In five years, most World War II veterans will be gone or out of functioning condition to communicate as I am with you. In the meantime, like the old warrior in Tennyson's *Ulysses,* we aren't yet ready to give up or give in. Rather, with hope for the future, we reflect back with pride and look forward—even in our nineties—to some years with health and family and friends and honoring the Gold Star families as we reflect on what it is like for those who died for the country. We know only our freedom is worth such a sacrifice and that we who are still living of the World War II generation, along with our fellow veterans, want to keep the message in the hearts and minds of our fellow citizens who are younger and who cannot comprehend the sacrifices given.

The World War II veterans aren't talking. Most of them are gone. With the help of Ken, I am sharing what they never shared but their offspring always wished they had. Now that you know, you feel both better and perhaps less pacified than you might have been had you never heard his words, which are so representative of what families wish they had heard from the veterans in their families.

The next time you see or hear or read about a Gold Star family, remember that this is what it is like to die for your country—and know that only our freedom is worth such a sacrifice. Those of us who believe that life without freedom is, for America, intolerable, remember that the willingness to accept the risks of the ultimate sacrifice is the price of our freedom.

# CHAPTER EIGHT

AGING

# I

# INTRODUCTION

One of Gen. MacArthur's best-remembered averments came on his seventy-fifth birthday—his quotation of the beautiful *Ode to Youth* by Samuel Ullman:

> Youth is not a time of life; it is a state of mind; it is not matter of rosy checks, red lips, and supple knees; it is a matter of the will, a quality of the imagination, a vigor of the emotions; it is the freshness of the deep springs of life.
>
> Youth means the temperamental predominance of courage over timidity of the appetite, for adventure over the love of ease. This often exists in a man of sixty more than a boy of twenty. Nobody grows old merely by a number of years. We grow hold by deserting our ideals.
>
> Years may wrinkle the skin, but to give up enthusiasm wrinkles the soul. Worry, fear, self-distrust bows the heart and turns the spirit back to dust.
>
> Whether sixty or sixteen, there is in every human being's heart the lure of wonder, the unfailing child-like appetite of what's next, and the joy of the game of living.
>
> You are as young as your faith, as old as your doubt; as young as your self-confidence, as old as your fear; as young as your hope, as old as your despair.
>
> In the center of your heart there is a wireless station; so long as it receives messages of beauty, hope, cheer, and courage, so long are you young.
>
> When the aerials are down, and your spirit is covered with snows of cynicism and the ice of pessimism, then, and only then are you grown old.

Age cannot be forestalled, but it can be delayed by remembering that old presumptions need not conform to those who refuse to follow the examples of history. "A certain age applies to all when some are not ready to accept the general rule of aging."

In my case, some students graduating under my presidency have retired or have begun to throttle down their life activities and adjust to a pace in keeping with their age as they perceive it to require long before their health suggests such a life adjustment as necessary.

In my case, as a lifelong educator for sixty-six years and a college and university president for twenty-two years, I do not yield to the old adages that are recorded everywhere, including in everyone's minds. Richard Armour's *Going Around in Academic Circles* suggests old age is for dozing and dreaming presumably by suggesting that when the president or old professor visits the campus:

> And meet old students who will say
> He looks exactly as the day They knew him first, and he will beam And go back home to doze
> and dream.

That is not my impression of myself, and it should not be anyone else's either.

The World War II generation presents evidence of the diverseness of lifestyles of those now in their nineties. Recently, I traveled with five others aged ninety-one and up to ninety-six. All were mentally active—and even with some physical limitation—and they did not let age stand in their way of being engaged.

The six of us were invited by the Greatest Generations Foundation to travel to London for three days with the purpose of interacting with veterans wherever we found them. We returned to New York on the *Queen Mary II* to interact with the three thousand or so passengers from all over the world about our World War II experiences. Four had served at Normandy, and two of us were marines in the Pacific at Iwo Jima and Okinawa.

Each, on assigned days, made presentations in the large theater, which was packed at every session. We wore hats highlighting our service so that we were engaged regularly by passengers. Each veteran was identified by a large poster, which, during the cruise, were fully autographed. Representative of the comments recorded on the poster are the following extracted from my poster and representing countries other than the United States.

- "Thank you for your service! Your stories were wonderful and inspirational. It was an honor to meet you." Owen and Helen, England
- "Thank you for sharing your story." BQ, St. Louis, Missouri
- "The best of times, the worst of times. That we remember, so we may know. Thank you!

- You touched my heart sir, with some of the most inspirational words I've ever heard. Thank you."
Ian Miller (Royal Navy Retired), Falklands, 1982
- "Thank you for going above and beyond." Morty and Iris, Germany

The entire world was at war, and everybody in every country knew the strength of the United States. Therefore, they give credit to the veterans for having maintained and sustained the struggle and overcome the enemies.

It was an enthusiastic crowd. We couldn't speak for being applauded, and all through the day and into the night, we would be stopped for discussions and to be paid compliments. We were proud to be Americans—marines, army, navy coast guard, air force—because we were all represented.

The *Queen Mary II* is not a cruise ship. It's an ocean liner that was built for actual voyages rather than for port hopping. The *QMII* is a classic of the type, sturdy and stately with lines that call to mind handkerchiefs flapping on the top deck or Kate Winslet repeatedly shouting, "Jack!" in *Titanic*. Built in 2003, it's the last of the great liners and the only ship still making that regular transatlantic crossing between England and New York. Along with its looks, the *QMII* has another bragging point: size. It is the largest ocean liner ever built: 10,138 feet long and 236 feet high with fourteen passenger decks, 1,360 cabins, a crew of 1202, and a capacity for 2,691 guests.

There are a variety of dining options depending upon which level of accommodation one has booked. Ours allowed access to the Britannia, but we veterans often went for the less glamorous places, particularly between meals, such as the Kings Court Buffet. On the selfimprovement side of the ship, they had various seminars. One of those was the World War II veterans sharing their experiences in the always-packed auditorium called the Planetarium.

As I plan on living to one hundred, I read whatever I can and do whatever I might do to add to that possibility. From an article entitled "Planning to live to 100," I draw the suggestion that one should volunteer. I interpret that as remaining busy. Don't draw in your own inclination to hide away and stop loving or even stop learning. Einstein said, "When you stop learning, you start dying."

"A ten-year-old child today has a 50 percent chance of living to be at least 104." The author questions what we might do with all that extra time on earth, suggesting that we should share our skills as volunteers. This is the "closest thing to a silver bullet we have discovered for personal and societal well-being." Those who volunteer have "lower mortality rates, less depression, along with a sense of control over one's life, and higher rates of self-esteem and happiness." Volunteering "can renew that sense of purpose and prevent the social isolation that is a recognized health hazard for our later years."

One thing that makes older age a happy time in life is the opportunity to follow one's passions to do whatever we want to do and have always wanted to do. It's what makes us light up with excitement. It's something in which we can immerse ourselves, get out of our routines, and get into activities and engagements that are completely different from what people think we ought to do. After ninety, it's not an age—it's an attitude. What is an unfilled ambition for one is a fulfilling satisfaction to another.

Aging is an adventure in itself, and it is not an excuse to back off from living life to the fullest. I now have more time to be adventuresome than when I was younger, and I could be wasting my time in front of a TV, thinking I am too old to ride a motorcycle. So many people assume that in my ninety-first year, I should be asleep on the couch somewhere and not out giving speeches or riding my Harley or serving some good organization's cause, but I rather like to use my life's topic: "If life is an adventure, why stop at ninety?" On one occasion, I rode to Sturgis, South Dakota, joining the chairman, president, and other Harley executives in Milwaukee for a three-day experience I won't soon forget.

What was I to do for my eighty-sixth birthday to match or exceed these experiences? My first motorcycle trip covered seven thousand miles, and the second covered five thousand. I charted a course that would cover in excess of nine thousand miles on that adventure. For my eighty-seventh birthday, I decided to fill in the blank spaces and covered six states and then the Lower 48, which meant passing through sixteen other states to make that happen. I was saluting the Greatest Generation when I covered the Lower 48 in a circle. When I chose to circle the country on my motorcycle to celebrate my eighty-first birthday, I had some misgivings, but that was a part of the challenge.

They say that with age comes wisdom. Some of my family and friends question that in my case, but I have lots of reasons for this journey—even if I don't have all the answers to the questions asked. This is not a low point in life. It is a high point in my life, filled with time, adventure, excitement, reflections, opportunities to interact with friends old and new, children, and grandchildren. Being busy is the best medicine for old age. The most tiring experience is in having nothing to do because you can't stop and rest.

I look forward to reaching ninety-five or even one hundred with passionate ambition. Being the oldest one living of the four surviving presidents of the University of Richmond is a position I want to claim long into the future. Conformity should not be our guideline. Instead, what makes life an adventure should be the guideline. This might involve taking risks, but life at any age is a risk—just being born is a risk. The greatest risk of all is to die bored or to fail to live life to the fullest.

"Don't be Ashamed of Your Age" is a country song by Kentucky Redd Foley. He is now deceased. In this generation, mature people apologize for being in the upper level of maturity. Many withdraw from activities they are totally capable of participating in. When we stand on the sidelines, we deny ourselves the joys that, in our younger years, were stimulating, fulfilling, and exciting. My long motorcycle rides provide more exercise by accident than many my age get on purpose. My adrenaline flows fast while exploring the landscape, learning about people, places, and things, and testing my agility, resiliency, and tenacity. Although we cannot add years to our lives, we can add life to our years. If we can't do anything about the length, we can do something about its breadth and depth.

\*\*\*

# II

## AGE AS PERCEIVED BY THOSE YOUNGER

*I am not made or unmade by the things*
*Which happen to me, But by the way I react to them.*
—*Saint John of the Cross*

I am entering my 93rd year and have come to the realization that the definition of old age has been the prerogative of those who have not yet experienced that condition. So, while I will seek to identify the general perceptions of age by those younger based upon historic assumption, I will also seek to correct some prevailing misconceptions.

Age doesn't matter when it comes to travel—whether by motorcycle, airplane, bus, ship, or whatever else. What we perceive that we can or can't do is more a matter of the mind than a physical limitation. Of course, health can be a factor, but fortunately, it's not for me.

Those my age and older, as well as some even younger, are generally categorized by impressions that restrict, confine, discount, and disregard them by relegating them, at best, to a second childhood. It is assumed that all of us are retired from almost anything productive or essential. People seldom ask me what I am doing, but how I enjoy retirement, when I've never even hinted about retirement. We are stereotyped as frail or disabled physically, intellectually, and emotionally—and incapable of operating at the same level as those at any younger age.

Those younger fail to recognize that many of us living at what is considered to be an advanced age have not yet recognized the limitations that, by historical standards, they impose upon us. So, how do I communicate to those who are younger the phenomenon that youth, whether for the young or for those who are older, is not a stage or an age in life but a state of mind and that life can be fulfilling at any age?

Samuel Ullman said, "Youth is not a time in life; it is a state of mind; it's not a matter of rosy cheeks, red lips, and supple knees; it is a matter of the will, a quality of the imagination, a vigor of the emotions; it is the freshness of the deep springs of life." With that in mind, why would anyone want to succumb to the mental acceptance of giving up youth for the supposed distress and depression of old age? That's not for me.

At one time or another, each, at any age, exhibits a weakness of mind. Forgetfulness should not be identified only with those of us who are older. One of my granddaughters remarked to her mother some years ago that they would "never know if Pawpaw had Alzheimer's because he already forgets our names." Along with racism, sexism, and all the rest of the isms, we need to add ageism.

Even Betty was guilty of political incorrectness on this issue. She complained that I never heard half of what she said. Finally, I called for an appointment with an ear doctor.

The young lady on the phone said, "But you sound so young."

I said, "Maybe I don't need this appointment after all. I heard that clearly." After an examination, the doctor told me that was nothing wrong with my hearing.

"But my wife keeps saying I hear nothing she says."

He responded, "My wife tells me the same thing."

The doctor shared the experience of another patient whose condition had been corrected with hearing aids. Upon his returning for a checkup, the doctor asked the patient whether his family was pleased. "I haven't told my family yet," he responded, "I just listen, and I've changed my will four times."

The age of ninety-one is not as old as it used to be. Only as we move closer to it do we recognize the fact that we all continue to strive to live beyond our current age to the next level because the alternative is not a happy one. The closer we come to that advanced age, the stronger is our ambition to attain it—and the less ancient it feels. Oliver Wendell Holmes said, "Being eighty years young is sometime far more cheerful and hopeful than being fifty years old."

Very little is expected of those of us over ninety—even though most of us still have our mental faculties and have moved beyond health risks. There isn't anything else to go wrong that can't be controlled by pills: allergies, thyroid, diabetes, high blood pressure, cholesterol, you name it.

Our teeth have all been transplanted or implanted, our rotator cuffs repaired, our hernias corrected, our prostates removed, and stints placed in the arteries to our hearts. Our appendixes have been long gone, our gall bladders are extracted, and our kidney stones are banished. What do we have to worry about?

Once you reach ninety-three, everyone wants to carry your bags and help you up steps. If you forget your name or anybody else's, or an appointment, or your telephone number, or promise to be three places at the same time, or can't remember how many grandchildren you have, you need only explain that you are ninety-three. At that age, you have a perfect excuse no matter what you do. If you act foolishly, it's your second childhood. Everybody is looking for symptoms of softening of the brain.

At age ninety-three, we have some benefits that younger people don't have. Patrick Henry said, "I have but one lamp by which my feet are guided; and that is the lamp of experience. I know of no way of judging the future but by the past."

Emerson said, "The years teach much which the days never know."

While it is often concluded that older people only think about the past, the reality is that the future becomes even more important because we have less of it. Thomas Jefferson said,

"Like the dreams of the future better than the history of the past."

We who have been around longer have learned more, have developed wisdom and knowledge, and hopefully no longer take ourselves too seriously. If we are going to succeed, we've done that, and if we are going to fail, that's already been a part of our makeup as well.

Many have crossed frontiers unprecedented and have taken advantage of challenges not before envisioned. Their vigor has been spent on new worlds conquered, and their imaginations have paid off in attaining new dimensions beyond their own imagination and the expectation of others.

Those who have arrived at an advanced age have more time, fewer responsibilities, more mature judgment, and the capacity—and often the resources—to take full advantage of the enjoyment that life offers. They can concentrate on good works, whether philanthropy or hospitality to their fellow man.

And just when they have accumulated enough in financial resources to be able to afford what they need, everybody wants to reduce their prices. Can you believe a 30 percent discount for a hotel room without blinking an eye? When at fifty-five, AARP said we were officially "a senior," everyone resented giving that discount. At sixty-five, they still checked our ages. And even at seventy, we could be suspect. But at ninety, when we walk up to the counter, lights start flashing and clerks throw up their hands in surrender and ask, "What are you willing to pay?"

Talk about a liberating experience! Add up the discounts, and you often can get up to 130 percent on a good day. That exceeds 100 percent, which suggests that you are due a refund.

I believe strongly that the most valuable life preserver is remaining actively involved— even to the point of having appointments beyond one's life expectancy. I decided to finance my new motorcycle for twenty years because I am legally obligated until I am 102. My credit rating is at stake.

In *Thoughts for a Vital Life*, Jerold Panas said, "Doing nothing is the most tiresome job in the world because you can't stop and rest." Much of self-esteem, which is a part of one's health, is involved in purposeful involvement.

Sixty-six years of my life have been devoted to education—twenty-one years of which I have served as a college and university president. There are very few professions that challenge the intellect, stamina, patience, and endurance as much as the presidency of a college or university.

I accepted the challenge of the presidency because I thought I could affect the lives of a great number of people. I also thought the presidency presented in one package a complete challenge to all that a human being could manage. It could be dangerous, it could be costly, and it could be exhausting. But it was adventuresome, it was refreshing, and it was invigorating.

# III

# IF LIFE IS AN ADVENTURE, WHY STOP AT EIGHTY?

My riding a motorcycle at age ninety-three attracts more attention and acclaim than all my years of work in higher education. Thus, for that fact and the personal satisfaction of riding, I share the nature of my stimulation from this experience.

Even at age ninety-three, each time I get astride my Electra Glide Harley-Davidson Ultra Classic and face the wind, it cleanses my mind of everything mundane. The world becomes my domain with the open road laid before me in ribbons of asphalt with panoramas on all sides offering visions of grandeur, aromas of the area, weather conditions as real as the openness that only a motorcycle allows. Large semis pass me even as I set my cruise control above seventy miles per hour. Many of the western interstates allow eighty miles per hour as the routine speed limit.

Adventure is defined as a "daring event or a bold occurrence." Thus, aging is an adventure in itself, and it should not be an excuse for backing off from living life to the fullest. I now have time to be more adventuresome than when I was younger. On Memorial Day two years ago, I rode with the Rolling Thunder—three hundred thousand motorcycles strong—through Washington DC. I was the only World War II veteran participating. Most would assume that at age ninety-three, I should be asleep on a couch somewhere—not out giving speeches or riding my Harley.

Periodically I set aside the dark suit, white shirt, and tie that have been my trademark to wear my leathers, representing a little bit of heaven on earth and to prove that life is more fulfilling after ninety-three for those who refuse to act their age.

When I chose to circle the country on my motorcycle to celebrate my eighty-sixth birthday, I had some misgivings. But that was a part of the challenge, a part of the adventure, and a part of the stimulation. Could I do it? Would I do it? I couldn't resist. I wanted to tell the world that when you are over the hill, you pick up speed. Two wheels help you get down the other side.

I was slightly apprehensive about traveling nine thousand miles out there all alone in the world. But like a baby taking its first step in learning how to walk, every mile traveled made the next mile easier. Pretty soon, I wondered why I was ever apprehensive.

I am often asked, "What's it like traveling nine thousand miles around the perimeter of the contiguous United States on a motorcycle?" The answer can be formulated only within the broader context of one's experiences. Having lived in a rural part of Kentucky in my early life and traveling only from farm to farm or to the county seat of only about four or five miles, what I have done now could not have been conceived. Traveling so many miles even in a lifetime would have taxed my imagination, much less the fact of doing it on two wheels in twenty-five days. Until I left home on a train out of Louisville for a four-day ride to San Diego in 1944 and the Marine Corps at age seventeen, I had no idea that the country was so large.

Traveling the periphery of the country touching thirty-four states that border the rest of the forty-nine emphasizes the magnitude of the country. At the same time, it's as if I have put my arms around the whole country—short of Hawaii and Alaska—in a matter of days.

One can travel the perimeter of the United States and feel at home. The I-10 goes from Jacksonville, Florida to Los Angeles, California, which is a mind-boggling grand adventure in itself. This never-ending piece of asphalt and concrete between those two cities provides a perspective of how the states are woven together.

One can pass through Florida, Georgia, Alabama, Mississippi, Louisiana, Texas, New Mexico, Arizona, and California—nine states—without incident. Different laws, regulations, policies, practices, prejudices, pride, or other considerations do not detract from a comfortable transition from one to the other. Except for minding a few regulations, there is no restraint to enjoying what is offered and for the most part being unnoticed and untethered for days at a time while absorbing all that is offered along the way.

From San Francisco, I traveled north to Oregon and Washington and then headed east to Idaho, Montana, North Dakota, Minnesota, Wisconsin, Illinois, Indiana, Ohio, Michigan,

Vermont, New Hampshire, and Maine. I turned south on I-95 to Rhode Island, Massachusetts, Connecticut, New York, Pennsylvania, New Jersey, Maryland, Delaware, the District of Columbia, and Virginia, bringing my total to thirty-four states.

The northern states were different from those in the South in temperature and landscape, but the people and their generosity of spirit were much the same. Traffic differed in congested cities, but Chicago and Houston weren't all that different from San Francisco and Los Angeles or Portland or Seattle. They were all crowded and full of hustle and bustle of travelers seeking to get where they wanted to go. Working a motorcycle into the midst of all the other vehicles was just a matter of matching their speed and fitting into the flow of traffic.

The fact that I could circle this fascinating landscape on a two-wheeler going through all these different states was unbelievable. Doing so in twenty-five days, some days covering as many as three different states, was hard to fathom. The highways were much the same throughout the states, the roadside stops are similar, and people—even of different origins—were not all that different in their actions and reactions.

Because I was about to experience my eighty-sixth birthday, I was a package of history, carrying with me the Great Depression, World War II, and principles and practices that were nourished in a rural setting in Kentucky and differing in many ways from most other travelers.

Yet none of this mattered as I made contact with others in incidental engagements.

The journey was fulfilling, stimulating, challenging, rewarding, socially broadening, geographically enlightening, physically uplifting, filled with anticipation, and I learned by *being there* that it doesn't snow year-round in North Dakota.

Was my cross-country journey educational? Yes, it was. Once dressed in full leather, gloves, a helmet cover, and traveling at seventy miles per hour, a bug flew down my collar. That immensely expanded my vocabulary!

Why wouldn't *more* people want to do such a thing? Good health certainly is important at my age, but beyond that, it's simply the desire to do it, the determination to prove to myself that I could, the enjoyment of it all, the contacts, the relationships, and the challenge that was met with little effort beyond that which could be called extraordinary. Yet many who hear my story think of it as unprecedented. To put it mildly, it was a piece of cake.

Ralph Waldo Emerson admonished, "Do not go where the path may lead; go instead where there is no path and leave a trail." Perhaps, for one of my age, I represented that. I learned that while the country is large, it can be embraced—and that the interstate system is a miracle in transportation, commerce, and social mobility. So many places to go and so much to see. I encountered no one in twenty-five days in thirty-four states in dozens of contacts who were my age or within ten years of it. I saw no World War II veterans riding motorcycles.

I am also often asked why I would do what I did at my mature age with the risks involved as if it were an unreasonable judgment. My response is that what seems outlandish to some becomes a source of great satisfaction to others. What is risk to some is challenge to others. What is an unfulfilled ambition for one is a fulfilling satisfaction to another. For me, the consideration was so full of anticipation that to not have met the challenge would have been an ambition unfulfilled and regretted.

Conformity should not be our guideline. That which makes life an adventure should be the guideline. This might involve taking risks, which the dictionary defines as "the possibility of loss" or "hazard" or "danger." Life at any age and anywhere is a risk. Just being born is a risk.

The greatest risk of all is to die bored or to fail to live life to its fullest.

This generation of mature people apologizes for being in the upper level of maturity. We demonstrate that by withdrawing from activities in which we are totally capable of participating. We stand on the sidelines and deny ourselves the joys that were stimulating, fulfilling, and exciting. We forego the human experiences that give fuller expression to our innermost yearnings for activities beyond the ordinary.

The definition of old age has become the prerogative of those who have not yet experienced that condition. Generally speaking, those who reach my age are categorized by that which restricts confines, discounts, and disregards so as to relegate all of us to the scrap heap of a second childhood.

Youth has tended to be defined by physical age, but the increase in life expectancy makes Samuel Ullman's perspective more realistic.

> It is not a time in life; it's a state of mind; it's not a matter of rosy cheeks, red lips, and supple knees; it is a matter of the will, a quality of the imagination, the vigor of the emotions; it is the freshness of the deep springs of life.

While it is often concluded that older people only think about the past, the reality is that the future becomes even more important because we have less of it.

Pluto, the Greek philosopher, said, "The mind is not a vessel to be filled, but a fire to be ignited." So, once it's been filled, the rest of it is just continuing to ignite it at whatever age.

I get up every morning by five and am actively engaged all the hours of the day. I am either at the university interacting with students, faculty, alumni, and other administrators or I am out in the world consulting or speaking or serving on one of the more than a dozen boards with which I am involved.

So, with five education boards, two foundation boards, three nonprofit boards, and three veterans' organization boards, I am fully committed personally and as a representative of U of R. Add my speaking schedule, and all I do on campus and off for U of R, I fill that five o'clock in the morning to evening schedule quite well.

On September 2, 2011, on the deck of the USS *Missouri*—the "Mighty Mo"—at Pearl Harbor, I stood in the footprints of General Douglas MacArthur where he accepted the Japanese surrender. Before me were hundreds of sailors, soldiers, marines, and dignitaries, including twenty World War II veterans in the front row.

What at age ninety-three keeps me energized and fired up? After all, I am ancient history. Born in 1926— along with Marilyn Monroe—I have lived through the Great Depression and World War II. I have seen and experienced much that those few or many years younger have not. I personally met Sergeant Alvin York from World War I and President Franklin Roosevelt. I have danced with Betty Davis and introduced Billy Graham to sixty thousand people in Copenhagen.

At an age when most have put aside such activities as motorcycle riding, I find it to be an elixir for stimulation, a sense of well-being, mental and physical wholesomeness, a release from the ordinary, and a challenge physically, mentally, socially, and intellectually. It lifts my selfconfidence, self-control, self-esteem, and physical competence.

While a motorcycle may not be on everybody's bucket list, other great adventures should be a part of the long-range anticipations in life. Motorcycling is only an example of life beyond the years of learning and leadership, making it a valued period of fulfillment.

Activity in old age keeps one's mind on positive things and off those perceived conditions that come to some with age. A few hours on a motorcycle or an activity of choice beats days of visiting a psychiatrist. Eighty and after is not an age—it's an attitude.

A couple of years ago, I was invited to Campbellsville, Kentucky, to give the eulogy for friend who fought on Okinawa. Bob Oldham was responsible for my becoming a student at the college.

We don't quit doing things because we get old. We get old because we quit doing things.

George Bernard Shaw said, "Life is no brief candle. It is a sort of splendid torch which I hold for a moment, and I want to make it burn as brightly as possible before handing it on to future generations."

I end with a letter from a student who served on the alumni board:

Dr. Heilman, I cannot express how thoughtful and inspirational your remarks were this morning. I am a 1975 graduate of UR and sit on the alumni board. You came to Richmond when I was a freshman and have always been someone I greatly admire. Not only are you a transformational leader of the school in building the foundation for its unparalleled success but you continue to set an extraordinary example for all of us.

Your lifelong involvement with the university and the Marine Corps, combined with your motorcycle travels reminds us that life is to be lived to the fullest and that we, as students, too often place artificial limits, including age, on ourselves and as a result never reach our full potential.

With Edwin Markham's I confirm the greatest lesson in human relations: "All that we send into the lives of others comes back into our own."

# CHAPTER EIGHT – AGING

"Age is a quality of mind. If you let your dreams behind, if hope is cold, you could no
longer look ahead. If you are ambitious, fires are dead when you are old"
—Shakespeare

## WITH PURPOSE WE HAVE REASON TO LIVE LONGER

Having a sense of purpose or having a reason to get out of bed has been a trait of many of the world's centenarians according to a project that has tracked the lifestyles of people who have lived past 100 years in Okinawa and other countries. "People who feel their life is a part of a larger plan and are guided by their spiritual values have stronger immune systems, lower blood pressure, lower risk of heart attack and cancer, and heal faster and live longer says Harrow Koenig, professor of Psychiatry and Behavioral Science of Duke University." "Purpose gives you fulfillment and joy he says and that can bring you the experience of happiness." I quote further – "a job is probably the easiest way to help you feel your life has purpose."

It turns out that the golden years really are golden. New research finds the happiest Americans are the oldest and older adults are more socially active than the stereotype of the lonely senior suggests. According to a recent article in the Associated Press, "the good news is that with age comes happiness. Older people generally have learned to be more content with what they have than younger adults so says the article while younger blacks and poor people tend to be less happy than whites and wealthier people, those differences faded as people aged. In general the odds of being happy increase 5% with every 10 years of age.

At my age of 93 conformity should not be the guideline, rather continuing to live life to the fullest in the spirit of Helen Keller who thought, born blind and deaf, declared "Life is either a grand adventure or it's nothing." With her attitude and spirit as the example why should those of us who are wholly capable fail to enjoy living life to the fullest irrespective of the presumed limitations of old age.

I am often advised by well-meaning people of the risks I take "at my age" in riding my motorcycle. Yes, I am aware of the risks of motorcycle riding but it has little to do with age. The dictionary defines 'risk' as "the possibility of loss, or hazard, or danger." So life, including motorcycle riding is a risk at any age. Just being born is a risk. But for me, the greatest of all risks is to die bored having failed to live life to the fullest.

I chose to set out across country on my motorcycle in my 83$^{rd}$ year and by age 88 I have travelled through 49 states. I had some misgivings at first, but that was a part of the challenge, a part of the adventure, and a part of the stimulation. Could I do it? Would I do it? I couldn't resist. I wanted to prove to myself and others, and to tell the world that 'over the hill' you pick up speed so that the most natural means for getting down the other side is on two wheels. After all, age is more an attitude than a restriction based upon a number.

With the right attitude most all of life at my age can be translated into an adventure and I am doing my best to take full advantage of exploring every aspect of that option.

At age 93 I can see both from the past and the present and I'm closer to the future than most. I know where I've been, what I've left behind, where I'm going and who I wish to be. I've had my satisfactions and lived with my mistakes. I know better what I want to do than I ever have in the past. And I don't intend to stop pursuing whatever may be on my bucket list.

The poet Edna Frederikson writes, "The trouble with being old is there is so little future in it." But at any age we may have only a few years, a few months or a few days to live so we should live for today and tomorrow for the day after that may never come. At age 92 there is a reasonable possibility of my living to be 95 or 98 or even 100. That's like living from birth through childhood to age 21 so I intend to use every day as if it could be the last or only the next of a series.

As long as I'm alive and not incapacitated. I want to represent a passion for life, an obvious desire to stay engaged with fire in the belly so as to ignore the reasons for not doing something. While I cannot add years to my life, I can add life to my years. While I cannot add length to my life, I enhance its breadth and depth.

Someone said, "The older I get the better I used to be." Perhaps that's positive affirmation that life's been good or at least we remember the good part and forget the bad. That's what makes older age satisfying and fulfilling.

Studies on aging and mental health have shown that except for dementia related diseases, mental health and emotional happiness generally improves with age. If we enthusiastically engage in what we continue to be able to do, if we are on fire with enthusiasm, people will come for miles around just to watch us burn. They gather on the curb to see if it's true that a 93 year old Great Grandfather really rides a motorcycle.

In an article entitled "The Best is yet to Be," Shari Roan of the Los Angeles Times stated, "For centuries sages have alluded to a richness in life's later years that is lost on the young. But only in the last decade have researchers begun to measure happiness across the life span and in doing so, try to understand why older people tend to be so content.

Among other things, "Older people are less likely to be caught up in their emotions and more likely to focus on the positive, ignoring the negative." "The insult that has our blood boiling for three days at age 20 may not even register a spike in blood pressure at age 93."

"The later stages of life also offer more opportunities to actively avoid those parts that are stressful or upsetting." We can surround ourselves with less negative people and events. I have always sought colleagues with positive outlooks on life who respond with an affirmative spirit in their voice, who see through rose colored glasses. I have such an assistant and every encounter lights up my day. She seldom sees things as problems, only opportunities.

## **Conditions of a good Life**

A good friend and former college president, Dr. Jim Fisher, a psychologist, agrees that "The three most important conditions for a good life, especially for seniors are engagement, forgiveness, and faith. Engagement involves work, volunteering, education, diet, exercise, attitude, checking bad habits (like drinking and smoking) and anything that challenges ones intellectual process. Forgiveness may be the most important condition of all. That includes those who have abused us, have offended us, been unfair or mean, and those who have taken advantage of us. All should be forgiven without any "yes, buts." This includes friends, business associates, parents, children, other relatives, spouses or former ones.

And having faith in things beyond our intelligence or rational thought is an essential condition. There may be room for skepticism but not cynicism.

Finally, it could all be summed up by the word love. All of our lives in the later days would be greatly enhanced if we applied these conditions to all aspects of our lives.

Edwin Markham:
> There is a destiny that makes us brothers
>
> None goes his own way alone
>
> All that we send into the life of others
>
> Comes back into our own.

# I V

## DEALING WITH THE AGING POPULATION

On an occasion when my father and I were in the presence of an acquaintance of mine, the individual very sincerely inquired as to whether my father was my brother. My father and mother were very healthy and active. They lived on a farm in Kentucky and worked hard every day at activities extending from looking after cattle and raising their feed to putting the harvest into the barns. My father also maintained a responsibility as a Sunday School Teacher and was active in the community, as was my mother and both enjoyed life in older age more than when they were younger. Neither of my parents stopped growing and developing and working. They never took the time to think about growing old. They always rose with the sun and went to bed tired as a result of their productive activity.

In the future, society may have to accept the fact that education is not a task to be completed but a process to be continued. This sets the stage for consideration of and concern for the increasing proportion of the population in the older age group in our society. We tend to perpetuate social customs of the past, and in the societies of the past, there have been too few older people to justify giving them much consideration. We have tended to assume that they are feeble, dull, and worthless because so few of them managed to survive in the middle years of life. If they did survive, they were worn out by repeated bouts of disease, poor diets, bad teeth, hormonal imbalance, and life-long overwork. But that is not true as often today. The aging are stronger; they are more vigorous; and they are more alert than they have ever been, gut still we retire them rather ruthlessly. We try to get them out of the way, and we leave them to wait out their life's endings on park benches or in nursing homes, if they are that fortunate. We have many easy excuses, among them the view that the aging are very conservative and that they are no longer capable of creative thinking. In our prejudiced point of view, only the young are fit to blaze new and innovative trails.

All of this could be circular reasoning. After all, we have tended to educate only the young. We have established a cut-off date, which we have taken for granted in education; and, as a result, we think of becoming educated rather than continuing to be educated. Thus, once we become educated, we never have to read a book again; we never have to learn anything more; and we never have to entertain another thought. Yet, supposedly we remain educated. Under conditions such as these, why shouldn't we expect people to grow old and become incapable of reading, learning or thinking? In the long life, low birthrate world of the future, things might have to change. Aging people will make up larger and larger percentages of the population. It will become more and more dangerous to permit them to remain non-thinking, dead weights on society. So educators must recognize that education will become not a task to be completed but a process to be continued. Older people can remain creative and innovative right up to the end of their lives.

Such a notion may be difficult for our youth to accept. It may be self-evident to young people that the workings of old age make individuals rusty and creaky. But that kind of self-evident proposition is only a guess based upon youth centered prejudices, youth chauvinism, so to speak. The actual fact is that our society has never tried a substantial process of adult education. We have never given the aging mind a chance to show what it can do, so we don't really know what it can do. A great deal of evidence suggests that we could be greatly surprised at what can be done with the aging and the aged to bring back youthful adaptability.

Since we have not included this subject in educational curricula over so many years of change and revision of educational programs, it seems fair to ask, "Why should educators be interested in it now?" A very academic answer is that wherever there is something to be studied, analyzed, and learned, education is concerned. Gerontology, which comprises a branch of knowledge dealing with aging in all of its aspects and processes, fills the requirements for the academic approach.

There are other very practical reasons for educators to turn attention to gerontology. Some of them are obvious. Among these considerations are: (1) the mounting numbers and growing percentage of our population who are in the age bracket of 60 years and older; (2) the changing economy which conflicts with established precedents for role assignment to older citizens; (3) technological developments that engage individual productivity based primarily on physical strength; and (4) a social value structure of age diametrically opposed to the realities of the society as it exists.

The question which should be asked is, "Why has gerontology so long been excluded from education?" In sociology, psychology, life sciences, economics, and other areas defined as liberal arts, a needed knowledge base has been compromised by this omission.

The place of gerontology in education is no less clear in the professions and specialty education. For example, at most universities, we have professional schools in law, business administration and education. In each of these areas our students need to acquire knowledge about aging, both for their personal benefit and for use as professional practitioners.

The attorney is engaged in protective services, and the types of legal services we require vary throughout life. In providing legal counsel, the attorney will need the understandings and the skills related to those to be served.

Business administrators must deal with many "people" facts of management, again mandating knowledge and compassionate understanding of those of all ages.

In education, the need is equally clear. In order to teach, one must first learn. But, including gerontology in our own special areas of teaching is not enough. Today, increasing numbers of older persons are coming to college to resume work on interrupted degrees, to study subject they have not had time to pursue, or simply to enjoy the stimulations and satisfactions they find in learning. This older group will require that educators understand their special needs and modify some of their teaching techniques to meet them. In so doing, they will be better teachers for all students.

It is easy to see that gerontology is multi-disciplinary. No area of education is outside its influence or unaffected by it. There is a place and a need for the competent, highly qualified specialist in gerontology who cross disciplines in his or her breadth of knowledge about aging. We need gerontologists as leaders, as planners and innovators. But, a more diffused need is for each of us in education to know the smaller area of the field as it relates specifically to our individual discipline or specialization.

Students have a need to know about aging while they are young. How we grow and develop, whether we find a satisfying role and place, will determine the level of fulfillment we reach. It is not difficult to accept that those who work with or for the aged must understand aging and age related changes. Equally obvious should be the universal need for each of us to know aging on a personal basis. The vast majority of us plan to live long and grow old, with the emphasis on growing. We can do it better if we understand it. A subject that has such personal meaning to so many has a rightful place in education.

Dr. Morton Lieberman, a University of Chicago psychiatrist, says "Perceiving one's self as the center of the universe seems most likely to insure survival. If we add attitude and self-esteem to heredity, diet, exercise, and mental alertness, the sum may equal long life." This is the consensus of the experts and education can do a great deal to add spice to life and also make better the life within the framework of its length.

In closing, let me share some lines form Tennyson's Ulysses relating to those of mature age, disposition and inclination.

> . . . for my purpose holds
> To sail beyond the sunset, and the baths
> Of all the western stars, until I die.
> It may be that the gulfs will wash us down;
> It may be we shall touch the Happy Isles,

And see the great Achilles, whom we knew.

Tho' much is taken, much abides; and tho'
We are not now that strength which in old days
Moved earth and heaven, that which we are, we are,
   -One equal temper of heroic hearts,
      Made weak by time and fate, but strong in will

To strive, to seek, to find, and not to yield.

# CHAPTER NINE

## MEASURING SUCCESS BY THE ACKNOWLEDGEMENTS OF OTHERS

## The World Meets Nobody Halfway
## But It Steps Aside For Those Who Know Where They Are Going

Seventy years ago, I left the farm in Kentucky for the Marine Corps and World War II after failing miserably in high school. Building upon the foundation of what the Marine Corps taught me, I have served sixty-five years on college and university campuses, two of which I served as president, having acquired my PhD along the way.

You may not know where you are going until you get there—so don't be surprised if you end up somewhere else. This idea fits the journey of my life and is the case of many veterans of World War II who were blessed by the G.I. Bill. We became the results of circumstances over which we had little control. The Great Depression and World War II shaped our lives.

Because my old high school burned down with all the records of the class of '44, no one can prove that I wasn't the smartest student on the planet. But one copy of a report card in my memoirs proves otherwise. How did I end up as a senior administrator in colleges and universities in four states for sixty-five years? It was not a likely outcome.

Irrespective of my lack of positive educational progress growing up, I was given outstanding examples of honesty, integrity, and the value of hard work from parents who, while dead broke, survived the Great Depression on character.

During the years prior to the attack on Pearl Harbor, the country was so chastened by depression hardships that it could hardly sink further. In fact, the new challenge of war and the stimulation of the economy extricated the country from the Depression and lifted our spirit of adventure and in many ways prepared the country for facing the challenges of a world at war.

Every day starts a new chapter in history, and its preservation is an important responsibility for each generation. What has been done by those of us who have made history will, when we are gone, perpetuate our experiences.

By now you have read much about my efforts at accomplishing my ambitions and fulfilling my destiny without confirmation from objective parties except by my own selective process. So you may be thinking, "This guy is the most self-possessed, immodest, narcissistic, braggadocio bag of wind I have encountered in a while. How can I believe half of what I am reading?"

Well, now that I have led you into such a frame of mind and you wonder what I am all about, let me review in paraphrase advice from the September issue of Fortune magazine. The article presents a question "Should leaders be modest?" It speaks about Jim Collins and his book "Good to Great" arguing that personal humility is a t5rait that distinguishes good to great leaders. But the article goes on to say, few leaders, particularly leaders of large organizations, actually seem to be very modest.

"Many of the most well-known and well regarded CEOs – including Bill Gates at Microsoft, Steve Jobs of Apple and Jack Welch of General Electric – exhibited narcissistic traits and behaviors. Immodesty in all its manifestations – narcissism, self-promotion, self-aggrandizement, unwarranted self-confidence – helps people attain leadership positions in the first place and then, once they are in them, positively affect their ability to hold on to these positions, extract more."

Further, says the article "because narcissists have a stronger bias for action and risk-taking – again a result of their higher levels of self-confidence – the study also found that more narcissistic CEOs led firms to bounce back more successfully during the post crisis recovery."

Yes, I am one of the restless and impatient and pushy CEOs who is never satisfied so that I am for3ver asking for the unusual in tandem with my board chair or at least with his blessing.

And, as a result, I have succeeded for 66 years as a CEO, a board chair, a dean, a coordinator of a state system of higher education and chief business officer by working 24 hours a day, up early to bed late, having so much vision that I never overtake its requirement and I push my board by way of its chair just to keep up with me, always to succeed in the long run. This approach has made for great progress and success. Hard work, long hours, good preparation, and knowing where I'm going is why the world has stepped aside to let me and my following pass.

Now in order to further prove my point and to give evidence of the fact that I am not bashful about exploiting the favorable and more objective impressions of my leadership and its style leading to the many successes being acknowledged in a variety of ways, I present the evidence in the following accolades and tributes.

# AWARDS, RECOGNITIONS, ACCOLADES, AND TRIBUTES

Love sought is good,
But given unsought, Is better.
*—Twelfth Night*

Because I have selectively published positive things which I offset in my book by some negative letters, I could have done so here but for the most part, in these later years of my life, anything I receive is reinforcing, positive, and in the spirit of goodwill.

That does not change my disposition to appreciate the goodwill by way of things said in good spirit from constitutencies allalong the way. Thus, I cite the following just to let those reading this book know that I understand how easy it is to cross the line between publishing a few positive comments about which I feel good for others to read and over doing it so that some may feel as this one who wrote to me but did not provide a name. Obviously it was someone who held resentment toward me and my obvious ego.

The note was as follows:

"The office Don Juan lost no time in trying to impress the new secretary, a young and pretty girl. He told her about his feats on the college football team, the dance floor, during the war, and in every other line of activity he could think of.

After weary of some recital of his achievements, the girl gave him a wide eyed smile asking 'have you ever had a group photograph of yourself?"

Sometime when you're feeling important;
Sometime when your ego's in bloom

Sometime when you take it for granted
You're the best qualified in the room,

Sometime when you feel that your going
Would leave an unfillable hole,
Just follow these simple instructions
And see how they humble your soul;

Take a bucket and fill it with water,
Put your hand in it up to the wrist,
Pull it out and the hole that's remaining
Is a measure of how you will be missed.

You can splash all you wish when you enter,
You may stir up the water galore,
But stop and you'll find that in no time
It looks quite the same as before.

The moral of this quaint example
Is do just the best that you can,
Be proud of yourself but remember,
There's no indispensable man.

Anonymous

The Bigger a man's head gest, the easier it is to fill his shoes.
*Henry Courtney*

So with these acknowledgements before me highlighting my vulnerability in sharing the many plaudits by people of goodwill, I leave it to others reading these pages to judge what might have been preserved only for the satisfaction of the benefactor.

I have never felt it essential to my self-esteem that a certain level or number of accolades be directed my way, yet I, like others who sometimes find themselves on the firing line, welcome enough approbation to offset the negatives directed our way.

Over the years, I have received some very negative, even rude, correspondence from those who have disagreed with me. Most have been related to actions I have taken as a president of a college and university. By virtue of positions I have held during my lifetime, I have also had the honor of receiving more than my share of awards and recognitions. Some of these have been related to positions held, and others have been for personal accomplishments.

Beyond my eightieth birthday, I have anticipated few, if any, awards and recognitions of consequence. Thus, I was greatly surprised when invited to a luncheon which led to my being selected for an American Veterans Tribute. At the luncheon, I listened to the conversation and waited for the next shoe to drop. When it did, it made a loud noise with the announcement that I was being invited to receive this high honor on July 4, 2015, as a veteran of World War II. For my family and the hundreds of others who gathered for this occasion at Lake

Gaston, it proved to be unique and commendable. This included a weekend at the Hilton Garden Inn in Roanoke Rapids, North Carolina, with delicious food, lots of entertainment, and a special presentation before many of my friends and family.

The objective of the program was to honor veterans for their service to the nation. This particular event, I was told, was to honor me as a Marine Corps veteran for my service to our nation. Among others who had received this award were Paul Galante and Bill Hanecke—both of whom served in very adverse conditions and held high the honor. I was truly touched to be placed among such great heroes as these two.

The program and festivities began around six. After skydivers dropped from the sky, dinner and fireworks lasted almost an hour—followed by a twenty-one-gun salute to honor our fallen heroes. The celebration went long into the evening. Breakfast the next morning continued the celebrations from the night before. A further purpose was to honor the country and all the men and women who have so bravely served her.

This event has proved to be an outstanding feature in the region. People from all over the country came to celebrate the Fourth of July with us and to testify that it was the most spectacular thing they had ever witnessed.

My family and I were provided with a boat seating twenty-two people with a captain for the event. It was a great honor to be selected to represent veterans of all services.

Following is the official definition of the award as expressed by the organization making the presentation:

Celebration Honoring Dr. E. Bruce Heilman
United States Marine Corps (Ret.)
July 4, 2015

Objective
Our objective in presenting the patriotic event is to honor Dr. Bruce Heilman US Marine Corps (Ret.) for his service to our nation.

Purpose

The show is to honor our country and the men and women who have so bravely served her. We feel that by putting on such an event, we are not only honoring those men and women, but we are also broadcasting this message to thousands of people. AVT wishes to honor you and tell your story of sacrifice and service to another generation.

With the production, AVT positively influences a great number of people to be more patriotic and to remember those men and women who have served our country in our armed forces. AVT does not know of a more patriotic event anywhere in our region. We honor our country and thank our veterans.

The festivities begin around 6:00 p.m. with a formal honoring of our veteran to family and friends. Following the semiprivate ceremony, skydivers depart from their plan in the Pete Luter jump. As soon as the skydivers land, we then honor and celebrate our war hero who has risked life and limb for the freedoms we enjoy. As soon as the awards ceremony is over, the entertainment begins. The fireworks show will last for approximately forty minutes. We will take a pause in the middle of the show to fire a twenty-one-gun salute in honor of all of our fallen heroes. We then conclude the show by playing the National Anthem followed by Taps.

People come from all over the country to celebrate the Fourth of July with us and testify that is the most special thing they have ever been witness to. We do not look for publicity. The goal is to make this an easy and enjoyable weekend celebration for the Heilman Family. Dr. Heilman and party will be provided with boat seating for up to twenty-two people with a captain for the event.

# American Veterans Tribute

# Honors

## Dr. Bruce Heilman,

## U.S. Marine Corps (Ret.)

### July 4, 2015

### Lake Gaston, VA

*Initiated* -- on April 30, 2014

PO BOX 9469
3114 SOUTHSIDE AVENUE
RICHMOND, VA 23228
Phone: 800-296-9641
Fax: 804-264-0251

## Dr. Heilman

If I were anyone else reading these accolades, I might be impressed, but only I know none of us live up to the goodwill exhibited in such commendations.

# OTHER ACKNOWLEDGEMENTS

Following the tribute, other accolades may seem small in comparison. However, to those making the presentations, they are not small or insignificant. I have selectively preserved such commendations at the risk of self-aggrandizement. Such remembrances and words of goodwill, however, especially from family members and special friends are worthy of acknowledging. In order to highlight my appreciation for the good will behind these accolades and compliments, I want to applaud those whose positive and supportive spirit give a boost to everyone.

I have sought to live as my disposition directs, leaning heavily toward believing that life will treat us right if we give it a chance. Because the world is filled with many of the same disposition, we can count on being reinforced by such as these. Thus, we need to concentrate on the positive thoughts of people of goodwill we encounter throughout life. Thus, I would admonish my readers to understand my personal pleasure in receiving and thus preserving and recording these citations of good will written by positive people. I thus complement their examples of affirmative reaction to what they observe as worthy of acknowledgement.

Thus, I present those reading as natural reactions by thoughtful friends, colleagues, family members, strangers whose paths crossed mine by accident or on purpose and whose intent was to express their feelings resulting from an action or expression which affected them in a special way.

I am a beneficial agent who caused the response to an action taken – a service rendered – a speech sparking an action, a response to a request, a complement on my part or an act not even remembered by me.

So please, in reading these which are representative of thousands over 65 years of senior leadership, reflect upon the goodwill and good spirit voluntarily displayed mostly by unamend good spirited humans who, not by request but by reaction to something they considered worthy of their acknowledgement,. It all comes down to recorded emotions of the moment.

## Letters and Other Expressions of Support and Goodwill

To be remembered for the positive things you did in life—or at least the things others remember as positive—is certainly satisfying. Sometimes, not-so-positive thoughts come from other sources, as nothing can be presumed as acceptable to every constituent or constituent group.

I have retained files on both the positive and the not-so-positive letters, cards, and comments in respect to what has happened under my watch. Following are representations of the many I have received over the years and each justify all the appreciation I can give.

From a story in the *Richmond Times Dispatch* highlighting positive progress and elicits pride in alumni and all who have interest in the university was this article:

"The University of Richmond Building for Tomorrow,"

"The University of Richmond would easily fit any Hollywood setting of an "ideal college," but Richmond was entering the 1970s with the prospect of a $1 million annual budget deficit. A drastic enough situation to rock the boat of even a stronger campus.

Shortly thereafter, there followed a major contribution from Claiborne and Lora Robins, and following that, a man described as dynamic and a go-getter was hired by the university. He would further alter the financial and academic picture with his administrative and thunderous skills. His name was Dr. E. Bruce Heilman. He was named the president of the University of Richmond in 1971. Richmond is now one of the top fifty universities in the country in terms of total endowments.

The idea of the gift was to make Richmond a finer university. One offering excellent and quality education—not to make it a little Harvard.

Says the president, "Maybe the South doesn't need another Harvard." Excellence and quality are the two areas both Robins and Heilman feel are paramount. The man selected to fulfill the goal of academic excellence and put the University of Richmond on the academic map is a trim, enthusiastic go-getter from Kentucky. Heilman is obviously a gregarious man. His enthusiasm matches Robins's, which may be one of the reasons the latter is so high on this high school dropout.

The way he handles crisis is to believe no crisis exists, and he said 99 percent of the time he is right. On days when people come into his office all fired up with emotion, he elects to stay cool. "I do think that one of the roles of the presidency is to maintain normality." When he became president in March of 1971, Heilman made a statement that he was prepared to run some risks for progress and in the process to make some mistakes.

Professors

Dear Bruce,

One in my position, having taught at only two institutions, sees a great deal of college traffic as teachers and administrators come and go. One comes to accept those comings and goings as just a part of it all and thinks little about it.

However, occasionally, one of those departures has more than the usual effect. Your leaving Georgetown happens to be one of those occasions. When you first came to Georgetown, some eyebrows were raised because you adopted some policies that we were not used to. However, those eyebrows settled back when it was found that you really had a policy and that your policy applied to everybody alike. We all came to take your efficiency for granted and never even stopped to offer a word of encouragement.

Now that you are leaving, we suddenly realize what you have meant to our college family, our community, and church. We are sorry to lose you. Of course, we want you to do the thing that seems best for you, and as you and your good family depart from our campus, though you remain firmly entrenched in our hearts, we say God bless you, every one.

Sincerely yours,
CR Alexander

Dear Bruce,

I suppose you will be gone by the time I return from vacation. I know it's customary to express regrets and best wishes to one who is leaving even when such expressions are not sincere. Allow me to express sincerely my regrets. I feel that your resignation is a very severe loss to the college, and I consider it a personal loss to me. I have been in the teaching profession long enough to realize that men in administration who are willing to do a job with integrity and above petty strife are hard to find.

Since I have been here, no individual has been added to the administration who deserved and received more respect from the faculty than you. There is a feeling that you have put a part of the college on a sound basis. We feel that your part of the college is so clearly defined that we know where we are and where we are going. If any of us did not recognize your worth, your little booklet here at Georgetown has emphasized our loss. When all the departments in the college are as clearly defined, Georgetown will be heading for the greatness that it merits.

I am sure I have not established myself as a person who resorts to insincere flattery. It is in this attitude that I express my regrets and wish for you and your family God's blessing and the very best of all good things in your new position. Very truly,

HY Mulligan

Along with these two letters, the full faculty passed a resolution expressing its appreciation for my services and its regrets at my departure. The president of Georgetown College, Dr. Leo Eddleman, sent a letter to the president of Peabody College, Dr. Henry Hill, upon my leaving Georgetown and moving to Peabody:

Dear Dr. Hill, your good fortune in securing Mr. E. Bruce Heilman as bursar is to be commended. He has meant much to us here at Georgetown College. He is a man of integrity, efficiency, dependability, loyalty, and sincerity. Congratulations on obtaining the services of so great a man.

The President of Another College who earlier served as my executive assistant

You are connected to whatever success my wife and I may have enjoyed during our time as president. We learned so many good things from you and Betty, particularly the part about big dreams and surrounding oneself with capable people who also dream big. Not a day goes by that I am not reminded of the lunch we had in Carrollton, Kentucky, and the seventeen years that followed.

A Speaking engagement

Dr. Heilman, I cannot begin to tell you how much the members of the club enjoyed and appreciated that presentation last night. It was the topic of conversation. Our members have long appreciated you as their near neighbor in your leadership in the past at the university, but your presentation enabled them to see another side of your life.

ENVIRONMENTAL AND PUBLIC PROTECTION CABINET

**Ernie Fletcher**
Governor

Capital Plaza Tower
500 Mero Street, 5th Floor
Frankfort, Kentucky 40601
Phone: (502) 564-5525
Fax: (502) 564-3354
www.environment.ky.gov

**LaJuana S. Wilcher**
Secretary

**NEWS RELEASE**

Contact: Gwen Holt
502-564-4496

## AWARD AS OUTSTANDING FOREST STEWARD
## GOES TO HENRY COUNTY LANDOWNER
### *Dr. Bruce Heilman has long record of accomplishments*

FRANKFORT, Ky. (Aug. 12, 2005)– Dr. Bruce Heilman, who for years has carefully tended 122 acres of forest land in Henry County, has received the Outstanding Forest Steward Award from the Kentucky Division of Forestry.

Heilman lives in Richmond, Va., where he is chancellor of the University of Richmond. But for 34 years, he also has been a Kentucky forest land owner and tireless advocate of good forestry practices. He has been a certified forest steward since 1993 and is a member of the American Tree Farm System.

Heilman was instrumental in getting the University of the Cumberlands involved in the division's Forest Stewardship Program. The university, at Williamsburg, Ky., now has a forest stewardship plan covering thousands of acres. Heilman also promotes the program to other landowners and has offered his own land as an example. His works include:

- Conducting timber stand improvement activities on 68 acres
- Hosting a forestry field day and conducting three timber harvests
- Hosting a logger education field day
- Establishing wildlife food plots
- Establishing three miles of roads for woodland access, recreational use and fire breaks.

The award, recognizing Dr. Heilman's lifetime of forest stewardship, was presented at the recent annual meeting of the Kentucky Association of Conservation Districts.

A Dean of the Leadership School

Your speech was funny and poignant, challenging and personal, informative and inspiring. Every student and family member who spoke to me after the ceremony remarked on how truly excellent your remarks were. Thank you for taking the time to mingle with them after the ceremony. This year's attendance was the largest with about four hundred students and family members in attendance. I know from speaking with those who attended that the word on campus is that Finale is a commencement event of choice.

Professors

Dear Dr. Heilman,

Your first year has been successful even beyond my expectations. Within the faculty, and I think within the student body, one can feel a new spirit on the move. We have all become a little more firmly loyal to the great university we serve.

Dear Dr. Heilman,

I just learned this morning through a casual conversation that Hilary and Natalie are your granddaughters. They were two of the best students in my organization behavior class, each earning one of a handful of As from among the forty students in that class. I found them to be not only conscientious, inquisitive, and thoughtful but also to be extremely positive and enthusiastic in class. You must be very proud of them and their parents. PS. One of them noted on her final paper in a section on gaining power and influence that "I have seen the power that treating others with respect and courtesy has. My grandpa is the greatest man I ever met. He treats the workers in the dining hall like he would treat the president of the United States and for that, everyone respects him and values his input. I have learned from his example, and I do believe, that being nice to others and treating them as unique individuals whether through listening to them honestly or offering sympathy and assistance is the most influential strategy in gaining power." Wow!

## RESOLUTION OF THE
## UNIVERSITY OF RICHMOND BOARD OF TRUSTEES
## TO MEMORIALIZE
## BETTY JUNE DOBBINS HEILMAN

**WHEREAS,** Betty June Dobbins Heilman was a native of Louisville, Kentucky and an alumna of Campbellsville University; and

**WHEREAS,** Mrs. Heilman served as First Lady of the University of Richmond from 1971 to 1986, during the distinguished Presidency of Dr. E. Bruce Heilman, giving generously of her time and talents; warmly hosting University guests, faculty, staff, and students in the President's Home; and accompanying Dr. Heilman on many of his extended trips on behalf of the University, all while rearing their remarkable family; and

**WHEREAS,** Mrs. Heilman was the mother of five children, all of whom are graduates of the University of Richmond; grandmother of eleven grandchildren, ten of whom are alumni; and great-grandmother to four great-grandchildren; and

**WHEREAS,** Mrs. Heilman established with Dr. Heilman the E. Bruce and Betty Heilman Scholarship to enable students with financial need to attend the University; and

**WHEREAS,** the University, in recognition of her extraordinary and generous service to the University and valued place in the Richmond family, was proud to designate her an honorary alumna in 1988; and

**WHEREAS,** Mrs. Heilman died on December 12, 2013, at age 85, after a remarkable life of accomplishment and dedication to her family, her faith, and the University;

**NOW, THEREFORE, BE IT RESOLVED,** that the Board of Trustees of the University of Richmond records with sadness the death of Betty June Dobbins Heilman, a beloved member of the University family; expresses its deep and lasting gratitude for her wonderful grace, friendship, and selfless service; and extends its deepest sympathy to her husband Bruce; her children: Bobbie Heilman Murphy, W'75; Nancy Heilman Cale, W'73, G'77; Terry Heilman Sylvester, B'76; Sandy Heilman Kuehl, W'77, G'86; and Timothy Bruce Heilman, R'86; and their families.

Charles A. Ledsinger, Jr.
Rector, Board of Trustees

February 28, 2014

matters of the head and heart

Answers to Parents' Questions

richmond

The Director of Public Relations

Dear Mr. President: I commend to your attentional Jack Wilberger's article in the current issue of the *Collegian*. It is an interview he conducted with the presidents of student governments of Richmond College, Westhampton College, and the business school. I was impressed with the enthusiasm of the three presidents and particularly with their cordial attitude toward the present administration. I have not known so much harmony on this campus in the past ten years.

Surely any such interview conducted at any time in the past ten years would have been devoted to a great extent to griping and, as we marines sometimes say, "bitching."

The students feel that this administration is interested in their problems. They are beginning to see the great future that extends beyond our present horizons. Sincerely,

Joseph E. Nettles

A former student

Dear president Heilman,

I have just read with great interest the University of Richmond magazine on your retirement. What a wonderful leader you have been. I can't think of any area in which you were not its best leader ever. How will we ever find a leader to follow you.

Heilman Response: "And of course, what I am writing today, many, many years later, refutes the idea that I could ever have been so good that having someone to follow me would be less than as good as I had been. That's always the fact but it is wonderful to be acknowledged positively by those you are trying to serve when one is in office.

**Brussels, Belgium**

**One laugh of a child will make the holiest day more sacred still.**

—*R.G. Ingersoll*

## Around the World 2008

Dear Mama and Papa,

You have truly given us the world, and we cannot thank you enough. We are so lucky to have grandparents who care so much about us and who want to spend time with us. We love you so much, and are so thankful for you.

We had an amazing time on the Around the World journey. From Neuschwanstein Castle, to the Taj Mahal, to Nepal, and to Hong Kong, we couldn't have asked for a better experience. Mama, you were greatly missed!

You have set the bar high for us all. We love you dearly.

Love,
Terry, Whitney, Hilary, Carly, Natalie and Nick

OLLIE S. TYLER
MAYOR

## OFFICE OF THE MAYOR
### SHREVEPORT, LOUISIANA

POST OFFICE BOX 31109
SHREVEPORT, LA 71130
(318) 673-5050 / (318) 673-5099 (FAX)

# Proclamation

**WHEREAS,** *the six-thousand (6,000) national motorcycle tour, led by Dr. E. Bruce Heilman, Chancellor of the University of Richmond, Virginia, will be making a stop in Shreveport, Louisiana; and*

**WHEREAS,** *Chancellor Heilman has been making his six-thousand (6,000) mile tour in honor of the Gold Stars of WWII and to raise awareness about the Seventieth Anniversary (70th) of the end of WWII; and*

**WHEREAS,** *Dr. E. Bruce Heilman, 88 years old, is a veteran of WWII, having served in Okinawa; and*

**WHEREAS,** *Dr. Heilman plans to complete his six-thousand (6,000) mile motorcycle tour when he appears and joins the Rolling Thunder motorcycle rally during the Memorial Day Parade in Washington, DC; and*

**WHEREAS,** *this intrepid road warrior will be looked after by members of the American Legion Riders along his six-thousand (6,000) mile journey;*

**NOW, THEREFORE, I, Ollie S. Tyler,** *Mayor of the City of Shreveport, do hereby proclaim* **Monday, April 27, 2015,** *as:*

### *"Dr. E. Bruce Heilman Day"*

*In the City of Shreveport and urge all residents to celebrate this special occasion.*

**IN WITNESS WHEREOF,** *I have hereunto set my hand and caused the Seal of the City of Shreveport to be affixed.*

*Ollie S. Tyler*
**Ollie S. Tyler**
*M A Y O R*

Alumni

Once in a past talk, you referred to the Boatwright Era, the Modlin Era, and suggested the next era would be the Robins Era. I agree that June 1969 will be known as the time of the gift, but I believe the next period of UR history will be the Heilman era.

The positive changes in the university's appearance, activity, the outlook, image since your inauguration have been many, and I feel that your leadership has been a dominant factor in bringing about these changes. I wish to say thank you for doing an excellent job in the difficult position of university president and express the hope that you may lead the university for many more years.

I hold you in highest esteem that I cannot put into words how sincerely I appreciate your praise. I feel very fortunate to have gotten to know you over the course of these few years, and I hope that my graduation will not mark the end of our relationship.

Thank you so much for sharing your stories, your joys, and your challenges, as UR president and your tales of bike riders to honor our veterans. Every minute was thoroughly enjoyable. Our OSHER students' comments ranged from wonderful to outstanding, to entertaining to terrific, consistently they request a sequel please. All of us continue to be grateful for your superb leadership throughout your years at UR.

Dear President Heilman:

This is a letter of apology from an alumnus who wrote to you back during the athletic department upheaval and said some pretty rash things that were not at all called for. I now find that not only was my original letter lacking in tact and diplomacy, but the position I took, the opinion that was the base of the letter, now seems to have been disproved. I don't even want to go back through my files to see what exactly I said, but whatever it was, I'm sorry. It seems I was wrong.

For me as a journalist, this has been a sobering lesson. I took what I read in the paper at face value, and it appears that was a mistake. So, please forgive me. Not just for being wrong but for not taking the time to consider all the facts and for not being at all civil to you. You deserve the benefits of the doubt, and henceforth, I shall try to remember to give it to you.

I would also like to thank you for being so kind to me in your reply to my original letter. You did not have to be so civil in answering such a letter, and that reply should in itself have been a sign that I had misjudged you. Again, my apologies, and I look forward to meeting you someday.

Dear Dr. Heilman:

As your time as president of the University of Richmond draws to a close, I wanted to write you and thank you for making this university what it is today. As you know, I am a "faculty brat" who has grown with the university. I can remember a time when you could drive across Westhampton Lake, you cheered at Spider basketball games in the Richmond Arena, you climbed to the very top of Maryland Hall to explore the greenhouse, you ordered a piece of pie in the basement lounge of Keller Hall, and you checked out library books in the tower section of Boatwright Library.

I carried these memories with me when I attended the University of Richmond between 1978 and 1982. At that time, few of my classmates could ever imagine the university without the Robins Center, Lora Robins Dormitory, or the Gottwald Science Center. During my stay at the university, I established many lasting friendships and received a very good liberal arts education.

Now that I have graduated and entered the workforce, I continue to watch the University of Richmond grow, with the addition of a new dining hall, our own football stadium, student apartments, and now the changing of the presidency. Just as these new buildings are permanently etched in my memories of U of R, so will you be. You will always be the president of the University of Richmond to me. You have helped make this university the strong institution that it is today and provided me with lasting memories. I thank you for this and wish you continued success in your new role as chancellor. With best regards,

Jennifer L. Decker, MA

A Neighbor in Kentucky

If it hadn't been for you taking a chance on me and trusting me and then helping me buy my home, I wouldn't be who I am today. The night before I moved from Maryland to Kentucky, it rained horribly, and the moving truck sank up to the axles in my parents' yard. Not having money for fuel and a tow truck, I traded my shotgun to get the truck winched out, and I was then Kentucky bound.

As hard as things were in the early years, it has produced some of the best memories of my life. The struggles of having no money to fill the propane tank and having to heat the house with the stove was outweighed by the pride of being on my own two feet.

Had it not been for folks like you and some others, I wouldn't have been able to do what I have done, and I thank you. You actually have served as more of an inspiration than you realize. During rough periods of my life, I've often thought of what you have accomplished in much harder conditions, and I soon stop my complaining and just do what is expected of me.

From Grandchildren

I try each year to bring my whole family together and that has become a large order. There are so many of them, but when I do bring them together, the kind of notes I receive from them justifies every cost and effort involved. Some examples from grandchildren follow:

Dear Pawpaw, my family, and I had a wonderful time with you and the family. We were blown away, especially this year, by the wonderful reception we received. Everyone there outdid themselves, and we were extremely grateful for how well they took care of us. Thank you so much for making the weekend possible. We just had a wonderful time.

I love you so much, Pawpaw, and I am so appreciative of everything you and Mawmaw have done for me over the years. There have been so many memories of my life that you have created for me, and I hope you know how special that is for me.

Christmas with you both was so great this year. You both are the best grandparents I could ever ask for. I love you more than words can describe. Love

Mawmaw and Pawpaw, you both mean the entire world to me. Your neverending love and sacrifice have been so important to the person I am becoming and to the person I have become. I love being with you and feeling the radiance and joy that you give to all people.

Thank you for a great graduation day. It was surreal to me because I had always imagined graduating at Richmond, not even realizing the day would actually come. I am so proud to finally call myself a Spider alumnus— without you, of course, it would not have been made possible.

We had such a wonderful time with you and the entire family in Richmond. I loved the change of venue, and enjoyed eating at the Heilman Dining Center and having a chance to walk around campus before the meal. A highlight for me was seeing all of the great-grandkids stand in front of your portrait for a picture in the dining center. While we didn't get a great picture (how could you with so many little ones), your legacy was so apparent.

I feel so fortunate to be your granddaughter. You have always been a role model for me, and my admiration for your endeavors seems to grow every year as you continue to work tirelessly, travel endlessly, and give generously. I hope that I can say the same when I'm in my later years.

A Daughter

Your generosity continues to amaze and inspire me. The gifts you have given me over the years have given me a sense of security I never had before. You have directly impacted our quality of life. We couldn't be more thankful.

A Little Girl in Hawaii

You are a hero.

If you hadn't fought what Hitler and Tojo sought, I wouldn't be able to say the United States lives happily today. You may not know, but you have made this country glow.

You've seen what horror really is, and I am thankful for this, Your embers will burn bright we won't ever lose sight Of what you did every faithful night.

But nobody could say how proud they really are of you today but here's a start. Please accept this poem from my heart. Here is a start so have this poem form my heart." (This is an early grade student.)

**Department of Veterans Affairs**

# Certificate of Appreciation

*Presented to*

## Dr. E Bruce Heilman

A Veteran of the Battle of Okinawa
and chancellor of the University of Richmond, Virginia.

Dr. Heilman stopped at Dallas-Fort Worth National Cemetery
on Tuesday, April 28, 2015, while he embarked on a
6,000-mile motorcycle ride across America to help raise public awareness
about the 70th anniversary of the end of World War II.

The staff members of Dallas-Fort Worth National Cemetery appreciate your
commitment to our Veterans and their families
as you continue on your journey.

Larry W Williams
Director

# "Our Time in History"

## A MESSAGE FROM DR. HEILMAN

*The Council for Financial Aid to Education reported recently that in addition to more than $26 million contributed by donors to all causes in 1975, an additional $26 million was contributed in goods and services by a vast group of volunteers. In fact, the free, private enterprise system in the nonprofit sector depends entirely upon volunteer leadership giving and working for the cause of their choice.*

*At the University of Richmond we too depend upon the gifts and services of volunteers to achieve the University's educational goals. Without the resources and advice and counsel of scores of individuals and other organizations, the University would not continue for long as a viable university.*

*In this, The 1975-1976 Report of Gifts, I am pleased to recognize the gifts, grants and services given to the University of Richmond during this past academic year.*

*This is a very special year in that the results of five years of planning are coming to fruition.*

- *The $4.0 million addition and renovation of the F. W. Boatwright Memorial Library will be complete in September 1976.*
- *The University Commons, costing $4.6 million, will open in the fall.*
- *Construction has started on the $8.0 million Science Center.*
- *The Lake Beautification Project is well under way, stimulated by the special gifts of many friends.*
- *Cannon Memorial Chapel is now being renovated.*
- *During this year the University received a major scholarship grant for the dramatic arts department; a gift to purchase a new harpsichord for the music department; a grant to assist with the purchase of scientific equipment for the chemistry department; and a major gift to support faculty salaries.*

*Volunteers played a key role by seeking gifts, serving on various boards, hosting at University events and providing the administration with valuable advice and counsel.*

*It is difficult in a few short paragraphs to express appreciation, to tell each of you — alumnus, parent, corporate executive, foundation director and Virginia Baptists — just how meaningful your gifts are to the well-being of the University of Richmond. Be assured, we take nothing for granted and we shall continue to make our case for support to each of you.*

*Thank you for your continuing interest.*

Respectfully,

E. Bruce Heilman
President

# CONTINUING ENGAGEMENTS MAKING UP
# AGENDAS THESE LATER YEARS

In reviewing my annual calendars for this extended 12 year period, I find myself still engaged in activities carried forward from my first 80 years. I entered this extended life period much as I closed out my first 80 years. Thus, my day schedule has yet to provide many open spaces for relaxation from the rather intense schedule which has defined my life from my days as a farm boy through my military years and into marriage followed by the rigors of catching up on my education.

Having six children while acquiring my professional undergraduate and master's degrees and entering a challenging profession which led to lifelong opportunities making it necessary to maintain an intense schedule set the stage for my habit of being a workaholic. Opportunities which have continued even to the age of 93 have provided the setting for full time engagement in satisfying activities.

Motorcycling continues to provide enjoyment that few others my age can claim for themselves. I am out and about at an age when most have long since given up this activity. During my life after 80, I have required radiation and chemotherapy for cancer of the esophagus and fortunately, it has been eradicated.

My children and grandchildren have become an even more important part of my life and interests. The addition of eleven great grandchildren adds a sense of starting all over again. It is a positive feeling to have my family helping to offset the absence of my late wife, Betty.

My first building Decision and a good one.

In the ten years since the publication of *An Interruption That Lasted a Lifetime: My First Eighty Years*, I have led a very active life. My schedule has remained busy, fulfilling, and challenging as I seek to successfully carry out my part of organizations in which I am engaged.

I continue to serve on a number boards in organizations for which I have a strong appreciation. These activities have kept me traveling across the nation and fulfilling leadership responsibilities. Some of the organizations I continue to serve are the Robins Foundation, the Virginia War Memorial, William Jewell College, Campbellsville University, the Marine Military Academy, and the Oldham County Historical Society. Most recently, I have been appointed an honorary trustee to the Virginia Home for Boys. Those are only some of what fill my days.

My schedule is continually packed with breakfasts, lunches, and dinners with boards, alumni, veterans, and other activities as a speaker and leader. Some are planned, and others are spontaneous. I am frequently recognized as either the Motorcycle Man or chancellor of the University of Richmond. I continue to work in fund-raising, meeting with influential people, which is essential to accomplishing projects I believe are worthy of being implemented.

Intertwined with all that I do on a daily basis are my motorcycle journeys representing the Greatest Generations Foundation, Gold Star families, and the Spirit of '45. These motorcycle trips are full of speaking engagements and meetings with politicians, veterans, and Gold Star families. Interacting with numerous and varied constituencies keeps me busy speaking and advising as young and old seek counsel on numerous subjects.

Very often, the most interesting conversations are with individuals who meet me on the road. They become intrigued about my engagements and purpose. At first, they are amazed that, at my age, I ride a motorcycle. When they learn why I ride, they quickly become interested in the purpose of my rides throughout the country.

During the past thirteen years, I have spoken at numerous commencements around the country, to civic organizations, and at military gatherings, especially as a representative of the World War II generation. Some request that I arrive on my motorcycle, dressed in my leathers, or my Marine Corps dress blues to display personal pride in an organization with which I am proud to identify as a part of who I have become.

Battleship Missouri Memorial
Battleship Row ~ Pearl Harbor, Hawaii

Certificate of Flag Presentation to

## Dr. Bruce Heilman

Of Virginia
In honor and commemoration of
your heroic and dedicated service in the United States Marine Corps
During World War II.

The United States flag accompanying this certificate is presented on
behalf of the grateful citizens of the states of Hawaii, Virginia,
and the United States of America, in honor and remembrance of
your service in the United States Marine Corps
during World War II.

The United States flag that accompanies this certificate
was flown aboard USS Missouri (BB-63) on

2 December 2011

Signed and authenticated this date, 2 December 2011.

Michael A. Carr
President and
Chief Operating Officer

Robert K. U. Kihune
Vice Admiral, USN (Retired)
Chairman of the Board

USS Missouri Memorial Association, Inc.

### THE GENERAL ASSEMBLY OF VIRGINIA

## Commendation

The Senate and the House of Delegates
of the
Commonwealth of Virginia

hereby offer sincerest congratulations to

## DR. E. BRUCE HEILMAN

in celebration of
his 90th Birthday and cross-country motorcycle journey
in honor of the 75th anniversary of World War II

Offered by Delegate M. Kirkland Cox
on May 25, 2016

# The Oldham Era
*Your News Since 1876*

## Oldham County native, veteran returns for talk at history center

Thursday, June 26, 2014 at 6:00 am *(Updated: June 26, 6:02 am)*

Join the Oldham County History Center in celebrating the life and adventures of WWII veteran and Oldham County native, Dr. E. Bruce Heilman on Friday, July 18. In 2008, Heilman published his memoir, An Interruption That Lasted a Lifetime: My First Eighty Years. He will present a short program based on his book and also have copies available for sale and signing. Lunch is included in the ticket price for this program.

Heilman was a Marine stationed in the Pacific during World War II and a survivor of Iwo Jima following combat on Okinawa. After completing four years of Marine Corps service during World War II he was educated under the GI Bill, earned three degrees from Vanderbilt University and went on to spend his life in higher education leading to a five-year presidency of Meredith College and 16 years as president of the University of Richmond followed by his current position as Chancellor. He also serves on several boards and foundations for the Marine Corps. A special honor he holds is National Spokesperson for the Greatest Generations Foundation, traveling coast to coast to bring attention to the contributions of World War II veterans.

In recent years he has rediscovered his passion for motorcycles. To bring attention to The Greatest Generations Foundation he began cycle trips across the United States. In 2008 at the age of 83, he rode his Harley cross-country from Richmond, Va. to San Diego and back, retracing route 66 which was the route he hitchhiked across country to return home after the war. A motorcycle adventure not long ago took him around the United States on over 9,000 miles in 25 days through 34 states. He has travelled to all the lower 48 states since his 83rd birthday. This summer, Bruce is on the road to Alaska and when he returns will celebrate his 88th birthday on July 16, 2014.

Heilman's career is featured in a current exhibit at the Oldham County History Center entitled, "I Pledge Allegiance: Honoring our WWII Veterans." He has been designated the 2014 Champion of Oldham County History and will received the J. Chilton Barnett Champion of History Award at the 2014 Oldham County Historical Society Gala in September. Heilman will also be a special guest of the Oldham County History Center on their float for the July 19 Oldham County Day Parade and take part in a meet and greet after the parade on the museum porch. On Aug. 8 Heilman will help kick off a fundraising campaign award for the History Center followed by a special river cruise on the Captain Quarter's Cruise Ship Princess.

Reservations are required for the luncheon program on Friday, July 18 which will include birthday cake. Tickets are $12 per person and payment must be made in advance. To make reservations please contact the History Center.

--Submitted info

MCU, BOARD OF VISITORS
NOVEMBER 5, 2007

To Dr.
Bruce Heilman
With Love
Loni Anderson

12-3-2016

Dear Mr. Earl Heilman

Thank you for

your Service in

the U.S Marine

Corps and please

enjoy your stay

in Hawaii

*While visiting
Schools in
Hawaii*

Sincerly yours,

Katie Heberlein from
Hickam Elemtary School

With Best Wish
HAPPY 64th BirthDAy.
It PAys to Be a GrandPaw
when you have Grandchildren

I Love You...

from. Corey Heilman

youare A Star

Wish everyone had
a Grandpa
as wonderful as you!

HAPPY BiRTHDAY
DEAR GRANDPAW,
Hope You had A Nice
trip ARound the
world!!! I missed you

# THE Richmond

# 100

*A select group of citizens who possess the ability to influence the people and events that shape this city.*

## The 100 Most Influential People In Richmond

| | Educators |
|---|---|
| Dr. Bruce E. Heilman | University of Richmond |
| Virginia Ritchie | Leadership Metro Richmond |
| Dr. S. Dallas Simmons | Virginia Union University |

**E. Bruce Heilman**, president, University of Richmond, later settled down to become editor of his junior college yearbook, but gave priority during his junior and senior years at La Grange High School, Kentucky, to the 1923 Model T touring car, for which he had paid the grand sum of $17.

"I used it until I wrecked it by tipping it over in crossing the railroad tracks—which put me in braces for quite some time," Heilman recollected. He also added that he was more interested in the Marine Corps than in his high school studies, and he went on to serve four years in the Corps between high school and junior college.

**E. BRUCE HEILMAN**
*"La Grange High School Annual," 1944*
*La Grange High School, La Grange, Kentucky*
Harmonica and guitar in string band; piano and violin; pitcher in county high school softball league; 4-H Club; Future Farmers of America.
*Present Position:* President, University of Richmond

**From the Podium**

457

## GEORGETOWN COLLEGE

*Office of Business Affairs*

March 29, 1971

Dr. E. Bruce Heilman, President
Meredith College
Raleigh, N. C. 27602

Dear Bruce:

I learned today that you have accepted the Presidency of
The University of Richmond.

I want to extend to you my heartiest congratulations!  I
know the Trustees of Meredith College are sad because of
your leaving.  If Joe Baker knew anything about your leaving,
he did not mention it to me last week while we were in Dallas
together.  I know Joe sure hates to see you leave because he
has said on numerous occasions that he had the best president
in the college field.  At one of the panel discussions in
our Dallas meeting, Joe told the group that one reason
Meredith College was not in a financial bind, as stated in
the Carnegie Commission's Report, was because Meredith had a
president that knew how a college should be run.

We are still looking for you and Betty to come by and visit
with us if you ever find time to do so.  Give Betty and the
rest of the family our best regards.

Sincerely,

Hubert E. Beck
Director of Business Affairs

P. S.  Mildred said to tell you that their friends in Durham
        informed them of this before the news release came.

                    H. E. B.

GEORGETOWN COLLEGE/Georgetown, Kentucky 40324/Telephone (502) 863-8011

Oldham
COUNTY SCHOOLS

*Continuing the Tradition of Excellence*

April 7, 2016

Dear Dr. Heilman:

It is a great pleasure to present you with the enclosed High School Diploma.
Thank you for your service to our country.

Sincerely,

Michael Williams
Director of Pupil Personnel

6165 W. Highway 146 • Crestwood, KY 40014 • Phone: (502) 241-3500 • Fax: (502) 241-3209 • www.oldham.kyschools.us

Kentucky Department
of Education

Kentucky Department
of Veteran's Affairs

*LaGrange High School*

(School)

# High School Diploma

Is hereby awarded to

*Earl Bruce Heilman*

An Honorably Discharged Veteran of **WWII**. This veteran was inducted
or volunteered to serve in the Armed Forces of the United States prior to
completing his high school course of study for a diploma.

In recognition of loyal and dedicated service to our country and on
behalf of the people of Kentucky this diploma is hereby awarded.

Given at ___Crestwood___, Kentucky by the ___Oldham County___ Board of Education.

Current Board Chairperson

Current Superintendent

# ROBINS FOUNDATION

### THIS CERTIFIES THAT

After 44 years on the Robins Foundation Board of Directors, serving as vice-president for almost two decades and providing years of invaluable expertise, we thank Dr. E. Bruce Heilman with a gift to the University of Richmond, specified for the

# DR. E. BRUCE AND MRS. BETTY D. HEILMAN SCHOLARSHIP

In the amount of

# $100,000

Given this 6th day of December, 2017.

**THE SECRETARY OF THE NAVY**
WASHINGTON, D.C. 20360-1000

6 August 1997

Dr. E. Bruce Heilman
4700 Cary Street
Richmond, VA  23226

Dear Dr. Heilman:

It is my pleasure to invite you to serve as a member of the Board of Visitors to the President of the Marine Corps University for a term ending September 2000.  As a member of the Board, you will advise and assist the Commanding General, Marine Corps Combat Development Command and the President, Marine Corps University in educational, doctrinal, budgetary, enrollment, and research policies and programs.

The Marine Corps University consists of eight institutions, including the Marine Corps War College, the Command and Staff College, the Amphibious Warfare School, the Command and Control Systems School, The Basic School, Officer Candidates School, the Staff Noncommissioned Officer Academies, and the College of Continuing Education.  The mission of the Marine Corps University is to develop, implement, and monitor the resident and distance learning Professional Military Education policies and programs for all Marines, regular and reserve.

The Board of Visitors meets annually, and occasionally as requested by the Commanding General, Marine Corps Combat Development Command.  The Board's opinions and recommendations are submitted directly to the Commanding General, Marine Corps Combat Development Command in order to assist him in accomplishing his mission more effectively.  The President of the Marine Corps University will contact you directly to make necessary arrangements for meetings.

I look forward to hearing from you in the near future concerning acceptance of this appointment.

Sincerely,

John H. Dalton

# Road Warrior Rally raises funds for WWII statue modeled after Dr. E. Bruce Heilman

**By Alexandria Swanger, communications assistant**

"It is said that nothing happens unless first a dream."

Dr. E. Bruce Heilman, a Campbellsville Junior College 1949 alumnus and Campbellsville University Board of Trustees member as well as chancellor at the University of Richmond, addressed a group of Harley Davidson riders at the Road Warrior Rally on Aug. 11 in Louisville.

Organized by the Oldham County Historical Society, the event's purpose was to raise money for a life sized World War II memorial statue that will be modeled after Heilman, a WWII Marine Corps veteran, riding his Marine issued Harley Davidson.

At 92 years old, he has ridden over 100,000 miles on his bike across the country and in all 50 states to raise awareness as a representative for Gold Star Families, families of United States military members who have died in battle, and as a spokesman for The Greatest Generations Foundation.

Heilman, a native of LaGrange, Ky, told the crowd,"I was unloading my things from my motorcycle at the hotel earlier when a woman passed by me. She went into the hotel and told the front desk staff that she 'thought they should know that an old man was stealing from one of their guest's motorcycles in the parkinglot.' To which the staff replied 'That's his motorcycle so he must be stealing from himself.'"

The group, with Heilman at the helm and a

**Heilman's WWII Marine Corps uniform is displayed at the Oldham County Historical Society. (CU Photo by Alexandria Swanger)**

police escort ahead of them, rode their motorcycles through 80 miles of scenic routes. After departing from the Bluegrass Harley Davidson in Louisville, they arrived at The Oldham County Historical Society in LaGrange, where Heilman is featured among the veterans who have submitted pieces of their past from the war and oral history accounts.

They rode to have dinner together at Gustavo's Mexican Grill where Heilman personally thanked the Jefferson and Oldham counties sheriff's departments for their "excellent service" during the ride.

The rally garnered the support of over 62 participants who arrived to ride and contribute to the project.

"I had people tell me that the only reason they came and participated today is because they saw his video," said Emily Stewart, an Oldham County Historical Society board member who was responsible for organizing the fundraiser.

The video, along with a GoFundMe page, has been used to raise awareness about the endeavor and to ask for support through donations so that they can begin construction. The statue will be interactive and will be placed on the corner in front of the Historical Society where guests can climb up and "take a ride with Bruce."

For more information or to make a contribution to the fundraiser, visit www.gofundme.com/the-road-warrior-sculpture or www.oldhamcountyhistoricalsociety.org.

**The clay model for the memorial statue was designed by Wyatt Gragg. (CU Photo by Alexandria Swanger)**

```
              UNITED STATES  MARINE CORPS
           Second Recruit Training Battalion
              Recruit Training Regiment
              Marine Corps  Recruit Depot
           San Diego, California  92140-5130
```

                                            8 February 1991

From:  Lieutenant Colonel Phillip E. Cotton, Commanding Officer
       Second Recruit Training Battalion

To:    Dr. Heilman, Chancellor University of Richmond, Richmond
       Virginia

1.  Sir, it was a privilege to have you review the graduation
parade of Company "E".  When we have such a distinguished Marine
such as yourself stand in front of our newest Marines it serves
to reinforce to them that with the right attitude and hard work
they can make a contribution while achieving personal and
professional satisfaction. I thank you for your example.

2.  I am most honored that you asked for a copy of my remarks
from today's graduation. I hope they will be of use to you.


     Welcome and thanks for joining us here today for this most
significant event in the life of our Marine Corps and the young
men graduating today.

     For over 215 years this Nation has had "Soldiers of the
Sea", MARINES. For those who have gone before, and those who
serve today the greatest honor one can bestow upon them is to
simply call them Marines. General Lejeune our 13th Commandant
once said, " Of all the awards and recognition I have received
throughout my career the thing I'm the most proud of is the
title, United States Marine".

     Today there are 380 young men who have earned the right to
be honored with the name Marine. Since their arrival over twelve
weeks ago they have been referred to as recruit or private but
never once have they been addressed as a Marine.  Today, as their
battalion commander I am honored and privileged  to be the first
to officially address them as Marines, "GOOD MORNING MARINES".

     Ladies and Gentlemen, today you will also be greeting your
young man as a Marine for the first time. I know you're going to
like what you see but so that you may have a better appreciation
for what your young man has become I'd like to share with you a
guide for understanding what a Marine is.

     The guide is easy to remember for it's the name Marine.

     M- Motivation. A Marine is always motivated to serve. Serve
his God, His family , his Country and his Corps. Motivated to
serve others vice self.

     A-Authority.  A Marine accepts and respects authority. He
understand the need for someone to be in charge, and the need for
instant and willing obedience to orders.

YOU   CAN

If you think you are beaten, you are;

If you think you dare not, you don't;

If you'd like to win, but you think you can't,

It's almost a cinch you won't.


If you think you'll lose, you've lost,

For out in the world you find

Success begins with a fellow's will--

It's all in the state of mind.


If you think you're outclassed, you are;

You've got to think high to rise;

You've got to be sure of yourself before

You can ever win the prize.


Full many a race is lost

Ere ever a step is run;

And many a coward fails

Ere ever his work's begun.


Think big and your deeds will grow;

Think small and you'll fall behind;

Think that you can and you will--

It's all in the state of mind.


[NEXT   PAGE . . .]

"The Heilman Family has been an ongoing force in the life of Meredith College, even though it has been over 40 years since Bruce Heilman served as President of Meredith College and his wife Betty served as distinguished "First Lady." Mrs. Heilman and their five children brought vivacity and laughter to the College. Mary Lynch Johnson's *A History of Meredith College* records Mrs. Heilman's demeanor: 'Her winsome friendliness and her calm poise make a charming combination.  That poise is not ruffled by a whirlwind of a husband, five lively children, a large house to keep, and dinners for various Meredith groups.'

Despite having left Meredith in 1971 for another successful presidency, the Heilmans have continued to contribute both financially and otherwise to Meredith College. Their scholarship fund makes possible an exceptional education for deserving undergraduate women. The College's ongoing gratitude to the Heilmans is matched only by our mourning the loss of this distinguished First Lady. Our hearts go out to her family and friends."

A memorial service celebrating Betty Heilman's life will be held on Saturday, December 21, 2013, at 2 p.m. at Cannon Memorial Chapel. The Heilman family has scheduled a visitation at Woody Funeral Home, Parham Chapel at 1711 Parham Road, Richmond, Va., from 2-4 p.m. and 6-8 p.m. on Thursday, December 19, 2013.

Photo Courtesy Meredith College Archives: Meredith's fifth president, Dr. Bruce Heilman and wife, Betty Heilman, during his presidency

SHARE

back

A-Z Listing | Emergency Planning | Contact Us
What Makes Us Strong | Accreditation & Nondiscrimination | F

3800 Hillsborough Street | Raleigh, NC 27607-5298
Phone: (919) 760-8600 or 1-800 MEREDITH

© 2013 All Rights Reserved.

"...it is incumbent upon all of us who love the University to make sacrificial giving a high priority." *Claiborne Robins*

To

Inser

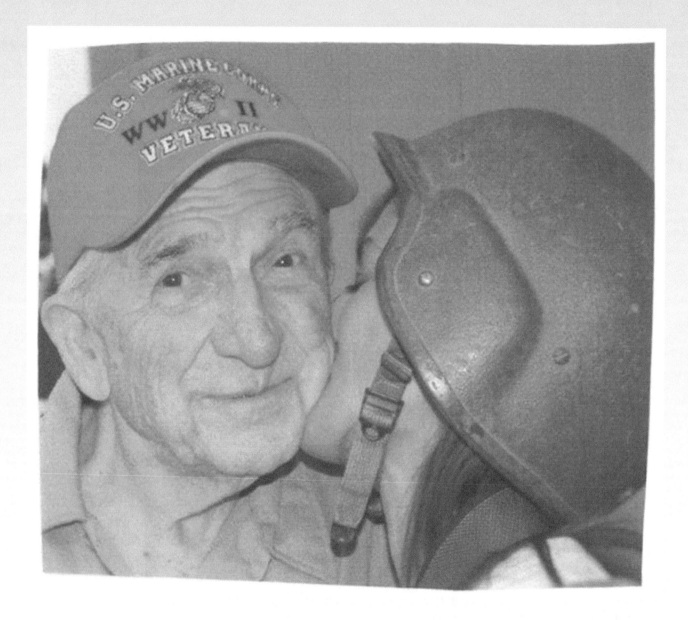

# AFTERWORD

A young marine corporal in Iraq, with his hands blown off and with a serious wound in his leg, continued to lead his men. When later asked why he didn't pass out, his response was, "I couldn't pass out. I was in charge." That Marine embodied the best of the value of responsibility, strength of character and commitment to purpose. Somewhere, either at home, at school, in his church or in the Marine Corps, this value was developed and when called upon, the mind and thus the body responded automatically to the responsibility at hand. Because the situation called for the impossible, the result was to get the best possible.

"The flesh may be weak" but it is stronger if the spirit is willing. The level of energy and, the resulting action is, to a large extent, determined by the level of passion for the committed purpose. State of mind has much to do with why some far outpace others. It makes a vast difference in how we deal with problems and opportunities. The spirit with which we face challenges is often more important than technique and know-how.

Longfellow expressed the resulting rewards of a willing spirit in his "The Ladder of St. Augustine":

The heights by great men reached and kept

Were not attained by sudden flight.
But they, while their companions slept,
Were toiling upward in the night.


Clearly the spirit is a component of the human condition which is the dynamo that propels actions. As President and Chancellor of at the University of Richmond for 48 years, it is no surprise to me that such an outstanding university as this could become a reality. In its almost 200 years of history, the University has developed traditions which continue to provide richness and preserve historical continuity. The spirit of the institution emboldened by its faculty, students, and alumni, fosters continuity of the best of what is carried from its past.

And a thought by JR Tolkien confirming Merriam Webster's definition of spirit seems relevant to my closing:

It is not the strength
Of the body that counts
But the strength
Of the Spirit


An afterword is a final reflection in respect to what the book is all about and as this book began with reference to a man who has been preeminent in the University of Richmond and in my life for the 48 years I have been associated with the University of Richmond, it appropriately should end with reference to him.

Claiborne Robins and his magnificent contribution fostered the dramatic and dynamic transformation toward his hope that his alma mater would become one of the finest small universities in the nation. One who reads this book completely, knows that his ambitions have been realized and that it has been recognized all over the world.

I chose to include in this Afterword, a paper which I recently rediscovered after some 30 years which reflects his impression of my leadership of the university during my 16 years as president.

The following is a page and a half of "Remarks for E. Bruce Heilman's recognition Dinner, March 7, 1986" which was my retirement from the Presidency to become Chancellor. The paper was given to me by Claiborne's secretary. I filed it away not realizing how significant it was and how it would fit into such a publication as this. I record it here precisely as I received it, with only one change which was a mark out by the author.

So I include Claiborne's comments by way of a copy of what he used at my retirement dinner from the presidency

REMARKS FOR E. BRUCE HEILMAN RECOGNITION DINNER, MARCH 7, 1986

WOW, WHAT A PRESIDENT!!!

WHEN BRUCE HEILMAN ACCEPTED THE CHALLENGE AT THE UNIVERSITY OF RICHMOND FIFTEEN YEARS AGO, WE KNEW WE WERE GETTING A GREAT PRESIDENT. HOWEVER, NO ONE COULD HAVE ENVISIONED THE AMAZING PROGRESS WHICH WOULD BE ACHIEVED IN SUCH A SHORT PERIOD OF TIME.

UNDER THE LEADERSHIP OF BRUCE HEILMAN, THE UNIVERSITY OF RICHMOND IS NOW IN THE TOP GROUP OF PRIVATE UNIVERSITIES IN THE NATION, AS EVIDENCED BY POLLS OF PRESIDENTS OF MAJOR UNIVERSITIES AND ARTICLES IN LEADING NEWS PUBLICATIONS.

WE HAVE SURGED TO THE FOREFRONT IN SO MANY AREAS THAT IT WOULD BE IMPOSSIBLE TO MENTION THEM ALL IN THESE BRIEF REMARKS. BRUCE'S ADMINISTRATION HAS BEEN CHARACTERIZED AND DISTINGUISHED BY WHAT I CALL THE EIGHT E'S.

1. ENERGY - STARTING WORK MOST DAYS AT 7 A.M. AND STILL GOING STRONG NEARLY 16 HOURS LATER.

2. ENTHUSIASM - WHICH INSPIRES OTHER TO GREATER HEIGHTS.

3. EXCELLENCE IN ALL CATEGORIES:
   ADMINISTRATIVE STAFF - PROBABLY ONE OF THE BEST IN THE COUNTRY.
   SUPERIOR ACADEMIC STANDARDS AND FACULTY.(91% OF FACULTY HAVE PHD'S).
   ATHLETIC ENDEAVORS.
   EXCELLENCE IN VIRTUALLY EVERY PHASE OF THE UNIVERSITY.

4. EXECUTIVE ABILITY - TO SELECT AND MANAGE GOOD PEOPLE IS THE TRUE TEST OF A GOOD EXECUTIVE. AND TO DEAL WITH THE VARIOUS CONSTITUENTS OF A UNIVERSITY REQUIRES EXTRAORDINARY DIPLOMACY, WHICH IS ONE OF BRUCE'S GREATEST ASSETS.

5. ENROLLMENT - RECORD NUMBER OF APPLICATIONS, APPROXIMATELY SEVEN FOR EACH OPENING IN 1986.

6. ENHANCEMENT:
   FACULTY AND ADMINISTRATIVE SALARIES HAVE GONE FROM THE 40th PERCENTILE TO THE 70th PERCENTILE.
   CURRICULUM IMPROVEMENT HAS BEEN SIGNIFICANT.
   HIGHEST REQUIREMENTS EVER FOR ADMISSION - WILL TAKE APPROXIMATELY A 1200 SAT SCORE TO BE ADMITTED IN 1986.

   AND I THINK ALL WILL AGREE THAT OUR REJUVENATED CAMPUS HAS NO PEER IN THE COUNTRY.

7. ENTERTAINMENT - BETTY AND BRUCE HAVE ENTERTAINED FACULTY, STUDENTS, ALUMNI, TRUSTEES, BUSINESS AND PROFESSIONAL LEADERS, DONORS AND POTENTIAL DONORS. THEY HAVE PROBABLY HOSTED MORE PEOPLE IN THE PRESIDENT'S HOME THAN ANY OTHER SIX PEOPLE IN THE STATE COMBINED, MAKING THIS HOME A MOST PROFITABLE INVESTMENT.

8. AND PERHAPS THE MOST IMPORTANT E OF ALL - ENDOWMENT. OUR PRESENT ENDOWMENT IS NEARLY $200 MILLION. WHO COULD HAVE FORESEEN FIFTEEN YEARS AGO THAT THIS SIGNIFICANT GOAL WOULD BE ACHIEVED.

AND LET US NOT OVERLOOK THE UNTIRING EFFORTS OF BETTY HEILMAN, WHO HAS PLAYED SUCH AN IMPORTANT ROLE IN THESE ACCOMPLISHMENTS. BETTY HAS BEEN AN ENTHUSIASTIC SUPPORTER AND A GRACIOUS HOSTESS, BESIDES BEING A DEVOTED MOTHER AND GRANDMOTHER. OUR DEEPEST THANKS TO THE FIRST LADY OF THE U OF R.

UPON BRUCE'S ARRIVAL AT THE UNIVERSITY OF RICHMOND, I SHARED WITH HIM MY DREAM OF SEEING THIS FINE SCHOOL BECOME ONE OF THE FOREMOST EDUCATIONAL INSTITUTIONS IN THE NATION. THE HIGHEST COMPLIMENT I CAN PAY HIM IS -- THIS GOAL HAS BEEN ACHIEVED AND THE ACCOMPLISHMENTS HAVE SURPASSED MY HIGHEST HOPES. HOW WONDERFUL IT IS TO SEE IN ONE'S LIFETIME A DREAM OF THIS MAGNITUDE COME TRUE.

IN CLOSING, I WOULD LIKE TO PARAPHRASE A POPULAR TELEVISION COMMERCIAL - "BRUCE, WE COULDN'T HAVE DONE IT WITHOUT YOU."

##############

Why do I show this draft? It has to do with my own self pride and my personal satisfaction that I have pleased the man who after my turning down the invitation of the university to be the president, convinced me that I should reconsider. So I find myself 48 years later writing these reflections and realizing that it was this man who gave me this grand opportunity in so many ways reflecting his comradeship, his confidence in me, and his continuing reinforcement and his support of everything I did and could do. So, to have him articulate in these words his satisfaction with the one who, in his judgement, was the right person to be the president at a time when his investment made all the difference is a special tribute.

With his satisfaction portrayed and my ego exposed, I have again accepted the realization that this man and his opinion, is the essence of measuring the university's success and my leadership during these days early in its transformation.

In my Afterword in closing I cite some verses and thoughts from others that have influenced my life including this letter representing many he wrote to me over the years.

E. Claiborne Robins
Chairman of the Board

A. H. Robins Company
1407 Cummings Drive
P. O. Box 26609
Richmond, Virginia 23261-6609
Telephone (804) 257-2000

Dr. E. Bruce Heilman
President
University of Richmond
Richmond, Virginia  23173

Dear Bruce:                    May 15, 1986

It is always thrilling for me to be on campus at the University of Richmond,
and last Sunday must have been the most exhilirating of all occasions.

I was looking forward to seeing Claiborne receive an honorary degree, as well
as being present for your commencement address.  Then, the surprise of my
being the recipient of the Paragon Medal was an emotional and overwhelming
experience.  This is truly one of the greatest honors I have ever received and,
even though there were a number of wonderful folks involved, I know that you
played a large role in the creation of this unique award.  I cherish the honor
and its definition.

As I said at your recognition dinner, there are few people who see a dream
come true in their lifetime, and I am fortunate to be in that rare group.
This was realized mainly through your talent and untiring efforts, the results
of which have and will continue to benefit those who have the good fortune
to attend the University of Richmond.  And how wonderful that the Cornerstones Campaign surpassed our goal by $4 million.  A fitting tribute to your
tenure as President.

Bruce, it has been such a joy these fifteen years to have you and Betty as
friends.  You are our kind of people, warm, caring and unpretentious.  We
look forward to many more years of this pleasant relationship, as well as
working with you as Chancellor.

With warmest regards,

                    Sincerely,

                    *E. Claiborne,*
                    E. Claiborne Robins

ECR/bb

And as I move on toward my closing ventures, I leave a large assemblage of young fertile minds and hearts bearing some inclination, hopefully, of all I have done and some of what I have left undone to make the world a better place and from the bits and pieces of these remembrances and reflection, these young minds will be impressed to draw some inclinations helping them to serve, to give and to build upon the best they can realize in the lives of their forebears.

I outpaced most presidential leaders but adhering to the principles as a first class person that first class people employ first class people while second class people employ third class people. I survived the presidency for 21 years in two presidencies because presidents don't get fired for raising too much money!

And finally a culminating statement about giving without which nothing much is apt to happen no matter the vision and ambitions.

Man's vital need is, as it has been throughout history, to have his generosity exploited. Generosity is a philosophy of life. When Jesus said, "It is more blessed to give than to receive," he not only taught a Christian tenant, but he summarized a concept which is basic to most of the world's religions. Wise men have stressed this truth since man first began to help his brother at the dawn of civilization.

Most of us, even if we believe in something, act upon it only when compelled to do so by certain prevailing circumstances. We are stimulated by the excitement of doing big things.

We are all motivated to serving with people and with organizations and institutions which are in a mode of confidence toward success. We don't want to miss the excitement of the journey and the new level of accomplishment. People want to be a part of a winning situation.

Specifically, people must believe in the mission of the organization. They must have confidence in the leader, and they must believe that their investment in time or money will make a difference. People tend to give because they believe in the people who are responsible for the organization into which they are giving. They must have reasons to which they can relate and people in whom they can believe and a cause which in their mind is unequivocally worthy.

Further, people give to people and to individuals in whom they deeply believe and who deeply believe in the cause that they have been invited to support. So those who are doing the inviting or soliciting must have themselves shown their great competence and their unwavering believe and their sacrificial giving as an example.

In Revelations 3:8 we read, "Behold, I have set before thee an open door and no man can shut it." If we truly believe that we hold the destiny of our cause in our hand and that the door is open that no man can close and that the window of opportunity is available to us at this time in history, there is no limit to the extent of our advancement through the door.

As Edgar Guest put it, "Life's battles don't always go to the stronger or faster man, but sooner or later the one who wins is the fellow who thinks he can."

# Thanatopsis

WILLIAM CULLEN BRYANT

*( Born November 3, 1794, died June 12 1878 )*

To him who, in the love of Nature, holds
Communion with her visible forms, she speaks
A various language: for his gayer hours
She has a voice of gladness, and a smile
And eloquence of beauty; and she glides
Into his darker musings, with a mild
And healing sympathy, that steals away
Their sharpness, ere he is aware. When thoughts
Of the last bitter hour come like a blight
Over thy spirit, and sad images
Of the stern agony, and shroud, and pall,
And breathless darkness, and the narrow house,
Make thee to shudder, and grow sick at heart,—
Go forth under the open sky, and list
To Nature's teachings, while from all around—
Earth and her waters, and the depths of air—
Comes a still voice:—Yet a few days, and thee
The all-beholding sun shall see no more
In all his course; nor yet in the cold ground,
Where thy pale form was laid, with many tears,
Nor in the embrace of ocean, shall exist
Thy image. Earth, that nourished thee, shall claim
Thy growth, to be resolved to earth again;
And, lost each human trace, surrendering up
Thine individual being, shalt thou go
To mix forever with the elements;
To be a brother to the insensible rock,
And to the sluggish clod, which the rude swain
Turns with his share, and treads upon. The oak
Shall send his roots abroad, and pierce thy mold.
Yet not to thine eternal resting place
Shalt thou retire alone—nor couldst thou wish
Couch more magnificent. Thou shalt lie down
With patriarchs of the infant world—with kings,
The powerful of the earth—the wise, the good,

Fair forms, and hoary seers of ages past,
All in one mighty sepulcher. The hills,
Rock-ribbed, and ancient as the sun; the vales
Stretching in pensive quietness between;
The venerable woods; rivers that move
In majesty, and the complaining brooks,
That make the meadows green; and, poured round all
Old ocean's gray and melancholy waste—
Are but the solemn decorations all
Of the great tomb of man! The golden sun,
The planets, all the infinite host of heaven,
Are shining on the sad abodes of death,
Through the still lapse of ages. All that tread
The globe are but a handful to the tribes
That slumber in its bosom. Take the wings
Of morning, pierce the Barcan wilderness,
Or lose thyself in the continuous woods
Where rolls the Oregon and hears no sound
Save his own dashings—yet the dead are there;
And millions in those solitudes, since first
The flight of years began, have laid them down
In their last sleep—the dead reign there alone!
So shalt thou rest, and what if thou withdraw
In silence from the living; and no friend
Take note of thy departure? All that breathe
Will share thy destiny. The gay will laugh
When thou art gone, the solemn brood of care
Plod on, and each one as before shall chase
His favorite phantom; yet all these shall leave
Their mirth and their employments, and shall come
And make their bed with thee. As the long train
Of ages glides away, the sons of men—
The youth in life's green spring, and he who goes
In the full strength of years, matron and maid,
And the sweet babe, and the gray-headed man—
Shall one by one be gathered to thy side,
By those, who in their turn shall follow them.

So live that when thy summons comes to join
The innumerable caravan that moves
To that mysterious realm, where each shall take
His chamber in the silent halls of death,
Thou go not, like the quarry-slave at night,
Scourged to his dungeon, but, sustained and soothed
By an unfaltering trust, approach thy grave
Like one who wraps the drapering of his couch!
About him, and lies down to pleasant dreams.

By special permission of
D. Appleton & Company.

# As night approaches, memories fill a void

Frost covers the window through which the honey-gold rays of the sun once smiled.

Delicate swirls of ice obscure the vision of children laughing and playing in the distance.

In a dark corner of the room, he sits all alone and stares into the future. The easy chair he loved is empty. The remote control and color television that kept him busy for the last several months are silent.

The pipe that was his constant companion most of his life lies untouched.

His overalls and flannel shirt that he loved so dearly are neatly folded and put away in a drawer. A hospital gown is now his leisurewear, a wheelchair is his throne and the four walls are his world.

He can no longer talk about yesterday or savor the taste of cornbread and beans. His meals are measured in cubic centimeters and delivered by a vinyl tube.

Sometimes when his daughter visits or his wife speaks of the past, his eyes twinkle ever so slightly before he slips back into the night.

Somewhere in his memories, a light spring rain is falling. He's 10 years old and running through a freshly mowed lawn. He picks his mother's favorite daffodils. She pretends to be angry before hugging him.

Somewhere in his memories, he's still a young boy running through a field of clover. Close behind him is Old Sam, the hunting dog he raised from a pup.

Somewhere in his memories, he's holding hands with the young girl who lives down the road. He's embracing her and they share their first kiss.

Somewhere in his memories, he's dressed in his best suit. That young girl is now the most beautiful woman he has ever seen. They vow to love one another forever.

Somewhere in his memories, he's pacing nervously in a waiting room, chewing on his pipe. A nurse summons him to his wife's side. She smiles and introduces him to their newborn daughter.

Somewhere in his memories, he's a proud new papa smiling brightly as his daughter takes her first steps.

Somewhere in his memories, he's holding his wife's hand, sharing a kiss, while they watch their daughter dancing with her husband.

Somewhere in his memories, he's standing in front of a glass window looking into the hospital nursery at his newborn granddaughter.

Somewhere in his memories, he's dressed once again in his best suit. Beside him is his still beautiful wife. They are celebrating their 75th anniversary.

Somewhere in his memories, there is no pain. The sun is smiling and he can hear the sound of children laughing and playing.

The frost grows thicker on the window as night begins to fall.

# I Shall Not Pass This Way Again
## A Symphony

EVA ROSE YORK

*(Born December 22, 1858)*

I shall not pass this way again—
  Although it bordered be with flowers,
  Although I rest in fragrant bowers,
    And hear the singing
    Of song-birds winging
To highest heaven their gladsome flight;
Though moons are full and stars are bright,
And winds and waves are softly sighing,
While leafy trees make low replying;
Though voices clear in joyous strain
Repeat a jubilant refrain;
Though rising suns their radiance throw
On summer's green and winter's snow,
In such rare splendor that my heart
Would ache from scenes like these to part;
    Though beauties heighten,
    And life-lights brighten,
And joys proceed from every pain,—
I shall not pass this way again.

Then let me pluck the flowers that blow,
And let me listen as I go
    To music rare
    That fills the air;
    And let hereafter
    Songs and laughter
Fill every pause along the way;
And to my spirit let me say:

"O soul, be happy; soon 'tis trod,
The path made thus for thee by God.
Be happy thou, and bless His name
By whom such marvellous beauty came."
And let no chance by me be lost
To kindness show at any cost.
I shall not pass this way again;
Then let me now relieve some pain,
Remove some barrier from the road,
Or brighten some one's heavy load;
A helping hand to this one lend,
Then turn some other to befriend.

    O God, forgive
    That now I live
As if I might, sometime, return
To bless the weary ones that yearn
For help and comfort every day,—
For there be such along the way.
O God, forgive that I have seen
The beauty only, have not been
Awake to sorrow such as this;
That I have drunk the cup of bliss
Remembering not that those there be
Who drink the dregs of misery.

I love the beauty of the scene,
Would roam again o'er fields so green;
But since I may not, let me spend
My strength for others to the end,—
For those who tread on rock and stone,
And bear their burdens all alone,
Who loiter not in leafy bowers,
Nor hear the birds nor pluck the flowers.
A larger kindness give to me,
A deeper love and sympathy;
    Then, O, one day
    May someone say—
Remembering a lessened pain—
"Would she could pass this way again."

Taken by permission from
*A Treasury of Canadian Verse.*
Published by E. P. Dutton & Co.

# BIBLIOGRAPHY

Acts 2:17. Bible: King James Version.

Armour, Richard. *Going Around in Academic Circles.* New York: McGraw-Hill, 1965.

Bartlett, John. *A Collection of Familiar Quotations.* New York: Philosophical Library, Inc., 1965.

Collins, J. *Good to Great and the Social Sectors.* Boulder, CO: Jim Collins, 2005.

"The Body Follows the Mind: The Flesh is Less Weak When the Spirit is Willing." Published speech presented to the American Association of Presidents of Independent Colleges and Universities, Phoenix, Arizona: Annual meeting, 1991.

"The Importance of Presidential Vision to an Educational Institution's Success," *The Southern Baptist Educator: News Journal of the Association of Southern Baptist Colleges and Schools*, Vol. LXV, No. 2, First Quarter, 2001.

"Keeping Your Head" or "Use it or Lose It." American Association of Presidents of Independent Colleges and Universities, Phoenix, AZ, February 1991.

"Now What? Where Do We Go From here?" *Fund-Raising for the Small College, Papers Presented at the 13th Annual CASC Workshop.*" Paper presented to The Council for the Advancement of Small Colleges, 1968.

"Thinking with Trustees." Proceedings of the 3rd Annual Conference of Texas Baptist College board of trustees, December 1966.

"The Heilman Years," *University of Richmond Magazine*, Vol. 48, No. 3, Spring 1986.

Giniger, Kenneth Seeman. *A Treasury of Golden Memories.* Garden City, New York: Hanover House, 1958.

Henry, Lewis C. *Five Thousand Quotations for All Occasions.* Garden City, NY: Doubleday, 1945.

Johnson, Mary Lynch. *A History of Meredith College.* 2nd ed. Raleigh, NC: Meredith College 1972.

Jones, Wilbur D. *Gyrene: The World War II United States Marine.* Shippensburg, PA: White Mane Books, 1998.

*Marine Corps Training Manual.* Washington, DC: Headquarters, United States Marine Corps.

*Meredith College Alumni Magazine.* Meredith College. Raleigh, NC: Office of College Communications.

Panas, Jerold. *Born to Raise.* Chicago, IL: Pluribus Press, 1988.

Panas, Jerold, Linzy & Partners, Consultants in Philanthropy, "Thoughts for a Vital Life—The Fourth in the Series."

Rhodes, Karl, Editor: *Richmond Alumni Magazine.* University of Richmond, Richmond, VA: Quarterly Publication, Summer 1976, Spring 1979, Spring 1986, Vol. 48, No. 3.

University of Richmond. *University of Richmond Bylaws.* Richmond, Virginia: University of Richmond, 2007.

# ABOUT THE AUTHOR

E. Bruce Heilman has been chancellor at the University of Richmond since 1988 after serving as president and chief executive officer for sixteen years. Having failed to pass enough courses to meet high school graduation requirements, he joined the Marine Corps during World War II. He was educated under the G.I. Bill at Campbellsville College and Vanderbilt University.

A respected educator, administrator, and much sought-after speaker and consultant in higher education, he has served on numerous boards of educational, religious, and nonprofit organizations. Among other numerous activities, he currently serves on the board of the Robins

Foundation and the President's Advisory Council of the Children's Home Society of Virginia. He is a trustee of Campbellsville University and William Jewell College. In addition, he is an honorary trustee of the Boys Home of Virginia.

Among other awards, he has received honorary doctorates from twelve colleges and universities as well as named buildings on three campuses. His varied leadership experiences in higher education in four states has included every defined administrative position including coordinator of higher education for Tennessee and president of Meredith College.

A marine "once and always," he is national spokesman for the Greatest Generations Foundation and the Spirit of '45. He is a founding member of the National Museum of the

Marine Corps at Quantico, a member and former chairman of the board of the Marine Military

Academy in Texas, member and chairman of the board of the Marine Corps University at

Quantico, and a member of the board of directors of the Virginia War Memorial Educational Foundation. He served for many years on the board of the Marine Corps Heritage Foundation and is an emeritus board member of the Families of the Wounded Fund. Among the numerous awards he has received, he is also the recipient of the Superior Public Service Award from the Department of the Navy presented to him by the commandant of the Marine Corps.

In addition to his experiences as a marine in World War II in the South Pacific and Japan, Dr. Heilman has traveled extensively, covering more than 145 countries, escorting travel groups annually for more than forty years.

In recent years, he has rediscovered his passion for motorcycles and has covered all fifty states since his eighty-third birthday. He has also ridden from coast to coast in the past two years, representing the Greatest Generation, Gold Star Families, and the Spirit of '45.

He and his late wife, Betty, have five children, eleven grandchildren, and nine greatgrandchildren. All the children, nine of the grandchildren, and three sons-in-law are University of Richmond graduates.

# E. BRUCE HEILMAN

Widely known for his active leadership, constant optimism, contagious enthusiasm, and untiring determination, E. Bruce Heilman had a transforming effect on everything with which he was associated. He was President and then Chancellor of the University of Richmond, and President of Meredith College in North Carolina. He made his Heavenly journey on October x, 2019 at the age of 93.

Born on July 16, 1926 into the family of a tenant farmer in Kentucky, Heilman learned to live on hard work, faith, and frugality. An uninspired student who dreamed of becoming a truck driver, he interrupted his farming life when, at age 17, he dropped-out of high school and enlisted in the Marines to serve in World War II. Compared to his daily schedule of farm and school activities, Boot Camp was good for him – he grew 4 inches and gained 35 pounds in his first four months in the service. Time "on the ground" in Okinawa was not as easy, as he saw countless friends and patriots give their lives for his country. The Marine Corps broadened his horizons, increased his confidence, and transformed his ambitions.

After an honorable discharge from the Marines Heilman embraced the GI Bill and restarted his education, ultimately pursuing a career in higher education administration. He advanced rapidly and was named President of Meredith College in North Carolina at the age of 40. Five years later the University of Richmond persuaded him to become their fifth president and help implement the $50 million gift recently made by E. Claiborne Robins of the A.H. Robins Pharmaceutical Company. Even though the largest capital campaign in the University's history was just $1.7 million, Heilman challenged the board of Trustees to support a $50 million campaign, saying that "We should all be able to do collectively, what Claiborne Robins did individually." That bold leadership defined Heilman's tenure.

Dr. Heilman was admired and appreciated for his fund-raising capabilities. Not only did he put Meredith College and the University of Richmond on solid financial footing, he was a major fund raiser and fund raising advisor for the Marine Military Academy in Harlingen, TX, the Marine Corps Museum in Quantico, VA, Campbellsville University in Kentucky, and many other small colleges throughout the U.S. As a result of his efforts, he has three buildings named in his honor at three universities: a dormitory at Meredith College, a dining center at the University of Richmond, and a student center complex at his alma mater, Campbellsville University. There are an additional two buildings at Campbellsville named in honor of his late wife, Betty.

A man of action in everything he chose to pursue, Heilman's greatest efforts and results were reserved for the University of Richmond. Before arriving in 1971, his predecessor had warned that the University was in danger of folding or being absorbed into another Virginia school. At that time UR's endowment was just $7 million. Sixteen years of tireless effort later, the University was vibrant with a growing national reputation, glistening new facilities, and a strong financial position. Today, Richmond has an endowment of $2.5 billion and ranks 10th in endowment per capita of all U.S. universities with over 3,000 students.

Even at the age of 93, Dr. Heilman was a sought-after speaker. He was tireless in his preparation of speeches which incorporated poetry, humor, and a rapid-fire delivery that kept audiences engaged and inspired. One of his most satisfying roles was that of the spokesperson for the Greatest Generation Foundation, where he traveled the globe to spread the history and lessons that shaped those in the Greatest Generation.

Heilman thought that exposure to other peoples and other cultures was an essential part of being well-educated. Soon after becoming President of Meredith he initiated a summer travel adventure, first inviting students, then friends and college supporters, and ultimately his family to join him as he traipsed the world and visited 145 countries.

At age 71 and looking for a new challenge, Heilman's wife Betty gifted him a Harley Davidson which he proceeded to ride and enjoy for the next 22 years. He took his Harley across the country multiple times and traversed all 50 states, including a solo trip to Alaska from Richmond at age 88. Along the way he picked up a new group of friends, all admiring his winsome spunk and ability to safely handle an 800 lb. two-wheeled "Hog".

Heilman was married to Betty June Dobbins for 65 years before she passed away in 2013. Preceded in death by his parents, Earl and Nellie Heilman, brothers Roland and Bob Heilman and sister, Nancy Ruth. He is survived by daughters Bobbie Murphy (Mike), Nancy Cale (Fred), Terry Sylvester (David) and Sandy Kuehl (Fred) and son, Tim as well as his 11 grandchildren, Chris Hudgins (Sarah), Matt Hudgins, Dylan Davis (Melissa), Morgan Davis (Allie), Whitney Christopoulos (Brett), Hilary Disher (Justin), Natalie Foy (Nick), Carly Parsons (Luke), Nick van der Meer, Corey Heilman, and Patrick Heilman. He is also survived by his 11 great grandchildren. He is the author of *An Interruption that Lasted a Lifetime*, an autobiography about his first 80 years. He loved his family deeply.

Printed in the United States
By Bookmasters